BEYOND THE CODICES

Published for the
UCLA Latin American Center
as Volume 27 in the
UCLA LATIN AMERICAN STUDIES SERIES
Series editor: Johannes Wilbert

Books published by the University of California Press in cooperation with the UCLA Latin American Center

1. Kenneth Karst and Keith S. Rosenn, *Law and Development in Latin America: A Case Book*, Volume 28, Latin American Studies Series, UCLA Latin American Center.

2. James W. Wilkie, Michael C. Meyer, and Edna Monzón de Wilkie, eds., *Contemporary Mexico: Papers of the IV International Congress of Mexican History*, Volume 29, Latin American Studies Series, UCLA Latin American Center.

3. Arthur J. O. Anderson, Frances Berdan, and James Lockhart, *Beyond the Codices: The Nahua View of Colonial Mexico*, Volume 27, Latin American Studies Series, UCLA Latin American Center.

(Except for the volumes listed above, which are published and distributed by the University of California Press, Berkeley, California 94720, all other volumes in the Latin American Studies Series are published and distributed by the UCLA Latin American Center, Los Angeles, California 90024.)

Beyond the Codices

THE NAHUA VIEW

OF COLONIAL MEXICO

Translated and edited by
ARTHUR J. O. ANDERSON
FRANCES BERDAN
and **JAMES LOCKHART**

With a linguistic essay by
RONALD W. LANGACKER

UNIVERSITY OF CALIFORNIA PRESS
Berkeley Los Angeles London

University of California Press
Berkeley and Los Angeles, California
University of California Press, Ltd.
London, England

ISBN: 0-520-02974-7
Library of Congress Catalog Card Number: 74-29801
Printed in the United States of America
1 2 3 4 5 6 7 8 9 0

Preface

The main sources of classical Nahuatl studies have been splendid, elaborately illustrated documents fully deserving their status as "codices." Their contents, often pre-Columbian in emphasis, are legends, annals, chronicles, and poems like those in Garibay's famous anthology.[1] Few are aware that there is another vein of Nahuatl texts equally rich and very different, more embedded in postconquest times, more reflective of the dynamics of social and cultural change. A mass of records concerning the everyday business of the Indian community of colonial Mexico exists in Nahuatl wills, land transactions, municipal council minutes, local tax records, and a rich variety of petitions and correspondence. This vast resource has been doubly out of the reach of the various disciplines—history, anthropology, linguistics—to which it would be of interest. Not only are the texts scattered and unpublished, but their forms and vocabulary are too unfamiliar to allow for their ready use.

With the present selection of representative texts, transcribed, translated, and to some extent commented upon, we hope to draw attention to this second world of classical Nahuatl, and also to provide a key with which scholars can open it up. Despite the initial difficulty, many of the records are standardized in the extreme, much like the Spanish ones on which they are patterned, and full understanding of a single model document will go far toward making others quickly comprehensible.

Our hearty thanks go to David M. Szewczyk. David gave the project its effective start when, in response to a request for Nahuatl notarial records, he sent Lockhart a copy of our present Document 1 as a Christmas present. Subsequently he located and sent us copies of the Coyoacan papers in Mexico's Archivo General de la Nación (AGN),[2] papers that are one of the two main sources of our selections. The other is the McAfee Collection of UCLA's Research Library, made available to us through the efficient cooperation of Sandra Taylor of Special Collections and Ludwig Lauerhass, Latin American Bibliographer. Mr. Lauerhass was also instrumental in UCLA's acquisition of the Tehuacan tribute records which are the basis of our Document 24.

[1]Angel María Garibay K., *Llave del Náhuatl.*

[2]Tierras 1735, exp. 2. The documents are concentrated after f. 105. They are accompanied by Spanish translations made in 1681, a hundred years and more after the composition of many of the originals. Despite frequent wild errors, the translations are most useful.

Contents

ILLUSTRATIONS

The Historical-Anthropological Potential of Nahuatl Documentation

We had once planned to write separate surveys of the ways in which our disciplines might use documents such as the ones in this volume. It is a testimony to the strength of interdisciplinary affinities that the chapter outlines for history and anthropology tended to converge; what was of interest to one was equally so to the other. We present therefore a single short discussion of some avenues of special promise for anthropological and historical studies, and also, from a layman's perspective, for philology and linguistics. To obtain a more professional view of the linguistic significance of such texts, we have asked Ronald W. Langacker for a brief assessment, which follows this section.

There is a specific disciplinary connection with history to the extent that our documentation represents, for the Indian world, material closely resembling that being used in recent research on the social and economic history of the European component of "colonial" or early modern Spanish America. This new work is built on close investigation of living, functioning entities, whether individual people or organizations. Although such research involves the discovery and analysis of social types, categories, functions, and processes, its raw material must be specific detail. For the Spanish world (cities, commerce, mines, and estates) coherent detail abounds, and there the studies have gone, bypassing the Indian towns that filled the hinterlands. Since the most concentrated and accessible documentation concerning Indians results from Spanish attempts to govern them, the approach to the study of colonial-period Indians has often been through the corporate community (even and especially in Charles Gibson's *Aztecs under Spanish Rule*). Much emphasis has been given to that community's relations with the outside. Nahuatl documents of the type presented here—wills, land sales, municipal records, petitions, and letters—offer the possibility of viewing *individual* Indians as well as the community, and *internal* as well as external relations.

Biographies or career sketches, put together from scattered materials, have been basic to recent social history. Even from the small selection presented here, it is apparent that Nahuatl documents contain the materials for multidimensional lives of important noblemen, possibly through several generations of the same family. Public or official attributes come through in great clarity and detail. For the mid-sixteenth-century ruler of Coyoacan we have extensive lists: of tributes paid him and services performed him; of the location, numbers, and duties of his retainers; also of lands he held, as ruler and as individual. He is frequently seen presiding over the Coyoacan council, or by himself making grants or confirmations. Correspondence, though quite rare, can be hoped for in the case of such individuals, and wills are common. For the ruling family of Coyoacan there are wills not only of the title holders, but of other male and female relatives over some generations. In one context after another, we see a person and a complex which are, so to speak, Indian on the inside and Spanish on the outside. All this information is not completely new. Prominent Indians have been portrayed successfully on the basis of Spanish sources alone by Charles Gibson, William Taylor, and Ronald Spores, among others, and Gibson has done much with this very dynasty of Coyoacan. It does seem that, if nothing else, the Nahuatl terminology will make it easier to distinguish between introduced patterns and older ones. And in these documents elements of the nobleman's staff or following begin to surface.

Beyond the high nobles, the records promise the recurring appearance of certain functionaries, especially the notaries and the church stewards or aides called *fiscales*. Our small net has not caught enough for full-scale lives, but in sixteenth-century Coyoacan it is clear, for example, that a whole family of Felicianos were notaries. In eighteenth-century Azcapotzalco we possibly have a glimpse of two generations of Sorianos acting as local attorneys.

But even where people appear only once, precluding the extended chronology and perspective that can come from tracking them through different times and situations, certain single documents alone, especially wills, can permit elements of a biographical framework. Let us take the example of Juan Fabián (Babia), subject of our Document 3, who flourished in the Coyoacan area in the early seventeenth century. We have only his will, with two accompanying memoranda of debts. Yet on this basis we can say a good deal about his social and economic position. We would need a dozen comparable cases in order to establish that his operations and problems fit a standard pattern or to divine whether the precedents for the pattern are mainly Spanish, mainly Indian, or a confluence of both. But the potential is there.

To illustrate the depth of information that can be readily seen or deduced, we will proceed to give a few details. Juan Fabián was more prosperous than the average, but an Indian commoner rather than being connected with the nobility. We know this because no municipal or other posts are mentioned, no relatives titled "don" or "doña," no high-sounding surnames. Juan Fabián thus emerged from within the local Indian community. He was typical in having lands at scattered locations, three in addition to the land around his home, some purchased and some probably not. In his will he divided his assets among wife, children, and grandchildren in the usual way. But Juan Fabián was also an entrepreneur, with ties to various Spaniards and to Indians outside his community. He sent zapote fruit, presumably grown in the orchard he owned, to other towns, using as an agent his son-in-law from the outside (if neighboring) area of Huitzilopochco. He owned horses and mules, as well as renting them from Spaniards, using them to transport his fruit and doubtless other commodities as well. He kept written records and accounts. He employed other Indians at least part of the time, like the carpenters he hired to prepare poles for him (doubtless in connection with his orchard). He had debts and credits within a circle that included both Spaniards and Indians. Yet no one Spaniard appears to have been his patron, and if some Spaniards were his creditors, in other cases the reverse was true. Juan Fabián tried to use family connections to operate and strengthen his enterprise, but with less than complete success, since both his son and his son-in-law dissipated money and goods entrusted to them. Whether exactly successful or not, Juan Fabián was operating in a manner and on a scale comparable to many Spaniards on the fringes of the urban market economy.

The specificity and informativeness of local Nahuatl documentation conjure up visions of studies of total Indian communities. This could give anthropology's ethnographical tradition a time dimension far beyond the reach of the interview technique and extend history's provincial studies to a level not accessible as long as only Spanish sources are used.[1] At the moment, the principal target visible for such an approach is Coyoacan; the reader will notice that both the McAfee Collection and the papers in AGN, Tierras 1735, our main sources, concentrate on that area. Hopefully other areas will prove as rich. Actually, even for Coyoacan, a greater volume of records than we now know to exist would be required in order for investigators to reap the full rewards of comprehensive, multidimensional local study. The systematic search for such documents has hardly begun. All that can be said at present is that the numerous professional notaries of Indian provinces like Coyoacan produced a varied and large enough documentation to make thorough going local studies immensely, uniquely valuable if enough of the original output has been preserved anywhere. To this we might add that local research should not rely on Nahuatl sources alone, but should supplement the Nahuatl core with all the formidable apparatus of Spanish documentation, to come as near as possible to a rounded whole. Indeed, documents of many of the types represented here are far more numerous in Spanish than in Nahuatl, and they lose little of their informativeness thereby, especially if one has access to a few close parallels in Nahuatl in order to grasp the original categories. We note, however, a strong tendency for the most revealing, intimate, unmasked information to be cast in Nahuatl, especially when it comes to glimpses of the lowest sectors. In the end, it is quite likely that no one Indian unit will have the documentary base necessary to show the interrelationships of the whole range of Indian activity and that specific regional studies should include a strong comparative element.

Nahuatl documents also offer the possibility of seeking out patterns attaching to topical categories or themes rather than to total functional units, whether lives or communities. Landhold-

---

[1]Lockhart's study of the local Spanish-language notarial and court records of late sixteenth-century Toluca, an area without an organized Spanish municipality, reveals overall provincial articulation as well as the internal structure of the Spanish sector. But only those Indians who were in some important way included in that sector could be portrayed in any detail. See "Spaniards among Indians: Toluca in the Later Sixteenth Century," in Franklin W. Knight, *Creole Societies in Africa and the Americas.* David Szewczyk's larger-scale doctoral project on Tlaxcala in the sixteenth and seventeenth centuries, with a similar documentary base, promises much information on ordinary Indians despite the Spanish documentary nucleus.

ing stands out among such topics, almost all of which are of interest to anthropologists and historians equally. Sales, grants, and confirmation of lands are among the Nahuatl documents most frequently found. Land also plays a large role in wills, and there one sees the testator's total holdings, sometimes with their manner of acquisition and utilization as well as disposition. Though maps are found occasionally, generally speaking there is not the kind of precision that would support a strictly geographical or quantitative approach. What the materials can readily do is to allow the establishment of basic patterns of tenure and use, as well as regional variations and trends over time, on the basis of analysis of potentially very numerous examples.

Not to anticipate the results of later extensive research, but to indicate an interesting direction or two, we will give here some of our impressions from the documents we have seen, both those reproduced in this volume and others in our principal sources. For one thing, from the mid-sixteenth century, as far back as our selections go, central Mexican Indians were measuring their lands very exactly, down to the yard in both dimensions, using quite sophisticated and individual terminology. At that time Spaniards in Mexico were still transferring land by the league, with no other description than the names of nearby owners or outstanding geographical features. Another important point is the apparent unity of landholding patterns in all levels of Indian society, from highest to lowest. Holdings were scattered; if there were only two or three fields, still they would be in separate places, or even in different districts. This was not something developing gradually over the colonial period, but was characteristic from the time of the earliest postconquest documents. Even more striking is the uniform structure of landholding, whether for a *tlatoani* and governor like don Juan de Guzmán or for a commoner like Juan Fabián. The scale varied tremendously, but in both these cases, as in most others, there was more permanent patrimonial land, *callalli*, at the core as opposed to scattered, alienable lands more specifically belonging to the individual, often purchased lands or *tlalcoalli*. That is, commoners as well as noblemen held what was in effect private landed property in addition to family land still residually under community control. Since all the terms are Nahuatl and the pattern appears in the earliest documents, one may at least wonder if it does not extend back into preconquest times; though proof would be difficult, the question is surely worth thorough investigation and consideration.

Yet another striking aspect of land documentation is the uniformly low money value of land from the sixteenth century to the eighteenth, only a few pesos being paid for good-sized fields. Some of this might be put down to Spanish exploitative pressure, but prices seem to have been no higher when transactions were purely among Indians. In wills, whenever money values mount, the important factors are livestock, equipment, marketable goods, improvements, or actual cash or debts—rarely land. It is hard to escape the provisional conclusion that land, whatever its necessity for sustenance or its social value, was simply not at a premium during the colonial period unless some special addition with market potential, such as an orchard or maguey stand, made it so.

A theme naturally well elucidated in a documentation studded with testaments is that of inheritance, with its implications for the nature of kinship and family organization. The materials for a study of this theme are as rich as for land; each will is a total description of a family and the apportionment of the property of one of its individuals. Our impression is of a very extensive division of the inheritance, just as was the practice among Spaniards. Yet where the important beneficiaries in Spanish wills were usually the testator's children, in Nahuatl wills the benefits were spread further. It seems to us that there was much more attention to brothers and sisters than among Spaniards, and also to grandchildren. We were surprised too by how much was given to wives. Amassing a good collection of wills should make it easy to delineate the patterns clearly and to pursue interesting questions such as the possible division of property along lines of sex, men's property to sons and women's to daughters, or the exact nature of *cihuatlalli*, "woman's land."

Another leitmotiv of Nahuatl documentation is the movement of people. Not as concentrated as with land and inheritance, information on movements turns up in records of every kind, reminding us that the myth of the closed, immobile Indian community lies a generation behind us and giving us a way to study patterns of movement, though hardly absolute quantities. In wills, we frequently find people living and owning land in communities not their birthplace, or whose spouses and in-laws are from the outside. In a sixteenth-century land investigation (Doc. 9), it turns out that one person after another, having been assigned land at Atenantitlan in the Coyoacan region, left it and went off to Xochimilco instead. Much of this movement was within the limits of city states like Coyoacan or between bordering ones, as with Coyoacan and Xochimilco. But there is no lack of reference to longer migrations. In the Tlaxcalan municipal records the council complains of the invasion of Indians not only from nearby Cholula, but from Texcoco, Mexico City, and other towns, people who come in and buy land or squat on it and do not fulfill community duties.

A major theme in Nahuatl documents is Spanish influence, aspects of which are, a little paradoxically, reflected better here than in Spanish documentation or in the purist writings of the Indian chroniclers. Social or economic ties to Spaniards are freely and specifically mentioned, as well as any Spanish terms, forms, or articles that Indians have adopted. For linguistic studies, documents like these are the primary corpus of evidence concerning Spanish loan words and linguistic interference in Nahuatl; there is hardly a one of our documents that is not full of relevant material. Nahuatl documents are also one of the few sources available for the history of the introduction of European material culture into the Indian world. Consider our Document 8, the inventory of the estate of a prosperous Indian of the mid-seventeenth century. Except for the house, all the items—the mares, the harness, the tools, the precisely detailed pieces of clothing—are of Spanish provenance and called by Spanish names. Indeed, Nahuatl documents are the first place to turn for that whole unwritten side of colonial Indian history, the all-pervasive internal adaptations of the Indian community to the Spanish presence.

In a sense, topics like land, inheritance, movement, or Spanish influence are only subdivisions of a broader question which Nahuatl documentation allows us to attack more directly: How did the Indian provincial unit function internally during the colonial period (with a multitude of implications for preconquest patterns as well)? Gibson has shown us the tenacity of the provincial entities or city-states, and how the Spaniards used them as the basis for the all-encompassing institutions of their early occupation of the countryside: the encomienda and the *doctrina* or parish. His jurisdictional analysis of cabeceras and *sujetos,* his study of interprovincial disputes, of officials and their duties, tell us a great deal about provincial organization. Much remains to be done; especially we need to see the parts in action and interaction.

Municipal records are among the best resources for this purpose, not only the council minutes themselves, but petitions, decrees, and grants issued by the municipality. Interest attaches not only to direct statements, like a decree of the Tlaxcalan council that attempts to increase market activity in Tlaxcala proper while discouraging surrounding smaller markets in the Tlaxcalan jurisdiction. Paying attention to personnel, to who does what, also yields rewards, in this case revealing functional organization. In early Coyoacan, one has the impression not of a Spanish-style city council where the *regidores* or councilmen are the backbone, with alcaldes shifting quickly and the corregidor or lieutenant governor a temporary outsider, but of a situation dominated by the permanent local *tlatoani*, now also "governor." As in preconquest times, he surrounded himself with a few of his judges when he needed to, leaving the body of councilmen in a secondary, passive position. In early Tlaxcala, on the other hand, the main body of councilmen and alcaldes was active and assertive, perhaps a function of the inclusion of the four separate districts within one entity. Here a Spanish corregidor from outside presided, and there was a division of spheres as the corregidor gave uncontested orders on matters relating to the central government while the council took the initiative and usually had its way in more purely local affairs. The time depth of municipal documentation is considerable. Records show the council of Azcapotzalco still in full operation, in Nahuatl, in the eighteenth century, its land titles respected by Spaniards as well as Indians. The documents also carry the possibility of obtaining a close view of the operation of a province's subdivisions. Document 9 shows two *sujetos* of Coyoacan involved in the same sort of jurisdictional dispute that took place between the larger towns. It also hints at the near-autonomy of the subdivisions in many respects, with the role of the cabecera confined to legitimizing local decisions and adjudicating disputes between the local units.

Municipal relations with resident priests also surface frequently in Nahuatl documentation, often in the form of complaints. These lack balance, but even so are most useful. The priest of Jalostotitlan in the early seventeenth century may not have been such a devil as the alcalde of the Indian council made him out (Doc. 27). In fact other Indian witnesses later said he was diligent and suffered mainly from a violent temper. But there can be no doubt that in this Indian town the council stood up to the priest, carrying on one appeal after another against him; that the alcalde was his sworn enemy; and that the council rather than the priest appointed the priest's chief aide.

New light on the nature of the provincial unit can come from internal tax records as well. Documents like the seventeenth-century records of the collection of royal tribute in the Tehuacan district (Doc. 24) contain entries for each of the many subdistricts every four months, with the exact amount delivered and by whom. Compilation would make it possible to determine which areas were most important and populous, which were gaining and which losing, whether the main cluster of settlement bore any relation to the cabecera, and so on. It is noteworthy that not all the villages have an entry every time; probably there is a pattern in the omissions that would tell us something about the nature of local Indian governments.

Equally instructive are such documents as the mid-sixteenth century market tax records for Coyoacan (Doc. 25), if in fact there are any others like them. They show the extent to which the cabecera, in the person of the tlatoani, was taxing the province's internal economy; the retention of traditional trades and the introduction of new ones; the fact that the market was operating on a money basis at an early time. Above all they show the economic organization of the province by detailing the specialties of subdistricts whose location further research could doubtless pinpoint. And here, as also in some of the tlatoani's other records (Doc. 26), there appears another principle of provincial organization: a division into two separate regions, an "upper" one (*acouic*) including the wooded hilly area, and one called *tlalnauac*, apparently the lower area near Coyoacan itself. Of course we still need to know to what use this distinction was put, beyond helping to subdivide tax and land lists. We must also try to establish whether the division is peculiar to Coyoacan or reflects some sort of dual organization in other central Mexican provinces, perhaps a distinction between an older core area and more recent acquisitions. In any case, this feature in Coyoacan would seem to have its roots in preconquest times.

Colonial Nahuatl documentation in general terms seems to have a good deal of relevance to the study of the pre-Spanish period. Preconquest cultural-social-economic history badly needs another data dimension. Present-day ethnographers have not only their subjects' formal descriptions of themselves, but a great deal of directly observed behavior and other objective data from which patterns and thoughts very different from those articulated can be deduced. Similarly colonial historians have not only laws, sermons, and synthetic reports of officials and travelers, but detailed information on careers and daily activity of people of that time. For preconquest times, there is no corrective available for sources which, in addition to being legalistic and tendentious, are largely posterior, nostalgic, and highly idealized. Archaeology retrieves reliable information from this time stratum, but can hardly yield full answers on matters of social organization. Materials such as those in the present volume (above all those of the sixteenth century, of course) are perhaps the nearest thing to a second dimension that will be forthcoming. It is true that they are from postconquest times, none of them untouched by European influence, and one cannot always achieve final certainty on what is new or old. Yet here we see, only a few years after the Spanish intrusion, a great many structures in the course of ordinary operation, in a perspective vastly different from that of the chronicles (which after all are a product of the same time).

All human documents have value as direct testimony of the culture and intellect of their originators; in this, Nahuatl documentation is no different from any other. But since we are dealing with people whose interior contours are so little known, it is well to leave no resource unused. Any Nahuatl document of a page or more contains signals that potentially place it quite exactly, not merely in time and space, but in relation to the classical Aztec tradition on the one hand and to the Spanish world on the other.

Look, for example, at the 1560 letter of the council of Huejotzingo (Doc. 29), the 1611 Jalostotitlan petition (Doc. 27), and the 1622 will of a member of the dynasty of Coyoacan (Doc. 4). The writer of the Huejotzingo document was surely conversant with the commonplaces of Spanish government and religion, but the letter's structure, syntax, and rhetoric belong to the well-developed art of central Mexican public discourse in preconquest times. With a slight dialectal variation or two, the letter could take its place among the speeches recorded by Sahagún. One recognizes the vocatives, reverentials, and dualisms, the general richness of language, the very turns of phrase. The writing of Juan Vicente, the alcalde of western Jalostotitlan, could hardly be in greater contrast. This is the Nahuatl of the periphery, regularized, skeletal, colloquial, naive, short of breath, lacking the rolling periods of the formal language of the central region. One or two mechanical formulas hark back to Aztec rhetoric, but the petition is based on Spanish conventions, and the context within which the writer operates is Spanish provincial governmental practice, that of the town council, the priest, the vicar general, the Audiencia. Also in the 1622 will of the nobleman of Coyoacan, preconquest forms of expression have given way to a document following Spanish models both in its structure and in the details of its provisions. Yet the language itself is that of the Aztecs: mature, resourceful, with characteristic traits of style and syntax, here elegantly integrated with a Christian and Spanish content.

Nahuatl documentation could readily support linear, systematic studies in intellectual history and historical philology. One could do an interesting book on the gradual transition of Nahuatl writing from a more pictorial-oral to a more textual orientation,[2] analyzing also the slow (never complete) assimilation of preconquest phraseology to Spanish prototypes. Changes in syntax and word use can be traced unusually well in documents such as the ones here and are of great interest for both philology and the history of culture. Below we will give some preliminary examples of the tracing of a few monetary and economic terms that were developing in the sixteenth and seventeenth centuries.[3] The whole set of operative concepts of the colonial Indian world can be studied in Nahuatl texts. Also, comparison with the very different set of categories displayed in Spanish translations of the time can serve to throw Nahuatl terminology into stronger relief.[4] As interesting as the concepts which are present are the ones which are lacking. Though Nahuatl speakers adopted many Spanish epithets, they did without one of the seemingly most important, *indio*.[5] Never in the earlier centuries does one see the term "Indian" itself, and only rarely circumlocutions like *nicantlacatl*, "person from here." The Indians' primary self-designations were based on the local ethnic unit or on the nobleman-commoner distinction.

Names also deserve close attention. There was a quite elaborate naming system among colonial-period Indians, on a Spanish model but somewhat distinct from that used by Spaniards. An Indian's name places him in a social niche, even if nothing else is known about him, and the general tenor of names says much

---

[2]See, for comparative purposes, Berdan, "The Matrícula de Tributos: Nahuatl Annotations"; the *Códice Osuna;* and the *Códice Sierra.*

[3]See pp. 27, 31, 32.

[4]See Appendix II.

[5]To the superficial glance, *indios* seems to be one of the most common words in Nahuatl documents, but this is actually *in dios,* "God."

about the character of a community.[6] It is also significant that in the eighteenth century Indian naming practices grew closer to those of the Spanish world, both sectors beginning to adopt the Jesus-Mary-Joseph name complex, as well as a new series of once-rare names like Anastasio, Rufino, and others.

Finally, colonial Nahuatl texts are a primary source for historical linguistics. They fill the gap between Sahagún and studies of twentieth-century dialects in the same way that for anthropology they mediate between archaeological and ethnographical materials. The texts display orthography so nearly phonetic as to allow for quite sophisticated work in phonology. Their great variety serves in the first instance as a control on the extent to which the chronicles, the principal corpus of texts studied to date, are idiosyncratic. In the second place it can allow for extensive study of regional dialectal variation and of the chronology of change. Once again, perhaps our first impressions can serve to indicate some avenues for investigation. There seems to have been a type of Nahuatl used on the western and southern fringe which contrasted with the language of the Valley of Mexico or Tlaxcala in a number of characteristics.[7] In addition to those mentioned just above in connection with the Jalostotitlan document, we might point to some miscellaneous features such as: regularized preterits; frequent substitution of [t] for [tl]; use of *inon* in addition to the center's main demonstrative *inin*; use of *-nauac* instead of *-tech* as the main prepositional connector; adoption of Spanish prepositions and adverbs. It seems no accident that these features are also characteristic of many present-day Nahuatl dialects. One wonders if it could be that today's dialects derive from a lingua franca rather than from the speech of the core area. Or could it be that the written language of the center was a formal, classical vehicle, and that even there a spoken vulgar dialect was current, much like the Nahuatl of the periphery? In any case, by the eighteenth century many such features were embodied in the written language of the center as well,[8] to such an extent that one might think that the eighteenth century was the time of the definitive emergence of the dialects we know today.

---

[6]See Lockhart, "Spaniards among Indians," for an attempt to analyze the social-cultural significance of Indian names in the Valley of Toluca.

[7]See Documents 8, 23, 27, 28, 30, 31.

[8]See Documents 6 and 17. UCLA's McAfee Collection contains several more examples.

Linguistic Significance of the Texts

Ronald W. Langacker
University of California, San Diego

These texts make a major contribution to Nahuatl linguistic studies. An assessment of their linguistic significance must nevertheless begin with a qualification. Nahuatl is a relatively well-studied language. Grammars, dictionaries, and texts for it abound, making it one of the most voluminously documented American Indian languages and by far the best documented one of the Uto-Aztecan family. From the linguistic standpoint, therefore, a collection of Nahuatl texts is in itself necessarily less than epoch-making and will not be greeted with the same voracious enthusiasm that would attend, say, the publication of texts for an otherwise undocumented language that was on the verge of extinction. However, this qualification in no way diminishes the interest and importance of this volume for linguists concerned with Aztec proper or with various related fields. Linguistic analysis based wholly or in part on these texts promises to yield results and conclusions of factual and theoretical interest for many aspects of the discipline.

The significance of this volume is due to the special character of the texts it contains in contrast to those readily available previously. Work on early Nahuatl has to date centered heavily on Sahagún's monumental *General History of the Things of New Spain.* Although this work in most respects offers a comprehensive and quite adequate picture of the classical language, the texts in the present volume differ in several important respects, though the difference is to be sure only one of degree.

One difference is that of subject matter. As working documents from everyday life (even though predominantly legal in character), these texts provide a selection of vocabulary and syntactic constructions rather different from those in Sahagún, if only in terms of frequency (a major consideration in text-based research). The texts represent a variety of dialects. They also cover a significant time span, making it possible to view certain structural features of the language in historical perspective.

Finally, they show the intimate and pervasive influence of Spanish, raising questions concerning language "borrowing." We are therefore presented with a comparatively realistic picture of the linguistic situation—a dynamic picture of linguistic variation and borrowing set in its immediate social context. Numerous avenues of linguistic research are possible only in terms of complex and heterogeneous data of this kind.

Linguists are interested in a wide variety of problems for which an analysis of these texts may prove to be of value. No attempt will be made here to consider any problem in full detail or to provide any comprehensive analysis of the data; the discussion will seek only to give a small sample of the kinds of questions that can be asked, and we will confine our attention to problems that bear in some direct way on matters of language structure. These can be categorized in either of two ways: according to the level of structure involved or according to the type of analysis undertaken.

Among levels of structure, we may distinguish the phonological level, the morphosyntactic level, and the lexical-semantic level. Phonological analysis pertains to the pronunciation of forms and the sound system of a language. Morphosyntax comprises morphology, that is, the structure of individual words and other lexical units, and syntax, that is, sentence structure. Lexical and semantic studies are in principle distinct (one can investigate vocabulary without engaging in deep semantic analysis, and semantic studies may pertain to units, such as clauses or sentences, larger than individual lexical items), but it will be convenient to group them together here. Among types of analyses, we may single out synchronic analysis (concerning the structure of a language at one point in time), diachronic analysis (concerning the historical evolution of a language), dialectical analysis, and the analysis of borrowing or the interaction of "languages in contact" more generally. Any given type of analysis can be undertaken with respect to any given level of structure. For example, a linguist might investigate the dialectical patterning of morphosyntactic elements or the synchronic structure of a phonological system. Of course these categories and distinctions must not be taken too seriously; languages and language structure resist neat dissection, and it is rarely possible to do insightful work in one area in complete oblivion of all others.

In the lexical domain, one can study the meanings of words and other lexical items, their phonological shapes, or their provenience. Extensive texts can serve to help pin down precisely the meanings of individual lexical items and to trace, through their occurrence in a variety of contexts, the full range of their alternate senses and the nuances that accompany their use. These texts should prove especially helpful in this regard due to their varied nature and down-to-earth subject matter. They will be particularly valuable for elucidating the subtle but crucial shades of meaning contributed by ubiquitous particles such as *ma, huel, yuh, ca, inic, çan,* and so on.

Since the orthography represents the phonetic form of lexical items fairly accurately (with certain obvious qualifications), serious questions of phonological shape arise primarily in regard to diachronic and dialectal analysis. For example, 'many' is repeatedly rendered as *miyac* in text 29, in contrast to the form *miec* we normally expect to find (*miequi* also occurs in 29). The most likely explanation (but not the only one possible) is that the form with *a* is historically more primitive, with *i(y)a* generally changing to *i(y)e* by assimilation of *a* to the preceding sound(s). Establishing the earliest form of this word is of some significance since it has cognates in other Uto-Aztecan languages (cf. Luiseno *muyuk* 'many, much' for example), and its original shape in Aztec will bear directly on how we reconstruct this quantifier for Proto Uto-Aztecan. A second example is provided by the use of *mich* in text 27 for the object prefix 'you' instead of the expected *mitz*. In this case, the more common form is doubtless the original one diachronically. The change of *mitz* to *mich* brings this element in line with *nech* 'me' and the other non-third person object prefixes, all of which end in *ch*. Here we have an excellent example of the interrelatedness of different aspects of grammar, for the phonological change from *tz* to *ch* in this prefix is conditioned by morphological factors serving to regularize the paradigm of object prefixes.

One may study in these texts the extension of existing Nahuatl lexical items to new situations, or the coinage, relying solely on Nahuatl lexical resources, of new lexical items to express new concepts. The pervasive Spanish borrowings catch the eye much more readily, however, and perhaps hold more theoretical interest in view of the current intense concern on the part of many linguists with the question of borrowing in all its forms, its relation to other kinds of language change, and its relation to language structure. Since lexical borrowing is discussed below in some detail ("Spanish Words in Nahuatl"), I will limit myself to a few general comments.

Although systematic investigation has been spotty, linguists have long been concerned with the question of what things can be borrowed and what things cannot. There is reason to believe that virtually anything can in fact be borrowed by one language from another given the proper conditions, but at the same time it is undoubtedly true that some features are borrowed more readily than others. For example, it is often held that lexical units are adopted from another language more readily than syntactic constructions and that, among lexical items, nouns, particularly those referring to concrete objects, are borrowed more easily than verbs or grammatical elements such as conjunctions, prepositions, subordinators, or affixes.

These texts appear to bear out these contentions and provide very useful material on which to base a careful and detailed study of the matter. In contrast to the pervasive lexical borrowing that they display, these texts attest to strikingly little syntactic influence from Spanish. Nahuatl syntax is preserved here in all its sometimes bewildering complexity and subtlety, for the appreciation of which these documents will be extremely valuable. Among the lexical borrowings, nouns clearly predominate, and as is to be expected, borrowed nouns pertain most commonly to elements of material culture introduced by the Spanish (*martillo, freno, cabayo*), legal and administrative concepts (*testamento, firma, juezes, regidor*), and the religious establishment (*christianos, santo*). Fewer borrowed grammatical elements are used in these texts than one might anticipate, though they are by no means lacking (e.g., *mientras, de*, and the seemingly redundant hybrid *para yc* in text 6 and *sin* in 8). Grammatical morphemes of Spanish origin are much more prominent in the modern Aztec dialects.

I will have little to say here about phonological analysis. In terms of a synchronic phonological analysis of the classical language, the material in this volume will do little more than supplement that already available. However, it is rich in data bearing on dialectal variations in Nahuatl phonology and on phonological change. One must not underestimate the very real difficulties in determining the phonetic values of various orthographic sequences—resolving them is a prerequisite for phonological analysis—but their resolution poses no real problem in principle given an intimate knowledge of orthographic practices supplemented by information on the phonological systems of the modern dialects.

Let us consider just one example. It is well known that Classical Nahuatl was characterized by a phonological assimilation rule to the effect that the sequence *l-tl* within a word was manifested phonetically as *l-l*. The form *no-cal-tlal* 'my house-land' would therefore be pronounced *no-cal-lal* by virtue of this rule. Text 20 suggests that an additional phonological process came to affect such sequences in the Coyoacan region, at least optionally. We find *no-can-lal* instead of *no-cal-lal* for 'my house-land', and *noyonlocopa* instead of *noyollocopa* for 'voluntarily'. Apparently this dialect had innovated a phonological rule whereby *l-l* dissimilated to *n-l*, at least on an optional basis (*ll* does occur in this text), assuming that the orthographic symbol *n* in fact stands for the sound *n*.

In the domain of syntax these texts are extraordinarily rich. They provide a wealth of material bearing on the analysis of a wide variety of syntactic constructions from the standpoint of synchronic, diachronic, and dialectal analysis. I will illustrate these by briefly examining topic constructions, detached perfective prefixes, and relative clauses.

Though it is found in Sahagún, topicalization occurs with such great frequency in these texts that it simply cannot be ignored. To topicalize a nominal, that is, to mark it as being what the remainder of the sentence "is about," one moves it to the beginning of the sentence, in Nahuatl as in many other languages. Since word order is relatively free in Nahuatl, sometimes we can only infer from the context that an initial nominal constituent has been topicalized. However, topicalization is often quite explicit and unambiguous due to the existence of various particles that normally occur in sentence-initial position; when a nominal precedes one of these particles, it clearly and consistently has topic value.

We will confine our attention to two of these particles, the exhortative *ma* and the negative *amo*. An excellent example involving *ma* is found in paragraph 12 of text 27. Right after requesting that a new priest be sent, the writer states *ynin tovicario, ma xicmoquixtili, ma quiça,* for which the most direct translation would perhaps be 'As for this vicar of ours, send him away, let him leave'; the 'as for' construction in English indicates the topicalization marked by special word order in Nahuatl. In text 5 we find the following example with the negative *amo: ynin notlatol, amo ytlacahuiz* 'This my command is not to be vitiated'. In this particular example the topicalization appears to have primarily emphatic value, but in the next one, from text 6, the fronted nominal is clearly being used to single out its referent as the individual that the following comment "is about"—this comment is one in a list of codicils, each pertaining to a different topic: *auh Yhuan Ynantzin Rofina Maria, ahmo aquin tlen quihtos mostlahuiptla* 'And as for his mother Rufina María, no one is to make any objections to her in the future'. These examples could be multiplied almost indefinitely.

From all indications, the perfective verb prefix *o* achieved prefixal status fairly recently. One indication of its recent attachment to the verb is the fact that it is the leftmost (or outermost) of the verb prefixes. Another is the fact that it interacts phonologically only weakly with the other, following verb prefixes, suggesting a rather loose connection, perhaps more in the nature of a proclitic than a true prefix. A third indication is that it sometimes occurs detached from the verb, usually near the beginning of the sentence.

Examples found in these texts support the claim that the prefixation of *o* is diachronically quite recent, and they provide possible clues as to the precise nature of the historical development that accomplished it. Besides countless examples in which *o* appears as a verb prefix in the expected manner, we find at least two other constructions. In this example from text 12, *o* appears as a sentence-initial particle, apparently standing alone: *o nican tixpan vallaque ipilhuan don luis cordes* 'Here before us came the children of don Luis Cortés'. In the following example from text 11, *o* follows the possibly topicalized nominal that begins the sentence; it is apparently cliticized to the postpositional expression *nispan* 'before me' and is of course not attached to the verb *necico: Nehuatl don juan de gusma onispan necico itocan maria* 'Before me, don Juan de Guzmán, appeared (a person) named María'. Text 33 provides another example of *o* in sentence-initial position (after *ca*): *Ca o nican notech onacico yn amamatzin nica granada* 'Your letter has come to me here in Granada'.

These examples suggest that *o* originated as a clause-initial particle, like many other modal and aspectual particles of Nahuatl. As particles commonly do, it tended to cliticize to the following element, which would often but not always be the verb. Eventually its preverbal attachment became frozen or "grammaticized," though its grammaticization as a true prefix has not yet been fully accomplished, since *o* still appears occasionally as an independent particle, or cliticized to some other element.

Relative clauses with *tleyn* 'something, what' will serve to illustrate the relevance of these texts to the analysis of dialectal variation in syntax. Normally in Nahuatl, relative clauses headed by *(in) tleyn* correspond to English "headless" relatives beginning with *that which* or *what*. Here are two examples, from texts 5 and 26 respectively (to facilitate interpretation, I use square brackets to mark the boundaries of the subordinate clause). In the first, the headless relative clause is also a topicalized nominal, since it precedes *ma: auh [yn tleyn nocamatica niquitoz] macayac quitlacoz* 'And what I shall say with my mouth, let no one go against it'. The headless relative may also be topicalized in the second example, but there is no explicit indication of this other than its occurrence in sentence-initial position: *[yn tleyn monequiz] quichyuazque yehuantin* 'They are to do what is needed'.

The important observation here is that relatives with *tleyn* generally never occur in Nahuatl with explicit head nouns, that is, these clauses are exhaustive of the nominal containing them. This is decidedly not the case in the modern Tlaxcala dialect, however, and the texts in this volume show that the dialectal difference is a long-standing one. To take just a single example, we find the following in text 22 (Tlaxcala, 1547): *amatl [tlen temacoz]* 'papers that are issued'. Here the clause containing *tlen* modifies an overt head noun, *amatl* 'papers', and *tlen* appears to function much like the relative pronoun *that* or *which* in English.

I hope these few brief remarks illustrate clearly the linguistic significance of these texts and answer the implicit question of why additional texts are desirable when there are already so many available. The vast documentation we possess concerning Classical Nahuatl does not by its mere existence supply us with full comprehension and appreciation of its remarkable complexity, subtlety, and nuance, particularly in the domain of syntax. True appreciation of this language requires long, detailed, sensitive study with a wide variety of materials. The variety of the materials represented in this volume will enable the dedicated scholar to advance toward this goal much more readily than will a relatively homogeneous body of texts.

A deep and true appreciation of Nahuatl naturally has vast

intrinsic interest for the Aztec scholar. Its importance for general linguistics, however, should also be mentioned. Linguistic scholarship profits greatly from deep and insightful analysis of a wide variety of languages. To a distressing degree, such analysis has been centered in recent years on various Indo-European languages, whereas work on more "exotic" tongues has tended to be more superficial. Because of the vast material available and the long tradition of Nahuatl scholarship, this language probably holds the greatest potential of all the American Indian languages for truly insightful analysis, particularly in the areas of syntax and semantics.

As I indicated previously, however, many of the most important problems of modern linguistics can be fruitfully attacked only in terms of a heterogeneous body of data that allows one to view the linguistic phenomena in diachronic, dialectal, social, and contextual perspective. Such data is the unique contribution of the present volume, and it offers the linguist an opportunity to make significant contributions in such domains as sociolinguistics, dialectology, language change, language universals, and syntactic and semantic theory.

Types and Conventions of Colonial Nahuatl Documentation

In this section we present a brief guide to the main genres of Nahuatl documentation, at least those presently known to us and represented in this volume. We describe some of the conventions of the documents' organization and expression, and we discuss matters related to their transcription and translation. In so doing, we both explain our procedures and try to provide readers with the tools for independent work on materials of this kind. Knowledge of some rudiments of Nahuatl grammar, above all recognition of the pronoun forms, is a prerequisite for such work.[1] It is our contention, however, that one can learn to understand and use these highly formulized records long before achieving full mastery of Nahuatl grammar, syntax, and vocabulary.

General Conventions

The quite varied documentation we are dealing with here was almost all produced by notary-secretaries attached to Indian municipal councils or to local parish churches. Thus some common notarial conventions and ways of identifying dates and people run through the whole corpus, whether written in the Valley of Mexico or the outlying districts, whether in the sixteenth century or the eighteenth. The notary usually called himself *escriuano* in some variant or abbreviation, though *amatlacuilo* also occurs. Most often he found occasion to say *(o)nitlacuilo*, "I wrote it," and/or *(o)nicneltili*, "I verified it." Running through the texts is *(o)moteneuh*, "(afore)mentioned," or *tlacpac (o)moteneuh*, "above-mentioned," the approximate equivalent of the Spanish *dicho*, "said." The various formulas

[1]Such knowledge may be sought in the grammatical sketch included in Siméon's dictionary, in Stanley Newman's article in the *Handbook of Middle American Indians*, or in Anderson's *Rules of the Aztec Language.*

used in speaking of signing can be recognized by the usual presence of the Spanish *firma*.

Dates cause relatively few problems, being predominantly in Spanish, with liberal use of Arabic and Roman numerals. Day, month, and year are given, with any Nahuatl terms usually repeated in Spanish, except often the number giving the day of the month. Toward the end of the documents one finds *(o)mochiuh*, "done," or "dated," followed by the place and either the full date or reference to a date previously given. "Witness" is always in Spanish (*testigo*); "before" or "in the presence of" is *ixpan*, with one of the possessive pronouns affixed in front.

As to names, first names and titles are of Spanish origin, used and written in the Spanish fashion, except that Nahuatl usage demanded something less than the iron consistency of the Spaniards in the application of titles.[2] In the early period many surnames are Nahuatl; these recede over time in favor of common Spanish surnames (or Christian names so used).

Principals in all kinds of documents are affiliated with a place of residence or origin. This is most frequently signaled by the term *chane*, "householder" or "citizen." *Nican nichane Aticpac*, "I (am) a citizen here in Aticpac." Actually, *chane* seems in certain instances to refer more to place of birth than to place of present residence. Spaniards sometimes translated it as *natural de*, "native of," and in some of our documents a person appears to be *chane* at a place where he is not now living. In view of uncertainties which we cannot resolve without much more contextual information, we have consistently translated *chane* as "citizen." An alternative expression was *nican nochan Aticpac*, which means "my home (is) here in Aticpac," not "here at my home." Citizenship was primarily in an *altepetl*, the name for any organized municipality from Mexico City to the smallest Indian town; the Spanish status, *villa* or the like, might also be given. After this often came some formulation related to *tlaxilacalli*, to give the person's quarter or district within the municipality. At this point or later in the document, any of a number of relatives may be mentioned, rather hard for a neophyte to recognize because they invariably appear in the possessed form. The accompanying table gives the lexical or absolute form as

---

[2]See Document 2, where the testator's daughter appears as both "Juana" and "doña Juana," something nearly unthinkable in a Spanish document until a much later time.

well as the form actually expected in the documents for the terms most commonly seen.

Testaments

Nahuatl wills, like those in other languages, have the advantage for the scholar of conveying very individual, intimate information in a systematic, coherent, usable way; furthermore, they exist not only for the nobility, but for poor people who had only a small house and one or two strips of land. It is not hard to extract the substance from them, since they are so standardized and follow Spanish models so closely. When it comes to subtleties and details, though, wills can be the most difficult of documents. As a result of their noncontinuous structure, ranging widely from item to item, a chance debt can plunge the reader into some unexplored technical specialty, say maguey culture, giving two or three terms not to be found in the dictionaries, without any repetition or explanatory context.

Wills begin with the traditional paragraph invoking the deity and reciting some tenets of faith, declaring the speaker to be ill of body but sound of mind, and commending his soul to God. A glance at our samples will show that the words varied little from the sixteenth century to the eighteenth, though slight modifications brought a change in flavor. After this introduction, the will proceeds item by item, one order or bequest at a time, signaled usually by a dash or indentation, plus ordinal numbering like that often seen in the *Florentine Codex*: *inic*, followed by the number proper in short or assimilated form, followed by the classifier *tlamantli*. Writers apparently viewed the whole thing as one unit; usually instead of *inic etlamantli*, "third," they put *iniquetlamantli*. Many individual items terminate with an exhortation for the command to be carried out: "My command" (*notlatol, notlanahuatil*) "is to be realized" (*neltiz, mochihuaz*).

The first items refer commonly to burial and masses; they are relatively easy to comprehend because they are liberally sprinkled with Spanish religious terms and names of churches and sodalities. If Indians were exempt from certain pious bequests mandatory for Spaniards, one would never know it from the testaments. *Toca* (or *tuca*), "to bury," also *tlamanalli* and *uentli*, "offering," are of frequent occurrence, as is *caua*, often "to

Some Nahuatl Kinship Terms

English	Nahuatl basic lexical forms	Nahuatl derived forms as found in documents
grandmother[1]	ci(tli)	noci, nocitzin[2]
grandfather[1]	col(li)	nocol, nocoltzin
mother	nan(tli)	nonan, nonantzin
father	ta(tli)	nota, notatzin
aunt	aui(tl)	naui, nauitzin
uncle	tla(tli)	notla, notlatzin
wife, husband	namic(tli)[3]	nonamic, nonamictzin
(older) brother[1] (cousin)	teachcauh, tiachcauh[4]	noteachcauh, noteachcauhtzin
(younger) brother[1] (cousin)	icauh(tli), Iccauh(tli)[4]	nicauh, nicauhtzin
(older) sister[1] (female cousin)	ueltiuh(tli), pi(tli)	noueltiuh, nouel-tiuatzin, nopi, nopitzin
(younger) sister[1] (female cousin)	icu(tli)	nicu, nicutzin

---

[1]The terms for grandparents, siblings, and grandchildren were frequently used for more distant relatives of the same generation.

[2]First person singular possessive pronouns, the most common in the documents, are used in the examples.

[3]These terms are often accompanied by *teoyotica*, "legitimate." Literally, *ichpochtli* and *telpochtli* mean only "young woman" and "young man."

[4]The "brother" forms are parallel. Formally they should be *achcauhtli* and *icauhtli*, should both permit of an impersonal *teachcauh* and *teicauh*, and of personal possessed forms *nachcauh* and *nicauh*. Yet *teachcauh* seems to have taken on independent existence, and instead of *nachcauh* one generally sees the double possessed form *noteachcauh*. For "my younger brother" we find both *nicauh* and *noteicauh*. There may still prove to be some distinction of meaning between the two types, but both seem to be used for brothers as well as cousins in the documents.

Some Nahuatl Kinship Terms (Continued)

English	Nahuatl basic lexical forms	Nahuatl derived forms as found in documents
child (of a woman)	cone(tl)[3]	noconeuh, noconetzin
child (of a man or woman)	pil(li)[3]	nopiltzin
daughter	ichpoch(tli)[3]	nochpoch, nochpochtzin
son	telpoch(tli)[3]	notelpoch, notelpochtzin
nephew, niece (of a woman)	pilo(tl)	nopilo, nopilotzin
nephew, niece (of a man)	mach(tli)	nomach, nomachtzin
grandchild[1]	yxuiuh(tli)	noxuiuh, noxuiuhtzin
mother-in-law	monnan(tli)	nomonnan, nomonnantzin
father-in-law	monta(tli)	nomonta, nomontatzin
sister-in-law (of a woman)	uezua(tli)	nouezui, nouezuatzin
sister- or brother-in-law (of a person of the opposite sex)	uepol(li)	nouepol, nouepoltzin
brother-in-law (of a man)	tex(tli)	notex, notextzin
son-in-law	mon(tli)	nomon, nomontzin
daughter-in-law	cihuamon(tli)	nocihuamon, nocihuamontzin
stepmother	chauanan(tli)	nochauanan, nochauanantzin
stepfather	tlacpata(tli)	notlacpata, notlacpatatzin

leave," but here meaning in effect to give or make an offering.[3] *Nohuentzin mocahuaz nahui tomin:* "my offering will be four tomines." Wills abound in important words related to the root *caua*; this *mocauaz* is distinct from *cahuilia*, "to bequeath." Also frequent are *(con)cauia* (*concauiz* is "he is to have it," i.e. be left with it) and *cauhtia*, to leave a person or persons behind at death.

After this, the body of most wills concerns real estate being bequeathed to relatives: houses, gardens, and fields, the last-named above all. They are most often called *tlalli*, or sometimes *cuemitl* or *milli*, terms with special reference to lands under cultivation. The fields are listed one after another, often enumerated by the formula *inic* [number]-*can*.[4] For most, measurements are given in terms of length and width (*huiac, hueyac* is "long"; *patlauac* or sometimes *coyauac* is "wide"; *necoc* is "on both sides" or "square"). The number can either follow or precede the dimension. Rather than the English "10 long by 7 wide," the Nahuatl is "how long 10, how wide 7": *(in)ic huiac matlactli (in)ic patlauac chicome.* The unit of measurement often fails to appear, in which case the governing local standard unit is meant, an apparently greatly varying quantity, but tending, it would seem, to hover between six and ten feet. Sometimes, at the end of a document, there is a more exact definition of the unit used. The principal units appearing are the *quauitl*, actually referring to the stick used in measurement, whatever length that might be, and the *matl* (from the word for "hand"), often meaning the distance between the outstretched hands, some five or six feet, the same as the Spanish "braza" (fathom), which itself appears in some late texts. On the one occasion when we have seen the two measurements distinguished, the *quauitl* was the larger. The units can be hard to recognize, preceded by an assimilated numeral, followed perhaps by a reverential: *cemmatzintli*, "one braza." We have uniformly translated *quauitl* as "rod," that being an analogous term though the English unit is much larger, and *matl* as "braza."

Often a field will be associated with one, two, or even three place names; in the central Mexican countryside every meadow and grove seems to have had its special name. A certain problem arises because many or most of these are the name of some physical feature characteristic of the place; *otlamaxalco* could be a settlement of that name at a road crossing or simply a crossing of roads. But one will not go far wrong in generously

[3]See Molina's alternate meaning for *caua*: "llevar alguna cosa a otra parte."

[4]Except that the first in such a series is frequently *inic cecni* rather than *inic ceccan.*

interpreting words which combine unclear reference and locative endings as place names. In the early texts there are few references to north or south; the terms for east and west, however, are of frequent occurrence and quite involved: *tonatiuh ycalaquiyampa (itzticac),* "on the west," "(facing) toward where the sun goes down," and *tonatiuh yquiçayampa (itzticac),* "on the east," "(facing) toward where the sun comes up."

For "house" the well-known *calli* was the term commonly used. Sometimes it seems to mean the main, sizable living and sleeping room, which in a sense *was* the house, plus *caltzintli* or smaller structures and *tlecopayotl* or storage places. These may in effect have been individual rooms built against the wall of the larger room or *calnepanolli* built on the roof, as in a picture accompanying the original of our Document 11. For permanent, built-up gardens or orchards, an item very frequently appearing, some form of the Spanish *huerta* is common.

Another standard item in wills is mention of debts owed or to be collected. Some of the words used in this connection can be found readily in the dictionaries. But as Nahuatl originally had no general word for "money," it also lacked a succinct expression for owing it. By the later sixteenth century *pialia,* given in the dictionaries as "to keep for someone," was taking on the meaning of "owe" while still retaining much of the earlier sense, since the two can overlap in many cases. By the seventeenth century it is occurring in positions where only "owe" is applicable (see Doc. 4). *Huiquilia,* "to carry for," was another common word for "owe" by the seventeenth century. There was also the expression *itech ca,* "he is charged with" or "he is owing" (lit. "with him is"). The common word for "pay" was *ixtlaua,* which underwent only a slight extension of its original meaning of "pay back" or "restore."

Towards the end of the will there is mention of the executors, usually the Spanish *albaceas*. The whole last section is full of Spanish terms and proper names, and with these guideposts, this part presents little difficulty.[5]

Land Documentation

The wills we have just discussed are very nearly land documents in many cases; we have already treated the basic manner

[5]An item of testament language is *catca*, the past tense of the verb "to be," along with the equivalent reverential form *mo(y)etzticatca*, both of which often translate as "the late," "the former" while also continuing to mean "was" or "who was," according to their position. The expression may be related to the Spanish *que fue*.

of the description of land holdings, this being the same in the instruments for confirmation or transfer of ownership which were issued by the municipal councils or the notaries. In this documentation there is greater emphasis on the status of the land. Some of the more common terms are: *callalli*, "house-land," a field appertaining to a person's house for the family's principal sustenance; *cihuatlalli*, land connected in some way with the woman of the family, in effect perhaps dowry-land, or land inherited through the female line (we have seen an example in which a man refers to "his" *cihuatlalli*);[6] *tlalcoalli*, land purchased individually and which therefore can be sold; *tlalnemactli*, land acquired by inheritance or donation; *calpullalli* and *altepetlalli*, land belonging respectively to the calpulli (however defined) and the town (the two categories not mutually exclusive).

Warnings to respect the owner's rights are standard fare in these documents; usually they begin with *ayac* (no one): *ayac (qui)cuiliz* (no one is to take it from him); *(qui)xitiniz* (is to harm or violate it); *(qui)quixtiliz* (is to evict him); *(qui)ixtoquiliz* (is to claim it from him). Also in constant use are terms for distribution and division: *(qui)mamaca, (qui)xexeloa*, and variants.

Because of their great variety and specificity, land investigations and confirmation procedures can be difficult to read. But the most common item, the bill of sale, is highly conventional. It says, at greater or lesser length: "Let all who see this know that I, of a certain name, town, and district, voluntarily sell to so-and-so land so described and to which I have full right, for a certain amount which I have received in my hand; I have given possession and now I cannot revoke the agreement." Donations vary more, but tend to run along the lines of a sale, and indeed "donations" to church entities especially were sometimes neither more nor less than sales.

Municipal Documentation

This branch of Nahuatl writing, including municipal council minutes, internal tax records, and many land documents, tends to

---

[6]Will of Tomás Feliciano, Coyoacan, 1579. McAfee Collection, UCLA Research Library, Special Collections.

consist to a large extent of lists of Spanish names and offices. If it is not immediately apparent who *tohueytlatocauh* is, it becomes clear when one sees the following *Rey in su mag*^{t} *nrō sr̄*. In this context, *audiencia* usually refers to members of the town council in session, rather than the high court in Mexico City, the Real Audiencia. A great variety of related forms based on *itech* (*itechpatzinco, itetzinco*, and so on) occurs on every hand, meaning "in the name of" or "on behalf of" some higher authority; *itencopa*, "by word or command of," has much the same effect. A repertory of reverential adjectives applied to officials recurs, the equivalents of the Spanish *ilustre* and *magnífico*; several are combinations with *mauiz-* *"honored, feared"* and *uecapa*, "high." A frequent item, not in the dictionaries, is *yoma*, meaning "in person." It appears to be a variant of *(y)noma*, as though Nahuatl speakers had interpreted the *n* as first person possessive, which would leave the root *oma*.

As to taxes, here too, much is in Spanish. *Tlacalaquilli* is tribute, especially in the sense of anything more or less tangible that is delivered, and *tequitl* also means tribute, especially in the sense of allotment, assessment, quota, or set task.[7] Tribute lists (and other lists) frequently begin with *nican icuiliuhtoc* "here is inscribed," related to *icuiloa*, "to inscribe or write," usually seen in the form *tlacuiloa*. The only similar form in the dictionaries is Siméon's *icuilotoc*, but the form with *-iuh*, based on the intransitive *icuiliui*, is the one used in documents. Tax entries like those for the royal tribute of the municipality of Tehuacan (Doc. 24) are so uniform that if one can read the first page one can read the whole manuscript.

Many of the special names for offices and taxes, in both Nahuatl and Spanish, can be found, clearly organized and well defined, in Charles Gibson's *Aztecs under Spanish Rule*.

The picture is different when one comes to tax lists for local market producers, specialists, and the like, such as those in our Document 25. In this mundane, half-hidden sphere, Molina and Siméon are not adequate. To compensate, one must be sure to search the analogous parts of Sahagún, comb through the *Estudios de Cultura Nahuatl* for some similar lists, consult Gibson, and use imagination.

---

[7]The meanings of the two words go far beyond tribute into ordinary usage, referring to anything brought or delivered and any kind of work.

Petitions, Correspondence, and Other Direct Statements

These documents are generally longer, more wide-ranging and varied than the preceding types, since they are directed to a certain person or instance rather than being records for the future, confined within a set form. Therefore they cannot be readily reduced to a standard formula, though they do contain many of the formulas of the documents we have treated above. They also have their own clear conventions and vocabulary, but these are of such a nature that elucidating them would be tantamount to the close study of whole sample documents, to which the reader is encouraged. We might mention that almost all messages begin with reverential salutations like *nimitznonepechtequililia*, "I bow down to you," and *nicnotennamiquilia in momatzin in mocxitzin*, "I kiss your hands and feet." The end is almost always signaled by *ye ixquich*, "that is all" or "enough."

There are two principal branches of this literature. One, mainly in letter-petitions of the larger towns to king or viceroy and in the correspondence of high nobles among themselves, is essentially the polished rhetoric of old Tenochtitlan and Texcoco, the style of the orations of kings and priests in Sahagún. The vocabulary and idioms are quite fully treated in the dictionaries, except that difficulties grow when the language becomes more oblique and allusive in private correspondence.

The second branch consists of petitions and narratives from smaller outlying towns. The style is colloquial, with a restricted vocabulary and simplified or regularized forms; one gets at times almost the feeling of a lingua franca, and indeed in the west and south, some of the people who produced the documents may not have been native speakers of Nahuatl.

Spanish Words in Nahuatl

From the earliest time, Nahuatl documentation is riddled with terms taken from the Spanish, a fact which all in all facilitates its study by scholars who usually already know Spanish, other romance languages, and the European tradition in general. Yet there are some pitfalls. One must be prepared for the changes caused by the difference between the Spanish and the Nahuatl phonemic inventories. Nahuatl lacked several sound distinctions made in Spanish. Above all it had no voiced stops and no labial fricative, causing the characteristic substitution of the nearest equivalent unvoiced stop: in writing, this meant putting *t* for Spanish *d*, and *p* for Spanish *b* and *f*. Also the only liquid in Nahuatl was [l], so that *l* often replaced Spanish *r*. Hence one frequently sees such forms as *capilto(n)* for *cabildo, pilma* for *firma, vicas* for *vigas*, or *poticalio* for *boticario*. The changes, however, went beyond these relatively straightforward equivalences. Nahuatl speakers did not readily hear any difference between [t] and [d]; yet the writers of our documents knew that the Spaniards had a letter *d* and that many sounds they heard as [t] were to be so written. It is natural that they should proceed through hypercorrection sometimes to write *d* for Spanish *t*, as well as *g* for *c* and *r* for *l*, even though [t], [k], and [l] existed in their own language; hence *desdigo* for *testigo* or *garavajar* for *Caravajal*. Nahuatl writers were as prone to add a syllable-final *n* to a Spanish word, or to subtract one, as with the words of their own traditional lexicon: thus *catella* for *candela, catalinan* for *Catalina, orancio* for *oración*. The accompanying table gives some idea of the most common substitutions.

Nahuatl speakers were likely to incorporate a word in the form they most frequently heard. Thus instead of *huerta* one may see *alahuerta* or *alaberda*; instead of *villa, alavilla*. Some writers of Nahuatl understood the operation of the Spanish plural and used the singular and plural in the standard Spanish fashion. But more frequently the *-s* ending was perceived as a singular and an additional Nahuatl plural in *-me* might be used: thus *alċaldes* (generally written *al̄l̄des*), "one judge," and *alcaldesme*, "judges." The monetary terms *peso* or *pexo* and *tomin* or *domin* did not vary according to number. Each writer would generally use either the singular or the Spanish plural for all cases. Most common of all were the abbreviations $p^{o}s$ and $t^{o}s$: "i $p^{o}s$ i $t^{o}s$," "1 peso and a tomín."

Once established in the Nahuatl lexicon, loan words from Spanish could take the usual affixes and endings, making them harder to recognize. Spanish nouns almost never received the absolutive suffix in *-tl* but could take plurals, as we have seen, and also frequently appear in possessed form (*nocauallo*, "my horse"). In one testament there is the form *mofirmatique*, "they signed," in which *firma* appears between a reflexive pronoun and a verbal ending indicating the causative in the preterit plural. Even when loan words appear exactly as in the Spanish, a certain alertness is required to recognize them. Thus we hesitated for a time when confronted with the string *cemula* before recognizing it as *ce mula*, "a mule."

The great dictionaries are not much help with Spanish loan words in Nahuatl. Molina recognized their importance and their status as a valid part of the language, yet he did his work at an early time when many Spanish terms were still not fully consoli-

Expected Equivalences for Spanish Letters in Nahuatl

Spanish	Expected primary Nahuatl substitution	Expected secondary Nahuatl substitution through hypercorrection or nondistinction
b or v (initial	p	f
b or v (medial)[1]	u[2] or p	..
c(qu)	..	g
d	t	..
f	p	b, v
g	c[k]	..
j	x[3]	..
l	(none, or ll)	r
ll	l,[4] ly	..
n	(often omitted)[5]	..
ñ	n	..
r	l	..
s	x[3]	..
t	..	d
u	o	..

[1]Often written *u* in Spanish in the sixteenth and seventeenth centuries.

[2]Even when both the Spanish and the Nahuatl were written *u*, there was a phonetic change from a bilabial obstruent to a glide, [w].

[3]In the situations where this occurs, it is probably that the Spanish consonant itself had that sound, [š]. One also sees *s* changed orthographically to *c* and *z* on rare occasions.

[4]*Ll* was often retained, though the sound would have been different, a true double or long [l].

[5]And frequently added in the Nahuatl where lacking in the Spanish.

dated in Nahuatl usage. In any case there is an ecclesiastical-scholarly emphasis in Molina, with a corresponding relative neglect of the technical and economic terms which are the loan word's special province. Siméon, the purist, is frankly hostile to loan words and does not even reproduce all the entries in Molina. That neither work is strong in this area is of no great consequence wherever the original Spanish meanings of loan words were retained, as they were more often than not. But there were important exceptions. Neither Molina nor Siméon gives a full definition of the just-mentioned word *tomin* or *tomines*, which from the mid-sixteenth century forward not only denoted a coin worth one-eighth of a peso, as it did in Spanish (though in Spanish before long *real* nearly displaced *tomín*), but more especially meant "money in coin," "cash," or simply "money." Another slightly transformed term is *medio*, usually appearing as *melio*,[8] abbreviated m^{o}, which specifically means half a real or tomín, even when the latter term is not specifically given; in other contexts indigenous words were used for "half."

Orthography, Transcription, and Translation

The paleography of colonial Nahuatl documentation will present few problems to anyone conversant with the epoch's Spanish script, of which it forms a part, even following the changes in style through the centuries. Over time the two traditions grew closer and closer, until by the eighteenth century there was hardly any calligraphic difference left at all between Nahuatl and Spanish documents. Most historians and some anthropologist-ethnohistorians will already know the Spanish paleography, so there is little need for us to go into detail in this respect. Perhaps, though, linguists and others can learn to read the Nahuatl documents without passing through a Spanish calligraphic apprenticeship. To that end we are including reproductions of the originals of several of our documents (in addition, facsimiles of Docs. 29 and 30 are published elsewhere). It seems fair to say that the eighteenth-century hand is quite easy for twentieth-century readers and that in the earlier period Nahuatl writing is overall distinctly easier than the Spanish notarial hand in which the bulk of Spanish documentation is written. Because of the newness of the tradition, or because of clerical influence in the Mexico City schools were it originated, Nahuatl writing of the sixteenth century is less cursive and more Italianate than the contemporary Spanish notarial-secretarial hand and far less plagued with abbreviations. In fact, the main ones found are taken over from the Spanish, for common Spanish names, titles, and monetary units. Place names are sometimes abbreviated, usually only after being written out once in full. The only strictly Nahuatl abbreviations we have seen are the ubiquitous tot^{o}, tt^{o}, or $tote^{o}$ for *totecuyo*, "our lord," and once or twice *che* for chane, "citizen," as well as a^{o} for *amo*, "not," and a superscribed $^{-co}$ at the end of a word to indicate *-tzinco*.

---

[8]Being alveolar segments, [d] and [l] would be susceptible to interchanging. In fact, this occurred in sixteenth-century Spanish itself, as in *Cáliz* for *Cádiz*.

A few peculiarities of the writing will bear mention; we will take this opportunity also to discuss our principles of transcription and to offer some hints for understanding the orthography of Nahuatl texts generally. In Spanish secretarial practice the line over or around *q*, to indicate *que* or at times *qui*, depending on the context, is a standard feature. Writers of Nahuatl did the same, but some of them went further to a consistent threefold distinction hardly used among Spaniards except in the ecclesiastical world and in printing: *q* with a vertical line over it (*q̍*) to indicate *qui, q* with a horizontal line (*q̄*) for *que*, and *q* with a line in zigzag pattern (*q̃*) to indicate *qua*. One also frequently encounters a device looking exactly like *qz*, to mean *que*. (The full spellings occur too, more frequently than the devices, and even frequently enough among the writers using the devices.) We have expanded these signs to their intended value in our transcriptions.

Like the Spaniards, writers of Nahuatl in the early period used a line over vowels to indicate syllable-final nasals. We have chosen for convenience and legibility to print the actual letter rather than the line, though certain problems arise. Nahuatl rules of phonetic assimilation called for an [m] instead of an [n] before [p] or [m]. In such situations we have therefore generally resolved the line as an *m*. Yet many writers in fact retained *n* before *p* and even before *m* when, as frequently, they wrote a letter instead of a line. When we had parallel examples of the unassimilated *n* in a given writer's practice, we have printed *n* instead of *m* in resolving the line. Therefore students of phonetics can draw no strict quantitative conclusions about syllable-final nasals from our texts, though all cases of unassimilated *n* are based on that writer's actual practice. It seems to us that *n* was more commonly left unchanged than assimilated, especially among writers without elaborate formal education; some writers used *n* or *m* indifferently in situations calling for assimilation. After all, writers of Spanish mainly used *n* in such cases, presumably with the phonetic value [m].

A final special sign of Nahuatl writing is a hook under a *t, ţ*, to indicate the sound [ts], generally written *tz*, occasionally *tç*. In the few instances of its occurrence in our texts we have resolved this *ţ* as *tz* or *tç* according to that writer's general usage. The *ç* which generally represented syllable-initial [s] before *a, o,* and *u* has been retained, and also the *tç* regardless of following vowel. But otherwise we have in the name of clarity removed the cedilla from the ç which was written sporadically, along with plain *c*, for [s] before *e* and *i*; this conforms with the practice of Molina and Siméon.

In all other respects we have followed the exact spelling of the original texts, not suggesting emendations except where a writer seemed to have made an obvious slip or oversight within the context of his own practice, however individual or variant that might be. In the printing of Nahuatl texts in general, we strongly advocate the retention of the ç before back vowels; this is the convention of both Molina and Siméon, and it was the practice of writers of Nahuatl at all levels through the sixteenth and seventeenth centuries. When it finally began to fall out of use in the eighteenth century, it was replaced in ordinary usage, not by the postreform *z* of today's Spanish canon, but by *s*.

Mastery of the system of orthography of Molina and Siméon is only the first of the skills necessary if one is to mediate successfully between Nahuatl texts and the dictionaries. One must also gain an understanding of the far-reaching effects of standard elisions and assimilations.[9] Even this is hardly adequate preparation for the great variety of Nahuatl speech and writing. There are common deviations from the dictionaries' orthographic system, of which the most important are:

Sound	Dictionary standard	Common variants
[i]	*i*	*y*[10]
[y]	*y*	*i*
[kw]	*qu*	*cu*
[s]	*ç, z*	*s* (18th cent.)
[š]	*x*	*s*
[w] (syllable-initial)	*u, v*	*o, hu, ho*
[w] (unvoiced, syllable-final)	*uh*	*hu, u, v*[11]
[ʔ]	—	*h*

[9]See Anderson, *Rules of the Aztec Language*, and Siméon's introduction.

[10]The letters *y* and *i* are not quite identical in usage in the texts. For the glide, *y* is much more common. With the syllabic vowel, there is a tendency to write *y* in the article *in* or at the beginning of words, and *i* within the word. Thus dictionary *inin*, "this," is most frequently seen as *ynin*; *inyn* would be an oddity.

[11]The [w]-equivalents yield innumerable variants. The single word *iuan*, "and," can also be *ihuan, ivan, ioan,* and *ihoan*, as well as *yuan, yhuan, yvan, yoan,* and *yhoan*.

And in general, an almost decorative *h* which is liberally sprinkled throughout Nahuatl texts, as it is in Spanish ones, must frequently be disregarded when looking up words.

Even some commonly seen variants that are doubtless not merely orthographic can be learned as though they were: *t* for standard *tl* (*matacti* = *matlactli*) or the interchangeability of *o* and *u* (*teotl* = *teutl*), *ia* and *ie* (*pia* = *pie*), *ye* and *e* (*yei* = *ei*). Syllable-final *n* and *m* are similarly equivalent, as seen above, and one could even view their free omission and insertion as orthographic. In any case, when a word is not to be found in the dictionaries, a reasonable hypothesis is that any syllable-final nasal in it may have been inserted, and that any open syllable may represent one ending in a nasal in the standard form.[12] Most aspects of consonant doubling and reduction can be seen in the same way. One must be prepared for any single consonant of the texts to represent a double one in the dictionaries, and vice versa. (For example, *ita* is often found instead of the standard *itta*, "see," and on the other hand, one finds *maquillia* instead of standard *maquilia*, the applicative of "give.")

But in fact all these variants have a phonetic dimension. Syllable-final *n* is more likely to be omitted before a consonant and even more likely before another nasal; it is doubled only between vowels. For standard *in tlacatl*, "the person," and *in amatl*, "the paper," some writers will quite regularly produce *ı̇ tlacatl* and *in amatl*; others, with equal regularity, put *in tlacatl* and *innamatl*.[13] Also, it appears that Nahuatl speakers were prone to insert glides between almost any two syllabic vowels. The dictionaries do not always recognize them, but glides may be expected whenever two vowels meet: [w] after *o* (or *u*), [y] after *a, i,* or *e*. Thus *tlatoua* = standard *tlatoa, puhua* = *poa, tlayocolli* = *tlaocolli, miyec* = *miec, teyotl* = *teotl.* Conversely, words without glides in the texts may appear with them in the dictionaries: *tlaecoltia* instead of the dictionaries' *tlayecoltia.*

---

[12]The dictionary word *oncan*, "there," can appear also as *ocan, onca,* or *oca*. These variants could equally well mean *oc can*, "another place"; *onca*, "there is"; or *o ca*, "behold." The string *ynopa* could be equivalent to *yn ompa*, "there," *yn nopan*, "for me," or *yn oppa*, "twice."

[13]The most persistent problems here have to do with the article *in*, the *n* of which very often geminates when the following word begins with a vowel. The important and sometimes difficult thing is to recognize the gemination and avoid analyzing the form *innamatl*, for example, as *in namatl*. On the other hand, when *in* precedes words beginning in *n*, including many first-person pronominal forms, one of the *n*'s is frequently lost, leaving legitimate doubt as to where the word begins. *Ineuatl* might be equivalent to either *in euatl*, "the hide," or *in nehuatl*, "I"; *inica* to either *in ica*, "with," or *in nican*, "here." The letter *n* is also especially omission-prone before glides and at the ends of phrases.

Beyond this, the best way to cope with the endless variants in the texts is to adopt, for pragmatic purposes of locating words in the dictionaries, the principle that the letters equal sound segments, and that any segment in a puzzling word may correspond to a phonetically neighboring segment in the word's dictionary form. Take the set of fricatives and affricates [s], [š], [ts], and [č], which are standardly written *ç* or *z, x, tz,* and *ch*. Almost any one of this closely related group can be a variant of any other:[14]

Standard	Variant
çotlaua	xotlaua
çan	tzan
mexica	mechica
tzontequi	çontequi
metztli	meztli
metztli	mextli
mitz	mich
choloa	tzoloa
pochtlan	poxtlan

There is also much interchanging of nasals, even in syllable-initial position, and of the members of the series *t, tl,* and *l*. With syllabic vowels, there is fluidity between bordering *i* and *e, e* and *a,* and it becomes even more marked between *o* and *u* (insofar as the latter phenomenon is not purely orthographic).

In our transcriptions we have not attempted to reproduce the word division or line segmentation of the original texts. Many writers, like their Spanish contemporaries, ran one word into the next until the pen went dry. Others did indeed leave spaces at intervals which were by no means random, but they still were far from consistent in respecting the "word." Particles and other short words were run together more often than not, articles were written together with nouns, and so on; no one set of rules maintained itself consistently, not even in any one writer's practice. An excellent example of this

---

[14]Actually, though one can probably find examples for all the possible switches, the main pattern is more specific than this. There are two points of articulation in this group, alveolar and palatal, and two manners of articulation, fricative and affricate:

	alveolar	palatal
fricative	s	š
affricate	ts	č

Interchanging is most common between segments which share one of the two characteristics and least common between the two sets which do not, [s] - [č] and [ts] - [š].

kind of quasi-word segmentation can be seen in Facsimile U* of the *Cartas de Indias*, the 1560 letter of the council of Huejotzingo which is our Document 29, and almost as pronounced in some of our illustrations. It appears to us that a thorough study of the subdivision of strings of letters in Nahuatl texts would be a rewarding enterprise, since in some cases the division seems to represent the writer's own conception of the organization of the language. There one can see much evidence to support the idea that the distinction between word and phrase was extremely tenuous in classical Nahuatl, that each type of structure partook of the characteristics of the other to a greater degree than in, say, English. Also one learns how the myriad short adverbial and connective particles were not words in the fullest sense, but were often attracted into the nearest sizable verbal or nominal agglutination, or formed fleeting, infinitely flexible combinations with each other.[15]

Of the two available dictionaries, Molina is a great deal closer than Siméon to sixteenth-century practice in this respect, generously adding up strings of associated roots to produce externally undifferentiated "words." Yet in our transcriptions we have chosen to follow the more atomistic procedures of Siméon, even though it does violence to the language by practically denying the possibility of the formation of new words by the extension of meaning beyond the mere combination of roots; in an English dictionary by Siméon, there would be no entry for "farewell" unless possibly "see *fare*." This does have the advantage of laying bare more of the structure of the language and facilitating lexical search for roots in a language which allows freewheeling combinations; therefore like Siméon we have printed as a separate word anything that can possibly be construed as standing independently. At the same time we have printed as one unit elements which are assimilated to each other. This occurs especially with the doubling of nasals, as discussed above. Thus we print *in atl*, "the water," but *innatl*, a form in which the *n* of the article has geminated and become the initial sound of the next syllable as well; *natl* by itself would be nonsense. The most important thing to remember is that word designation is not a standard feature of Nahuatl script, which is best thought of as an undivided string of letters, and that our segmentation into words is an interpretation.

Nor do Nahuatl texts (in this like coeval Spanish texts) have any uniform system of punctuation, as we have recognized by eschewing punctuation of any kind in our transcriptions. The obligatory incor-

---

[15]In this resembling the common behavior of clitics, but to a greater degree than in most European languages.

poration of subject and object into verbs makes it extremely difficult to determine whether a Nahuatl phrase is grammatically dependent on or conjoined with another. Intensive study of word order and connector use can probably clear up this matter, but for the present we do not wish through periods and commas to make any definite, possibly misleading statement that "a sentence ends here," or "this phrase is dependent on the preceding one." It seems conceivable that classical Nahuatl was able to achieve semantic precision while leaving the question of clause relationship in a relative limbo of flexibility and, seen from the perspective of English, ambiguity. The sentences in our translations obey practical considerations of subdividing an English paragraph and carry no implication that the sentence structure of Nahuatl is at all the same.

Various nonalphabetical marks do occur in the texts. A period-like dot occurs frequently; some writers put such dots in the spaces between word-sized units, but never at all consistently. The only fairly consistent use of the dot which we have seen is after *s* to indicate an abbreviation for *san* or *sant*, and this we have reproduced. There is also a double diagonal line (//) such as was used by the Spaniards to indicate paragraph divisions or radical changes of topic. In Nahuatl texts it sometimes occurs at such junctures; then other times where one might expect a sentence division; other times to separate the items of a list; and once in our experience, in the middle of a word. Therefore, we have viewed the sign as a potentially confusing element to be ignored in transcription. We have seen one example of a perfectly formed colon used as it would be used today, and were so impressed that we have printed it (Doc. 35), but this is an isolated instance. Also there are two or three marks in the early seventeenth-century will of don Juan de Guzmán (Doc. 4) that seem to be acting as commas, but it is hard to be sure of the intention, so we have omitted them. The essential thing to keep in mind when confronting punctuation-like markings in Nahuatl texts is the possibility that they may not indicate any syntactical break at all.

Many Nahuatl writers followed their Spanish contemporaries in using only one set of characters and making no distinctions at all between upper and lower case. Even with those who did have some distinctive capital letters in their repertoire or who on occasion made clear attempts to write certain letters large, the distinction was in no way basic to the calligraphy, necessary to understanding, or a uniform convention. Nevertheless, in the transcriptions we have reproduced recognizable efforts to write capital letters. Insofar as there is any pattern in their occurrence, they tend to fall at the beginning of documents or paragraph-like segments. From the late sixteenth century names are increasingly capitalized, usually the first word of the name only. Also the large letter representing Spanish double *r* appears in the Nahuatl texts; we have reproduced it in upper case, though there is no intention of capitalization per se in this character. Syntactically the most significant use of capitals is the persistent capital *A* of the word *Auh*, which seems to coincide with its frequent (far from invariable) use as a marker of the beginning of a new independent phrase. Both *auh* and its capitalization are invaluable guideposts for the practical translator.

By the eighteenth century, Nahuatl texts had a full set of upper- and lower-case characters, used as capriciously as in Spanish texts of that time, even in the middle of words. But since these capitals are easy to recognize and contribute to the general flavor, we have printed them. The resultant comic impression holds as much for the originals as for the transcriptions; it is ephemeral in both cases. One recognizes a tendency to capitalize all proper names and important words, almost as we do today in English in the titles of books, and in addition there is an exuberant glorying in the capital letter for its own sake independent of significance, unless esthetic significance.

In our translations, we have given priority to meaning; our primary purpose is to show scholars the potential of the documents. To produce a readily understandable English version, we have when necessary translated present tenses as past, subjects as objects, and passive verbs as active. We have supplied the copula, since that is the English practice; we have often omitted elements like *-quiuh*, "to come to do," which are left unexpressed in English. Nevertheless, since our second purpose is to provide a guide or key for those who would utilize documentation of this type, we have stayed as close to a literal translation as is consonant with a readable English text, even when this goes somewhat against English idiom. Though *oncan mani Acaltitlan* probably means neither more or less than standard English "it is at Acaltitlan," we have written the more literal "it is there at Acaltitlan," since this is at least possible in English. We have used the same procedure with Nahuatl metaphors. Thus the word *yollotl,* "heart," had come to signal emotional-volitional states in general. A phrase like *tle quinequi moyollo?* could best be rendered as "What is your wish?" Yet we have tended to write the more literal "What does your heart desire?"

Within this framework, we have made as accurate a translation as we presently can, but we wish to underline the speculative nature of the rendition of many passages which are without close parallel among previously published texts. A much larger corpus of texts must exist and a great deal of close philological investigation must be done before translations from older Nahuatl can be as subtle and accurate as, say, those from one European language to another. We do believe, however, that that goal can be attained, with considerable benefit for historical-anthropological analysis and for universal linguistics.

In our Nahuatl transcriptions we have used brackets to indicate (1) words and letters which are unclearly written or dubious in the original or (2) missing elements we have supplied from the context. In the English translations, renderings included within brackets are more than ordinarily speculative, while those in parentheses are items necessary for understanding which are clearly implied in the Nahuatl but not actually contained in it.

DOCUMENTS

I. Wills and

1. Testament of don Julián de la Rosa, Tlaxcala, 1566.[1]

traslado del testamento de don julian de la rosa

Ytechpatzinco dios tetatzin yxquichiuelli yuan ipiltzin yuan espū sancto yey personas çan uel ce nelli dios ma quimatican in ixquichime quitazque yn notestam^o yn nehuatl don julian de la rosa nican nichane ciudad de tlaxcalan nipoui ytech cabecera[2] ocotelulco yquac yn maçoyui nimococoua[3] yca notlalnacayo auh yn noceyaliztica uel nipactica niqueleuiya ynic uel niccencaua yn noyoliya yn nanima[4] ymactzinco nictlaliya yn notlatocauh in jhū x^o no itech nipoui yn notepantlatocatzin ytlaçohnantzin ciuapilli Sancta maria muchipa uel nelli ichpochtli niquitoua nicnocuitiya yca yn axcan nicchiua notestam^o yc tla[m]i noceyaliz yehuatl yn

— Yn achto itech nictlaliya yn nanima[4] dios yxquichiuelli oquiyocox oquimaquixti ica ytlaçohyezçotzin Auh yn yehuatl notlalna[ca]yo nicnomaquiliya in tlalli yehica ytech oquizqui intla yehuatli cocoliztli yc miquiz nonacayo nicnequi oncan nitucoz in teopan Sancta maria tlx̄n[5] teopan yglesia yxpan crucifixo tecalco[6]

— quito cocoxqui yn niquintlatlauhtiya teopixque[7] macuiltetl misa nechtlaocolizque nopan quitozque yn notlamanal yezqui monamacaz nocavallo çayyauh aoctle silla yn ipatiuh yezqui cavallo nochi ipan poliviz ynic misa mochivaz yuan centetl nepaniuhqui[8] notilma monamacaz no ipan pouiz ynic misa mochivaz yuan centetl nihuitilma patosyhuitl no monamacaz çannoye ipan poliviz ynic misa mochivaz tlamanalli yez yvan ontetl ayatzitzintin namacozque no

---

[1]Museo de Antropología, microfilm collection, series Tlaxcala, roll 1, item 21. The will is accompanied by a Spanish translation of c. 1580, mainly good though not quite complete. The originals of the documents are in the Tlaxcalan state archive. At the bottoms of pages, the copy of the testament, like Spanish notarial documents, contains notations to indicate corrections. The main terms are *tlilvavaqui*, "deleted," *tlatzalan ca*, "inserted between lines," and *noyeh*, "stet."

[2]The four "cabeceras" of Tlaxcala were districts or subdivisions of the province rather than head-towns as elsewhere.

[3]The *m* is not a mistake since *mo* had come to be the universal reflexive pronoun in

Related Documents

Copy of the testament of don Julián de la Rosa.

In the name of God the father omnipotent and his son and the Holy Spirit, three persons yet one true God, know all who see my testament that I, don Julián de la Rosa, a citizen here in the city of Tlaxcala and belonging to the Ocotelulco cabecera,[2] though at this moment I am ailing in my earthly flesh, yet in my mind I am very healthy; I desire, in order to prepare well my spirit and soul, to commend it to the hands of my lord Jesus Christ; I am also devoted to my intercessor his precious mother lady Saint Mary, eternally very true virgin. I declare and acknowledge herewith that now I make my testament and last will as follows:

— First I commend my soul to God omnipotent who created it and redeemed it with his precious blood. And as to my earthly body, I return it to the earth, since from there it came. If this is a sickness from which my body will die, I wish to be buried there at the church of Santa María in Tlaxcala,[5] in the church, before the crucifix [in a stone tomb].[6]

— The sick person said: I request the priests[7] to do me the charity of saying five masses for me. My offering will be that my horse be sold, it goes without saddle; the price of the horse will all go for saying masses. And a plaited[8] cloak of mine will be sold, it will also be devoted to saying masses, and a feathered cloak of mine, with duck feathers, will also be sold, it too will go for saying masses and be an offering. And two very fine cotton cloaks will be

---

some areas. Molina in his *Arte* (f. 24) specifically mentions that the Tlaxcalans used *mo* in the first person.

[4]The original is *naīa*. Lines to represent nasals are standard, but rare intervocalically. The intention may have been *naniman*.

[5]The Spanish translation is *en el monesterio desta dicha ciudad*.

[6]Molina defines *tecalli* as "casa de bóveda." Perhaps the *capilla mayor*, or main altar area, is what is meant, though to our knowledge there was never any vaulting in the Tlaxcalan monastery church. The Spanish translation has simply *junto al cruciffijo*.

[7]The Spanish translator considers the priests to be the friars of the monastery.

[8]See *Florentine Codex*, Book 9, p. 8. In the Spanish translation, *vna manta labrada*.

oncan pouiz yn ipan misa mochivaz centetl ychcacoztli cetetl uahcalxochiyo[9] auh yn nochi omonamacac yn ixquich ipatiuh yn iquac oquizqui macuiltetl misa yn oc quexquich mocauaz tomines yn oc quenman quimilnamiquizque teopixque tlaocolilozque[10]

— Auh in ica nochanyo nicnequi yn teoyotica nonamic ytoca maria cozcapetlatzin nican yezqui nochan centlahcoltica yezqui Auh yn caltitlan onpa yezqui yn niccauhtzin baptista cuicuitlapan ynauac yezqui yn nonamic ynic yezque yeh tlahmah in tepantli xochitecochtenco yn nonamic ohtenco ahciz auh yn nicmaca cuemitl nonamic tecpatepec napoualpatlauac centzontli yc ueyac yuan centetl mani chiyauhtla acxoteca cuentla[11] yc tepal oncan titlacati yca tocihtzin[12] tlalteuahcan yepoualpatlauac macuilpoualli ueyac oc centetl mani atenco çauapan[13] contlan tlayacac[14] cenpoualmatzintli onmacuilli yc ueyac cenpoualmatl oncaxtolli oquixoxocoque noye quipiaz yn nonamic auh inic oquixoxocoque ipan tlatoz yn baptista ixpan just[a] Oc centetl mani nepaual ohtlamaxalco[15] panotecatl ixpan çan cuenmantica chichicocalactica[16] intepanco teixuiuan[17] quauhquiyauac[18] ceccapal acxotecapan[11] oc centetl çacatl çan inauac cenpoualmatzintli onpoualhueyac nochi quipiyaz yn nonamic

— Auh yn nicmaca baptista yn cuemitl onpa amaxac onpoualpatlauac centzontli yc ueyac

— Auh yn amiztlato[19] diego yn nicmaca cuemitl acolco necoc onpoualcoyauac[20] oc tlahco actica Ju[o] ximenez ycuen no cepa nocuen çanno necoc onpoualcoyauac noyeh quipiyaz in di[o] amiztlato oc cepa nepa ça pitzauatica at chiconmatl chicuematl ic patlauac ynic ueyac at macuilpoualli çannoyeh quipiyaz in diego

---

[9]See *Florentine Codex*, Book 8, p. 24. In the Spanish translation, *dos mantas de toldillos labrados*.

[10]Or "they will remember the priests who are to receive charity"?

[11]*Acxoteca Cuentla* is given by the Spanish translator as the name of a place, but it might be interpreted as "next to the fields of the Acxotlan people."

[12]The Spanish translator omits mention of birth, rendering the whole passage from *Cuentla* through *tocihtzin* as *que las huue de parte de mi abuela*.

[13]We can give no meaning for *çauapan* unless it is yet another place name. The Spanish translator ignores it. *Atenco* itself could be "at the water's edge," but the translator seems to know the place as "Atengo."

[14]The Spanish translator considers Contlan Tlayacac a place name. It might mean "in the district of Contlan." See Molina's *cecentlayacapan*, "en cada barrio," an entry which was brought to our attention by Luis Reyes.

[15]Possibly "road crossing" rather than a set place name, though the Spanish translator considers it the latter.

sold and will also be devoted to saying masses, one of them of yellow cotton, and one with basket-flower design.[9] And when it has all been sold, all of its price, when five masses have been taken out of it, (with) however much money remains [the priests will at times remember those who are to receive charity].[10]

— And as to matters of my household, I want my legitimate wife named María Cozcapetlatzin to be here at my home. She will be with half of it, and my younger brother Bautista will be there at the house in the back; he will be next to my wife. He knows how they will be. The dividing line is at the edge of the garden; my wife's (half) will reach to the road's edge. And I give my wife a field at Tecpatepec, 80 (brazas) wide, 400 long; and one at Chiyautla, (in the part) Acxoteca Cuentla[11] where we were born and (that we inherited) through our grandmother[12] at Tlaltehuacan, 60 (brazas) wide, 100 long; and another one at Atenco [. . .][13] in Contlan Tlayacac,[14] 25 brazas, 35 brazas long. They invaded it, (but) my wife is to have it also, and Bautista is to bring suit before the law about what they invaded. There is another one there in the vicinity of Otlamaxalco[15] facing the Panotlan people; it is a cultivated field going back and forth irregularly[16] at the borders of the dependents.[17] At Quauhquiyauac,[18] near one part of Acxoteca,[11] is another one, an uncultivated field, right next to the (other one), 20 brazas, 40 long. My wife will have it all.

— And I give Bautista the field there at Amaxac, 40 (brazas) wide, 400 long.

— And as to Diego Amiztlato,[19] I give him a field at Acolco, 40 (brazas) wide on both sides;[20] in the other half lies Juan Jiménez' field, then again a field of mine, also 40 (brazas) wide on both sides; Diego Amiztlato will have it too. Also there is just a narrow strip there maybe 7 or 8 brazas wide, maybe 100 long; Diego will have it likewise.

---

[16]The Spanish version here is *ques vna suerte redonda que no estan los linderos [derechos?] que vnos entran y otros salen a la linde de los teyxihuas.*

[17]The *teixuiuan*, literally "someone's grandchildren," were a group directly connected with and subordinated to the noble houses. Their exact status has been a subject of doubt in both the sixteenth and twentieth centuries. In some descriptions they are considered as lower nobility themselves; in others they seem closer to the status of the *macehualli* or commoner. A 1554 land suit (in this same roll 1 of the Tlaxcala microfilm series, item 2), in which don Julián de la Rosa was himself involved, speaks of the *maceguales que dizen texiguas*. As just seen in note 16, the Spanish translator of don Julián's will retains the word *teyxihuas* throughout.

[18]Thus the Spanish translator, but one may wonder if "at the gate" is not what is intended.

[19]An honorific title given to the master of the hunt in preconquest times; see Durán, *Historia*, I, 281. Here it is apparently being used primarily as a name.

[20]Presumably square, and so interpreted by the Spanish translator.

— Oc no oncan quipiaz baptista cuemitl onpoualli çanyano ixquich yn chiconmatl

— Auh in callah cuemitl tecpan[21] ya ytech pouhtica[22] in benito tequacuilli[23] çaniuh quipixtiyez[24] yuan ontetl calli

— Auh in uey calpolli in at oc ymixpan uetziz[25] noteachcauh diego amiztlato yuan baptista niccauh yehuan tlahmatque quen quichivazque

— Auh in ipiltzin benito tequitotol ytoca mīn yn quenin quipiya cuemitl ma çaniuhtiye çan tel nochi quimocuillitah ayac quimacac auh in solar ipan catca oncan tlatenco nehuatl nicpatlac yca notlal auh çan oncan tocontlalica in benito tequitotol auh in axcan motequiz cequi ytech pouiz yn mīn macuilmatl auh yn oc chiquacenmatl nican pouiz nochan onpoualmatl yc ueyac

— Auh in amiztlato[26] achi onictlapan inotlal yn oncan yc omotlalli tepozpitzqui çaniuh quipixtiyez[24] at nanmatl yc patlavac çan quitocatiyez[28] nepa yahtiyez yeh tlahma ynic oquinacazti ycal çaniuh tlamelauhtiyez ytech ahcitiuh mīn ytepanco ohtentli quitocatiyez

— Auh in teixuiuh tepiltzin yn iuh otechmotlacamachitiyaya tiuan niccauh[29] juº ximenez çaniuh yezque ynic quintlacamatizque in diº yuan baptista ocotitlan cate yuan tlilhuacan chiyauhtenco contlan

[21]In the Spanish version, *tierras solariegas de tecpa.* Molina gives *calla* as "población" or "casería." The sense of the phrase might well be "the land around the chiefly household's complex." *Tecpan* means both a royal or chiefly palace and the household or lineage that holds it, as well as having yet broader meanings; below, it apparently refers to the whole district of San Pedro. The Spanish translator retains the Nahuatl word in his version.

[22]It is not clear in which direction *ytech pouhtica* refers. An alternate translation would be "And as to the land with houses belonging to the chiefly household, Benito Tequacuilli . . ."

[23]"Stone image"; the word had also been the title of a minister charged with the education of girls for the temples (Simeón, p. 455), and thus even here might refer to some official function. The Benito Tequitotol just below is presumably the same person.

[24]The phrase *çaniuh quipixtiyez* occurs in the text three times. The *pix-* in *pixtiyez* derives from *pi(y)a*, the *a* being lost in combined form, and the *y* in syllable-final position changing to *x*, as for example *calpixqui. Pia*, glossed in Molina as *guardar*, is here well on its way to meaning "have" as well as "keep," and the Spanish version is usually *tener.* The form *-tiyez* is a sort of future progressive much used in Tlaxcalan documentation. Thus presumably the literal meaning is "he will be having or

— Also Bautista will have a field there, 40 (brazas), all of it the same 7 brazas (wide).

— And as to the chiefly household's land with houses,[21] already belonging to[22] Benito Tequacuilli,[23] he is to take care of it as he has been,[24] along with two houses.

— And as to the greater calpulli, if perhaps it still [is to come to the attention of][25] my older brother Diego Amiztlato and Bautista my younger brother, they know how they will do it.

— And Benito Tequitotol's son named Martín, as to how he has land, let it be as it has been, though he just seized it all, no one gave it to him. And the lot on which he was there at Tlatenco, I exchanged it with my land, and there we settled Benito Tequitotol, and now it is to be divided. Five brazas of it will belong to Martín, and the other 6 brazas will belong to my house here; it is 40 brazas long.

— And I took a little of my land there [for?][26] Amiztlato, on which a blacksmith settled; he[27] is to keep it as it has been,[24] perhaps 4 brazas wide. He is only to follow[28] where it will extend, as he knows, as far as the corner of his house; (then) it will just go straight ahead as far as Martín's fence; it will follow the edge of the road.

— And as to the dependents who have obeyed us, my cousin[29] Juan Jiménez and me, they are to be as before, so that they will obey Diego and Bautista. They are at Ocotitlan and Tlilhuacan, Chiyauh-

---

keeping." Yet a distinction is apparently being made between *quipiaz* and *quipixtiyez. Pia* is often used here in contexts where "have" is appropriate, not that it necessarily means full ownership any more than English "have," but that attention is being drawn to the aspect of having. *Pixtiyez*, each time qualified by *çaniuh*, apparently in the sense "just as is," seems to convey something more akin to custody, and indeed the translator uses *guardar* in this case (though reverting to *tener* in the other two, below).

[25]See Molina's entry *nixco uetztiuh*, "ir abriendo los ojos y el entendimiento, para entender los negocios." The Spanish version of this passage, which as far as we can see is fanciful, runs in its entirety: "y el capule grande y la casa del mayorasgo si murieren los dichos bautista y diego amistlato ellos saben lo que an de hazer dello."

[26]It appears to us that don Julián might have taken the land *from* rather than *for* Amiztlato. *Onictlapan* is literally "I broke off." The Spanish version is *a amistlato le di un pedazo de tierra.*

[27]Whether "he" is Amiztlato or the blacksmith is not quite clear to us; the Spanish translator decided in favor of the former.

[28]Or "to sow it"?

[29]The terms for brothers were used also for cousins. The Spanish translator puts *hermano* here, but the land suit mentioned in n. 17 says *Juan Ximenez e don Julian su primo.*

amaxac yvan panotlan ça quezqui calli izqui tlayacatl in omoteneuh[30]

— Auh in calpolli ythualco yn calli[31] ynnecuitlauil yezqui in di° amiztlahto yvan baptista amo yhtlacauiz quimocuitlauizque yehica techan

— yn teixuivan oc cequin cate chiqualoapan

— Auh in chimalli yuan matlacpoualli quetzalli ma çaniuhtiyez ynpiyal yezqui in di° yuan baptista yvan centetl coyotl ytzontecon yuan patzactli çanno yuh mopiyaz

— Auh in oçomahtli ytlacayo[32] yuan coxcox ytzontecon xiniz mochivaz cirios onpa monequiz tecpan[21] teopan sant p°

— yn oc centetl quetzaltototzintli ycuitlapil yyahtlapal[33] çanno yuhtiyez mopiyaz

— quito cocoxqui yn iquac momiquiliz teoyotica nonamic yn cuemitl çan nican quicauhteuaz yn nochan yc mopiyaz yn ithualli quiyauatl[34]

— yn noalbaceas yezque antonio mocatl yuan ant° tahua teoyotica nechpaleuizque yuan nochanyoyca

— yuan quito cocoxqui cuemitl niquinmacac teixuiuan cate atlantepec yn teyacantica ytoca fr^co xiuhtototl ynic nechtlacamati yn iquac pasqua natiuitas yuan pasqua resurrecion yuan corp^os xp̄i yuan sancta maria assunpcion yn nechmaca cecentetl vexolotl matlacpoualli cacauatl yuan tamalli chilli quauitl auh in iquac sant pedro ylhuiuh yn nechmaca ontetl vexolotl matlacpoualli cacauatl yuan tamalli quauitl chilli çanno yuh quichiuazque quimacazque teoyotica nonamic yuan quitlay cuemitl tecpatepec yuh quichiuazque ynic niquinmacac cuemitl quipiya sentencia

---

[30]There are various possibilities here. The Spanish translation runs ". . . y panotlan que seran pocas casas son conthenidas arriba." In this case the translator does not take *tlayacatl* for a place, as above. An alternate translation might be ". . . and Panotlan. (There are also) a few houses belonging to the Tlayacac people mentioned above." Or Tlayacac could be construed as part of Panotlan. The "few houses" could refer to Panotlan directly or to the whole preceding passage, and the last part could mean "these are all the mentioned districts." Or the translation could be "there are a few houses at each of the mentioned districts."

[31]The words seem to lend themselves to this construction, yet we have also seen *ithualco* in the meaning of a large complex of houses under one head; there may well be some metaphorical or kinship meaning here that escapes us. The Spanish translator turns the matter in a completely different direction from our version: "y el

tenco, Contlan, Amaxac, and [at Panotlan the mentioned district with a few houses?].[30]

— And the house at the calpulli courtyard[31] will be under the care of Diego Amiztlato and Bautista. It is not to go to ruin, they are to take care of it, because it is someone else's home.

— There are more dependents at Chiqualoapan.

— And the shield with 200 quetzal plumes, let it be as it is; it is to be in the keeping of Diego and Bautista, and a coyote's head (headdress) with crest device will also be so kept.

— And the monkey [of feathers][32] with the pheasant's head (device) will go to make candles needed there at the district[21] church of San Pedro.

— Another quetzal bird's plumes[33] will also be kept as they are.

— The sick person said: when my legitimate wife dies, she is to leave the fields to my household here [so that the patio and door will be kept].[34]

— My executors will be Antonio Mocatl and Antonio Tahua; they will aid me with churchly things and with my household.

— And the sick person said: I gave fields to the dependents who are at Atlantepec; a man named Francisco Xiuhtototl supervises them so that they obey me. At Christmas and Easter and Corpus Christi and the Assumption of Mary, they give me one turkey cock each, 200 cacao beans, and tamales, chiles, wood; and on St. Peter's day they give me two turkey cocks, 200 cacao beans, and tamales, wood, chile. They are also to do and give the same to my legitimate wife. And they work the fields at Tecpatepec; they are to (continue to) do the same, since I gave them the fields (and) they have the court order.

calpul que esta en el patio de cassa los tengan a su cargo diego amistlato y bautista para que no sea maltratado porques de todos los teyxihuas."

[32]In the Spanish, *vn mono de plumas con la cabeça de oropel*. The translator apparently took *itlacayo* to be from *tlachcayotl*, "la pluma mas delicada y blanda del ave" (Molina). Alternatively, it might represent *ytlacyo*, "trunk" or "body."

[33]Literally "tail and wing." The Spanish translator interprets *quetzaltototzintli* as a diminutive, speaking of a *pajaro pequeño*.

[34]Presumably metaphorical: "so that the family will keep the symbols of its identity." The Spanish translation goes much further: "las tierras y sementeras las dexe en mi casa para [sic] se guarden y tengan en el calpul grande donde se juntan los teyxihuas."

— yn notla fran^{co} chichimecayaotequiua[35] nicmacac cuemitl couaqualocan otonpan[36] çaniuh quipixtiyez[24] aoctle quimitaviliz[37]

— quito cocoxqui nicneltiliya notestam^{o} yc tlami noceyaliz ixpan mochiuh mag^{co} $\overline{sr}$ blas osorio a$\overline{ll}$de hordinario yn nican mihtoua ciudad y su proui^{a} de tl$\overline{xn}$ por su mag^{t} yuan ymixpan p^{o} de la cadena andres de herera leonardo contrellas regidores tl$\overline{xn}$ ypan quitlalique infirmas yntoca yuan nixpan di^{o} de soto escr^{o} tl$\overline{xn}$ ipan nictlalli nofirma notoca yn cocoxqui auel quitlalli ytoca ipanpa a^{o} quimati leer quitocayoti andres ḏe herera mochiuh ychan don julian ipan diez y nueve de mayo de mil y quini^{o}s y sesenta y seis años don julian de la rosa blas osorio pedro cadena andres de herera leonardo contrellas nixpan mochiuh diego de soto escrivano tlaxcallan

Ypan mui noble y mui leal ciudad de tlaxcalan macuililhuitl mes de junio de mil y quini^{o}s y sesenta y seis años ymixpan mag^{cos} señores don ju^{o} m$\overline{in}$ gou^{or} yuan blas osorio don domingo marmolexo julian de silva a$\overline{ll}$des hordinarios yn nican mihtoua ciudad y su proui^{a} de tl$\overline{xn}$ por su mag^{t} yuan nixpan di^{o} de soto escr^{o} tl$\overline{xn}$ mopouh in itestam^{o} don julian de la rosa catca chane nican ciudad omihto poui tecpan[21] sant pedro ipan cabecera ocotelulco cacoc nican audi^{a} tl$\overline{xn}$ yn $\overline{sr}$ gou^{or} yuan a$\overline{ll}$des tlanauatique yuh mopiaz neltiz yn iuh tlanauatita don julian catca yuh quipiazque yn iuh quintlamamacata yuanyolque ymixpan testigos buenauentura de paz tatheo de niça toribio maldonado joachin de la corona[38] yn $\overline{sr}$ gou^{or} yuan a$\overline{ll}$des yuan testigos mofirmatique motocayotique don ju^{o} m$\overline{in}$ blas osorio don domingo de marmolejo julian de silva bu^{ra} de paz nit^{o} tatheo de niça toribio maldonado joachin de la corona nixpan mochiuh diego de soto escr^{o} tl$\overline{xn}$

Yn iz catqui ytech moquixti yn original ytestamento don julian de la rosa catca çan uel yuhtica atle yc mopatili çan neneuhqui ymixpan moquixti pasqual tziuhtecatl ju^{o} baptista pedro quauhtli br^{do} mixcouatl yn nies[cr^{o}] omoteneuh nican nictlalli nofirma notoca yquac mochiuh macuililhuitl mes de henero de mil y quini^{o}s y setenta y tres años

doy fee di^{o} de soto scr^{o} tl$\overline{xn}$

[35]"Chichimec war captain."

[36]In the Spanish translation, *en los otomies*; yet *Otonpan* would also be a good place name.

— As to my uncle Francisco Chichimecayaotequiua,[35] I gave him a field at Couaqualocan among the Otomis;[36] he is to keep it as it is[24] and say nothing more.[37]

— The sick person said: I certify my testament and last will. Done before the magnificent lord Blas Osorio, alcalde ordinario here in the said city and its province of Tlaxcala for his Majesty, and in the presence of Pedro de la Cadena, Andrés de Herrera, Leonardo Contreras, councilmen of Tlaxcala, whereon they placed their signatures and names, and before me, Diego de Soto, notary in Tlaxcala, whereon I put my signature, my name. The sick person could not put his name because he does not know how to read; Andrés de Herrera signed for him. Done at don Julián's home on the 19th of May of the year of 1566. Don Julián de la Rosa. Blas Osorio. Pedro Cadena. Andrés de Herrera. Leonardo Contreras. Done before me, Diego de Soto, notary in Tlaxcala.

In the very noble and very loyal city of Tlaxcala, on the 5th day of the month of June of the year 1566, before the magnificent lords don Juan Martín, governor, and Blas Osorio, don Domingo Marmolejo, Julián de Silva, alcaldes ordinarios here in the said city and its province of Tlaxcala for his Majesty, and before me, Diego de Soto, notary in Tlaxcala, was read the testament of don Julián de la Rosa, late citizen of the said city here, belonging to the district[21] of San Pedro in the cabecera of Ocotelulco. When it was heard here in council in Tlaxcala, the sir governor and alcaldes ordered that it be kept and carried out as the late don Julián ordered; his relatives are to keep it as he distributed it to them. Before the witnesses Buenaventura de Paz, Tadeo de Niza, Toribio Maldonado, Joaquín de la Corona.[38] The sir governor and alcaldes and witnesses signed and wrote their names. Don Juan Martín. Blas Osorio. Don Domingo de Marmolejo. Julián de Silva. Buenaventura de Paz. I am a witness, Tadeo de Niza. Toribio Maldonado. Joaquín de la Corona. Done before me, Diego de Soto, notary in Tlaxcala.

The above was copied from the original of the testament of the late don Julián de la Rosa; it is just like it, with no changes, just exactly the same. It was copied in the presence of Pascual Tziuhtecatl, Juan Bautista, Pedro Quauhtli, Bernardino Mixcouatl. I the aforementioned notary put here my signature, my name; the time it was done was the 5th day of the month of January of the year 1573.

I attest. Diego de Soto, notary in Tlaxcala.

---

[37]I.e., "make no more claims."

[38]The Spanish translator renders this as *de la Coruña*.

2. Testament of doña Catalina de Sena, Coyoacan, 1588[1]

Nehuatl doña catalinan de gena[2] nicnoneltoquitia yn ssantisima trinidad yn dios tetatzin yn [dios] tepiltzin yn dios espu^{o} santo yn ixquich quimoneltoquitia yn tonantzin santa yglesia ca ixquich nicnoneltoquitia yn ixquich quimoneltoquitia yn christianosme ca no ixquich nicnoneltoquitia yn axcan notech oquimotlalili yn tt^{o} dios yn cocoliztli cenca ninococohua auh yn noyolo çan pactica noyolocopa yn nictlalia notestamento yn iquac yntla oninomiquili y[n] naniman nicnocemmaquilia yn notecuiyo yn dios ca itlachihualtzin ma quihualmani[liz]

— ynic centlamantli nitlanahuatia yn iquac yn oninomiquili oncan ninotocaz yn ichantzinco s^{or} san ju^{o} bap^{ta} calitic nohuentzin mocahuaz nahui tomin yc nechmaniliquihui teopantl[aca] nahui tomin orancio nopan mitoz yn otlica[3] ome tomin momacazque teopantlaca santo Comonio mocahuaz ome tomin ynic nitlilpolihuiz[4] yhuan ome tomin nohuentzin noestra señora del rosario yhuan nahui tomin nohuentzin ynnompa tepeacac yn itechtzinco pohuiz yn totlaçonantzin santa m^{a}

— ynic ontlamantli nitlanahuatia nicnitlanitiuh ontetl missa manior nopan mitoz monamacaz tlali onpa mani tepeticpanc nechmomaquilitia notatzin yc ocan monamacaz notlal chinampan[5] yn quezqui [in?] auiz oncan quizaz nicnotlanehui tomin cenpohuali oncan moxtlahuaz yhuan nictlanehuili ome peso maria catalinan no oncan quiçaz ynic moxtlahuaz yhuan ce tomin yc tlatziliniz ospital yhuan ce tomin santa catalinan yc tlatziliniz auh yn iquac nopan mitoz yn ontetl missa mayor momac[az]que teopantlaca nahui tomin ynic nopan quitozque onrras huentzintli motlaliz ymixpan tompa yn [on]tetl mitoz nahui tomin nohuentzin ynic ontetl nahui tomi tomin mocahuaz nohuentzin

— Yniquetlamantli nitlanahuatia yn teoyotica noconeuh yn itoca bal^{sar} garauajar nicmaca huerta cali çan quicencuiz yehuatl yn icaltzin yhuan yn ihuertatzin teoyotica nonamictzin auh yn [om]pa

---

[1]AGN, Tierras 1735, exp. 2, f. 107. A Spanish translation of 1681 is on ff. 144-145.

[2]Sena is the Spanish form of Siena. The lady has taken the name of St. Catherine of Siena.

[3]Possibly metaphorical, though the Spanish translator put "el responso que me digeron en el camino."

I, doña Catalina de Sena,[2] believe in the most Holy Trinity, God the father, God the son, God the Holy Spirit. All that our holy mother church deems true, all that I believe; all that Christians believe, also all that I believe. Now our Lord God has visited me with an illness; I am very ill, yet my spirit is healthy; of my free will I order my testament. For the time when I have died, I give my soul entirely to my Lord God, since it is his creature; may he take it to himself.

— First, I order that when I have died I am to be buried there within the house of lord St. John the Baptist. My offering will be four tomines so that the church people will come to take me; four tomines for prayer to be said for me [on my way];[3] two tomines will be given to the church people of the Holy Communion; the two tomines will be given when I die;[4] and two tomines is my offering to Our Lady of the Rosary, and four tomines is my offering to be devoted to our dear mother St. Mary there at Tepeacac.

— Second, I order and request that two high masses be said for me. The land there at Tepeticpac, that my father gave me, is to be sold, and additionally my land at Chinampan[5] is to be sold. However much is needed will come from there. I borrowed 20 tomines, it is to be paid back from there; I borrowed two pesos from María Catalina, also from there enough is to be taken to pay it back; and one tomín to ring the bells at the hospital; and one tomín to Santa Catalina to ring the bells; and when the two high masses are said for me, the church people are to be given four tomines to say honors for me; the offering is to be agreed on; the two (masses) are to be said before the tombs; four tomines is my offering; [for the second] (also) four tomines in money will be my offering.

— Third, I order: to my legitimate son named Baltasar Caravajal I give the orchard and house, he is to take all of it, it was the house and orchard of my legitimate husband; and as to the land there, I

[4]We take this for the equivalent of *nitlalpolihuiz*. The Spanish translator has "para que me boren de la memoria."

[5]This appears to be a place name as elsewhere in these papers, though conceivably an actual field of the *chinampa* type might be meant. The Spanish translation is "otras tierras que llaman la chinanpa."

tlali nicmacatiuh yn nochpoch yn itoca juana nocihuatlal[6] auh yn notelpoch cempantzin oncan n[ic]maca yn itoca ca bal^{sar} auh yn teoyotica nonamictzin catca yn itlaltzin ynnompa palpan nicmacatiuh yn notelpoch yn itoca bal^{sar} garavaiar

— Ynic nauhtlamantli nitlanahuatia yn notelpoch yn itoca bal^{sar} nicmacatiuh nocaltzin tonatiuh yquizayampahuic ontetl yhuan yn tlapancali çanno ontetl çan ipan ca yhuan yn ithualco yn tonatiuh ycalaquiampa ytzticac yn cali nicmacatiuh yn nochpoch yn itoca juana auh yn [itle]copayo yhuan yn ontetl mexicopa ytzticac yhuan yn itlecopayo[7] niccemmacatiuh yn notelpoch yn itoca bal^{sar} yhuan yn huerta nicmacatiuh yn nochpoch yn itoca juana çan niman ayac quicuiliz

— Ynic macuilamantli nitlanahuatia notlaltzin mani tetliyacac nicmacatiuh yn notelpoch yn itoca bal^{sar} tonatiuh ycalaquiampahuic ytech azi yn otli yhua yn nochpoch yn itoca juana nicmacatiuh yn ixeliuhca yn tonatiuh yquizayampahuic yhuan yn nopilotzin ynnitoca juan nicmaca matlaccuemitl[8] yn itech yn nochpoch yn itoca juana quimacaz yhuan yn cont[on]co mani tlali nicmacatiuh yn nochpoch yn itoca juana ca itlaltzin catca yn itatzin ayac quicuiliz yhuan yn i[c]quich nocihuatlatqui niccemmacatiuh yn quexquich yn nocalitic onoc moc[hi] niccemmacatiuh yn nochpoch doña juana

— ynic chiquacentlamantli nitlanahuatia yn nopan motlatoltizque niquinnonahuatilia alfaceas yn ipa[n] motlatoltizque naniman ynic ce tlacatl fray gaspar de vargas fray dḡo de contreras yhuan don feliphe de guzman nopan motlatoltizque yhuan yntla mochalanizque nopilhuan yhuan yn nochpoch yn doña juana yntechtzinco nicauhtiuh yn totlaçotatzin fray gaspar yhuan yehuatzin don feliphe de guzman yhuan nicmacatiuh yn nocal yn nochpoch yn onicteneuh yn quauhtlacopa yn huerta yquixohua niccenmacatiuh ca ye isquich yn niquitohua

ascan omicuilo 17 dias del mes de enero 1588 año nehuatl onicneltili yn ytlatol cocoscatzintli juan de san lazaro

---

[6] See "Types and Conventions of Colonial Nahuatl Documentation," p. 28.

[7] I.e., the same two small houses or rooms referred to at the beginning of the paragraph. The terminology for buildings and rooms is both interesting and, as yet, little known. *Tlapancalli* is composed of *tlapantli*, "flat roof" or "terrace," and *calli*, "house" or "large room." It could by its roots equally well mean "flat-roofed house" or "upper room." We have tentatively decided in favor of the latter, in view of the Spanish translation, *altos* (see also Doc. 11, n. 6). On the other hand, we have not followed the translation of *tlecopayotl* as *cocina*, in view of Molina's entry for *tlecopa*: "oficina

am giving my daughter named Juana my woman's-land,[6] and to my son whose name is Baltasar I give a strip there, and as to my late legitimate husband's land there at Palpan, I am giving it to my son named Baltasar Caravajal.

— Fourth, I order: I am giving my son named Baltasar my two small houses facing east, with [upper rooms], likewise two, right above them, with a patio facing west. I am giving the (main) house to my daughter named Juana, but as to its storage place and the two (houses) facing Mexico City with their storage places,[7] I am giving it all to my son named Baltasar; and I am giving the orchard to my daughter named Juana; no one at all is to take it from her.

— Fifth, I order: as to my small piece of land at Tetliyacac, I am giving my son named Baltasar (the part) facing west, reaching the road, and to my daughter named Juana I am giving her half facing east; and to my nephew named Juan I give ten furrows[8] next to (the land of) my daughter named Juana; she will give it to him; and at Cont[on]co is land that I am giving to my daughter named Juana, since it was her father's land; no one is to take it; and I give her all my household possessions; whatever is in my house, I give it all to my daughter doña Juana.

— Sixth, I order: as to those who will speak for me, I appoint as my executors who can speak for my soul first fray Gaspar de Vargas; fray Domingo de Contreras; and don Felipe de Guzmán; they are to speak for me also if my children argue among themselves; and I leave my daughter doña Juana with our dear father fray Gaspar and also with don Felipe de Guzmán; and I am giving my house, [the one toward the forest], to my daughter whom I mentioned. I am giving it all to her, (including) the orchard and its exit. That is all I have to say.

Written today, 17th day of the month of January, year of 1588. I verified the sick person's words. Juan de San Lázaro.

---

o cámara donde algo se guarda." The Spanish translation of *caltzintli* as *aposento* is also of interest. It seems quite possible that doña Juana's "house" and Baltasar's "small houses" were all part of the same building.

[8]The logic of the bequests seems to demand the interpretation "furrows" rather than "fields." Besides, plots and fields in the documents of the Valley of Mexico are generally *tlalli* or *milli*, and only in the Tlaxcalan Document 1 have we seen *cuemitl* with that meaning. The Spanish translator also gives *surcos*.

3. Testament of Juan Fabián, San Bartolomé Atenco, 1617[1]

Axcan lunes yc i dias del mes de augustus 1617 años

yn ipan axcan sanctissima trinidat dios tetatzin dios tepiltzin dios espū sancto y ça ce huellnelli dios yxquichyhuelli yn oquiyocox yn ilhuicatl yn tlalticpac yn ixquich itallo yhua yn amo ytallo ca mochi yehuatzin oquimochihuilli Auh yn axcan ca notech oquimotlalilli yn ijustitiatzin yn tt° dios yn nehuatl notoca juan babia nican nochan san bartholome atenco huel oc noyollocopa nictlallia notestamento canel ochicahuac yn notlallo noçoquiyo[2] ca ça nicnochielilia yn itlatoltzin yn notlaçotatzin dios yn quemman nechmotlatzontequililiz ynic nicahuaz yn tlalticpac yntla nechmopolhuiz yn tt° dios ca ymactzinco nocontlalia yn noyollia yn nanima ypanpa ca ytlamaquixtiltzin ca oquimomaquixtilitzino auh yn notlallo noçoquiyo ca ytech pouhqui yn tlalli ypanpa ca ytech quiz ca nitlalli ca niçoquitl ninocuepaz çanninoyollia nanima ma quihualmaniliz ca noconnocemmaquillia yn tt° dios yntla hualtotocaz yntla hualyetiez yn notlallo noçoquiyo yntla ninomiquiliz yntla nechmopolhuiz yn tt° dios yc tlatziliniz yn ichantzinco nuestra señora i t°s yc tlatziliniz san jacinto 2 t°s yc tlatziliniz yn onpa nocha san bartholome i t°s yc quimatizque yn nopilhua yc tlatziliniz santa maria natiuitas i t°s yc quiças candelas 2 t°s niman teopantlaca momacazque 4 t°s yhuan nitlanahuatia nicnitlatiuh centetl missa mayor yc palehuiloz naniman

— ynic centlamantli yc nitlanahuatia yn onpa nocha sant bartholome yn yehuanti nopilhua yn yehuatl nocihuamotzin mariana nicnomaquillia tlalli oncan mani xaxalpa yhuan yehuatl noxhuiuhtzin p° jacobo yhuan yehuatl notetlpoch juan babia quimoxelhuizque quiquauhtamachihuazque ixquich pouhqui yn nocihuamo yhuan noxhuiuh yhuan yehuatl notelpoch yn iquac yntla motlaliz quiniquac macoz yntla ye quichihua yn tlacoyotl tequiyotl[3] Auh yntlacamo motlaliz ahuel macoz

— ynic ontlamantli yc nitlanahuatia yehuanti noxhuihua ynic ce tlacatl cecilia anastacia ynic omenti ysabel niquinmacatiuh yn callali yhua cecni notlatl oncan mani otenco notlaocoliloca quecahuizque[4] yntla quimmochicahuiliz yn tt° dios

[1]McAfee Collection, UCLA Research Library, Special Collections.

[2]Literally, "my earth, my clay," a solemn formula meaning the body.

Today, Monday, first day of the month of August of the year 1617.

Now by the most Holy Trinity, God the father, God the son, God the Holy Spirit, yet indeed one true God omnipotent who created heaven and earth, and everything visible and invisible; he fashioned it all. Now that our lord God has issued his sentence upon me, I, named Juan Fabián, my home being here in San Bartolomé Atenco, still truly of my free will, order my testament, since my earthly body[2] has grown old and I am only awaiting the word of my dear father God when he will sentence me to leave the earth. If our Lord God removes me, I commend my spirit and soul to his hands, for it is something redeemed by him, that he freed, and my earthly body belongs to the earth because from there it emerged; and I will turn to earth and clay again, but may our Lord God take my spirit and soul to himself, for I give it entirely to him. If my earthly body worsens or weakens, if I die, if our Lord God removes me, then 1 tomín is for ringing the bells at the church of Our Lady; 2 tomines to ring the bells at San Jacinto; 1 tomín to ring the bells there at my home, San Bartolomé; my children know about it; 1 tomín to ring the bells at Santa María Nativitas; 2 tomines from which will come candles; then the priests are to be given 4 tomines, and I order and request one high mass for the aid of my soul.

— First I order: There at my home of San Bartolomé I give to my children (the following): to my daughter-in-law Mariana, the land there at Xaxalpan, and also to my grandson Pedro Jacobo and to my son Juan Fabián; they are to divide it and to measure it by rods, all belonging to my daughter-in-law, grandson and son. At that time if they agree among themselves, then it is to be given, if they do the service and tasks;[3] and if they do not agree among themselves then it cannot be given.

— Second I order: to my grandchildren, the first Cecilia Anastasia and Isabel, both of them, I am giving the house-land and a separate piece of my land there at the road's edge, [granted to me?]; they are to keep it[4] if our Lord God gives them strength.

---

[3]Note that this is not the familiar term *coatequitl*.

[4]Here one would expect *concahuizque* as at similar junctures in this document.

— yniquetlamantli yc nitlanahuatia notlalcohual oncan mani acatitla 4 p^{os} ypatiuh nicmacatiuh yn yehuatl noxhuiuh p^{o} jacobo yhuan nitlanahuatia yn yehuatl noxhuiuh mariana nicmacatiuh cecni tlalli oncan mani acatitlan

— ynic nauhtlamantli yc nitlanahuatia oncan mani tlalli tlalpechco nicnomaquilitiuh yn yehuatl teoyotica nonamictzin ju^{a} maria ayac quicuiliz yhuan nicnomaquilitiuh alahuerta yn onca onoc xocoquauhtzintli ayac quicuiliz yhuan nitlanahuatia yn yehuatl ytoca ju^{a} maria yhua yehuatl notelpoch juan niquinmacatiuh cecni tlalli onpa mani ocotitla concahuizque

— ynic macuillaman yc nitlanahuatia yn yehuatl notetlpoch juan babia centetl cauallo oquihuicac çan oquichtequico amo nicmaca amo nicteochihuilli 5 p^{os} ypatiuh yhuan nitlanahuatia notomines oquipiaya quauhxinque yc oquiquixtizquiya quahuacatl ynic ce tlacatl ytoca juan clemente quipiaya i p^{os} yc ome tlacatl augustin quipiaya 4 t^{os} yniquey tlacatl bablo quipiaya 4 t^{os} ynic nahui tlacatl matheo quipiaya 5 t^{os} mochi oquicuic ymatica amo nicteochihuilli yn nehuatl nitatzin ca cenca miyec yn itech ca yn tlahueliloc yntla quequemmania tlahuellilotiz ca nechixtlahuiliz

— ynic chiquacentlamantli yc nitlanahuatia quipia felipe chane atliytic i p^{os} 2 t^{os} yc moxtlahuiliz ytomines gabriel sanchez i p^{os} 2 t^{os} yhuan quipia ytoca babia chane tlacochcalco 4 t^{os} yhuan nitlanahuatia nechpielia notomines ytoca $fran^{co}$ quipia i p^{os} chane santo dḡo yc moxtlahuiliz ytomines yehuatl señor bartholome delez nicpielia i ps

— ynic chicontlamantli yc nitlanahuatia yn yehuatl españor andres te tabia nechpielia 5 p^{os} quixtlahuaz yn iquac yntla oquixtlauh yc mochihuiliz centetl missa mayor yn yehuatl nonamic catca ytoca cecilia anastacia yhuan nitlanahuatia yn yehuatl matheo xuarez quauhxinqui nicpialia 2 t^{os} moxtlahuiliz

— ynic [chi]cuentlamantli yc nitlanahuatia yn yehuatl nomo diego $fran^{co}$ onechpolhui centetl mulla yhuan mochi xalma auh ypatiuh 40 p^{os} yhua centetl macho xxxv ypatiuh yhuan centetl cauallo 7 p^{os} ypatiuh yhuan nicmacac 6 t^{os} yc nechcohuizquia tlaolli cenquahuacalli amo quineltili çano quipollo yhua yn iquac ohuia acalhuaca chicuey tonatiuh[5] onpa quichiuh atle oquitlaxtlahui yn nocahuallo yxquich i p^{os} quixtlahuaz yhua ce cuitlaxmecatl oquipollo 4 t^{os} ypatiuh yn ye mochi ytech ca nauhpohuanlli peso yhuan nahui peso yhua ome tomi Auh yn axcan nictlapopolhuia 40 p^{os} 4 p^{os} ça yxquich quixtlahuaz 40 p^{os} yc ninomaquixtitiuh yxpantzinco yn tt^{o} dios

[5] This term may be the Spanish *ocho días*, a week.

— Third I order: I am giving my purchased land there at Acatitlan, worth 4 pesos, to my grandson Pedro Jacobo, and I order that I am giving my granddaughter Mariana a separate piece of land there at Acatitlan.

— Fourth I order: I am giving the land there at Tlalpechco to my legitimate wife Juana María; no one is to take it from her; and I am giving her the orchard where there are fruit trees; no one is to take it from her; and I order that I am giving to (my wife) named Juana María and to my son Juan a separate piece of land there at Ocotitlan; they are to have it.

— Fifth I order: My son Juan Fabián took a horse, he just stole it, I am not giving it to him nor have I absolved him; it was worth 5 pesos. And I order: the carpenters [were to have] my money to make poles; the first named Juan Clemente, who [was to have] 1 peso; the second Agustín, who [was to have] 4 tomines; the third Pablo, who [was to have] 4 tomines; the fourth Matheo, who [was to have] 5 tomines. He took it all himself. I his father have not absolved him, for there is a great deal of badness in him. If sometime his badness diminishes, he is to pay me back.

— Sixth I order: Felipe, citizen of Atliytic, has 1 peso and 2 tomines with which to pay Gabriel Sánchez his money, 1 peso and 2 tomines; and (a man) named Fabián, citizen of Tlacochcalco, has 4 tomines. And I order: (a man) named Francisco, citizen of Santo Domingo, owes me money; he has 1 peso with which to pay Señor Bartolomé Téllez his money; I owe him 1 peso.

— Seventh I order: The Spaniard Andrés de Tapia owes me 5 pesos; he is to pay it. And when he has paid it, a high mass is to be held for my late wife named Cecilia Anastasia. And I order that 2 tomines that I owe Mateo Juárez, carpenter, is to be paid to him.

— Eighth I order: My son-in-law Diego Francisco lost me a female mule and all its pack-gear, worth 40 pesos; and a male mule worth 35; and a horse worth 7 pesos; and I gave him 6 tomines with which to buy me half a fanega of maize; he did not carry it out, he lost that too. And when he went to Acalhuacan for eight days,[5] there he did (this): he paid nothing (to maintain) my horse, he is to pay back a total of 1 peso; and he lost a leather strap worth 4 tomines. All that he is charged with is 84 pesos and 2 tomines; and now I pardon him 44 pesos, and he is to pay only 40 pesos, with which I will release him before our Lord God.

ye yxquich ynic nitlanahuatia yn imixpa aluaciasme yehuanti ytoca juan bicente fiscal dgo cihuatzitzinti ynic ce tlacatl juana viatriz ana maria chaneque san bartholome

onicneltilli yn itlatol cocoxcatzintli nehuatl nixpan nican nictlallia nofirma balthasar xuarez[6]

memoria

Yn ixquich yn itech ca Diego fran^{co} chane san matheo huitzilopochco

— yacachto quipollo macho ypatiuh onpohualli
pesos ytlatqui Espannor bar^{men} delez — xl p^{o}s

— ynic ontetl çan no macho ypatiuh cenpohuali
Oncaxtonli ypan ce peso çan quitlexixil — xxxvi p^{o}s

— ynicquetetl çan cavalo quimicti ypatiuh chicome
peso ytlatqui Espannor fuente — vii p^{o}s

— yhuan tlacotli catca ynic quixtlauh tomines ynic
quiz matlactli ypan Ome peso ytomin jacobo manuel — xii p^{o}s

— yniccouhpa oquimotlacui chiuhnahui [sic] pesos
ytomin jacobo manuel — ix p^{o}s

— yhuan xalma quipoloto yhuan preçada yhuan
coxtal mochi mecatl[7] ypatiuh tomines yey pesos — iii p^{o}s

— yhuan yc quicohuaz tlaonlli chiguacen tomin
yhuan Acha yc quicohuasquia nahui tomin — 1 p^{o}s ii t^{o}s

— yhuan yn ixquich tlacalaquinlli ynic moxtlahua
nauhxiuitl yn omoxtlahuilli yehuatl diego fran^{co}
mocentlalia — xiiii p^{o}s

memoria

Yn ixquich yn ye quicui tzapotl quinamaca yn yehuatl Diego fran^{co} chane san matheo huitzilopochco

— ynic ceppa Oquitec tzapotl — ce cabalo
— ynic ouhpa Oquitec tzapotl — ce caballo
— ynicquexpa oquitec tzapotl — ce caballo
— ynic nauhpa Oquitec tzapotl — ce caballo
mocentlalia chicuey coxtal — viii
amo ytlatqui amo iaxca

---

[6]Written on the outside, in another hand: *ytestamento ju^{o} phapia che s. bar^{me}.* "the testament of Juan Fabián, citizen of San Bartolomé."

This is all I command, in the presence of the executors, whose names are Juan Vicente, fiscal, and Domingo, and the women, first Juana Beatriz, and Ana María, citizens of San Bartolomé.

I verified the sick person's words (said) in my presence; here I put my signature: Baltasar Juárez.[6]

Memorandum

All that is charged to Diego Francisco, citizen of San Mateo Huitzilopochco.

— First, he lost a male mule worth 40 pesos, the property of the Spaniard Bartolomé Téllez.	40 pesos
— Second, another male mule worth 36 pesos; he just overworked it.	36 pesos
— Third, a horse he killed, worth 7 pesos, the property of the Spaniard Fuente.	7 pesos
— And [as to the helpers, he was to pay them the money, to produce 12 pesos], Jacobo Manuel's money.	12 pesos
— A second time he borrowed 9 pesos, Jacobo Manuel's money.	9 pesos
— And a packsaddle he lost, and a horse blanket and sacks [all of cord][7] worth 3 pesos in cash	3 pesos
— And to buy maize, 6 tomines; and to buy an axe, 4 tomines.	1 peso, 2 tomines
— And all the tribute to be paid for four years, that was paid for Diego Francisco, adds up to . . .	14 pesos

Memorandum

All of the zapote fruit that Diego Francisco, citizen of San Mateo Huitzilopochco, took to sell.

— The first time he cut zapote	1 horse(load)
— The second time he cut zapote	1 horse(load)
— The third time he cut zapote	1 horse(load)
— The fourth time he cut zapote	1 horse(load)
It adds up to 8 sacks.	8

It is not his property, not his possession.

---

[7]Possibly "and all the cord" is meant.

4. Testament of don Juan de Guzmán, Coyoacan, 1622[1]

yca yn itocatzin tote^{o} dios ma yxquich tlacatl quimati yn quenin nictlalia ynin memoria testamento yn ça tlatzacan notlanequiliz yn nehuatl don Ju^{o} de guzman nichane nican ypan altepetl villa cuyohuacan ypan tlaxillacalli s^{t}tiago xuchac niquitohua ca nicnoneltoquitia yn santissima trinidad dios tetatzin dios tepiltzin dios espiritu s^{to} can[2] ce huel nelli dios yxquichyhueli yn oquiyocux yn oquimochihuili yn ilhuicatl yn tlalticpac yn ixquich ytalo yhuan yn amo ytalo ca mochi nicneltoca yn ixquich quimoneltoquitia yn tonantzin s^{ta} yglessia catolica

yn axcan cenca ninococotica huel mococohua ynonacayo amo pactica yece yn notlamachiliz cenca pactica yn iuhqui nechmomaquili yn tote^{o} dios amo nitlapolohua auh yn axcan yntla nechmohuiquiliz dios yntla ninomiquiliz ca ymactzinco noconcahua yn noyolia yn naniman ma quihualmaniliz ca cenca nicnotlatlauhtilia yn tlaçocihuapilli s^{ta} m^{a} cemicac ichpochtli ma nopan motlatoltiz yn ixpantzinco ytlaçoconetzin tote^{o} Jesu x^{o} ma nechmocnoyttiliz ca nopampa omomiquili cruztitech omamaçohualtiloc oquimonoquili yn itlaçoyezçotzin ynic ninomaquixtiz yhuan yehuatzin s^{t} Ju^{o} bap^{ta} nosantotzin ma nopan motlatoltiz yn ixpantzinco dios

— ynic centlamantli nitlanahuatia niquitohua yn iquac yntla oninomiquili ompa ninotocaz yn huey teupan s^{t} ju^{o} bap^{ta} oncan yxpantzinco Entierro ymiquiliztzin tote^{o} dios oncan tonetocayan oncan mochintin toctitoque notatzin noteachcahuan noteyccahuan mocahuaz huentzintli yn iuh ca tlatecpantli yhuan hualmohuicaz ce totatzin capa quimotlaliz nechmaniliquiuh yhuan teupantlaca mocahuaz huentzintli yn iuh mocahuani ynic tlatziliniz auh ynin catley onca tomines nicpia ca ytech quiçaz calli monamacaz ompa mani tetla ycalteputzco s^{or} don ju^{o} cortes yhuan yni tlalli mochiuhtica temilli[3] ypan mamani tzapoquahuitl yhuan metl yhuan tecomuli[3] oncan mamani durasnos yhuan[4] atlacomulli yhuicallo yez in calli yhuan oncan quiçaz yc nitlaxtlahuaz notech ca missas chiquacentetl huehuey misas cantadas ypampa yaniman Doña ysabel micatzintli quauhtitlan cihuapilli yhuan ypampa ynamic catca don hernando estrada

---

[1]McAfee Collection, UCLA Research Library, Special Collections.

[2]For *çan*.

[3]See Molina's entry *centemilli*, defined as *sementera*. As to *tecomuli*, the prefix *te-* should be the root "stone" rather than the impersonal possessive, since the absolutive suffix surfaces; *comuli* does not figure as such in the dictionaries, though one

In the name of our Lord God, may all persons know how I am issuing this memorandum and testament as my last will; I don Juan de Guzmán, citizen here in the city and town of Coyoacan, in the district of Santiago Xochac, declare that I believe in the most Holy Trinity, God the father, God the son, God the Holy Spirit, yet only one true God omnipotent who created and fashioned the heaven and the earth, all that is seen and not seen; I believe all that our mother the holy Catholic church deems true.

Now I am very sick, my body is very ill and not healthy, but my understanding is very sound, as our Lord God gave it to me, and I have not lost it. If God now takes me away and I die, I leave my spirit and soul in his hand; may he take it to himself, for I greatly implore the dear lady St. Mary, eternal virgin, to speak on my behalf before her dear son our Lord Jesus Christ; may he view me compassionately, because he died for me; he was stretched out on the cross and spilled his precious blood so that I might be redeemed; and may also St. John the Baptist, my saint, speak for me before God.

— First I command and declare that when I die I am to be buried at the main church of St. John the Baptist, there facing the burial and death of our Lord God; there is our burial place where they all lie buried, my father and my older and younger brothers. The offering is to be as is arranged, and one of the priests will come wearing a cloak to take me; and the offering usually given to the church people will be made to ring the bells; and [what money I (will) have] is to come from the sale of a house there at Tetla behind the house of señor don Juan Cortés; and this land is made into a cultivated field,[3] on which are zapote trees and maguey and [. . .],[3] and there are peach trees there and a well; it will pertain to the house, and from there will come the means for me to pay for the masses incumbent on me: six high masses to be sung for the soul of doña Isabel, deceased, a lady of Quauhtitlan, and for her husband, who was don Hernando Estrada.

---

can deduce from related entries that it means "hole." The word thus bears some analogy to *teatlauhtli* below.

[4]In the manuscript *yhuan* is written twice, once at the end of a page and again at the beginning of the next.

— yhuan niquitohua nicmelahua nicnocuitia ca nechpialtitia[5] 8 p^{o}s ylamatzin Ana ytoca catca ye omomiquili ycnocihuatl chane tlacopac

— yhuan niquitohua nicnocuitia yn yehuatzin nohueltihuatzin catca doña Ju^{a} de guzman xuchmillco namiqueticatca ynamic catca don p^{o} de sotomayor yei missas cantadas mochihuiliz ypampa yAniman ye huecauh omomiquili

— yhuan niquitohua ca yn nonamictzin catca doña fran^{ca} ye huecauh momiquili ytech catca ytomin magdalena ynamic catca español luys hidalgo mocahuaz teupan chiquacen p^{o}s missas yc mochihuiliz yn omoteneuh magdalena

— yhuan nitlanahuatia niquitohua ca yn ompa tetla mani huerta peras oncan mani yhuan ahuacatl higos oncan pehua ynic tontemo yuhqui teatlauhtli[3] ompa onnaci yn techinamitl mani ymil catca miguel ayeuhtzin oniccohuili concahuizque yn omentin nochpochuan doña Ana dona m^{a} tepotzontlan ca yomextin quicuizque quimonepantlaxelhuizque

— yhuan nitlanahuatia yn itech çaliuhtica ycenmanca huerta tetla çanno xocoyotoc peras ypan mamani nicmaca yn notelpoch don lorenço de guzman quicuiz

— yhuan nicmelahua niquitohua domingo tlaxupan sebastian ytex homac ychan s^{ta} catalina nechpialia macuilli p^{o}s yc tlatequipanozquia nicmamacac quezquipa

— yhuan niquitohua nicmelahua yehuatl Ju^{o} tlaxcalchiuhqui[6] s^{ta} catalina homac ychan ompa quinemiti chiquacen metztli ce mula yhuan ynechichihual xalma yancuic gerga nicmacac yei p^{o}s ypan motlali auh yn ye mochi quixtlahuazquia cempohualli onmatlactli ypampa ycnotlacatl çan ixquich quixtlahuaz caxtolli p^{o}s yntla aca[7] quitlaniz ytla nicpialia tomines ome p^{o}s anoço yei p^{o}s oncan yc moxtlahuaz çan ica juramento quichihuaz yc tlaneltiliz momacaz auh yn oc cequi missas Reçadas yc mochihuaz yehuan quimati ynoalbaceashuan niquimixquetzaz

— yhuan nitlanahuatia niquitohua yehuatl juan de la cruz platero morisco nechpialia ompohualli onmatlactli p^{o}s nechpialia nicmacac huel tomins ymatica conan quezquipa nicmamacac quixtlahuaz yhuan ce Relicario oro bajo ypatiuh cempohualli onmacuilli p^{o}s mochi quixtlahuaz quitlanilizque ynoalbaceashuan niquimixquetzaz

[5]*Pialtia* is listed in the dictionaries as meaning to deposit something with someone for safekeeping, or the like. It could well mean that here. However, if *pialia* has come to mean "owe," as it clearly has to the writer of this document, then *pialtia*

— And I declare, explain, and acknowledge that an old woman whose name was Ana lent 8 pesos to me.[5] She is dead now; she was a widow, citizen of Tlacopac.

— And I declare and acknowledge that my older sister was doña Juana de Guzmán, who was married in Xochimilco; her husband was don Pedro de Sotomayor. Three masses are to be sung for her soul; she died long ago.

— And I declare that my wife was doña Francisca, who died long ago; she owed money to Magdalena, whose husband was a Spaniard, Luis Hidalgo. Six pesos are to be given to the church for masses to be said for the aforementioned Magdalena.

— And I pronounce and declare that there at Tetla is an orchard, where there are pears and avocados and figs; it begins there as you go down toward something like a water hole;[3] it reaches the stone wall there. It was the field of Miguel Ayeuhtzin, and I bought it from him. My two daughters are to have it, doña Ana and doña María at Tepotzontlan; they are both to take it and divide it among themselves.

— And I pronounce that adhering to and united with the Tetla orchard is another stand of pear trees; I give it to my son don Lorenzo de Guzmán; he is to take it.

— And I explain and declare that Domingo at Tlaxopan, brother-in-law of Sebastián, whose home is in Santa Catalina Homac, owes me 5 pesos that I gave him at times with which to do his work.

— And I declare and explain that a Juan Tlaxcalchiuhqui,[6] whose home is in Santa Catalina Homac, maintained a mule there for six months with its harness and packsaddle of new cloth. I gave him 3 pesos when the agreement was made, and he was to pay 30 altogether; because he is a poor person he is to pay only 15 pesos. If anyone should demand any money I owe him, (up to) two or three pesos, he is to be paid back; with only taking an oath to certify it, it is to be given to him. And as to the additional low masses to be said, my executors know about it, I leave them in charge of it.

— And I pronounce and declare that a Juan de la Cruz, Moorish silversmith, owes me; he owes me 50 pesos; I gave him good money and he took it in his hand; several times I gave him money, and he is to pay it back. And there is a reliquary of low-grade gold worth 25 pesos. He is to pay it all back and my executors are to demand it from him; I charge them with it.

---

would mean "to make someone an ower," i.e., "lend."

[6]The word means "baker" and may be so intended here.

[7]*Aca* is written twice in the manuscript, apparently a careless repetition.

— yhuan niquitohua ca nicofrade Sta Veracruz yhuan Rosario yhuan Entierro de x^{o} yntla yquac ninomiquiliz mocahuaz huentzintli nanahui t^{o}s yn excanixti ce p^{o}s yhuan nahui t^{o}s aço quimonequiltizque quiçaz cera candelas yc ninotocaz

— ye ixquich yn niquicuilohua yc nitlanahuatia yn ipan ynin notestam^{to} nictlalia yn ça tlatzacan notlanequiliz yehuatl neltiz mochihuaz auh mochi nicpolohua yn oc cequi aço onictlali testam^{tos} aço memoria cobdicilio atle ypan pohuiz yehuatl neltiz yn axcan nictlalia

— yhuan niquitohua nitlanahuatia yehuatzin doña Augustina de guzman ye huecauh omomiquili ynamictzin catca don cost^{o}[8] huitzimengari michuacan tlatohuani motlanahuatilitia ypan ytestam^{to} nimacoz caxtolli yhuan yei p^{o}s ytech quiçaz yn xocotl ypatiuh yn mochihua huey tecpan huerta ynin t^{o}s omoteneuh nechmopialilia yn don phelippe de guzman achto ynamictzin catca quitlanizque yn noalbaceashuan niquimixquetza don lor^{ço} de guzman doña Ana nopilhuan ymixpan testigos melchior ju^{o} yhuan Ju^{o} fran^{co} chaneque nican ypan altepetl villa cuyohuacan onicchiuh ynin ça tlatzacan notlanequiliz notestam^{o} niquinmaca nohueltiliz yn nopilhuan omoteneuhque ynic yehuantin quichihuazque yn ixquich monequi ypalehuiloca naniman yhuan ynic quicuizque quitlanizque yn tleyn nechpialia ynican onicteneuh onicmelauhcayto axcan matlaquilhuitl omome mani ytlapohual Junio de mill y seiscientos y veynte y dos años

por testigo fr alonso de paredes

5. Testament of Angelina, San Simón Pochtlan, 1695[1]

Jesus M^{a} y Juceph

ynehuatl angelina nican notlaxilacaltian san simon pochtlan niquitohua yn axcan notech quimotlalilia yn ijusticiatzin ynoteotzin notlatoca Dios cenca yetie ynotlallo noçoquio auh ynanimantzin motlachieltitica auh yehica yn axcan nocenyollocacopa notlanequiliztica ynic nictlalia notestamento auh yn tleyn nocamatica niquitoz macayac quitlacoz neltiz mochihuaz

---

Document 4

[8] Don Constantino, alive in 1615, was at various times governor of Coyoacan and Xochimilco (AGN, Tierras 1735, exp. 2, ff. 78, 89, 92). He was closely connected with the don Antonio Huitzimengari mentioned in Doc. 15 (ibid., f. 87). Apparently two

— And I declare that I am a member of the sodalities of the Holy True Cross and the Rosary and the Burial of Christ; when I die an offering of four tomines is to be given to each of the three, 1 peso and 4 tomines; perhaps they will desire that the wax candles for my burial will come from this.

— This is all that I am writing, wherewith I pronounce that in this my testament I set forth my last will. It is to be carried out and performed, and I revoke any other testaments, memoranda, or codicils I may have issued; they are to have no validity; the one I now issue is to be carried out.

— And I say and pronounce that doña Agustina de Guzmán, who died long ago and whose husband was don Constantino[8] Huitzimengari, ruler of Michoacan, ordered in her testament that I was to be given 18 pesos from which was to come the price of the fruit trees to make the greater royal house's orchard, and don Felipe de Guzmán, whose first wife she was, owes me this aforementioned money; my executors are to request it. I leave don Lorenzo de Guzmán and doña Ana, my children, in charge of it. In the presence of the witnesses Melchor Juan and Juan Francisco, citizens here in the city and town of Coyoacan, I made this my last will and testament. I give power to my aforementioned children to do all that is needed for the aid of my soul and to take and request what is owed me. What I have said here I have said truly. Today on the 12th day of the month of June of the year of 1622.

As witness: Fray Alonso de Paredes.

Jesus, Mary, and Joseph.

I, Angelina, my district being here in San Simón Pochtlan, declare that now God my divinity and ruler has issued his sentence upon me. My earthly body has grown very heavy, yet my spirit is aware; wherefore now it is with all my heart and volition that I order my testament, and let no one go against what I shall say with my mouth; it is to be carried out and performed.

Huitzimengaris of Michoacan married women of the ruling family of Coyoacan at nearly the same time.

Document 5

[1]McAfee Collection, UCLA Research Library, Special Collections.

— ynic centlamantli niquitohua onca ce noxhuiuhtzin ytoca tomas de los santos auh niquitohua yn axcan nicnomaquilitiuh ynotlaçomahuiznantzin candelaria[2] quimotequipanilhuiz yntla quimochicahuiliz dios ynin notlatol neltiz mochihuaz

— ynic ontlamantli[3] niquitohua oncatqui tlaltzintli ompohualpa nican mani ycampatzinco ynotlaçomahuiztatzin s^{to} domingo auh yn axcan niquitohua ça no yehuatzin nicnomaquilitiuh ynotlaçomahuiznantzin candelaria yc quimotequipanilhuiz ynoxhuiuhtzin onicteneuh ytoca tomas de los santos yntla quimochicahuiliz Dios ynin notlatol neltiz

— yniquetlamantli niquitohua yn yehuatzin ylhuicac ychpochtli s^{ta} catalina nicnomaquilitiuh ynic ome noxhuiuhtzin yn itoca teresa de jesus quimotequipanilhuiz yn[tla] quimochicahuiz dios ynin notlatol amo ytlacahuiz neltiz mochihuaz yhuan oncatqui tlaltzintli ompohualli nicnomaquilitiuh ynotlaçonantzin s^{ta} catalina yc quimotequipanilhuiz yn onicteneuh ytoca noxhuiuhtzin teresa de jesus neltiz mochihuaz

— ynauhtlamantli niquitohua oncate omentin pipiltzitzinti yce tlacatl ytoca jacinto ventura ynic ome ytoca jucepa de la yncarnacion auh niquitohua yn axcan nica mani tlaltzintli caltitla matlactlo [sic] yhuan nahui ynic huiyac auh ynic patlahuac matlactloce quahuitl niquinmacatiuh ynoxhuihuan onicteneuh ytoca jacinto ventura yhuan jucepa de la yncarnacion yntech pouhqui concahuizque ayac huel quinquixtiliz ynin notlatol mochihuaz neltiz

— ynic macuillamantli niquitohua oncatqui centetl caltzintli tlacopa[co]pa ytzticac nicmacatiuh yn itoca juceph [sic] de la yncarnacion ytech pouhqui ayac huel quiquixtiliz ynin notlatol neltiz mochihuaz

— ynic chiquacentlamantli niquitohua nican mani callatiltontli tepiton auh niquitohua yn axcan nicmacatiuh ynoxhuiuhtzin tianquiztenco ca nicolasa jacinta yc quimotequipanilhuiz ynotlaçomahuiznantzin Rosario ytech pouhqui ayac huel quiquixtiliz ynin notlatol neltiz mo[chi]huaz

---

[2]Throughout this document saints' names appear without specific mention of the organizations referred to. In each case we have tried to determine whether a church or a cofradía is meant.

— First, I declare that there is a grandchild of mine named Tomás de los Santos, and I declare now I am giving him to (the cofradía of)[2] my dear honored mother (of) Candelaria; he is to work for it if God gives him strength. This my command is to be carried out and performed.

— Second,[3] I declare that there is a small piece of land of 40 rods here behind (the church of) my dear honored father St. Dominic, and I now declare that I am also giving that to my dear honored mother (of) Candelaria so that my grandson whom I mentioned, named Tomás de los Santos, will work (the land for the cofradía) if God gives him strength. This my command is to be carried out.

— Third, I declare that to (the church of) the celestial virgin St. Catherine I am giving a second grandchild of mine named Teresa de Jesús, who is to work (for it) if God gives her strength. This my command is not to be vitiated; it is to be carried out and performed. And there is a small piece of land of 40 (rods) that I am giving to my dear mother St. Catherine so that the grandchild I mentioned named Teresa de Jesús will work there (for it). This is to be carried out and performed.

— Fourth, I declare there are two small children, the first named Jacinto Ventura, the second named Josefa de la Incarnación; and I declare that now there is a small piece of land here near the house, 14 rods long, 11 wide, that I am giving to the aforementioned grandchildren of mine named Jacinto Ventura and Josefa de la Incarnación to belong to them; they are to have it; no one may evict them. This my command is to be performed and carried out.

— Fifth, I declare there is a small house looking toward Tacuba; I give it to the one named Josefa de la Incarnación, to belong to [her]; no one may evict her. This my command is to be carried out and performed.

— Sixth, I declare there is a small bit of land here with buildings on it. And I declare that I am now giving it to my grandchild at Tianquiztenco, Nicolasa Jacinta, to work on it for (the cofradía of) my dear honored mother (of the) Rosary, to belong to her; no one may evict her. This my command is to be carried out and performed.

[3]Between the first and second items appears, in another hand: *yni tlalli motenehua monamaca yc mopatla alahuerta tlaco*, "This land mentioned here is being sold to be exchanged for half an orchard."

— ynic 7 contlamantli niquitohua yn caltzintli ypan mani matlacquahuitl yhuan tlaco ynic huiyac inic tlacopancopa auh ynic patlahuac chicuequahuitl yhuan tlaco ynic quauhtlacopa tlalpatlalli auh yn axcan oncan nicauhtia ynomontzin yn itoca tomas peres yhuan inamic francisca jacinta ayac huel quinquixtiliz yntech pouhqui ynin notlatol mochihuaz neltiz

— ynic 8 tlamantli niquitohua yn tlayxpan calli yn quauhtlacopa ytzticac çan oncan nicnocahuilitiuh yn ilhuicac ychpochtli sta catalina çan ichantzinco yez ayac huel quimoquixtiliz ynin notlatol mochihuaz neltiz

— ynic chicunauhtlamantli niquitohua yn ipanpatzinco sto san nicolas yn ompa quimopielia Domingo Ramostzin quimochihuiliz centetl misa cantata yntech pouiz mimicatzitzin ynin notlatol mochihuaz neltiz

yc nictlamiltia ynotlatol atle ma ytla nicnopielia ca çan ixquich ynican onicteneuh ca nicnotlacatzintli ymixpan testigos yn ice tlacatl ytoca juceph andres ynic ome tlacatl ytoca juan matias yniquey tlacatl ytoca pedro de los angeles ynic nahui tlacatl ytoca juan andres cihuatzitinti ana de la cruz pedronila

yn tehuantin tonecuitlahuil sta yglesia fiscal tixpan omochiuh in itestamento cocoxcatzintli oticaquilique yn itlatol yc ticneltilia nican tictlalia totoca tofirma axcan martes a 16 de agosto de 1695 años

Don Diego Juarez fiscal de la sta yglesia juan domingo teopan topile ante mi Don nicolas pelipe escrivano Real de la audiencia

6. Testament of Miguel Jerónimo, Metepec, 1795[1]

Jesus Maria Y Josef Año de 1795 aos

Axcan Miercules a 9 de Dbre Xiuhtlapuali 1795 aos ninomachiotia yca ytlasomahuistocatzin Dios tetahtzin Yhuan Dios tepiltzin Yhuan Dios Espiritu Santo Ma yn mochihua Amen Jesus Maria y Jósef

Document 6

[1]McAfee Collection, UCLA Research Library, Special Collections. As emerges in the document, this is the Metepec near Toluca.

— Seventh, I declare that the small house is on (land) 10½ rods long toward Tacuba, and 8½ rods wide toward Quauhtla and the land of Tlalpan; and I now leave there my son-in-law named Tomás Pérez and his wife Francisca Jacinta. No one may evict them; it is to belong to them. This my command is to be performed and carried out.

— Eighth, I declare that I am bequeathing the house in front, looking toward Quauhtla, to (the church of) the celestial virgin St. Catherine; it will be her own house; no one may evict her. This my command is to be performed and carried out.

— Ninth, I declare that [in] (the church of) St. Nicolás where Palm Sunday is kept, a mass is to be sung, dedicated to the dead. This my command is to be performed and carried out.

With this I end my words. May I keep nothing to myself; I have mentioned everything here, for I am a poor person. In the presence of witnesses, the first named Josef Andrés, the second named Juan Matías, the third named Pedro de los Angeles, the fourth named Juan Andrés, and the women Ana de la Cruz and Petronila.

We the fiscales in whose charge is the holy church, before us the sick person's testament was made, we heard her words. To attest to it we place here our names and signatures, today, Tuesday, on the 16th of August of the year 1695.

Don Diego Juárez, fiscal of the holy church. Juan Domingo, church constable.

Before me, Don Nicolás Felipe, royal notary of the council.

Jesus, Mary, and Joseph. Year of 1795.

Today, Wednesday, the 9th of December of the calendar year of 1795, I take as my sign the dear honored name of God the father and God the son and God the Holy Spirit. May (their will) be done, Amen. Jesus, Mary, and Joseph.

Nican nicpehualtia notestamento nehhuatl notoca Miguel Jeronimo yhuan nosihuauhtzin metzticatca Ytoca pasquala Josefa Auh ca nican tichanehque San Ju^{o} Baup^{ta} Metepec Yhuan totlaxilacalpan Santa Cruz tianquistenco Yese niquihtoa Ca huel senca mococoa no[tla]lo nosoquio pero noanimantzin Ca san huel pactica Yntla onechmotlatzontequilili yn noteotzin notlahtocatzin Dios Ca ysenmactzinco ninoCahuilia Yn totecuyo Jesu Christo

— Yhuan niquihtoa Ca nichuenchihua Melio Santos lugares de Jerusalen motemacas

— Yhuan canpa toctos notlalo nosoquio Ca onpa tiopan Calititic Yhuan noquimiliuhca yes Ca Dios quimonextil[is] Yhuaniquihtoa Ypalehuiloca yes noyoliantzin noanimantzin sentetl [misa] Cantada de Cuerpo presente nechmotlaocolilisque neltis notlanahuatil

— Yhuan niquihtoa Caltzintli muchica Solar Yhuan Yxiptlayotz[in] Dios Ca oncan [ni]quinCauhti Omentin noxhuihuan se ytoca Jil A[ntonio y]huan oc se ytoca Rafael Balentin Yehhuantin tlatequiPan[osque in]tla Dios quimonemiltilis Yntla noso se Dios quimoCuepilis D[. . .] se mocahuas neltis mochihuas notlanahuatil

— Yhuan niquihtoa se tlali nahpual mani Oncan Onoc Capultitla[n] ohtli Ymilnahuac Ju^{o} de Dios Bitoriano Ca niquinCahuilitiu[h] Ynin motenehque Jil Antonio Yhuan Rafael Ant^{o} Para yc tlatequipanosque Oncan Calititic neltis notlanahuatil

— Yhuan niquihtoa oc se tlaltontli de mactlacquahuitl Oncan Onoc milnahuac D^{n} Cruz de los Santos Ca nicMactiti nocxpoch ytoca Petrona Martina Para yc Nechylnamaquis mostlahuiptla neltiz no[tlatol]

— Yhuan niquihtoa Oc se tlali de mahtlacquahuitl Oncan Onoc Ca[pultitlan?] Ohtli Ymilnahuac fran^{co} Mateo Ca san no yehhuatl nochpoch Petrona Martina nicMactiliti neltis mochihuas notlanahuatil

— Yhuan niquihtoa Oc se tlali senpoal mani Oncan Onoc tohloca Ohtli Ymilnahuac Dionisio Cosme reJildo Ca nicCahuilitiuh noxhui Ytoca Rafael Balentin neltis mochihuas notlanahuatil

— Yhuan niquihtoa Ca onniquinCauhti nomontzin Yhuan nocxpoch Ytoca Petrona Martina OnniquinCauhtiPan cali Para quinmoCuyhu[. . .]que[2] Mientras Dios quimmoneMiltilis neltis mochilhuas notlatol

— auh Yhuan Ynantzin Rofina Maria[3] Ahmo aquin tlen quihtos mostlahuiptla neltis mochihuas notlanahuatil

---

[2]Possibly *quinmocuilisque*.

[3]While the phrase might more regularly mean "Rufina Maria's mother," this would

Here I commence my testament. My name is Miguel Jerónimo and my late wife's name was Pascuala Josefa; we are citizens of San Juan Bautista Metepec, and our district is Santa Cruz Tianquiztenco. I declare that my earthly body is very ill, but my mind is perfectly sound. If God my divinity and sovereign has condemned me, I leave myself in the hands of our Lord Jesus Christ.

— And I declare that I offer half (a tomín) to be given for the Holy Places of Jerusalem.

— And as to where my earthly body is to lie buried, it is there at the church, inside. And my burial clothing will be as God manifests. And I declare that the aid for my spirit and soul will be one high mass in the presence of the body that they will do me the charity of performing. My command is to be carried out.

— And I declare a small house with lot and an image of God; there I have left my two grandsons, one named Gil Antonio and the other one named Rafael Valentín. They are to keep it up if God gives them life; if perhaps God should take one back, [. . .] one will remain. My command is to be carried out and performed.

— And I declare that there is a piece of land of 80 (rods) located there at the Capultitlan road, next to a field of Juan de Dios Vitoriano, which I am bequeathing to these aforementioned Gil Antonio and Rafael Antonio [sic], so that they will keep up the house. My command is to be carried out.

— And I declare that another small piece of land of 10 rods is there next to a field of don Cruz de los Santos; I am giving it to my daughter named Petrona Martina so that she will remember me in the future. My command is to be carried out.

— And I declare that another piece of land of 10 rods is there at the Ca[pultitlan?] road next to the field of Francisco Mateo which I am also giving to my daughter Petrona Martina. My command is to be carried out and performed.

— And I declare there is another piece of land of 20 (rods) located there on the Toluca road next to the field of Dionisio Cosme, councilman, which I am bequeathing to my grandson named Rafael Valentín. My command is to be carried out and performed.

— And I declare that I have left my son-in-law and my daughter named Petrona Martina at the house, for them to [have] while God should give them life. My order is to be carried out and performed.

— And no one is to make any objections to [his mother], Rufina María,[3] in the future. My command is to be carried out and performed.

---

involve the abrupt introduction of two unexplained and unrelated individuals, whereas most others, especially beneficiaries, are meticulously identified.

— Auh Yhuan niquihtoa Canpa niquincAuhti Nochpoch Yhuan nomontzi Cayetano Salvador Oncan Caltech Mochantisque Ahmo quintlenquitos mostlahuiptla neltis mochihuas notlanahuatil

— Auh Ca sannichquich Onicmachisti Yxpantzinco Dios Yhuan aquihque nopan motlatoltisque noalbaseas Ca yehhuantintzitzi Marselino Antonio Yhuan Pasqual de los Reyes yntla quali quimochihuilisque Ca Dios quinMotlaxtlahuilmaquilis neltis mochihuas notlatlautitilis

— Auh Ca tehhuanti tixpan Omochiuh Ynin testamento fiscales de la Santa Yg^{a} fiscal Mayor Juan de leon fiscal Mexicano Leonardo Antonio Fiscal EECatepec Antonio luis Nehhuatl OnitlaCuylo Es^{no} de la Santa Yg^{a} Ju^{o} de D^{s} B^{no}

7. Statement of the executor of an estate, c. 1632[1]

— Ca nican nicmachiyotia Yn icuac omomiquilli yn Juana a 21 dias del mes de marҫo 1629 años yn iquac omomiquilli auh yn inamic grabiel rraphael Ca yehuatl Oquipatiaia yn tequitl ce xihuitl yn ohualtequihuicac ҫa icel auh yn iquac omomiquilli ca quinicuac onechcahuillitia yn tequitl yn nehuatl Juan bap^{ta} rreg^{or} ma^{or} yhuan yn nonamic Susana maria Ca tonehua otiqualtequihuiquillique

— Axcan nican momachiyotia Ca in iquac Omomiquilli auh ynic omotocac Ca netlacuilli omochiuh 12 p^{o}ss auh ynic opatic Omotemacac metl matlactli auh ynic omochiuh missas 10 p^{o}s Oconcahuique yn inamic grabiel Raphael yhuan Juana m^{a} Ic nahuilhuitl mani metztli Decienbre 1630 años auh niman tlacallaquilli yc opatic 3 p^{o}s 4 ts niman cohuaҫacatl[2] yc opatic 6 ts auh niman Cohuatequitl yc opatic yye mochi mocentlallia yn ce xihuitl 24 pe^{o}ss auh yn totoltetl yc oc opatic 6 ts

Document 7

[1]McAfee Collection, UCLA Research Library, Special Collections. While place is

— And I declare that at the place where I have left my daughter and my son-in-law Cayetano Salvador, they are to dwell there at the house; no one is to make any objections to them in the future. My command is to be carried out and performed.

— And this is all that I have stated before God; and those who are to speak for me, my executors, are Marcelino Antonio and Pascual de los Reyes. If they do this well for me, God will give them the reward. My request is to be carried out and performed.

And we in whose presence this testament was made are the fiscales of the holy church; chief fiscal Juan de León; Mexican fiscal Leonardo Antonio; fiscal for Ehecatepec Antonio Luis. I wrote it, notary of the holy church, Juan de Dios Vitoriano.

— Here I make manifest when Juana died; the time she died was on the 21st day of March of the year 1629, and her husband Gabriel Rafael paid the tribute for a year; he alone made the payment, and when he died then he left the tribute to me, Juan Bautista, chief councilman, and to my wife Susana María, and we have made the payment for him together.

— Now is made manifest here that when he died, a debt of 12 pesos was incurred for him to be buried, and to make it good 10 (rods) of maguey land were given up; and with it masses costing 10 pesos, which Juana María and her husband Gabriel Rafael had reserved for themselves, were held on the 4th day of the month of December of the year 1630, and then there were 3 pesos, 4 tomines to make good the (royal) tribute, then 6 tomines to make good the [community fodder supply duty],[2] and 24 pesos to make good the total community works obligation for one year, and 6 tomines to make good the egg duty.

---

not specified, the document is found among a group of papers from the Coyoacan region.

[2]We presume that *coaçacatl* is analogous to *coatequitl*.

— Axcan nican momachiutia yn iquac Omochiuh yn imissas grabiel Raphael yhua yn inamic Juana m^{a} 10 pe^{o}s niman tlacallaquilli yc opatic 3 p^{o}s 4 ts niman Cohuatequitl yc opatic ynic ce xihuitl mocentlallia 24 p^{o}ss niman cohuaçacatl yc opatic 7 ts niman totoltetl yc opatic 6 ts auh yn icuac omochiuh yn inmissas mimique yc nahuilhuitl mani metztli mayo 1631 años

— Axcan nican nicmachiyotia ynic omochiuh in inmissas grabiel Raphael yhua yn inamic Juana m^{a} oconcahuique 10 p^{o}s niman oc cepa ocalac 5 p^{o}s yhuan yntech puqui quimocuillico yn fiscal nima ytatzi ynantzi yhua ycoltzin ycitzin yntech opouh 5 p^{o}s yc omochiuh ynmissas yn mochinti auh niman tlacalaquilli yc opatic 3 4 ts niman cohuaçacatl 7 ts niman totoltetl yc opatic 6 ts niman cohuatequitl yc opatic ynic ce xihuitl mocentlallia 24 p^{o}ss auh yn iquac omochiuh missas a 7 dias del mes de Julio 1632 años

— auh niman Omonec milpa 7 p^{o}s yc Oquichitonique metzontetl yhua yc ocaquique metl yhuan yc onicanato yn pil^{ton}tli Juan xacinto ocholloca Onpa Oticanato atl molloya 3 p^{o}s yhua 2 ts auh niman yteycauh yn iquac ohualla Santiago[3] onenca ça ytatapa yc onicchichiuh 3 p^{o}s

8. Inventory of the estate of Francisco Felipe, with funeral expenses and auction of effects, Analcotitlan, 1652[1]

Axcan [5]3[2] tonali febrero yn xihuitl de 652 anos omochihua ynin memoria yn imixpan al̄l̄des ordinarios ypan ynin altepetl analcotetan de san fran^{co} yn itechcopa yn ten quimopieliyaya mihcatzintli fran^{co} phelipe catca ynic neltis nican mofirmatiya

ju^{o} mīn de sespedes alcalde ju^{o} bernabe l̄l̄de di^{o}lucas destigo esteban clemente fran^{co} ernandes ju^{o} bernabe frioste di^{o} peliphe prioste ju^{o} matheo testigo por tes^{o} Don diego mīn de gusman[3]

Document 7

[3]While we think this the most likely interpretation, it seems possible that Santiago is a place where the boy had been living, or even that the boy came on the day of Santiago, though in that case, in standard classical Nahuatl, *ipan* or some such word would seem to be needed.

— Now is made manifest here that when the masses of Gabriel Rafael and his wife Juana María were held, it was 10 pesos; then 3 pesos, 4 tomines to make good the (royal) tribute; then 24 pesos to make good the total community works obligation for one year; then 7 tomines to make good the [community fodder supply duty]; then 6 tomines to make good the egg duty; and the time the masses for the deceased were held was on the 4th day of the month of May of the year 1631.

— Now I make manifest here how their masses that Gabriel Rafael and his wife Juana María had reserved for themselves were held, costing 10 pesos; then came in additionally 5 pesos belonging to them that the fiscal took; then with 5 pesos belonging to his father and mother and his grandfather and grandmother, were held masses for all of them; and then 3 (pesos), 4 tomines, to make good the (royal) tribute; then 7 tomines [community fodder supply duty]; then 6 tomines to make good the egg duty; then 24 pesos to make good the total community works obligation for one year; and the time the masses were held was on the 7th day of the month of July of the year of 1632.

— And then at the field 7 pesos were spent with which they trimmed the maguey growths and transplanted maguey, and for me to take the boy Juan Jacinto to Ocholloca where we went to take the spring waters, it was 3 pesos, 2 tomines; and then when his younger brother [Santiago][3] came, who had been living in ragged clothing, I dressed him up for 3 pesos.

Today, the [5]3[2] day of February of the year of 1652, this memorandum was made before the alcaldes ordinarios in this town of Analcotitlan of San Francisco, concerning what the late deceased Francisco Felipe possessed; to verify it they sign here.

Juan Martín de Céspedes, Alcalde. Juan Bernabé, Alcalde. Diego Lucas, witness. Esteban Clemente. Francisco Hernández. Juan Bernabé, cofradía steward. Diego Felipe, cofradía steward. Juan Mateo, witness. As a witness: don Diego Martín de Guzmán.[3]

Document 8

[1]McAfee Collection, UCLA Research Library, Special Collections.

[2]The 53rd day of February is a most unlikely date, yet paleographically the first digit cannot pass for a 1 or 2.

[3]Most or all of the signatures were written by the notary, except that don Diego de Guzmán clearly signed for himself.

— huel achtopa mopiya[4] ce cali ycalnahuac [man?] justina beatris

— no yhuan mopiya matacti yuan ome yehuas mopiyas[5] — 12

— no yhuan mopiya ce capoti yuan ropilla yhuan ce calsonis paño

— no yhua ce xobon ya soltic yuan ce sonbrero soltic

— no yhuan medias berdes soltic

— no yhuan ce mancas raso asul mopiya

— no yhuan ce pares ligas asules

— no yhuan ce palona[6] soltic mopiya

— no yhuan ome martillo teposti[7] mopiya

— no yhua ce tenaza tepostli mopiya

— no yhua mopiya chicuacen limas tepostli — 6

— no yhuan ponsones teposti mopiya — 11

— no yhuan ce tenaza mopiya

— no yhuan silla xinete yca coxinillo sin estribus yhuan Almardiga mopiya sin freno

— yz ca tehuiquililistli ynahuac santicimo çacramento ca mochintin quimatitica tle yxquich — 15 1 p^{o}s 2 ts
deue 17 p^{o}s 2[8]

— yhuan altepetl quihuiquiliya — 5 p^{o}s

— yhuan nel quitehuiquilia ynahuac ju^{o} matheo oquitlaneuhtic ixquich — 5 p^{o}s

Axcan nican oquimotilique tlatuque l̄ldes mochintin principales ypan ynin altepetl analcotetlan y huel neli ca nican mofirmatiya

ju^{o} mīn de sespedes Alcalde ju^{o} bernabe l̄lde por test^{o} Don diego mīn de gusman ju^{o} matho testigo ju^{o} bernabe prioste di^{o} pelipe prioste grabiel mendes testigo nixpan nehuatl niamatlacuilo ju^{o} baltasar

gasto

— yz ca omocohua sera de castilla yn icuac ypan yntiero huel ixquich omocohua — 6 p^{o}s

— no yhuan omomacaque cantores limosna yxquich 1 p^{o}s

---

[4]Literally, "it is kept."

[5]This verb, if referring to the mares, should be the plural *mopiazque*.

[6]*Palona* is Spanish *valona*.

[7]Originally this term would have referred to copper, but it was readily applied to the European-introduced iron and undoubtedly means that here.

— First of all, there is[4] a house near the house of Justina Beatriz.

— And also there are 12 mares; [they are to be kept].[5] —12
— And also there are a cloak with doublet and a pair of trousers of woolen stuff.
— And also a jacket, already used; and a hat, used.
— And also green hose, used.
— And also there is a pair of sleeves, of blue satin.
— And also a pair of blue garters.
— And also there is a large soft collar,[6] used.
— And also there are two hammers of metal.[7]
— And also there is a pair of tongs, of metal.
— And also there are 6 files, of metal. — 6
— And also there are punches, of metal. —11
— And also there is a pair of tongs.
— And also there is a riding saddle with saddle-pad, without stirrups, and a halter without bridle.

— Here is the debt to (the cofradía of) the Most Holy Sacrament, as all know, (it is) a total of .... 16 pesos, 2 tomines
(he owes 17 pesos, 2 tomines)[8]
— And he owes the town .... 5 pesos
— And indeed he owes to Juan Mateo, who lent it to him, a total of .... 5 pesos

Here now the lords alcaldes and all the nobles in this town of Analcotitlan considered it; in truth here they sign.

Juan Martín de Céspedes, Alcalde. Juan Bernabé, Alcalde. As a witness: don Diego Martín de Guzmán. Juan Mateo, witness. Juan Bernabé, cofradía steward. Diego Felipe, cofradía steward. Gabriel Méndez, witness. Before me the notary, Juan Baltasar.

Expenses.
— Here is the Castilian wax bought for the occasion of the burial; the total bought was .... 6 pesos
— And also the singers were given a donation totaling .... 1 peso

---

[8]The "deue 17 p^{o}s 2" is written in a different hand. The odd "15 1" seems to be the equivalent of *caxtolli once*, or "16." The "17 p^{o}s 2" is thus a correction adding one peso to the total.

— no yhuan omochihua missa omocavac huencintli yxquich 4 ts

— no yhuan cofradia otitemacaque limosna conception sulidat yxquich 4 ts

Axcan 17 tonali motoca metztli març̧o yn xihuitl de mil y seis sientos y cincuenta y dos años oncan mochihuac almoneda difunto fran^{co} felipe nican tecpantoc yn monamacatiyahu[9]

— y huel achto se sonbrero y solti omonamacac ce peso yhuan chiquacen ts 1 p^{o}s 6 ts

— no yhuan omonamacac ce martillo yhuan yey sinseles oquihuica juan ber^{be} yca 0 6 ts

— no yhuan omonamacac ce silla xineta yca coxinillo yhuan almartiga yca mochi Reata oquihuica miguel angel escriu^{o} soledad yca macuili pes yhuan macuiltomines 5 p^{o}s 5 ts

[9]The form *monamacatiyahu* is unfamiliar to us. The *-tiyahu* probably represents *-tiyauh*, in turn perhaps representing *-tiuh*, a progressive form of the verb.

— And also a mass was held; an offering was given totaling .... 4 tomines
— And also we gave a donation to the cofradías of the Conception and the Solitude totaling .... 4 tomines

Today, the 17th day of the month of March of the year 1652, an auction was held for the deceased Francisco Felipe here at the courthouse; what was sold[9] (was the following):
— First of all a used hat was sold for 1 peso and 6 tomines .... 1 peso, 6 tomines
— And also a hammer was sold with three chisels; Juan Bernabé took it for .... 6 tomines
— And also a riding saddle with saddle-pad was sold, and a halter with all its rope; Miguel Angel, notary of the Solitude, took it for 5 pesos and 5 tomines. .... 5 pesos, 5 tomines

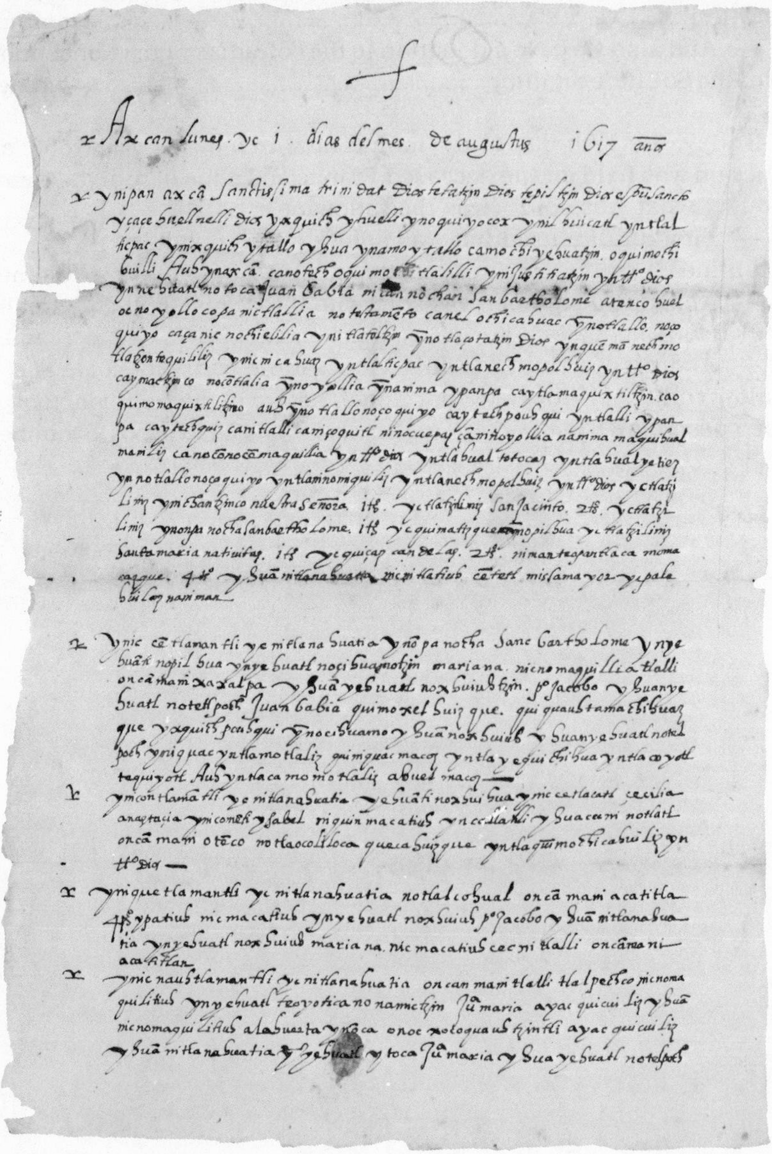

x Axcan lunes yc i dias del mes de augustus 1617 años

x yn ipan axcã Santissima trinidat Dios tetatzin Dios tepiltzin Dios espiritu sancto
ycemce huelnelli Dios yxquich yhuelli yno quiyocox ynilhuicatl yn tlal
ticpac yn ixquich ytallo yhua ynamo ytallo camo chi yehuatzin. oquimochi
huilli. Auh ynaxcã. canotech oquimo[illegible] tlalilli yn ijustiticatzin yn tt° dios
yn nehuatl notoca Juan fabia nican nochan San bartholome atenco hual
ce noyollo cepa nictlallia notestamento canel ohuicahuac yn notlallo, noço
quiyo caça nic nochielilia yn itlatoltzin yno tlaçotatzin Dios ynquẽ mã nechmo
tlaçontequililiz yn icmicahuiz yn tlalticpac yn tlanechmopolhuiz yn tt° dios
caymactzinco nocotlalia yno yollia ynanima ypanpa caytlamaquixtiltzin. cao
quimomaquixtilitzino Auh yno tlallo noço quiyo caytech pouhqui yn tlalli ypan
pa caytechquiz canitlalli camiçoquitl ninocuepaz camiyollia nanima maquihual
maniliz canoconocemaquilia yn tt° dios yntlahual totocaz yntlahual yehicoz
yn notlallo noço quiyo yn tlaninomiquiliz yn tlanechmopolhuiz yn tt° dios ychtlatz
liniz ynichan tzinco nuestra señora. 1 ts. yctlatziliniz San Jacinto. 2 ts. ychtlatzi
liniz yno onpa nochãn San bartholome. 1 ts yc quimatziquetzamopilhua yctlatziliniz
Santa maria natiuitas. 1 ts yc quiçaz candelas. 2 ts. ninantequiyutlaca moma
caquic. 4 ts y hua nitlanahuatia nicmitlatiuh cetetl missa mayor yepale
huiloz nanima

x ynic cẽ tlamantli ye nitlanahuatia yn onpa nochãn Sanc bartholome ynye
huatl nopilhua ynyehuatl noçihuamotzin mariana. nicnomaquillia tlalli
oncã mani xaxalpa y hua yehuatl noxhuiuhtzin. p° Jacobo y huanye
huatl notelpoch Juan fabia quimoxelhuiz que. quiquauhtamachihuaz
que yxquich pouhqui yno cihuamo y hua noxhuiuh y huanyehuatl notel
poch ynic quac yntlamotlaliz quinquac macoz yntla yequichihua yntlacoyotl
tequiyotl Auh yntlacamomotlaliz ahuel macoz

x yn icontlamantli ye nitlanahuatia yehuatl noxhuihua ynic cetlacatl cecilia
anastacia yn icontli ysabel niquinmacatiuh ynce tlalli y hua cecmi notlatl
oncã mani oteco notlaocoltloca quecahuizque yntla quimochicahuiliz yn
tt° Dios

x yn iquetlamantli ye nitlanahuatia notlalcohual oncã mani acatitla
ypatiuh nicmacatiuh ynyehuatl noxhuiuh p° Jacobo y huã nitlanahua
tia ynyehuatl noxhuiuh mariana. nicmacatiuh cecni tlalli oncã mani
acatitlan

x ynic nauhtlamantli ye nitlanahuatia oncan mani tlalli tlalpechco nicnoma
quilitiuh ynyehuatl teoyotica nonamictzin Juana maria ayac quicuiliz y huã
nicnomaquilitiuh alahuerta yn oca onoc xoloquauhtzintli ayac quicuiliz
y huã nitlanahuatia y yehuatl ytoca Juana maria y hua yehuatl notelpoch

Document 3. Testament of Juan Fabián, San Bartolomé Atenco, 1617. Page 1.

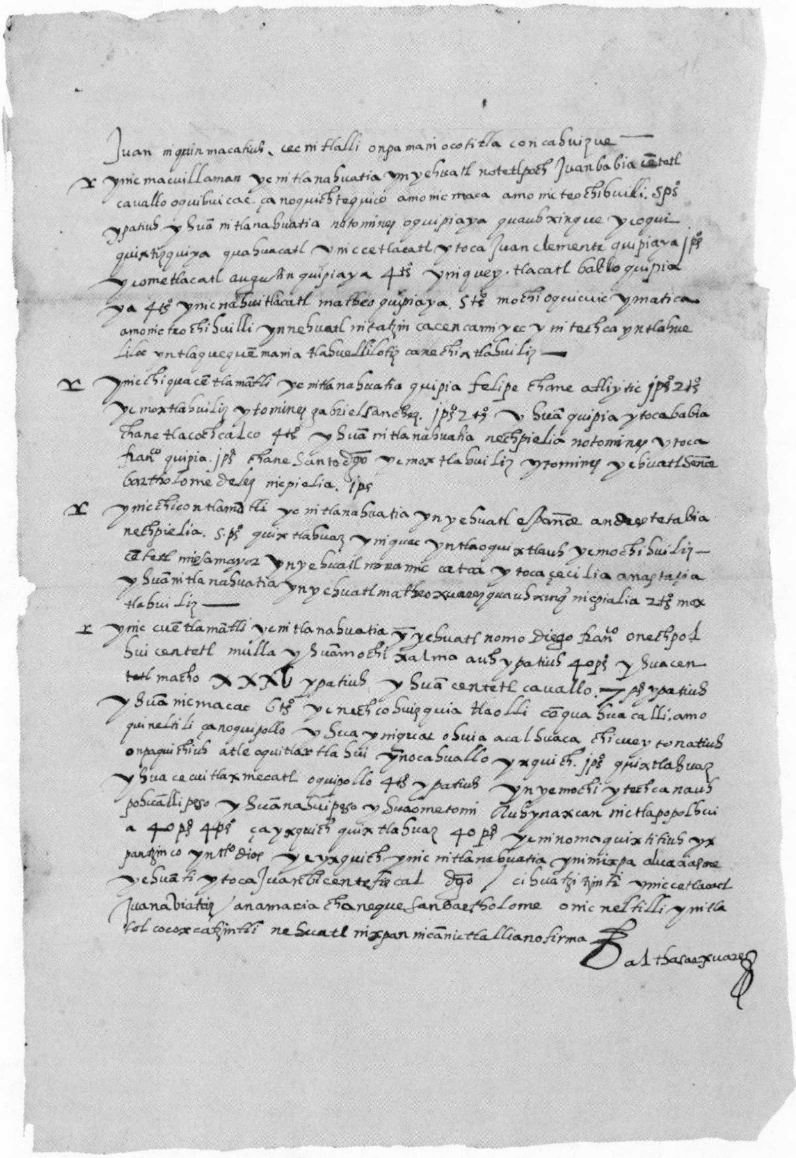

Document 3. Testament of Juan Fabián, San Bartolomé Atenco, 1617. Page 2.

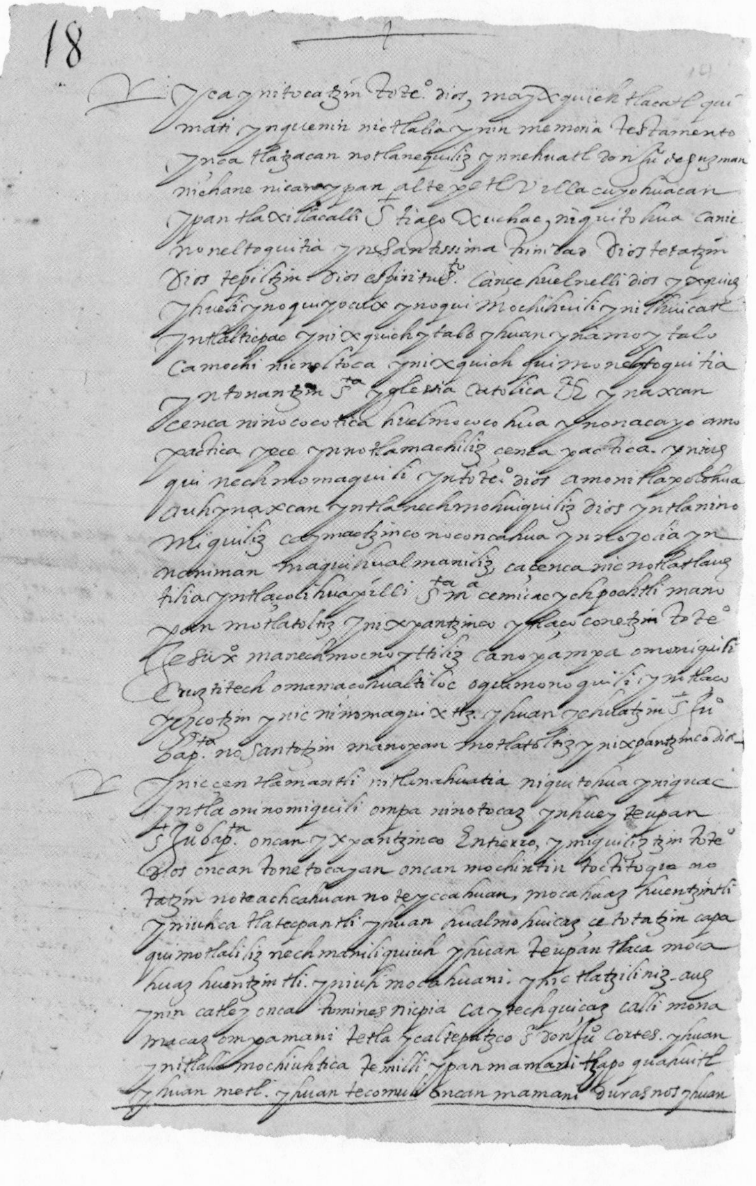

Document 4. Testament of don Juan de Guzmán, Coyoacan, 1622. Page 1.

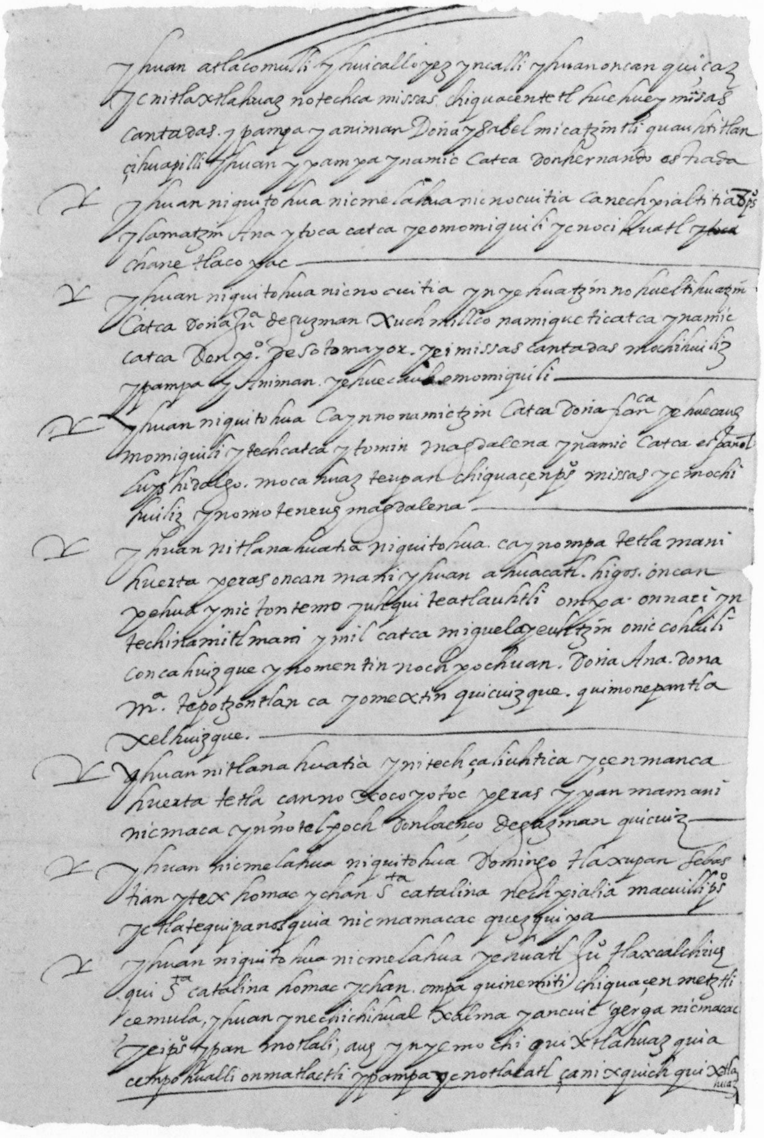

Yhuan atlacomulli y huicallo yez ynealli yhuan oncan quiçaz
yc nitlaxtlahuaz notechca missas. chiquacentetl huehuey missas
cantadas. ypampa yanimantzin Doña ysabel micatzintli quauhtitlan
cihuapilli yhuan ypampa ynamic catca don fernando astriada
Yhuan niquitohua nicmelahua nicnocuitia ca nechpialtitiad ps
ylamatzin Ana yteca catca ycomomiquili ycnocihuatl yteca
chane tlacoxpac
Yhuan niquitohua nicnocuitia yn yehuatzin nohueltihuatzin
catca doña Jua de guzman Xuchmilco namique ticatca ynamic
catca don xpo de sotomayor. ycimissas cantadas mochihuiliz
ypampa yanimantzin. ye ihuecauh omomiquili
Yhuan niquitohua ca yn nonamictzin catca doña franca ye huecauh
momiquili ytechcatca ytomin magdalena ynamic catca español
luys hidalgo. mocahuaz teupan chiquacen ps missas ye mochi
huiliz ynomoteneuh magdalena
Yhuan nitlanahuatia niquitohua. ca yn nompa tetla mani
huerta peras oncan mani yhuan ahuacatl. higos. oncan
pehua ynic tontemo yuhqui teatlauhtli onhuia. onnati yn
techinamitl mani yn il catca miguela xeuhtzin onic cohuili
concahuizque yn omentin noch xochuan. doña Ana. doña
ma tepotzontlan ca yomextin quicuizque. quimonepantla
xelhuizque.
Yhuan nitlanahuatia yn itech çaliuhtica yçen manca
huerta tetla canno Ococototoc peras ypan mamani
nicmaca yn notelpoch don lorenço de guzman quicuiz
Yhuan nicmelahua niquitohua Domingo tlaxupan Sebas
tian ytex homac ychan S.ta catalina nechpialia macuilli ps
yc tlatequipanosquia nicmamacac quezqui ya
Yhuan niquitohua nicmelahua yehuatl Juo tlaxcalchiuh
qui S.ta catalina homac ychan. ompa quinemiti chiquacen metztli
cemula, yhuan ynechichiual Xalma yancuic Jerga nicmacac
ycips ypan nototali; auh yn yzemo chi quixtlahuaz quia
cempohualli onmatlactli ypampa yenotlatlatl cani xquich quixtla huaz

Document 4. Testament of don Juan de Guzmán, Coyoacan, 1622. Page 2.

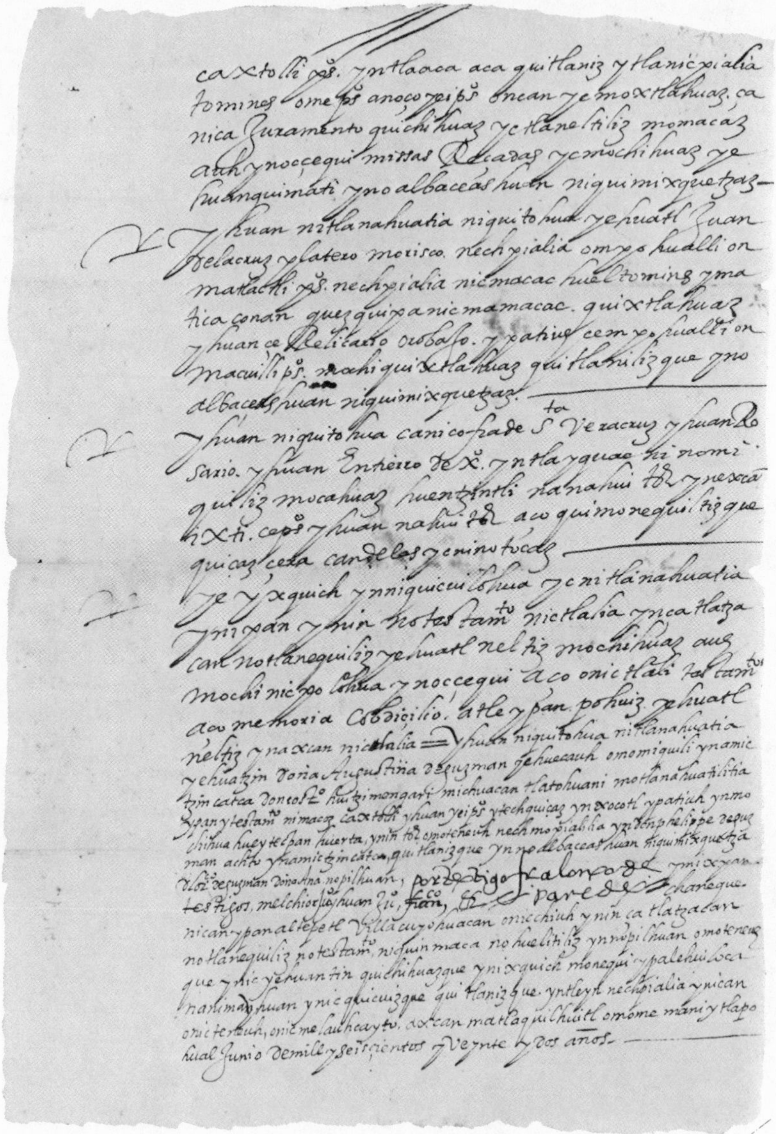

caxtolli p̃s. yntlaocca aca quitlaniz ytlanicxpialia
tomines ome p̃s anoço yei p̃s oncan yc moxtlahuaz, ca
nica Juramento quichihuaz yc tlaneltiliz momacaz
auh yn oc çequi missas Rezadas yc mochihuaz yc
huanquimati yno albaceas huan niquimixquetzaz—
yhuan nitlanahuatia niquitohua yehuatl Juan
Velacruz ylatero morisco. nechxpialia om p̃s huallion
matlactli p̃s. nechxpialia nicmacac huel tomines yma
tica conan quezquixpa nicmamacac. quixtlahuaz
yhuan ce Relicario orobasso. ypatiuh cem p̃s huallion
macuilli p̃s. mochi quixtlahuaz quitlatiliz que yno
albaceas huan niquimixquetzaz.
yhuan niquitohua canicofrade Sta Veracruz yhuan Ro
sario. yhuan Entierro de Xo. yntlayquac ni nomi
quiliz mocahuaz huentzintli nahuahui tor ynexca
hxti. ce p̃s yhuan nahui tor aco quimonequiltizque
quicaz çera candelas yc ninotocaz
ye yxquich yn niquicuilohua ycnitlanahuatia
yn ixpan yhuin notestamento nictlalia ynca tlatza
can notlanequiliz yehuatl neltiz mochihuaz auh
mochi nicxpolohua yn occequi aco onictlali testamentos
aco memoria Codiçilio. atle ypan pohuiz yehuatl
neltiz yn axcan nictlalia — yhuan niquitohua nitlanahuatia
yehuatzin Doña Augustina de guzman ye huecauh omomiquili ynamic
tzin catca Don costantino huitzimengari michuacan tlatohuani motlanahuatilitia
yxpan ytestamento nimacoz caxtolli yhuan yei p̃s ytechquiçaz yn exocotl ypatiuh ynmo
chihua huey tecpan huerta, ynin tor omoteneuh nechmoxpialilia yn don phelippe de guz
man achto ynamictzin catca, quitlanizque yn no albaceas huan niquimixquetza
Dn Lorenzo de guzman doña Ana nopilhuan, por testigo Juan Alonso de [illegible] yn ixpan
testigos, melchior de S. Juan, Diego, Franco, [illegible] pared [illegible] charegue.
nican ypan altepetl Villa cuyohuacan onicchiuh ynin ca tlatzacan
notlanequiliz notestamento niquinmaca nohuelitiliz yn nopilhuan omoteneuh
que ynic yehuantin quichihuazque yn ixquich monequi ypalehuiloca
nanima yhuan ynic quicuizque quitlanizque. yntleyn nechxpialia ynican
onicteneuh, onicmelauhcayto. axcan matlaquilhuitl omome mani ytlapo
hual Junio de mile y seiscientos y veynte y dos años.

Document 4. Testament of don Juan de Guzmán, Coyoacan, 1622. Page 3.

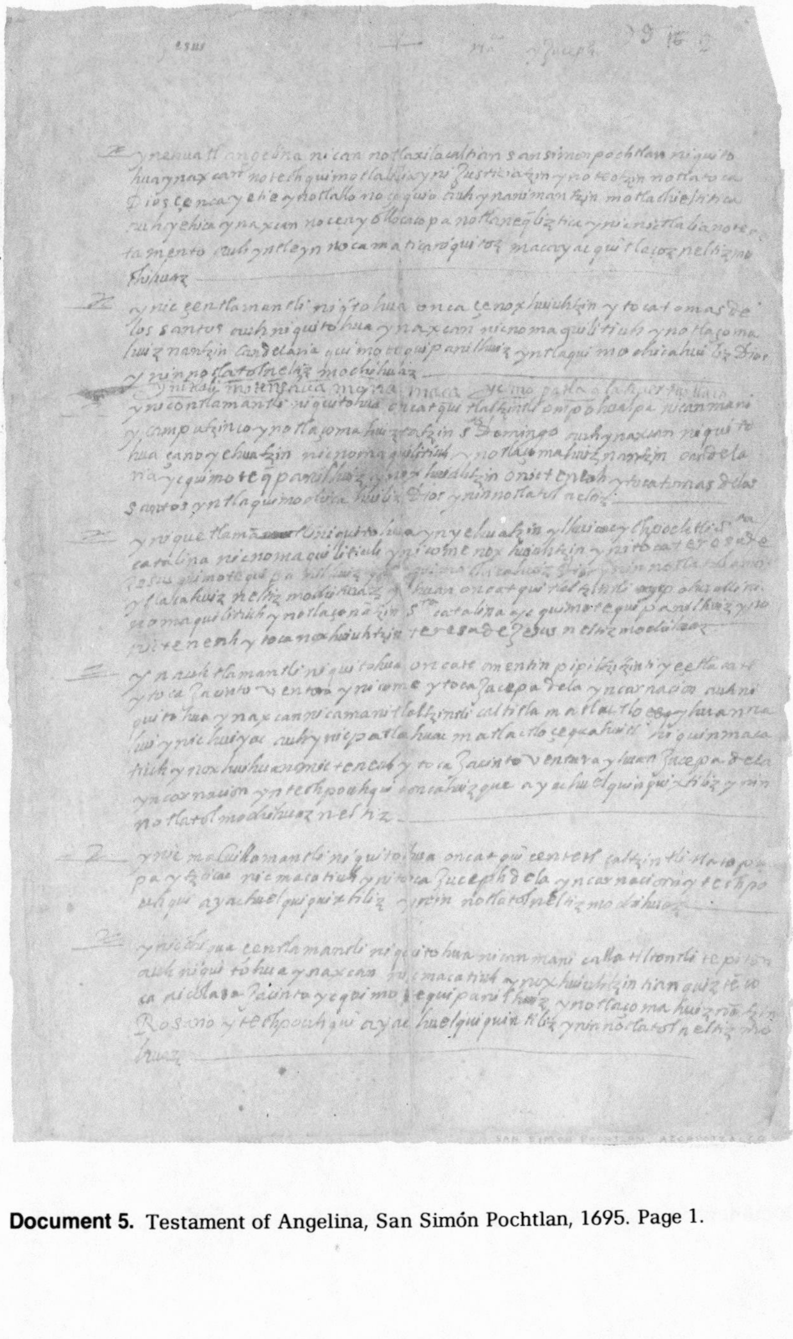

Document 5. Testament of Angelina, San Simón Pochtlan, 1695. Page 1.

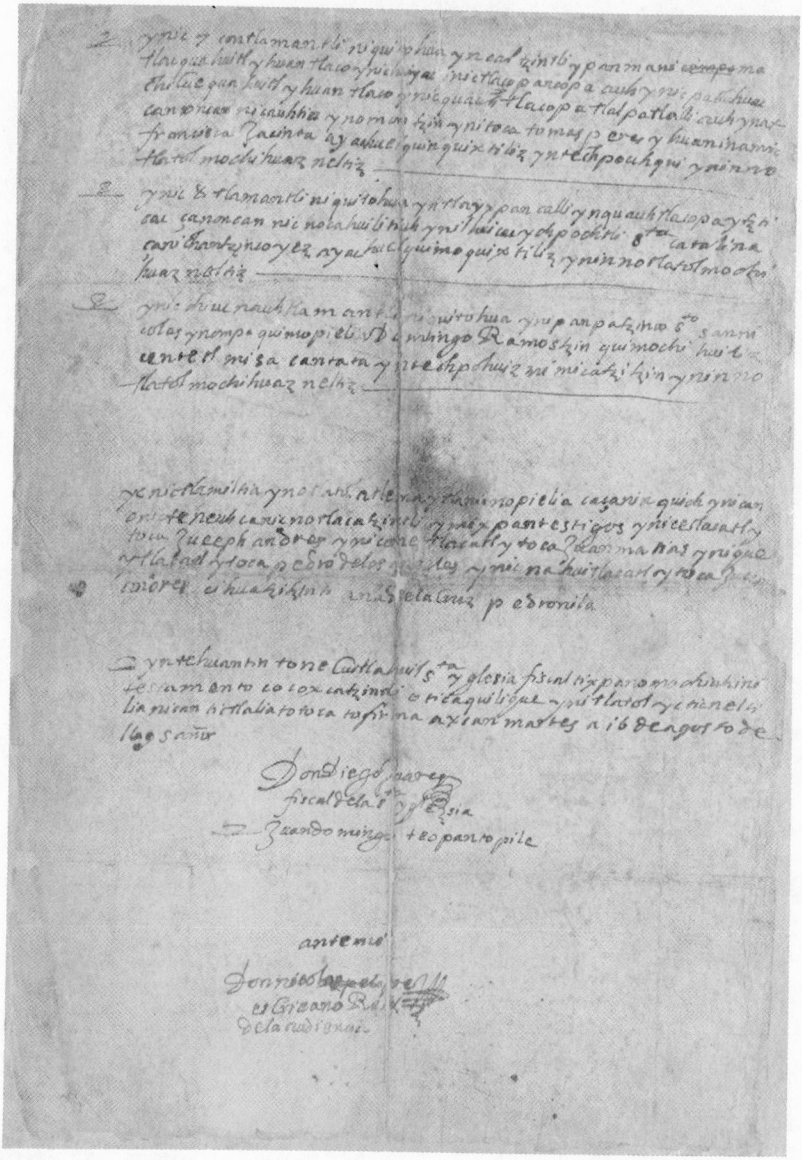

Document 5. Testament of Angelina, San Simón Pochtlan, 1695. Page 2.

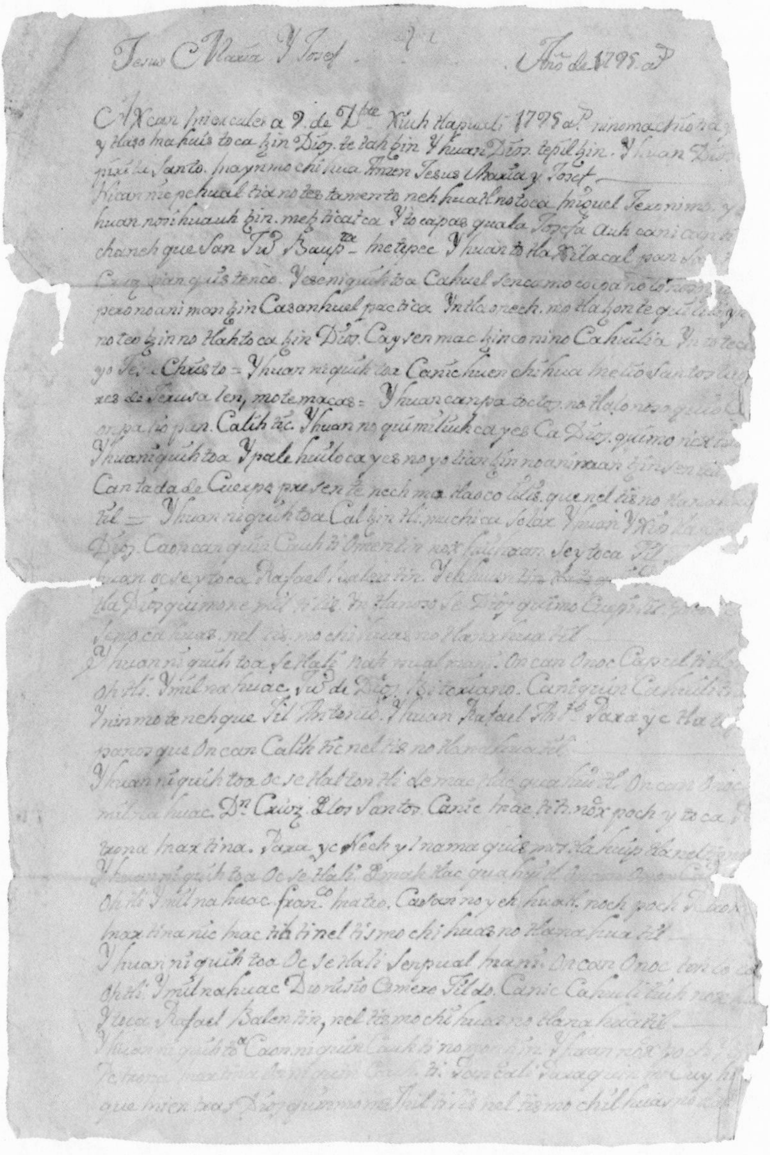

Document 6. Testament of Miguel Jerónimo, Metepec, 1795. Page 1.

Document 6. Testament of Miguel Jerónimo, Metepec, 1795. Page 2.

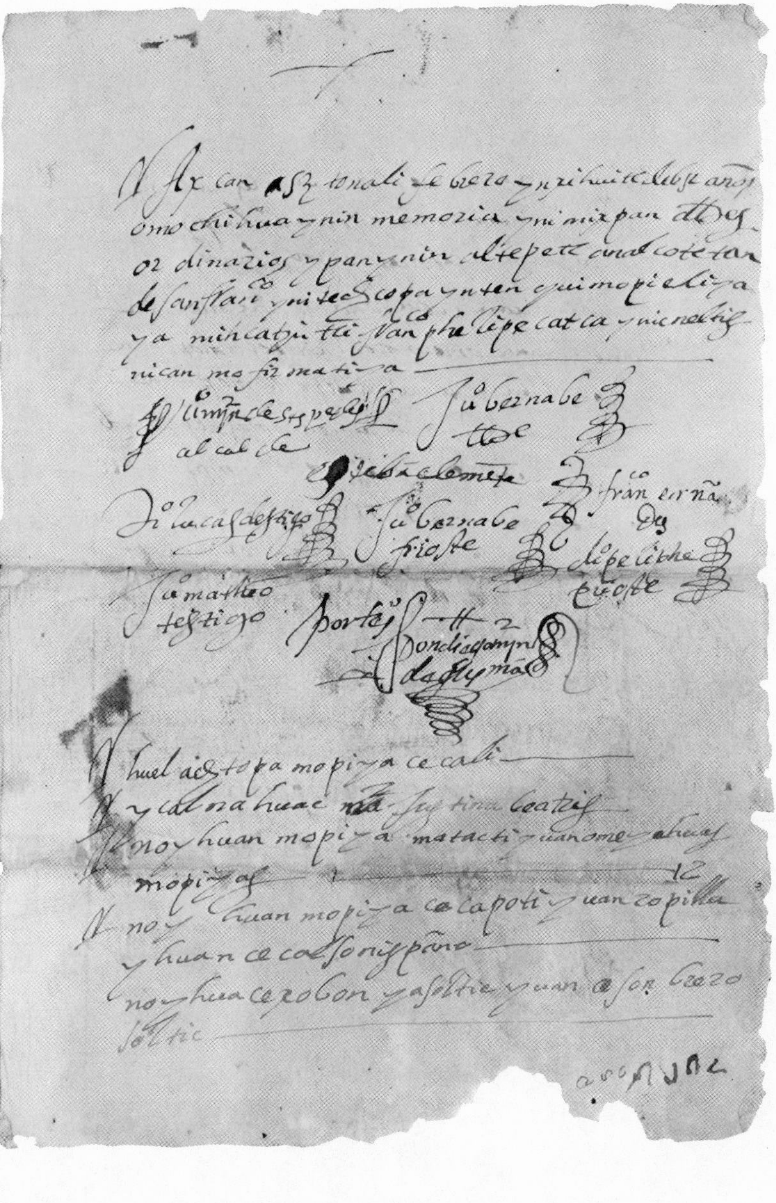

Document 8. Inventory of the estate of Francisco Felipe, with funeral expenses and auction of effects, Analcotitlan, 1652. Page 1.

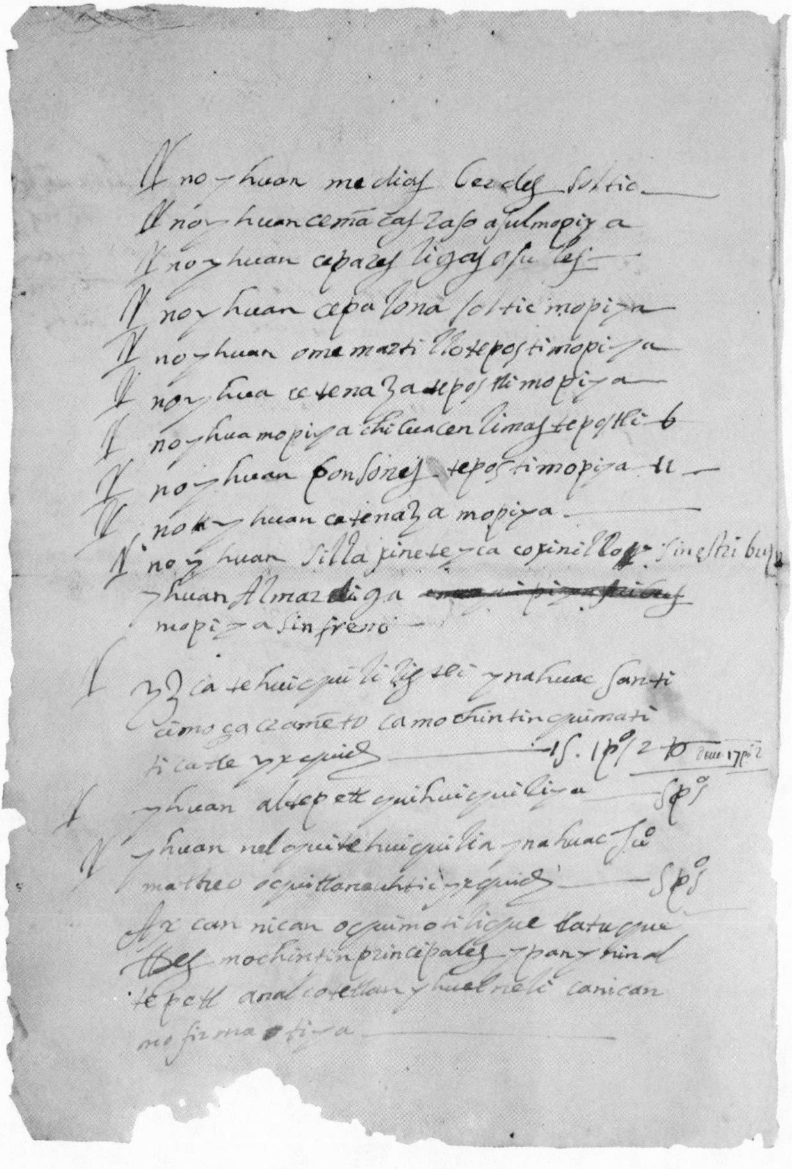

Document 8. Inventory of the estate of Francisco Felipe, with funeral expenses and auction of effects, Analcotitlan, 1652. Page 2.

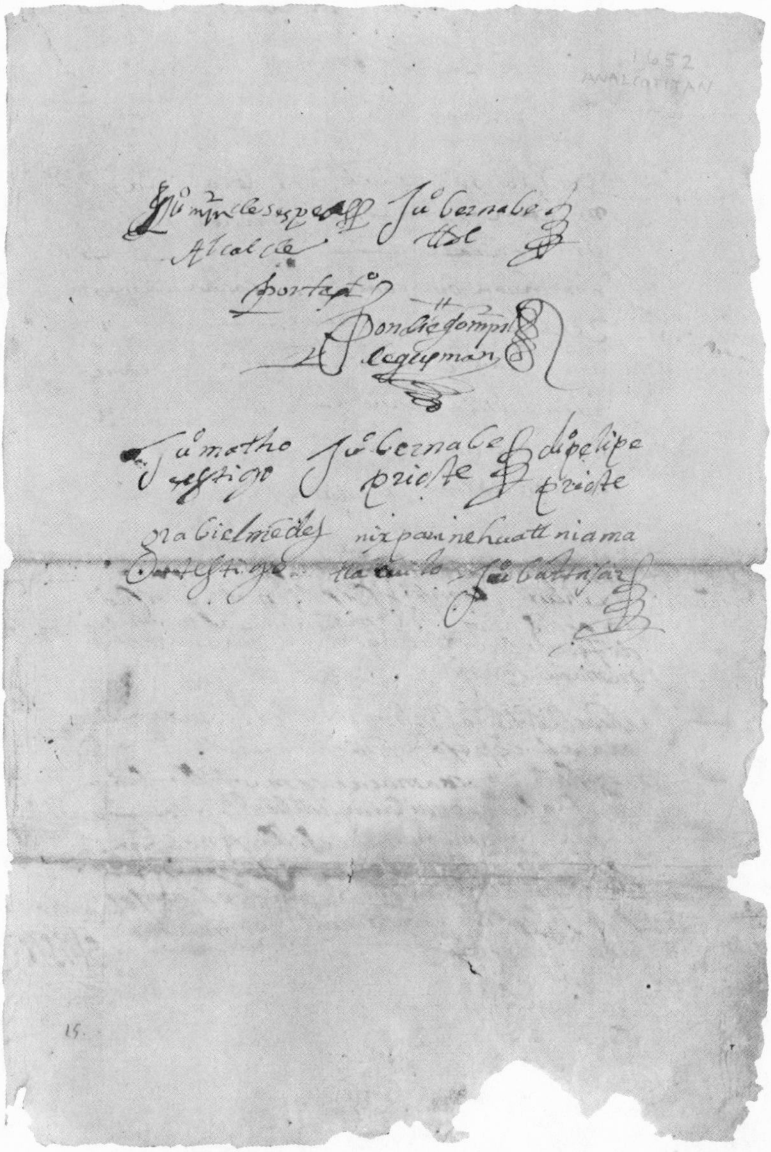

1652
ANALCOTITLAN

Alcalde

Juº bernabe
alc

por testº

Don diego

Juº matheo
testigo

Juº bernabe
prioste

diº phelipe
prioste

gabriel mendez
testigo

nixpan nehuatl niamatlacuilo
Juº baltasar

15

Document 8. Inventory of the estate of Francisco Felipe, with funeral expenses and auction of effects, Analcotitlan, 1652. Page 3.

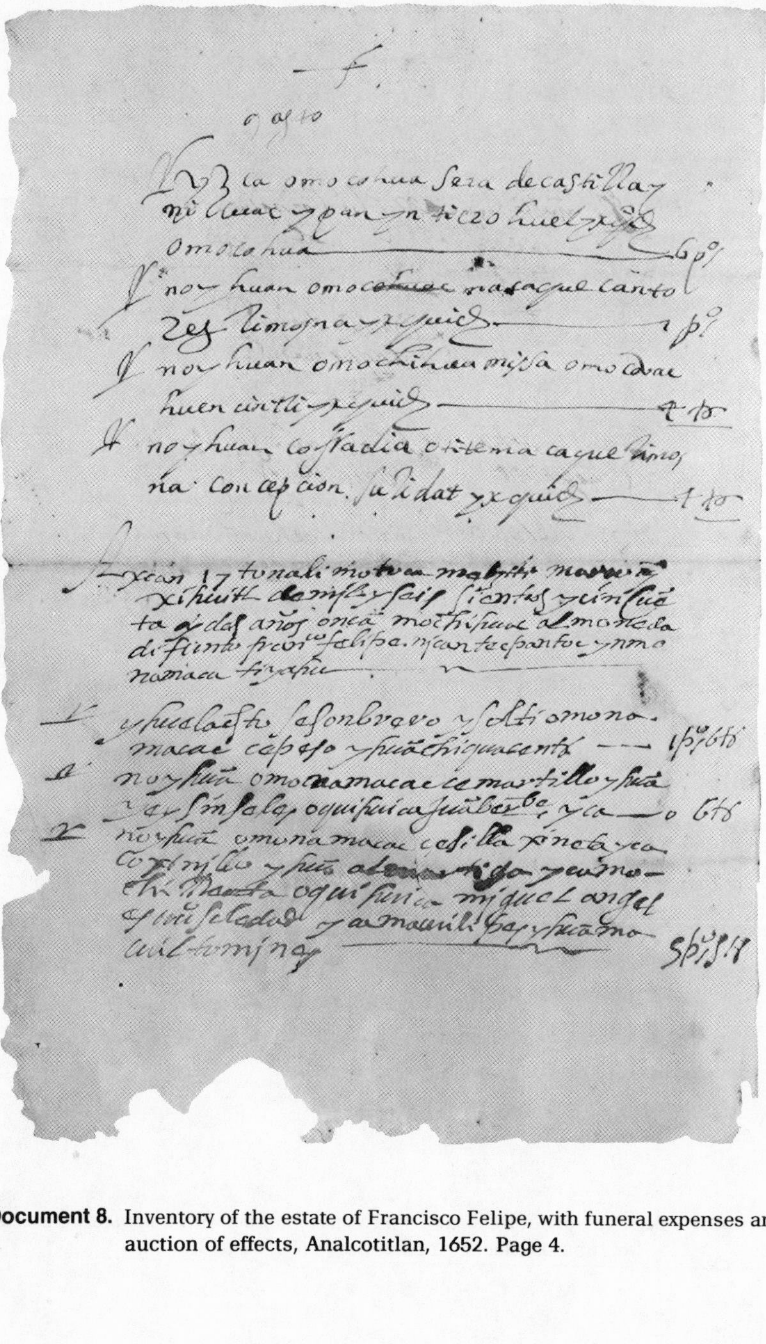

— f.

9 ps 10

ynic ça omocohua sera de castilla y
nic tlacatl yxpan yn tecpo huel yxquich
omocohua ———— 6 ps

noyhuan omocohuac ... caquel canto
res limosna yxquich ———— 1 ps

noyhuan omochihua missa omocohua
huan cintli yxquich ———— 4 ts

noyhuan cofradia otitema caquel limos
na concepcion sufidat yxquich ———— 1 ts

axcan 17 tonali motenca mahtlactli marzo yn
xihuitl de mill y seis sientos y cincuen
ta y dos años oncan mochihua almoneda
difunto franco felipe ytlatecpantoc ynmo
namaca ...

ypatiuh sonbrero ... omona
macac ... ———— 1 ps 6 ts

noyhuan omonamacac ce martillo ypatiuh
... ———— 0 6 ts

noyhuan omonamacac ce silla ...
... ... miguel angel
... ypatiuh mo
cuil tomines ———— 5 ps 5 ts

Document 8. Inventory of the estate of Francisco Felipe, with funeral expenses and auction of effects, Analcotitlan, 1652. Page 4.

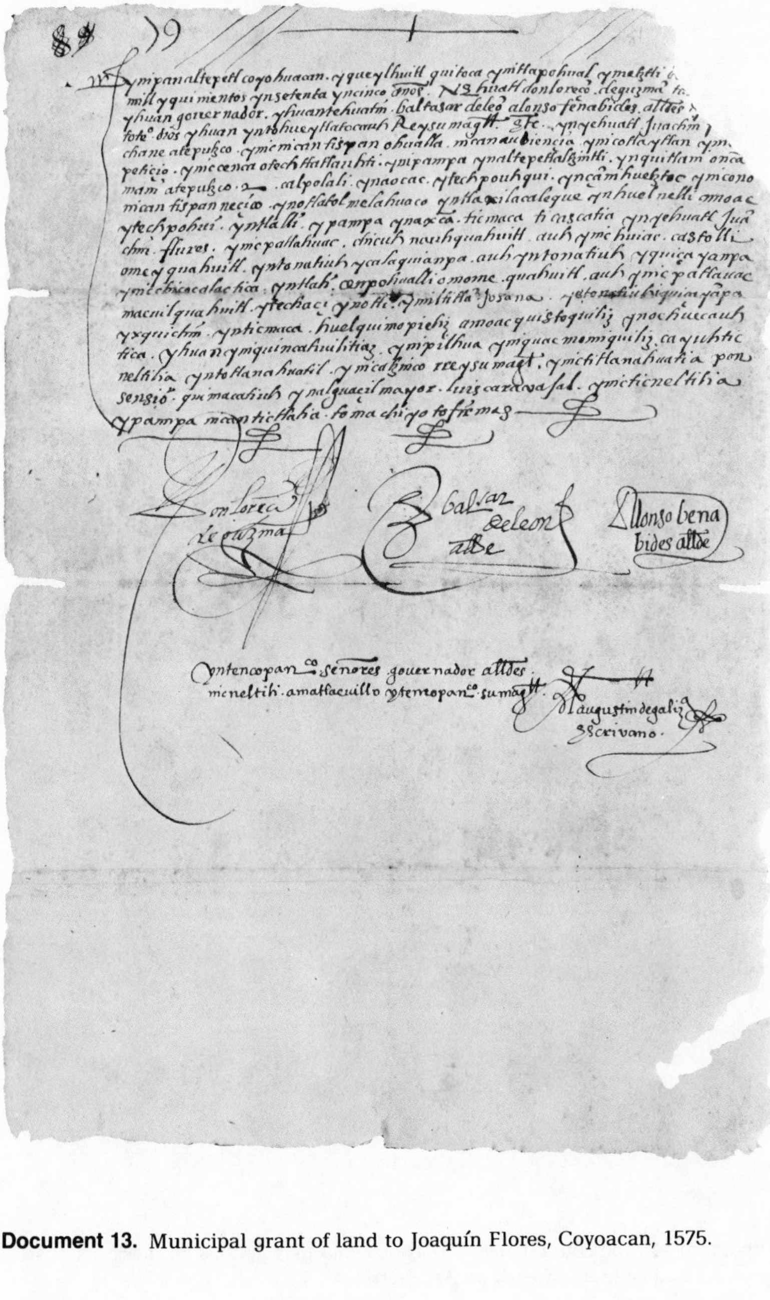

Document 13. Municipal grant of land to Joaquín Flores, Coyoacan, 1575.

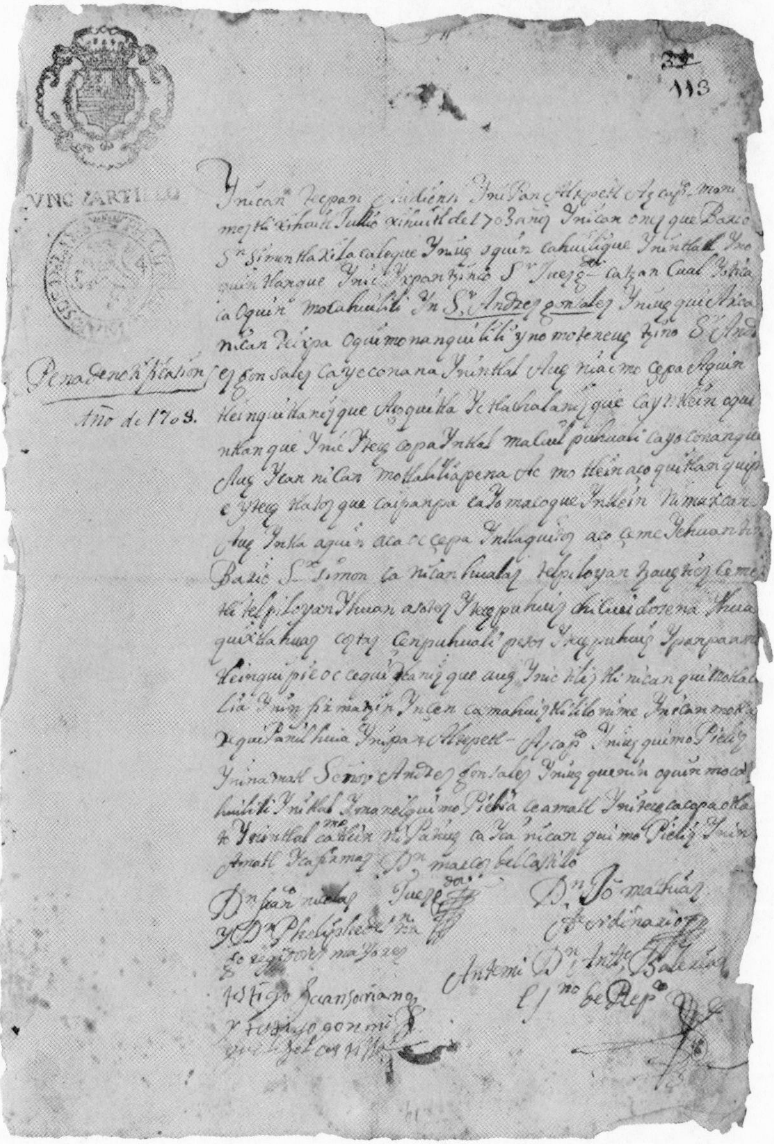

Document 14. The council of Azcapotzalco enjoins penalties on those not observing a land agreement, Azcapotzalco, 1703.

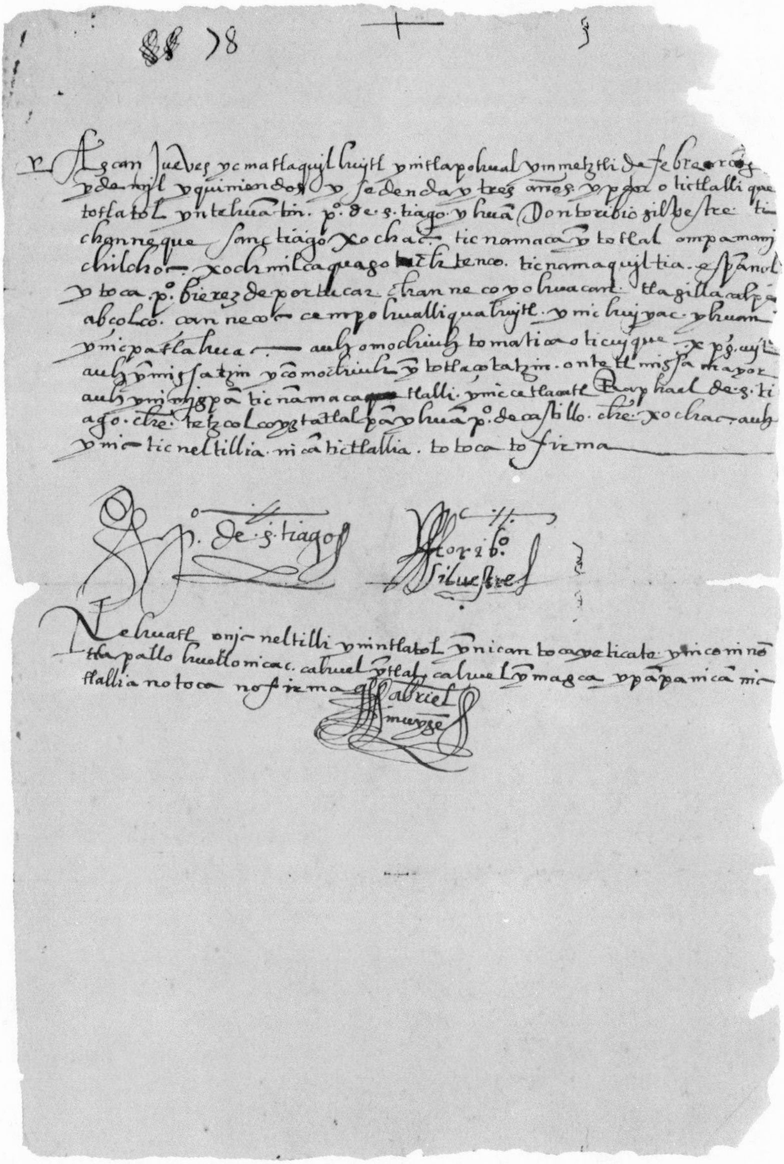

Document 16. Sale of land to a Spaniard, Coyoacan, 1573.

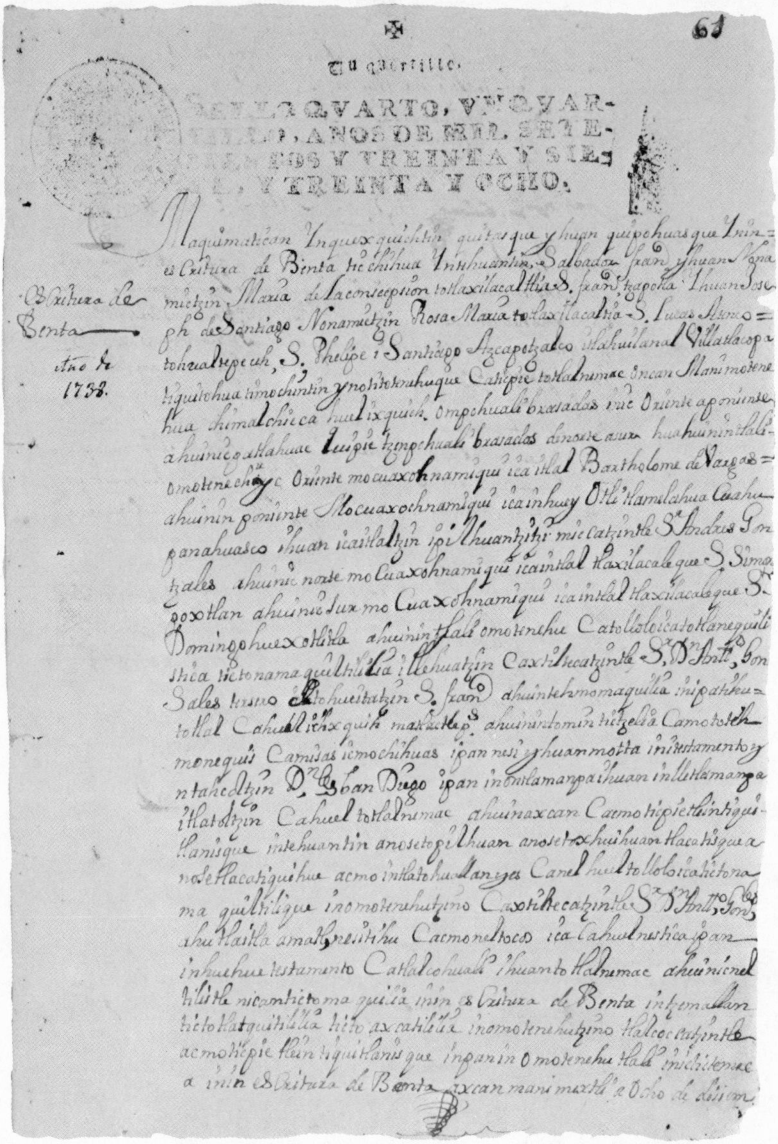

✠ 61

Un quartillo.

SELLO QUARTO, UN QUARTILLO, AÑOS DE MIL SETECIENTOS Y TREINTA Y SIETE, Y TREINTA Y OCHO.

Escritura de Benta

año de 1738.

Maquimatican Yn quexquichtin quitasque yhuan quipohuasque Ynin escritura de Benta ticchihua Inthuantin Salbador fran yhuan Nonamictzin Maria de la consepsion totlaxilacal Ytlia S. fran tzapotla Ihuan Joseph de Santiago Nonamictzin Rosa Maria totlaxilacaltia S. Lucas Atenco tohuiltepec, S. Phelipe i Santiago Azcapotzalco ...

Document 17. Sale of land, with all the acts of investigation, confirmation, and possession; will attached, Azcapotzalco, 1738. Page 1.

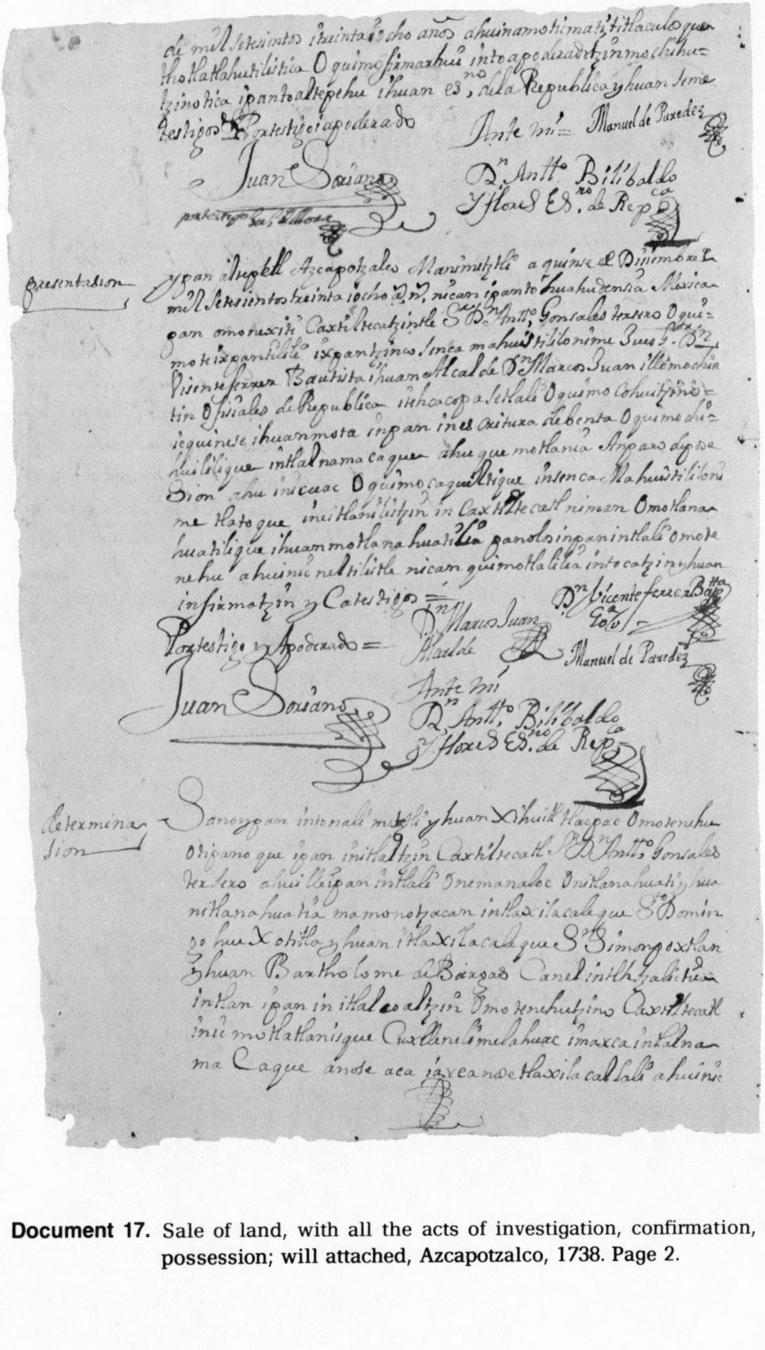
de mill setesientos i treinta i ocho años ahuinamo ticmati titlaculoque
tito tlatlahutilitica Oquimofirmarhui into apoderadotzin mochihutzinotica ipan to altepehu ihuan Esno, dela Republica y huan teme
testigos por testigo i apoderado Ante mi = Manuel de Paredes
Juan Soriano Dn Antto Bilibaldo y Flores Esno de Repca
por testigo Luis Flores

Presentasion
ypan altepetl Azcapotzalco Manimetztli a quinse de Diziembre de mill setesientos treinta i ocho años nican ipan to huahudensia Mexicano omonexiti Caxtiltecatzintle Sr. Dn Antto Gonsales tersero Oquimo tixpantilile ixpantzinco inca mahuiztililoni Jues Sr. Dn Visente ferrer Bautista ihuan Alcalde Dn Marcos Juan ille mochi tin Ofisiales de Republica ithcacopa setlali Oquimo cohuitzino iquinse ihuan nota in pan in es critura debenta Oquimo chihuililique in tlalnamacaque ahu que motlania Amparo de posesion ahu in icuac Oquimo caquiltique insenca tlahuiztililoni me tlatoque in itlanilitzin in Caxtiltecatl niman Omotlanane huatilique ihuan motlanahuatilia qanolsi ipan in tlali Omote nehu ahuinic nel tilitle nican quimotlalilia into catzin y huan in firmatzin y Cates digos = Dn Vicente ferrer Batta
Por testigo y Apoderado = Dn Marcos Juan Alcalde Manuel de Paredez Ante mi
Juan Soriano Dn Antto Bilibaldo y Flores Esno de Repca

Determinasion
Sanoyqan in tonali mextli y huan xhuitl tlacpac Omotenehu Otipano que ipan in itlaltzin Caxtiltecatl Sr. Dn Antto Gonsales tersero ahuilleipan in tlali Onemanaloc Onitlanahuati y hua nitlanahuatia mamonotzacan in tlaxilacalque Sto. Domingo huexotitla y huan itlaxilacalque Sn Simon pochtlan y huan Bartholome de Bargas Canel in tlh yaltitica in tlan ipan in itlal coaltzin Omotenehutzino Caxtiltecatl inic motlatlanisque Cuix llenelo melahuac imaxca in tlalnama Caque ahose aca iarean de tlaxilacal tlali ahuinic

Document 17. Sale of land, with all the acts of investigation, confirmation, and possession; will attached, Azcapotzalco, 1738. Page 2.

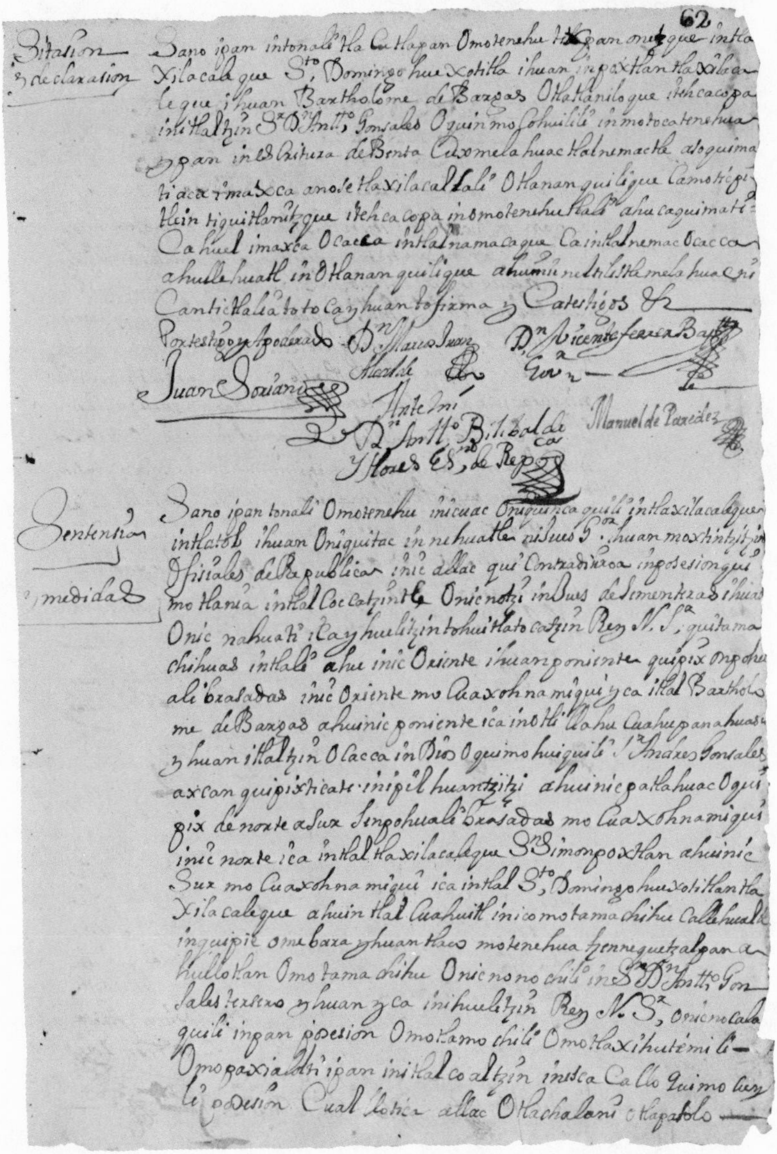

62.

Citasion y declarasion

Sano ipan intonali tlacatlapan Omotenehu [illegible] ipan oneque intla-
Xilacalque S.to Domingo huexotitla ihuan inpaxtlan tlaxilacaleque ihuan Bartholome de Bargas Otlatlanilo que ithcacopa
initlaltzin S.r D.n Anto. Gonsales Oquin mocohuilili in motocatenehua
ipan in escritura de Benta Cuxmela huac tlalnemactli aloquima-
tiaca imaxca anoce tlaxilacaltlali Otlanan quilique camo tiqui-
tlein tiquitlanitzque ithcacopa in omotenehu tlali ahu caquimati-
ca huel imaxca Ocacca intlalnamacaque ca intlalnemac Ocacca
ahuelle huatl in Otlanan quilique ahuinin neltililistlimela huacni-
Cantictlalia to to ca yhuan tofirma y Catestigos &c.

Portestigo y Apoderado D.n Marcos Juan Alcalde — D.n Vicente ferrer Baptista Gov.or

Juan Soriano

Ante mi
D.n Ant.o Bilibaldecar y flores Es.no de Rep.ca

Manuel de Paredes

Sentensia y medidas

Sano ipan tonali Omotenehu inicuac Oniquinca quili in tlaxilacalque in
intlatol ihuan Oniquitac in nehuatl el [illegible] ihuan moxtintzitzin
Ofisiales de la Republica inic ayac qui contradicio a in posesion quimotlania in tlal Coccatzintli Onicnotzi in bues de sementeras ihuan
Onic nahuati ica yhuelitzin tohuitlatocatzin Rey N. S.r quitamachihuas in tlali ahu inic Oriente ihuan poniente quipix onpohuali brasadas inic Oriente mo cuaxohnamiqui yca itlal Barthol-
me de Bargas ahuinic poniente ica in otli [illegible] cuahuepanahuas-
y huan itlaltzin Olacca in Dios Oquimohuiquili S.r Andres Gonsales
axcan quipixticate inipil huantzitzi ahuinic patlahuac Oquipix de norte a Sur Sempohuali brasadas mo cuaxohnamiqui
inic norte ica in tlal tlaxilacalque S.n Simon poxtlan ahuinic
Sur mo cuaxohnamiqui ica in tlal S.to Domingo huexotitlan tla-
Xilacalque ahuin tlal cuahuitl inic omotamachihu callehualli
in quipie ome bara yhuan tlaco motenehua tenneguetzalpan a-
huillotlan Omotamachihu Onicnonochili in S.r D.n Anto. Gonsales terxero y huan y ca inihuelitzin Rey N. S.r Onicnocalaquili in ipan posesion Omotlamo chili Omotlaxihuitemili-
Omopaxialti ipan initlalcoaltzin inteca callo quimo hue-
li posesion Cuallotica allac Otlachaloni otlapatolo —

Document 17. Sale of land, with all the acts of investigation, confirmation, and possession; will attached, Azcapotzalco, 1738. Page 3.

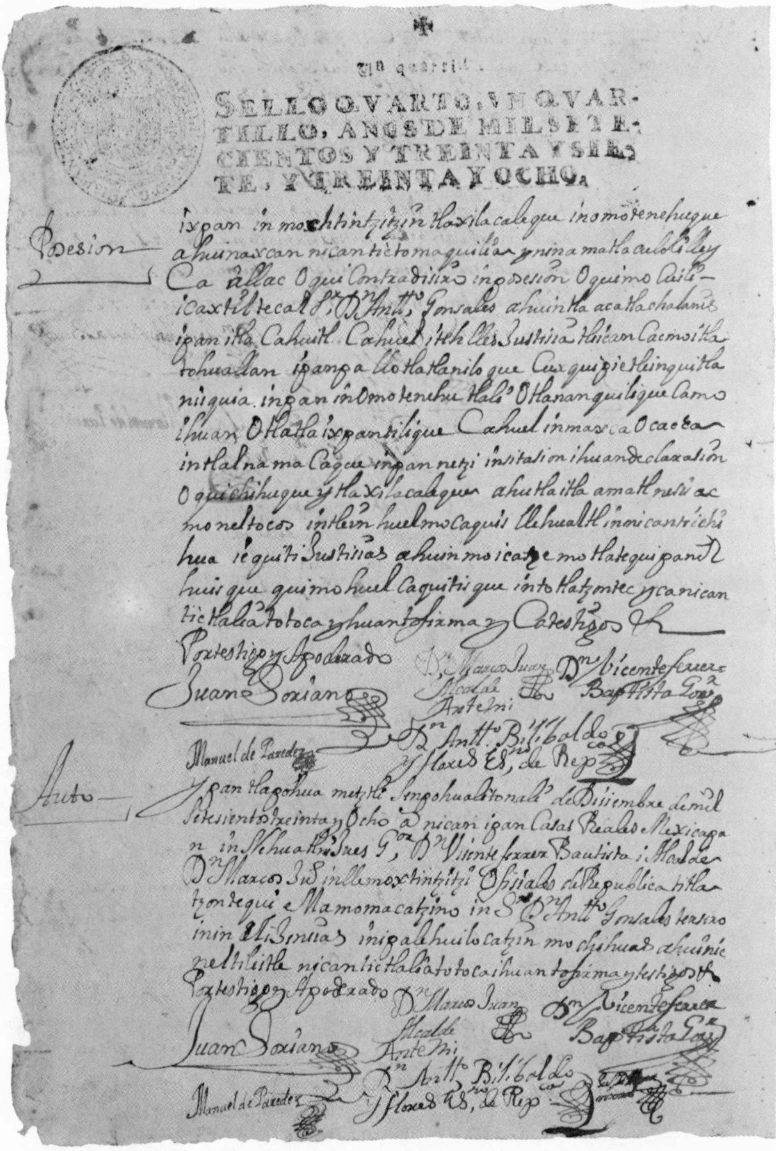

Document 17. Sale of land, with all the acts of investigation, confirmation, and possession; will attached, Azcapotzalco, 1738. Page 4.

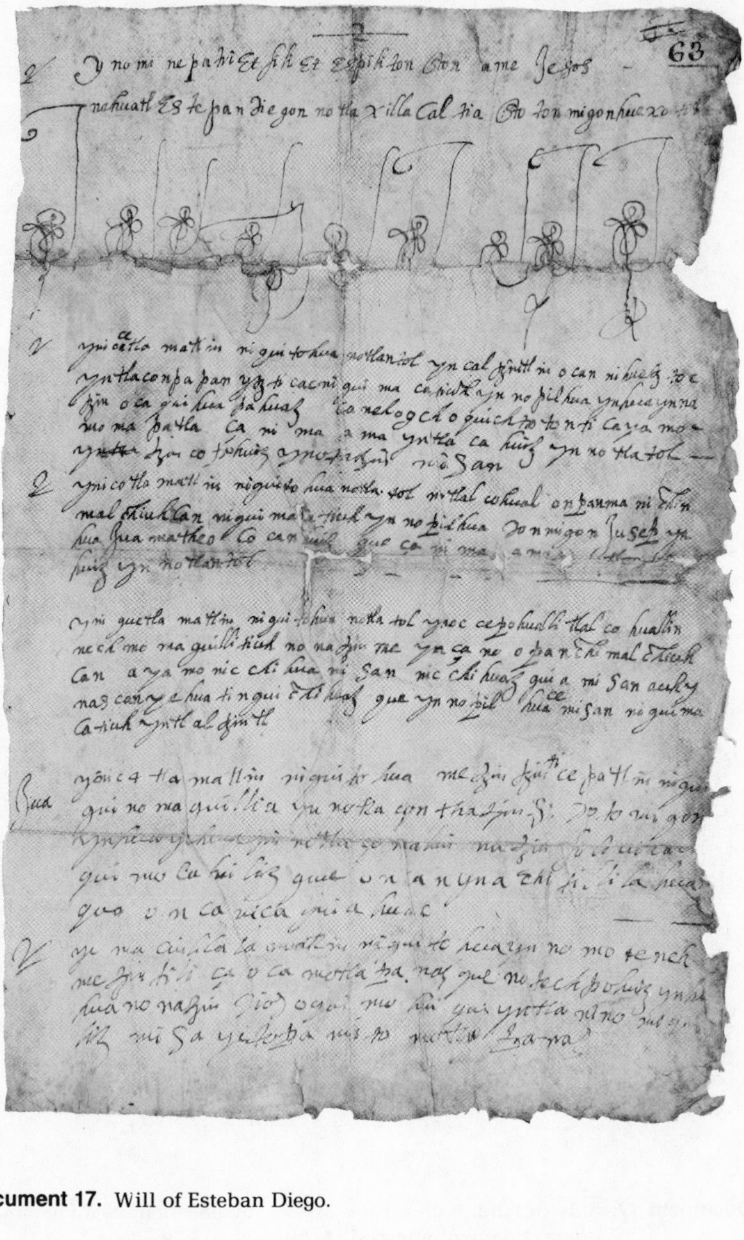
63

Yn nomi ne patri Et fili Et Espiliton Con ame Jesos

nehuatl Estepan diegon notlaxillacaltia Con ton migonhuexo[illegible]

[illegible]

Document 17. Will of Esteban Diego.

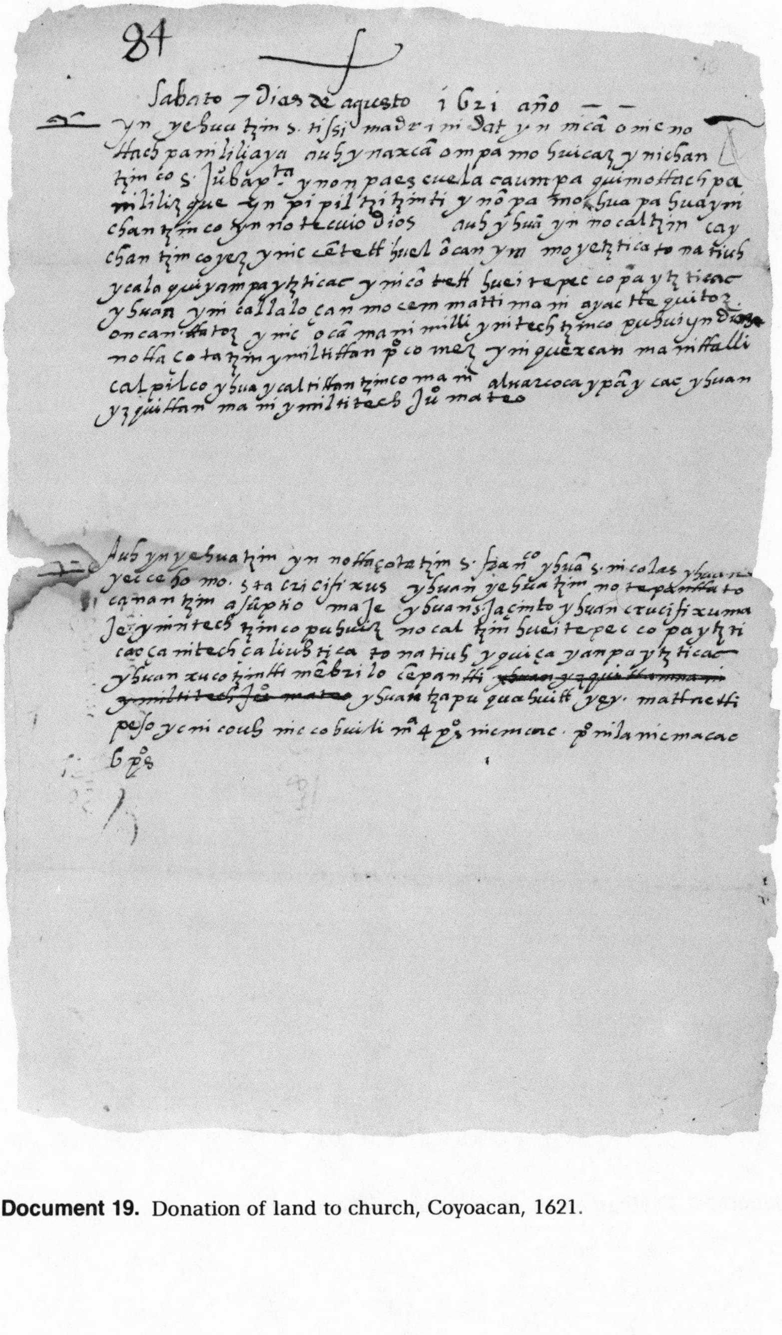

84

Sabato 7 dias de agusto 1621 año — —

yn yehuatzin s. tissi madre i mi dat yn mica omic no ttachpa milliaya auh yn axca ompa mo huicaz yn ichan tzinco s. Ju baptª. y non paesquela caumpa quimottachpa milliz que yn pipiltzitzinti y nopa mokhua pa huay michantzinco yn notecuio dios auh yhuã yn nocaltzin cay chantzincoyez ynic cētetl huel ocan ym moyetztica tonatiuh ycalo quiyampa ytztica ynicō tetl huei tepec co pa ytzticac yhuan ym callalo çan mocem matti ma yn ayac ttequitoz oncan ittatoz ynic ocā ma ni milli yn itech tzinco pouhui yn diego notta co ta tzin ymiltitlan pº comez yn iquezcan ma mitalli calpilco yhua ycaltitlan tzinco ma m alvarcoca ypāy cac yhuan yzquittan ma ni ymiltitech Juº mateo

Auh yn yehuatzin yn nottaçotatzin s. franco yhuā s. nicolas yhuan i yeicehco mo. sta crucifixus yhuan yehuatzin no tepantlato canantzin asuption maje yhuan s. Jacinto yhuan crucifixu ma Je ymitech tzinco pohuiz no cal tzin huei tepec copaytztica çan itech çaliuhtica tonatiuh yquiça yanpa ytzticac yhuan xucotzintli mēbrillo çe pantli ~~yhuan yzquittan mani ymiltitech Juº mateo~~ yhuan tzapu quahuitl yey. matlactli peso ycni couh nic cohuili mª 4 pºs nicmacac. pºrila nicmacac 6 pºs

Document 19. Donation of land to church, Coyoacan, 1621.

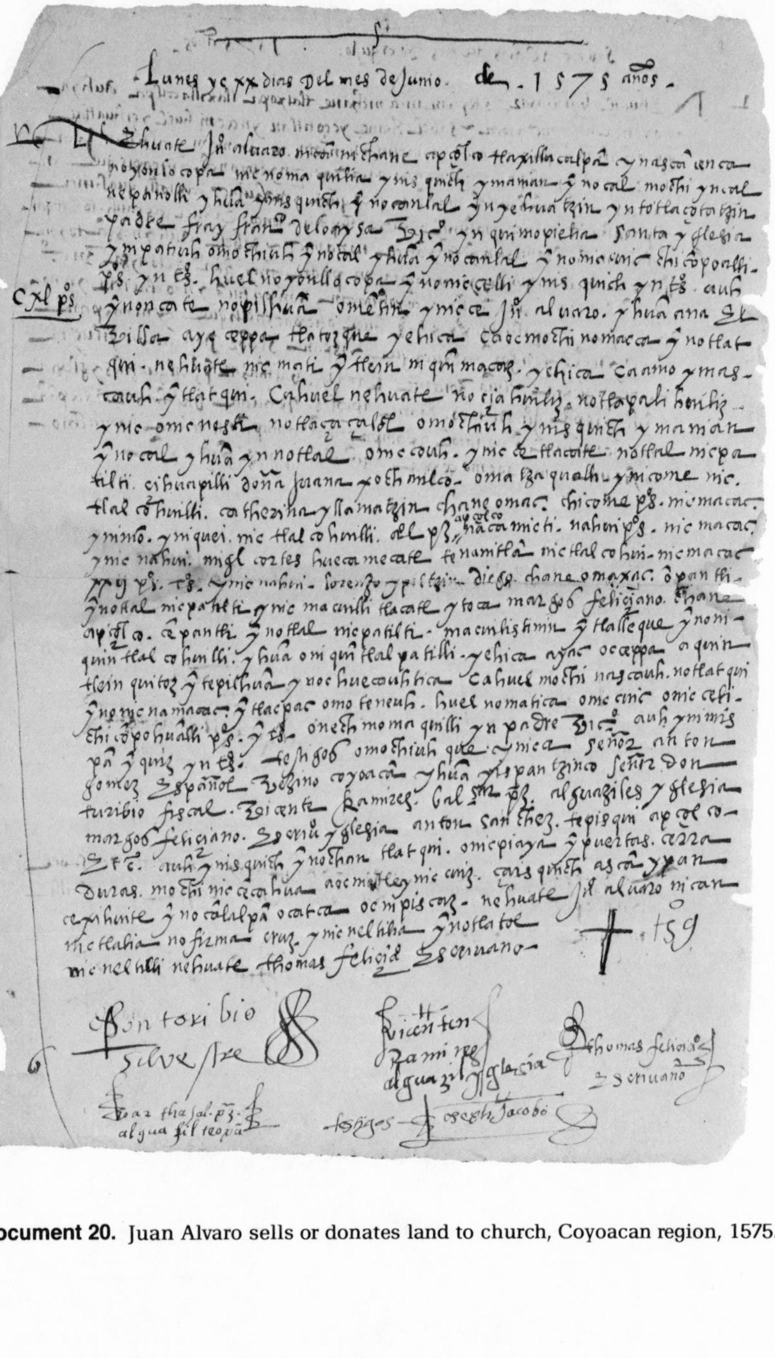

Document 20. Juan Alvaro sells or donates land to church, Coyoacan region, 1575.

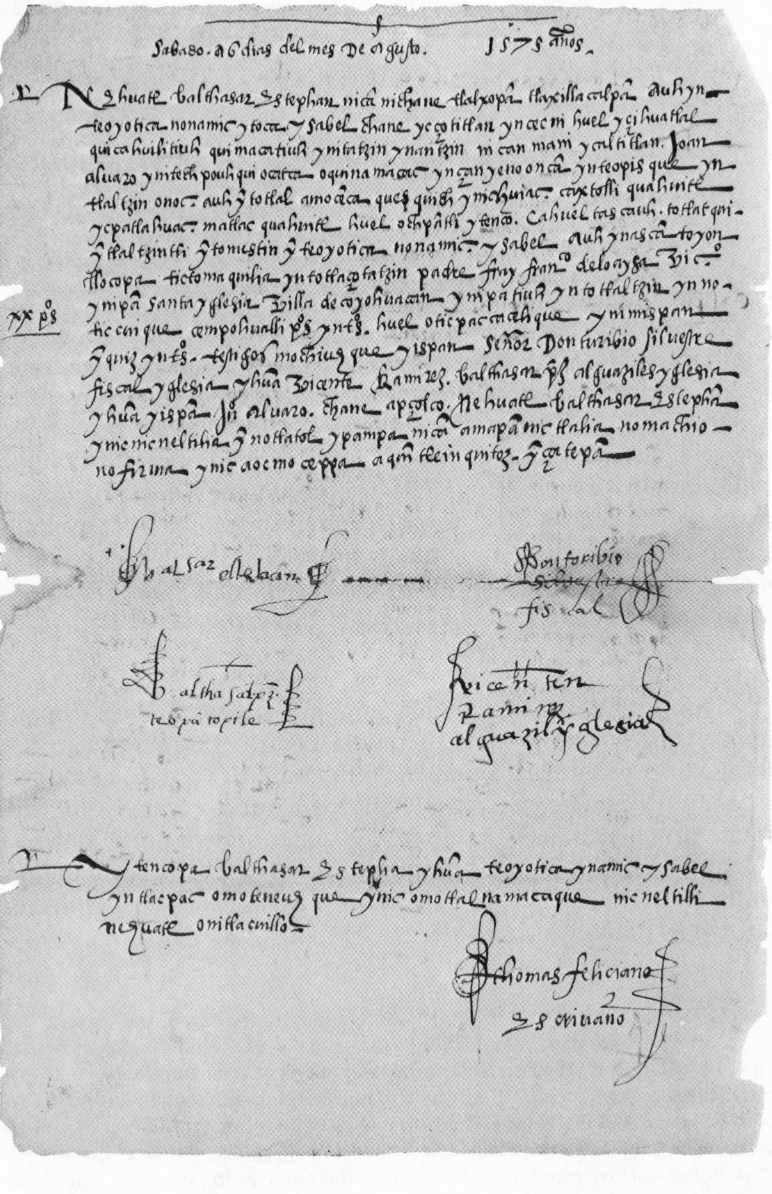

Document 21. Baltasar Esteban and wife sell or donate land to church, Coyoacan region, 1575.

II. Land

9. Land investigation and distribution at Atenantitlan, 1554[1]

xiii dias de hebrero 1554 años

Nehuatl p^{o} de paz regidor oniquitlatlani in palpanueuetque ynic ce mi̅n tlacuchcalcatl[2] inic ome miguel itzcotecatl ju^{o} tzonen fran^{co} moysen p^{o} helias quitoua yn ye cempoualxiuitl yn ie castolxiuitl yn ie matlacxiuitl ca yeppa ticencalle yeppa ticcenchiua in totequiuh Auh yn icuac vitza miguel garcia juez quinicuac tlatzoncaualpan[3] motlalique In axcan ic omovicatza in tlatoani doctor santillan omomacuiltecpantlalique[4] veipulco canel yc omotlalli çan yeuatl ic tonteilvia ompa mani totlal ynnatenantitlan v tlacatl yn opa tlalchiua ynic ce fran^{co} ciuaivinti ini ii ju^{o} tonal ini iii ju^{o} icnoiotl inic iiii ycnopiltzintli itoca ju^{o} inic v icnociuatl in iconeuh ju^{o}[5]

— Oniquitlatlani in chaneque atenantitlan a^{o}l tepanecoc miguel ixquen fran^{co} xico p^{o} tochtli quitoa ca in icuac tetlalmacoc ye matlacxiuitl yancuican momacac mi̅n cuauhtli yn tlalli çan exiuitl in conchiuh niman ya xuchmilcatlalpan Auh yn fran^{co} ciuaivitin niman quimacaco in tlalli mi̅n topille chane atonco çan yc iuh mani ie ixquich cauitl axcan oquimoçancamolvi fran^{co} xico quitoua quinio axcan onicnoçacamolvi amo ac onechmacac auh yn tlali ynic viac xiii ic patlauac xi

[1]AGN, Tierras 1735, exp. 2, ff. 105-106. A Spanish translation of 1681 is on ff. 142-144. A bit of explanation may facilitate the reader's understanding in either language. Palpan and Hueypulco were apparently towns of some importance in the Coyoacan jurisdiction; Atenantitlan was a hamlet or subunit at the edge of the two towns' spheres. Having belonged previously to Palpan, Atenantitlan at the time of this document has recently been reassigned to Hueypulco's sphere. Councilman Pedro de Paz of Coyoacan has come to regularize and confirm the local inhabitants' rights to disputed or unused land and to liquidate the claims of Palpan in the area. Hence the presence of the Palpan elders, and the fact that the Atenantitlan people are one moment identified with, the next moment distinguished from, the people of Palpan.

[2]Many of the Nahuatl surnames are also (former) titles, or derive from calendrical items, or have other meanings. For example, Tlacuchcalcatl, "spear-house person," title given to military leaders and judges; Itzcotecatl, possibly based on a place name; Tzone(n), "hairy"; Ciuaiuinti, "woman-crazy"; Tonal, "day"; Icnoyotl, "mis-

Documentation

13th day of February, year of 1554.

I, Pedro de Paz, councilman, interrogated the Palpan elders: the first Martín Tlacuchcalcatl,[2] the second Miguel Itzcotecatl, Juan Tzonen, Francisco Moysen, Pedro Elías. They said: it was twenty years ago, and fifteen years ago, and ten years ago, that we heads of households before now have united to perform our duty. And when Miguel García came as judge, then [tributes?][3] were arranged. Recently Judge Dr. Santillán came in order for them to be organized by hundreds[4] at Hueypulco. Since it was so arranged, we have been claiming that our land is there at Atenantitlan. There are five people working land there: first, Francisco Ciuaiuinti; second, Juan Tonal; third, Juan Icnoyotl; fourth, an orphan called Juan; fifth, a widow's son, Juan.[5]

— I interrogated the householders at Atenantitlan, Alonso Tepanecoc, Miguel Ixquen, Francisco Xico, and Pedro Tochtli. They said that when the land was assigned to them ten years ago, this land was newly given to Martín Cuauhtli; he only worked it three years, then he went to the country of the Xochimilca. And then Martín the constable, citizen of Atonco, came to give the land to Francisco Ciuaiuinti. It lay idle thus all the while until recently Francisco Xico broke the ground for himself. He said: just recently I broke the ground for myself, no one gave it to me. And the land is 13 (rods) long, 11 (rods) wide.

---

ery"; Ixquen, "face covering"; Xico, "bee"; Tochtli, "rabbit" (Pedro Tochtli = Peter Rabbit); Cuauhtli, "eagle"; Xochitl, "flower"; Opoch, "left hand"; Tepantemoc, "person scaling a wall, besieging"; Mimich, "fish"; Hueytecuhtli, "great lord" (or "judge"); Auacatitlancalqui, "living near the avocados" (or "at Auacatitlan"); Couatl, "serpent"; Metzon, "leg-hair." Some of the other surnames are taken from Spanish, including Moysen, "Moses."

[3]The term *tlatzoncahualli* is unfamiliar to us, but in AGN, Tierras 1735, exp. 2, f. 74, we have seen it apparently equated with the delivery of maize, fowl, wood, hay, and money to an overlord.

[4]I.e., to reorganize at the community level. *Tlatoani*, of course, means "ruler" rather than "judge" but was used frequently for the judges of the Royal Audiencia, as in Doc. 12 as well.

[5]Or "a widow, whose son is Juan"? Perhaps the orphan Juan just mentioned? The Spanish translation is "una viuda con su hijo llamado Juan."

— Oniquitlatlani in chaneque palpantlanca quitoua yn icuac tetlalmacoc yancuican ieuatl macuc mīn xochitl çan niman icuac mic auh ynnomic niman concalaltique ju^{o} icnoiotl ye ixquich cauitl aic quichiua çan quicaualtitinemi yn atenantitlantlaca quitoua yn axcan oquimomaquili in tlacatl miguel opoch ipan tequipanoz in tlalli ic viac xix ic patlauac xii yeuatl oquipouh mīn tepantemoc alguazil

— Quitoua in palpanueuetque yn iancuican tetlalmacoc yeuatl macoc bernadino cuauhtli xuchmilcatlalpan oya ynnicuac yan niman commacaque a^{o}l mimich quimacaco ju^{o} ueytecuhctli alcalde chane tequemecan yn axcan omic yn ipiltzin itoca ju^{o} quitoua yn atenantitlantlaca camo ac quicuilia çaniuh mani canel itlal ma concui auh yn tlalli inic viac xxx ic patlauac xii

— Quitoua ynnatenantitlantlaca tlacpac omoteneuhque ynni tlalli yancuican macoc mīn aciquiuhnemi ynnaxcan temilco oya yn icuac ya niman quimacaco gabriel çacatzonatl yeuatl quimacaco ju^{o} ueytecuhctli alcalde chane tequemecan yn oquichiuh chicuace xiuitl auh yn axcan oticmacaque mīn choquima ypan tequipanoz ynic viac in tlalli xiii ic patlauac xii yc ocan xii inic viac xv yeuatl oquipouh mīn tepantemoc algazil

— Axcan martes oniquitlatlani yn atenantitlantlaca yn ipampa inic ca tlalli çaniuh vetztoc ye ixquich cauitl ynic viac c ynic patlauatoc yn itzintlan xlvi in icpac xiiii oniquimilvi quen anquitoua in ipampa inic ca tlalli hi ca amechixtoquilia in palpantlaca cuix quinequi amoyollo anquimonepanxelvizque niman oquitoque ca ye cualli ma iuhqui mochiua ma xitechmomamaquilli ma yc concuican in tlatzonco oniquimilvi ca ye cualli inic amo oc ceppa anquicuepazque amotlatol xicchiuacan juramento niman oquichiuhque inic ce a^{o}l tepanecoc miguel ixquen fran^{co} xico ju^{o} cuauhtli Auh yn o iuh quichiuhque ymixpan in palpanueuetque mīn tlacuchcalcatl fran^{co} moyse p^{o} helias ju^{o} tzone yn testigosme mīn tepantemuc alguazil chane aticpac yoan gonçalo hernandez alguazil chane chimaliztacan yzquintin ymmixpan yn o iuh quitoque ynnatenantitlantlaca

xvii dias de hebrero 1554 años axcan saba^{o} Axcan omomacaque tlali atenantitlantlaca palpan opouia axcan poui veipolco

— miguel opuch ycalal omacoc ic patlauac x ic viac xviii yn milco catca don mīn de paz aocmo cepa ompa yaz ipan tequipanoz yc ocan xii xxiiii

— I interrogated the householders from Palpan, who said that when the land was assigned to them, this piece was newly given to Martín Xochitl, but then he soon died, and when he had died then they made it the house-land of Juan Icnoyotl. All the while he never worked it, he just left it abandoned. The Atenantitlan people said, recently it was given to a Miguel Opoch to work on. The land is 19 long, 12 wide. The person who measured it is Martín Tepantemoc, constable.

— The Palpan elders said, when land was newly assigned to people, it was given to a Bernardino Cuauhtli, who went to the country of Xochimilca; when he went, then they gave it to Alonso Mimich. Juan Hueytecuhtli, alcalde, citizen of Tequemecan, came to give it. Recently he (Alonso Mimich) died. His son is named Juan. The Atenantitlan people said that no one is taking it from him, it lies idle; since it is his land, let him take it. And the land is 30 long, 12 wide.

— The above-mentioned Atenantitlan people said, this land was newly given to Martín Aciquiuhnemi, who now has gone to Temilco. When he went, then it was given to Gabriel Çacatzonatl. The person who came to give it was Juan Hueytecuhtli, alcalde, citizen of Tequemecan. He worked it for six years. And now we have given it to Martín Choquima to work on. The land is 13 long, 12 wide. Another place is 12 (wide), 15 long. The person who measured it was Martín Tepantemoc, constable.

— Today, Tuesday, I asked the Atenantitlan people why the land thus lies idle all the time, 100 long, being 46 wide below, 14 above. I said to them: what do you say about this land that the Palpan people claim from you? Do your hearts desire that you divide it between you? Then they said: very well, let it be done thus, distribute it to us, and let them take it then. Finally I said to them: very well, so that you will not go back on your word again, take the oath. Then they did it: first, Alonso Tepanecoc; Miguel Ixquen; Francisco Xico; Juan Cuauhtli. And they did this in the presence of the Palpan elders Martín Tlacuchcalcatl; Francisco Moysen; Pedro Elías; Juan Tzonen. Witnesses were Martín Tepantemoc, constable, citizen of Aticpac, and Gonzalo Hernández, constable, citizen of Chimaliztacan. In the presence of all these, thus spoke the Atenantitlan people.

17th day of February, year of 1554, today being Saturday. Today the Atenantitlan people who belonged to Palpan and now belong to Hueypulco were given land.

— Miguel Opoch was given his house-land, 10 wide, 18 long, where the field of don Martín de Paz was. He is not to go away again, he is to work on it. Another place is 12 (by) 24.

— fran^{co} xico yc ocan itlal[6] omacoc x ic patlauac xii ic viac

— p^{o} tochtli yc ocan itlal xiii ic patlauac xxi ic viac

— min̄ choquima yc ocan [i]tlal xiii ynic patlauac xx in itzintla yn itzonco xiii

— a^{o}l tepanecoc yc ocan ytlal xvi ic viac xi ic patlauac otenco

— filiphe cuauhtli yccocan ytlal xiiii ic viac xi ic patlauac

— ju^{o} auacatitlancalqui yc ocan itlal x ic viac xiiii

— simon couatl ycalal yancuican momaca ytlal xii ic viac xxix imilco ocatca do min̄ de paz nican ipan tequipanoz

— p^{o} xochitl ycalal yancuican momaca yn milco ocatca don min̄ yn icalal x ic patlavac ynnic viac xxxvi ipan tequipanoz aocmo ceppa yaz

— miguel ixquen omomacac tlaltzontli apantentli vii inic viac xiii

x tlacatl

Nehuatl p^{o} de paz regidor oniquimmamacac yn intlal yeuantin atenantitlan calle yn iuh quineque inyollo o iuhqui mochiuh yc onicneltilli ynic omotlaytlanique ixpan capilton de coyouacan axcan onicneltillico inic oniquinmamacac yntencopa in señor don ju^{o} yoan senores alcaldesme don antoni^{o} ju^{o} de s lançaro Auh ynicconiquimmamacac çan intlatol onictocac ynic oquimomamacaque ymmixpan palpantlaca ju^{o} tzone fran^{co} moysen p^{o} helias yoan p^{o} chane totoltepec yoan yeuatl otlalpouh min̄ tepantemuc alguazil chane aticpac yoan fran^{co} metzon chane veipulco yoan don ju^{o} de marrigue de çayulan Auh yṅ cuauitl yc omopouh yeuatl yn matlactlacxitl nican mopia[7] etc ymetztli omoteneuh tlacpac yoan xiuitl

---

[6]Land in a second or another place, i.e., in addition to the house land.

[7]Or perhaps "is observed here," rather than being physically preserved at the

— Francisco Xico was given additional land,[6] 10 wide, 12 long.
— Pedro Tochtli, additional land, 13 wide, 21 long.
— Martín Choquima, additional land, 13 wide, 20 (long) below, 13 above.
— Alonso Tepanecoc, additional land, 16 long, 11 wide, at the road's edge.
— Felipe Cuauhtli, additional land, 14 long, 11 wide.
— Juan Auacatitlancalqui, additional land, 10 (wide), 14 long.
— Simón Couatl was newly given his house-land; his land is 12 (wide), 29 long, where the field of don Martín de Paz was; he is to work here on it.
— Pedro Xochitl was newly given his house-land where the field of don Martín was; his house-land is 10 wide, 36 long; he is to work on it, he is not to go away again.
— Miguel Ixquen was given the end of the field at the edge of the canal, 7 (wide), 13 long.
(There are) ten people.

I, Pedro de Paz, councilman, distributed their land to those Atenantitlan householders as their hearts desired; it was thus done in order for me to verify it as they requested before the council of Coyoacan; now I have come to attest how I distributed it on the command of lord don Juan and the lords alcaldes don Antonio and Juan de San Lázaro. And in the manner of how I distributed it to them I merely followed their word as to how they had distributed it among themselves, in the presence of the Palpan people Juan Tzonen; Francisco Moysen; Pedro Elías; and Pedro, citizen of Totoltepec. And the person who measured the land was Martín Tepantemoc, constable, citizen of Aticpac, and Francisco Metzon, citizen of Hueypulco, and don Juan de Manrique, of Çayulan. And the rod with which it was measured was the ten-foot-measure that is kept here.[7] Etc., on the above mentioned month and year.

---

council building. The Spanish is "la brasa de dies pies que es la que acoztumbra este pueblo."

10. Division of a plot of land, Coyoacan region, 1554[1]

Axcan fiernes i dias de junyo mdliiii años Nevatl don ju^{o} gouer^{dor} in ipan altepetl yoan p^{o} de paz regidor tixpan oualla imach julia vixtopolcatl ynniiichpuch ana oncan chaneque tetitlan in itlal ompan mani copilco oniquinepantlaxelvi matlatlacmatl concui ic pa^{oc} x matl concui fran^{ca} no x matl concui ynnana ynic viac xv çanno ixquich concui in ana omextin niquimmacan ipampa aocmo ceppa quixtoquiliz ynniichpuch vistopolcatl ynnimixpan ju^{o} de s. lazaron a$\overline{ll}$de bar^{m} leon regidor luis daniel alguazil diego uecamecatl ju^{o} coiouan diego ramirez domingo laçaron yeuatl quicuaxuchtito m$\overline{in}$ tepantemuc alguazil

pedro de paz Regidor   nehuatl onitlacuilo d$\overline{go}$ lazaro escri^{o}

11. Confirmation of property rights, Coyoacan region, 1568[1]

Nehuatl don juan de guzma onispan necico itocan maria hueytetitlan chanen yn iuh tlacauhtian p^{o} tlahuilatl çaniuh yez ayac tlaxitiniz[2] nicascatian ymarian ipanpa nican nictlalia nomachiouh notocan nopilman imispan niquinauatia desticosme diego delez juan gr^{a} niquipialtian ytlahuan yntocan domingo p^{o} diego de s. meguel juan pabtistan ayac hue quixitiniz y calli auh y cihuacalli[3] omatl ipan ce yollotli[4] yn quauhtectli[5] xxxiiii i tlapanco calnepanolli[6] tonatiuh ycallaquiyapapa itzticac ce matl ipan ce matl[7] auh in tonatiuh yquiçayapa itzticac necoc ce mac ah yn ithualco icac ça no necoc ce matl ipan del mes dias ii d d[es]ediembre mdlxviii años

don juan de guzman   ju^{o} g$\overline{a}$

Document 10

[1]AGN, Tierras 1735, exp. 2, f. 112. A Spanish translation of 1681 is on f. 148.

Document 11

[1]AGN, Tierras 1735, exp. 2, f. 108. A Spanish translation of 1681 is on f. 145.

[2]An alternative translation might be: "Since Pedro Tlahuilatl has left, she will be alone; no one is to harm (the place)." The Spanish translator gives "pidio que ce guardase lo que dejo ordenado Pedro tlalhuilatl por lo que toca a una casa en que no Se dezbaratase."

[3]Literally, "woman's house." Sonia Lombardo de Ruiz, *Desarrollo Urbano de*

Today, Friday, the first day of June of the year 1554, before us, don Juan, governor in the town, and Pedro de Paz, councilman, came the niece of Julián Uixtopolcatl, whose daughter is Ana, citizens of Tetitlan, his land being there at Copilco. I divided it among them, each taking 10 brazas: Francisca takes 10 brazas wide, Ana also takes 10 brazas (wide), 15 long; Ana takes an equal amount. I give it to both of them, wherefore Uixtopolcatl's daughter is not to claim it again from (Francisca). In the presence of Juan de San Lázaro, alcalde; Bartolomé León, councilman; Luis Daniel, constable; Diego Uecamecatl; Juan Coyouan; Diego Ramírez; Domingo Lázaro. The person who went to measure the boundaries was Martín Tepantemoc, constable.

Pedro de Paz, councilman. I wrote it: Domingo Lázaro, notary.

Before me, don Juan de Guzmán, appeared (a person) named María, citizen of Hueytetitlan. [So that it will be as Pedro Tlahuilatl ordered and no one will harm the place],[2] I make it the property of María, wherefore I put here my rubric, name, and signature. I order it before the witnesses Diego Téllez and Juan García. I make guardians her uncles named Domingo Pedro, Diego de San Miguel, (and) Juan Bautista. No one may harm the house. And the common room[3] is 2½ brazas;[4] the clearing[5] is 34. On the roof, the room[6] facing west is one braza [by one braza],[7] and the one facing east is one braza square, and the patio is also one braza square. On the 2d day of December, 1568.

Don Juan de Guzmán. Juan García.

Mexico-Tenochtitlan, p. 186, says that the *cihuacalli* was a common room where family tasks were performed. The Spanish translator gives *cosina*.

[4]*Cinco baras* in the Spanish.

[5]*Solar* in the Spanish.

[6]Molina gives *calnepanolli* as "sobrado de casa," "attic or garret." See also Doc. 2, n. 7.

[7]In such phrases *ipan* usually introduces another, smaller unit of the same measurement rather than a new dimension. This appears to be the case in *omatl ipan ce yollotli* above, though if so we are left with the second dimension unstated. On the other hand, in *ce matl ipan ce matl* the two measurements are identical.

12. Distribution of land to heirs of don Luis Cortés. Coyoacan, 1557[1]

neuatl don juan g^{or} in ipan altepetl coiouacan yoan teuanti tal̅l̅dsme don antonio mi̅n̅ d.s.tiago titlaixquetzalhuan in tlatouani don luis de uelasco visorrei o nican tixpan vallaque ipilhuan don luis cordes acuecuesco chane ipampa omoteixpanhuique ymispantzinco yn tlatoque ompa yn mex^{co} audiencia Real in ipampa in ixquich imil[2] in iaxcan[2] vel oquimmottilique auh totech oquimocavillique ynic tevantin ticneltilizque tiquinxexelhuizque in imil[2] yn ieuatl doña ana ynamic juan d. s. lazaro conana macuilcan ynic cecni yieiocan inic patlavac xxxv quauitl auh in centlapal çan cempoualli ommacuilli auh inic huiac chicompovalli omei quauitl ynic occan xomacuilco inic p^{ac} ompoualli ynic huiac ompoualli ommatlactli yniquexcan chilchoc ynic p^{ac} xviii quauitl inic huiac cempovalli ynic nauhcan [ch]inampan inic p^{ac} cempoualli ynic huiac ompoualli ynic macuilcan atliztacan inic p^{ac} viii quauitl inic huiac xii quauitl yzquican inyn conana vel quimopieliz[3] amo ac quicuiliz ipanpa ticneltilia ca oquimotzontequillique yn tlatoque inic vel quimopieliz[3] inic tiquinxexelhuia nican audiencia imixpan Regidorme bartholomen atempanecatl a^{o}l daniel fran^{co} flores di^{o} Ramirez augustin gallego domingo d. s. sevastian no ixpan turibio silvestre miguel de la cruz auh in oquipovato tlalli yioma al̅l̅de mi̅n̅ ds.tiago ioan fran^{co} flores a^{o}l daniel amatlacuillo mi̅n̅ jacobo

in omochiuh ipan metztli junio x dias mdlvii años ynic ticneltilia nican tictlalia tomachio totoca tofirma

don juan de coyoacan don antonio al̅l̅de mi̅n̅ ds.tiago al̅l̅de

neuatl namatlacuillo yn nican coiouacan yntencopatzinco yn cenca maviztililoni yn tlatouani don luis de uelasco visorrei domingo Ramos escr^{o} audiencia

[1]AGN, Tierras 1735, exp. 2, f. 111. A Spanish translation of 1681 is on ff. 147-148.

I, don Juan, governor in the town of Coyoacan, and we alcaldes don Antonio and Martín de Santiago, we officers of the ruler don Luis de Velasco, viceroy: here before us came the children of don Luis Cortés, citizen of Acuecuexco, because they complained before the judges there in the Royal Audiencia in Mexico City on account of all his[2] fields that are his[2] property; they considered it well, and they delegated it to us so that we would carry it out and divide them among them. His[2] fields which doña Ana, wife of Juan de San Lázaro, takes (are in) five places: first at Yieiocan, 35 rods wide, though on one side only 25, and 143 rods long; second at Xomacuilco, 40 wide, 50 long; third at Chilchoc, 18 rods wide, 20 long; fourth at Chinampan, 20 wide, 40 long; fifth at Atliztacan, 8 rods wide, 12 rods long. These are all the places she receives. She will be able to keep it,[3] no one is to take it from her, since we verify what the judges ruled, so she will be able to keep it;[3] thus we divide it here in session before the regidores Bartolomé Atempanecatl, Alonso Daniel, Francisco Flores, Diego Ramírez, Agustín Gallego, Domingo de San Sebastián; also before Toribio Silvestre, Miguel de la Cruz. And those who went to measure the land personally (were) Alcalde Martín de Santiago and Francisco Flores, Alonso Daniel; notary Martín Jacobo.

Done in the month of June, 10th day, year of 1557. To verify it here we place our rubrics, our names, our signatures.

Don Juan de Coyoacan. Don Antonio, alcalde. Martín de Santiago, alcalde.

I, notary here in Coyoacan in the name of the very honored ruler don Luis de Velasco, viceroy, Domingo Ramos, court notary.

---

[2]"His" probably refers to don Luis Cortés.

[3]This may mean either "she will be able to keep it" or "she will keep it well."

13. Municipal grant of land to Joaquín Flores, Coyoacan, 1575[1]

yn ipan altepetl coyohuaçan yqueylhuitl quitoca yn itlapohual ymetztli d[. . .] mill y quinientos yn setenta yn cinco años Nehuatl don loreçon de guzman t[latohuani] yhuan gouernador yhuan tehuatin baltasar de leon alonso fenabides alldes [ytencopan^{co}] tote^{o} dios yhuan yn tohueytlatocauh Rey su mag^{tt} Etc yn yehuatl juachin [flures] chane ateputzco ynic nican tispan ohualla nican audiencia ynic otlaytlan yni [. . .][2] peticio ynic cenca otechtlatlauhti yn ipampa yn altepetlaltzintli yn quitlani oncan mani ateputzco calpolali yn aoc ac ytech pouhqui yn çannihuetztoc ynic o no nican tispan necico yn otlatolmelahuaco yn tlaxilacaleque[3] yn huel nelli amo ac ytech pohui yn tlalli ipampa yn axcan ticmaca ticascatia yn yehuatl juanchin flures ynic patlahuac chicuhnauhquahuitl auh ynic huiac castolli omey quahuitl yn tonatiuh ycalaquianpa auh yn tonatiuh yquiçayanpa ynic chicocalactica yn tlali cenpohualli omome quahuitl auh ynic patlauac macuilquahuitl ytech aci yn otli ymiltitlan josana yc tonatiuh iquiçayanpa yxquichin yn ticmaca huel quimopieliz amo ac quistoquiliz yn oc huecauhtica yhuan yniquincahuilitiaz yn ipilhua yn iquac momiquiliz ca yuh ticneltilia yn totlanahuatil yn icatzinco rrey su magt ynic titlanahuatia ponsension quimacatiuh yn alguacil mayor luis caravajal ynic ticneltilia ypannpa nican tictlalia tomachiyo tofirmas

don lorenço de guzman bal^{sar} de leon al̅l̅de Alonso benabides al̅l̅de

yntencopan^{co} señores gouernador al̅l̅des nicneltili amatlacuillo ytencopan^{co} su mag^{tt} augustin de galiz^{a} escrivano

[1]McAfee Collection, UCLA Research Library, Special Collections.

[2]The page is torn here. There may or may not be an *in*, "the," or *ce*, "an," missing.

In the town of Coyoacan on the third day, following the count of the month of [December] of the year 1575, I don Lorenzo de Guzmán, ruler and governor, and we Baltasar de León and Alonso Benavides alcaldes in the name of our Lord God and of our great sovereign king His Majesty, etc.: there came a Joaquín Flores, citizen of Ateputzco, before us here in council to make a [. . .][2] petition with which he greatly implored us concerning a piece of town land that he requests there at Ateputzco, calpulli land no longer belonging to anyone, but lying idle; as also here before us have appeared leading dwellers in the district[3] and come to explain that indeed truly the land belongs to no one, wherefore now we give it to Joaquín Flores and make it his property, 9 rods wide and 18 rods long on the west, and on the east, where the land enters at an angle, 22 rods and 5 rods wide, reaching the road next to the field of Susana on the east. All this we give him, to be guarded well, no one is to claim it from him for a long time to come, and so that he will bequeath it to his children when he dies, for thus we confirm our order on behalf of the king His Majesty that we order the chief constable Luis Carvajal to give him possession, wherefore to verify it we put here our rubrics and signatures.

Don Lorenzo de Guzmán. Baltasar de León, Alcalde. Alonso Benavides, Alcalde.

In the name of the lords governor and alcaldes I verified it: notary in the name of His Majesty, Agustín de Galicia, notary.

---

[3]We presume that *tlaxilacaleque,* by analogy with *calpuleque. tianquizhuaque* and *altepehuaque,* can refer to the leaders of the district rather than average citizens.

14. The council of Azcapotzalco enjoins penalties on those not observing a land agreement, Azcapotzalco, 1703[1]

Pena de notificasion[2] Año de 1703

Ynican tecpan Audensi Yn iPan Altepetl Azcap^{co} mani meztli Jullio xihuitl de 1703 añoz Ynican onezque Bario S^{n} Simon tlaxilacaleque Yn iuh oquincahuilique Yn intlal Yn oquintlanque Ynic Yxpantzinco Sr Juez g^{dor} ca tzan CualYotica ca Oquinmocahuilili Yn Sr Andrez gonsalez Yn iuhqui Axca nican Teixpa Oquimonanquilili yn omoteneuhtzino Sr Andrez gonsalez ca ye conana Yn intlal Auh [ni]acmo [sic] cepa Aquin tlein quitlanizque Açoquitla[3] Yc tlachalanizque ca yn tlein oquintlanque Ynic Ytechcopa Yntlal maCuilpuhuali ca yoconanque Auh Ycan niCan motlalilia pena Acmo tlein aço quitlan quipie ytech tlatozque ca ipanpa ca Yomacoque Yn tleinnimaxcan Auh Yntla aquin aca oc cepa Yntla quitoz aço ceme Yehuantin Bario S^{n} Simon ca nican hualaz telpiloyan tzauhtiez Ce meztli telpiloyan Yhuan asotez Ytech puhuiz chiCuei dosena Yhua quixtlahuaz coztaz cenpuhuali pesos Ytech puhuiz Ypanpa amo tlein quipie oc ce quitlanizque auh Ynic [nel]tiliztli nican quiMotlalilia Yn infirmatzin Yn cenca mahuiztlililonime Ynican motlatequiPanilhuia Yn ipan Altepetl Azcap^{co} Yn iuh quimoPieliz Ynin amatl Señor Andrez gonsalez Yn iuh quenin oquinmocahuilili Yn intlal Ymanel quimoPielia ce amatl Yn itechcacopa otlato Yn intlal ca^{mo} tleinniPatiuh ca Yca nican quimoPieliz Ynin Amatl Yca firmaz

D^{n} marcoz del Castillo Juez g^{dor} Don fran^{co} nicolaz y D^{n} Pheliphe de S^{n}tiago regidorez mayorez D^{n} Jo^{u} mathiaz A^{de} ordinario testigo Juan soriano y testigo por miguel del castillo Ante mi D^{n} Antt^{o} Baleriano Es^{no} de Rep^{ca}

[1]McAfee Collection, UCLA Research Library, Special Collections.

[2]The literal meaning of the Spanish, of course, is "penalty of notification." It would appear that the writer was not completely fluent in Spanish.

Notification of penalty.[2] Year of 1703.

Here in the courthouse in council in the town of Azcapotzalco in the month of July, in the year of 1703, there appeared here inhabitants of the district of San Simón who had just been conceded their lands that they had demanded, so that before the lord judge and governor might be approved what señor Andrés González had conceded them. Thus now the aforementioned señor Andrés González replied here publicly that they are already taking their lands and none of them are to demand anything again or dispute anything,[3] since they have taken what they demanded concerning their land, 100 (rods). And herewith the penalty is set here: no one who had any demand is to make claims about it, because they were already given what belongs to them, and if anyone, perhaps some of those of the district of San Simón, should make claim again, he will come here to jail and be confined a month in the jail, and will be given 6 dozen lashes, and will have to pay 20 pesos in costs, because they have nothing further to demand. And to verify it the very esteemed sirs who officiate here in the town of Azcapotzalco affixed their signatures. Thus, señor Andrés González is to keep this document as to how he conceded them his land; though they should have a document speaking about their land, it has no validity, because he will keep this signed document here.

Don Marcos del Castillo, judge and governor. Don Francisco Nicolás and Don Felipe de Santiago, chief councilmen. Don Juan Matías, alcalde ordinario. Witness, Juan Soriano, and witness for Miguel del Castillo. Before me, Don Antonio Valeriano, notary public.

---

[3]We construe this form as *aço oc itla*.

15. Bill of sale: land sold by Mateo de la Cruz, Coyoacan, late sixteenth or early seventeenth century[1]

Ma quimatica yn ixquichti y quitazque yhua y quipohuazque yni namacacuiloli carta de benta y queni nehuatl notoca matheo de la + yhua nonamic maria mag^{na} nica tocha yn ipa altepetl villa coyohua notlaxilacalpa tehuitzco niquitohua nozielizcacopa yhua nonamic totlanequilizcacopa auh amo aqui nechcuitlahuiltia ynic nimitznamactia y nimitzaxcatia y notlal y nehuatl matheo de la + onechcahuililia y nozitzin yn itoca catca ju^{a}tzin omomiquili axca ye cepohuali xihuitl auh yc neli ticnanaquiltia y zihuapili dona [dgoa ana?][2] ynamictzin catca donnat^{o} huitzinmecari[3] yeyca techmomaquili yn itomines 2 p^{o}s ipan macuili pesos[4] yc ticpatizque y totlacalaquil hua tonetlacuil ticelia yn tomines tomatia[5] auh yeyca ahuel ticuepazque y totlatol yhua amo huel ticxitinizque yni carta de benta ypampa ca ye oquimocuili y tlali ca oticaxcatique auh ticmaca huelitiliztli y justizia ynic quimopalehuiliz y dona [dgc̅a̅?][2]

16. Sale of land to a Spaniard, Coyoacan, 1573[1]

Ascan jueves yc matlaquilhuitl yn itlapohual ymmetztli de febrero y[. . .]y de mil y quiniendos y sedenda y tres años ypan otictlallique totlatol yn tehuantin p^{o} de s.tiago yhuan Don toribio silvestre tichanneque sanctiago xochac ticnamaca yn totlal ompa mani chilchoc xochmilcaquasochtenco ticnamaquiltia español ytoca p^{o} bierez[2] de portucar channe coyohuacan tlasillacalpan abçolco çan necoc cempohualli quahuitl ynic huiyac yhuan ynic patlahuac

---

Document 15

[1]AGN, Tierras 1735, exp. 2, f. 122. A Spanish translation dating from 1681 is on f. 152.

[2]Undecipherable. Probably an abbreviation. The Spanish translator also threw up his hands.

[3]We presume this is the don Antonio Huitzimengari, nobleman of Michoacan, mentioned in Paso y Troncoso, *Epistolario*, VII, 376. See also Doc. 4, n. 8.

[4]The string *2 p^{o}s ipan macuili pesos* must be in error. To us it seems most probable that the second *pesos* is a mistake for *tomines*. The Spanish translator, on the other hand, presumed that the error was in the first number, which, if the denom-

Know all who see and who read this sale letter, (this) bill of sale, how I, named Mateo de la Cruz, and my wife María Magdalena, our home being here in the city of Coyoacan, my district Tehuitzco, declare of my free will and that of my wife, both voluntarily, and no one is forcing me to, that I sell to you and give you possession of the land of me, Mateo de la Cruz, that my late grandmother named Juana left me, who died 20 years ago now. And so we truly sell it to lady doña [. . .],[2] whose husband was don Antonio Huitzinmecari,[3] because we were given her money, 2 pesos and 5 [tomines],[4] with which to pay up our tribute and our debts. We receive the money knowingly,[5] and therefore we cannot go against our word and we cannot annul this bill of sale because the land was already taken and we gave possession of it, and we give power to the law officers to favor doña [. . .].[2]

Today Thursday, on the 10th day of the count of the month of February [. . .] of the year of 1573, we issued our statement that we, Pedro de Santiago and don Toribio Silvestre, citizens of Santiago Xochac, are selling our land there at Chilchoc, bordering on Xochimilco. We are selling it to a Spaniard named Pedro Pérez[2] de Portugal, citizen of Coyoacan in the district of Apçolco; (it is) 20 rods on both sides, in length and width.

Document 15 (cont.)

inations are right, should have been 20 in the Nahuatl system. Thus he arrived at 25 pesos, a solution fully as logical as ours.

[5]Parallel documents usually have at this juncture *tomatica*, "in our hands," i.e., personally and physically. The Spanish translation renders *tomatia* as *con efecto*.

Document 16

[1]McAfee Collection, UCLA Research Library, Special Collections.

[2]In another document in the collection, the name appears as "Pierres de Portugal" and again as "yn señor Perez."

auh omochiuh tomatica oticuique x p^{o}s iiii t^{o} auh ymmispatzin[3] yc ommochiuh yn totlaçotatzin ontetl missa mayor auh yn imispan ticnammaca tlalli ynic ce tlacatl Raphael de s.tiago chē tetzcolco yztatlalpan yhuan p^{o} de castillo chē xochac auh ynic ticneltillia nican tictlallia totoca tofirma

p^{o} de s.tiago   torib^{o} siluestre

Nehuatl onicneltilli yn intlatol yn nican tocayoticate ynic oninontlapallo huellonicac ca huel yntlal ca huel ymmasca ypampa nican nictlallia notoca nofirma   gabriel muysen

17. Sale of land, with all the acts of investigation, confirmation, and possession; will attached, Azcapotzalco, 1738[1]

escritura de Benta año de 1738

Ma quimatican Yn quexquichtin quitasque yhuan quipohuasque Ynin esCritura de Benta ticchihua Yn tehuantin Salbador fran^{co} yhuan Nonamictzin Maria de la consecpsion totlaxilacaltlia S. fran^{co} tzapotla Yhuan Joseph de Santiago Nonamictzin Rosa Maria totlaxilacaltia S. Lucas Atenco tohualtepeuh S. Phelipe i Santiago Azcapotzalco itlahuilanal Villa tlacopa tiquitohua timochintin yn otitotenehuque Ca ticpie totlalnemac oncan Mani motenehua chimalchi[e]ca[2] huel ixquich ompohuali brasadas inic Oriente a poniente ahu inic patlahuac Quipie[3] tzenpohuali brasadas de norte a sur huahuinin tlali omotenechu yc Oriente mocuaxohnamiqui ica itlal Bartholome de Vargas ahu inin [sic] poniente Mocuaxochnamiqui ica in huey Otli tlamelahua Cuahupanahuasco ihuan ica itlaltzin ipilhuantzitzi miccatzintle Sr Andres Gontzales ahu inic norte moCuaxohnamiqui ica intlal tlaxilacaleque S. Simon poxtlan ahu inic Sur moCuaxohnamiqui ica intlal tlaxilacaleque S^{to} Domingo huexotlitla ahu inin tlali omotenehu Ca tolloloica totlanequilistica tictonamaquiltililia illehuatzin Caxtiltecatzintle Sr D^{n} Antt^{o}

Document 16

[3]*Ymmispatzin* seems misplaced and without a referent; we have speculated that the intention might be *in* or *inin ipatiuhtzin*.

Document 17

[1]McAfee Collection, UCLA Research Library, Special Collections. Throughout the document *ll* seems to have a value somewhat like Spanish *ll*, being used where one

And in fact we took in our hands 10 pesos and 4 tomines and with [its price?][3] were said two high masses for our dear father. And those in whose presence we sell the land are first, Rafael de Santiago, citizen of Tetzcolco Iztatlalpan, and Pedro de Castillo, citizen of Xochac; and to verify it we put here our names and signatures.

Pedro de Santiago. Toribio Silvestre.

I verified the words of the here named, as I stepped forward and heard it well; it is indeed their land and their property; wherefore I put here my name and signature. Gabriel Moysén.

Instrument of sale, year of 1738.

Let those know who should see and read this instrument of sale made by us, Salvador Francisco and my wife María de la Concepción, our district being San Francisco Tzapotla, and Josef de Santiago and my wife Rosa María, our district being San Lucas Atenco, our town being San Felipe y Santiago Azcapotzalco, subject to the town of Tacuba, that all of us aforementioned declare that we have a piece of land that was given us located there at the place called Chimalchi[e]ca,[2] measuring a full 40 brazas from east to west, and in width it measures[3] 20 brazas from north to south. And this aforementioned land on the east abuts on Bartolomé de Vargas' land, and on the west it abuts on the highway going to Quauhpanahuasco and with the land of the children of the deceased Señor Andrés González, and on the north it abuts on lands of the citizens of the district of San Simón Pochtlan, and on the south it abuts on lands of the citizens of the district of Santo Domingo Huexotitlan. And voluntarily and willingly we sell this aforementioned land to the Castilian Señor don Antonio

---

would expect *y*. Azcapotzalco consisted of two subdivisions, Mexicapan and Tepanecapan, of which the former figures in the present document (see Gibson, *Aztecs*, p. 38).

[2]Despite the *e* that seems to be written in the manuscript, the name is doubtless Chimalchiuhcan as in Esteban Diego's will at the end of this document.

[3]Several times *pia* occurs in this document in conjunction with numbers in a meaning that is translated by English "measures" or "is," like Spanish *tiene*.

GonSales tersero de tohueitatzin S. fran^{co} ahu in tehmomaquilia in ipatihu totlal Ca huel ichxquih matlactle p^{s} ahu inin tomin tictzelia Camo toteh monequis Ca misas ic mochihuas[4] ipan nesi yhuan motta in itestamento yn tahcoltzin [sic] D^{n} Esban Diego ipan in ontlamanpa ihuan in lletlamanpa itlatoltzin Ca huel totlalnemac ahu in axcan Cacmo ticpie tlein tiquitlanisque in tehuantin anose topilhuan anose toxhuihuan tlacatisque anose tlacatiquihue acmo in tlatohuallan yes Canel huel tolloloica tictonamaquiltilique in omotenehutzino Caxtiltecatzintle Sr D^{n} Antt^{o} Gon^{es} ahu tla itla amatl nesitihu Cacmo neltocos ica Ca huel nestica ipan in huehue testamento Ca tlalcohuali ihuan totlalnemac ahu inic neltilistle nican tictomaquilia inin esCritura de Benta in tzemallan tictotlatquitililia tictoaxcatililia in omotenehutzino tlalcoccatzintle [sic] acmo ticpie tlein tiquitlanisque inpan in omotenehu tlali inic tictemaca inin eSCritura de Benta axcan mani mextli a Ocho de disiem[bre] de mil setesientos i treinta i ocho años ahu in amo ticmati titlaculosque thotlatlahutilistica Oquimofirmarhui in toapoderadotzin mochihutzinotica ipan toaltepehu ihuan es^{no} de la Republica yhuan seme testigos

Por testigo iapoderado Juan Soriano   Manuel de Paredez
por testigo Ju^{o} de Mora   Ante mi D^{n} Antt^{o} Bilibaldo y flores
Es^{no} de Rep^{ca}

presentasion

ypan altepetl Azcapotzalco Mani metztli a quinse de Disiembre de mil setesientos treinta i ocho añ^{os} nican ipan tohuahudensia Mexicapan omonexiti Caxtiltecatzintle Sr D^{n} Antt^{o} Gonsales tersero Oquimoteixpantilili ixpantzinco senca mahuistililonime Jues Sr D^{n} Visente ferrer Bautista ihuan Alcalde D^{n} Marcos Juan i lle mochintin Ofisiales de Republica itehcacopa Se tlali OquimoCohuitzino icqui[5] nese ihuan mota inpan in escritura de benta Oquimochihuililique in tlalnamacaque ahu quemotlania Anparo de poseSion ahu in icuac Oquimocaquiltique in senca Mahuistililonime tlatoque in[e]itlanilistzin in Caxtiltecatl niman Omotlanahuatilique ihuan motlanahuatilia panolos inpan in tlali omotenehu ahu inic neltilistle nican quimotlalilia intocatzin yhuan infirmatzin yCa testigos

Por testigo yApoderado Juan Soriano   D^{n} Marcos Juan Alcalde   D^{n} Vicente ferrer Ba^{tta} Govr Manuel de Paredez
Ante mi D^{n} Antt^{o} Bilibaldo y flores Es^{no} de Rep^{ca}

4An alternative translation might be "which we will not need for saying masses." Though syntactically less probable, this statement would be more expected in such a context.

González, member of the Third Order of our great father St. Francis, and he is giving us the price for our land, a full 10 pesos, and we receive this money, which we will not need; it is for saying masses.[4] It appears and is seen in the testament of our grandfather don Esteban Diego in the second and third of his commands that it is indeed our land by gift, and now we no longer have any demands to make. Our children and grandchildren who will be or should come to be born will no longer have a voice in it, for truly very willingly we sold it to the aforementioned Castilian Señor don Antonio González. And if any paper should appear it is not to be believed, since it well appears in the old will that it is purchased land and our land by gift. And in order to verify it we here issue this instrument of sale, we give him perpetual ownership and possession of the aforementioned purchased land, we no longer will have any demands to make concerning the aforementioned land, wherewith we issue this instrument of sale today on the 8th of the month of December of the year of 1738; and since we do not know how to write, on our request our proxy signed for us. Done in our town with the notary public and some witnesses.

As a witness and the proxy, Juan Soriano. Manuel de Paredes. As a witness, Juan de Mora. Before me, don Antonio Bilibaldo y Flores, notary public.

Presentation.

In the town of Azcapotzalco on the 15th of the month of December of the year of 1738, here in our Mexican council appeared the Castilian Señor don Antonio González, member of the Third Order, and notified the very honorable judge Señor don Vicente Ferrer Bautista and Alcalde don Marcos Juan and all the town officials about a piece of land he bought, as[5] appears and is seen in the instrument of sale that the sellers of the land issued; and he demands affirmation of possession. And when the very honorable lords heard the Castilian's demand, then they ordered and do order that everyone go over to the aforementioned land. And as verification here they put their names and signatures, with witnesses.

As a witness and the proxy, Juan Soriano. Don Marcos Juan, alcalde. Don Vicente Ferrer Bautista, governor. Manuel de Paredes. Before me, don Antonio Bilibaldo y Flores, notary public.

---

[5]The puzzling form *icqui* occurs twice in the document. Professor R. Joe Campbell has brought to our attention words in present-day dialects that are presumably related: *ihquin*, "this way," and *no ihqui*, "also," both evolved from classical *iuhqui*.

determinasion

Sano ypan in tonali metztli yhuan xihuitl tlacpac Omotenehu otipanoque ipan in itlaltzin Caxtiltecatl S^{r} D^{n} $Antt^{o}$ Gonsales tersero ahu ille ipan in tlali Onemanaloc Onitlanahuati yhua nitlanahuatia ma monotzacan in tlaxilacaleque S^{to} Domingo hue-Xotitla yhuan itlaxilacaleque S^{n} Simon poxtlan yhuan Bartholome de Bargas Canel inteh tzalictica[6] intlan ipan in itlalcoaltzin Omotenehutzino Caxtiltecatl inic motlatlanisque Cux lle neli melahuac imaxca in tlalnamaCaque anose aca iaxca nose tlaxilacallali ahu inic[7]

Sitasion y declarasion

Sano ipan in tonali tlaCutlapan[8] Omotenehu tixpan onetzque in tlaxilacaleque S^{to} Domingo hueXotitla ihuan in poxtlan tlaxilacaleque ihuan Bartholome de Bargas Otlatlaniloque itehcacopa in itlaltzin S^{r} D^{n} $Antt^{o}$ Gonsales OquinmoCohuilili in motocatenehua ypan in esCritura de Benta Cux melahuac tlalnemactle aso quimati aca imaxca anose tlaxilacallali Otlananquilique Camo ticpi[e] tlein tiquitlanitzque itehcacopa in omotenehu tlali ahu ca quimati Ca huel imaxca Ocacca in tlalnamacaque Ca intlalnemac Ocacca ahu llehuatl in Otlananquilique ahu inic neltilistle melahuac niCan tictlalia totoCa yhuan tofirma yCa testigos

Por testigo yApoderado Juan Soriano D^{n} Marcos Juan Alcalde D^{n} Vicente ferrer Bap^{tta} Govr Manuel de Paredez Ante mi D^{n} $Antt^{o}$ Bilibaldo y flores Es^{no} de Rep^{ca}

Sentensia y medidas

Sano ipan tonali Omotenehu in icuac Oniquincaquili in tlaxilacaleque intlatol ihuan Oniquitac in nehuatle ni Jues G^{or} ihuan moxtintzitzin Ofisiales de Republica inic allac quiContradisiroa in posesion quimotlania in tlalcoccatzintle Onicnotzi in Jues de Sementeras ihuan Onicnahuati iCa yhuelitzin tohuitlatocatzin Rey N. S^{r} quitamachihuas in tlali ahu inic Oriente ihuan poniente quipix onpohuali brasadas inic Oriente moCuaxohnamiqui yca itlal Bartholome de Bargas ahu inic poniente ica in otli llahu Cuahupanahuasco yhuan itlaltzin OCacca in Dios Oquimohuiquili Sr Andres

[6]*Çaloa*, "to adhere," is probably intended, as the land in question borders on the lands of the persons mentioned. See the nearly identical configuration *itech çaliuhtica* in Doc. 4.

[7]Broken off at the end of a page, this statement doubtless would have been con-

Determination.

Likewise on the day, month, and year above mentioned, we went over to the land of the Castilian Señor don Antonio González, member of the Third Order, and at the time the land was shown, I ordered and do order that the citizens of the district of Santo Domingo Huexotitlan and the citizens of the district of San Simón Pochtlan and Bartolomé de Vargas be called, [since it is next to them,][6] to see if they have demands concerning the aforementioned Castilian's purchased land, if it was truly the property of the sellers of the land, or if perhaps it was someone else's property or was district land. And in order[7]

Citation and declaration.

Likewise on the day mentioned [above][8] there appeared before us the citizens of the district of Santo Domingo Huexotitlan and the citizens of the district of Pochtlan and Bartolomé de Vargas, who were asked about the land of Señor don Antonio González that he bought from those whose names are mentioned in the instrument of sale, whether it was truly land given them or if they know it to be someone's property or district land. And they answered that we have nothing to demand concerning the aforementioned land and that they know that it was indeed the property of the sellers of the land, that it was land given them, and that is what they answered. In order to verify it as true we put here our names and our signatures, with witnesses.

As a witness and the proxy, Juan Soriano. Don Marcos Juan, alcalde. Don Vicente Ferrer Bautista, governor. Manuel de Paredes. Before me, don Antonio Bilibaldo y Flores, notary public.

Judgment and measurements.

Likewise on the day aforementioned, when I the judge and governor and all the town officials had heard the words of the district citizens and seen how no one contradicts the requested possession of the purchased land, I summoned the lands judge and with the power of our great sovereign king our lord I ordered him to measure the land. And from east to west it measured 40 brazas, on the east abutting on Bartolomé de Vargas' land and on the west on the road going to Quauhpanahuasco and the land that belongs to Señor Andrés

---

tinued as at the end of the next section: "in order to verify it as true we put here our names and signatures, with witnesses."

[8]Although *tlacütlapan* only vaguely resembles *tlacpac*, the position and the appearance in combination with *omoteneuh* strongly suggest that this meaning was intended.

Gonsales axcan quipixticate in ipilhuantzitzi ahu inic patlahuac Oquipix de norte a Sur Senpohuali brasadas moCuaxohnamiqui inic norte ica intlal tlaxilacaleque S^{n} Simon poxtlan ahu inic Sur moCuaxohnamiqui ica intlal St^{o} Domingo huexotitlan tlaXilacaleque ahu in tlalCuahuitl inic omotamachihu Ca llehualtl in quipie ome bara yhuan tlaco motenehua tzennequetzalpan[9] ahu llotlan Omotamachihu Onicnonochili in Sr D^{n} Antt^{o} Gonsales tersero yhuan yca in ihuelitzin Rey N. S^{r} onicnocalaquili inpan posesion Omotlamochili Omotlaxihutemili Omopaxialolti[10] ipan in itlalcoaltzin inescaCallo Quimocuyli posesion Cualllotica allac Otlachalani Otlapalolo[11]

Posesion
ixpan in mochtintzitzin tlaxilacaleque in omotenehuque ahu in axcan nican tictomaquilia ynin amatlaculoli lleyca allac OquiContradisiro in posesion OquimoCuili i caxtiltecal Sr D^{n} Antt^{o} Gonsales ahu intla aca tlachalanis ipan itla Cahuitl Ca huel iteh lles Justisia tleican Cacmo itlatohuallan ipanpa llotlatlaniloque Cux quipie tlein quitlanisquia inpan in Omotenehu tlali Otlananquilique Camo ihuan Otlatlaixpantilique Ca huel inmaxca Ocacca intlalnamaCaque inpan netzi in sitasion ihuan declarasion Oquichihuque y tlaxilacaleque ahu tla itla amatl nesis acmo neltocos in tlein huel moCaquis llehualtl in nican ticchihua icqui[5] ti Justisias ahu in moicatze[12] motlatequipanilhuisque quimohuelCaquitisque in totlatzontec yca nican tictlalia totoca yhuan tofirma yCa testigos

Por testigo yApoderado Juan Soriano D^{n} Marcos Juan Alcalde D^{n} Vicente ferrer Baptista Govr Manuel de Paredez Ante mi D^{n} Antt^{o} Bilibaldo y flores Es^{no} de Rep^{ca}

Auto
Ypan tlapohua metztli Senpohuali tonali de Disiembre de mil Setesientos treinta y Ocho a^{os} nican ipan Casas Reales Mexicapan in Nehuatl ni Jues G^{or} D^{n} Visente ferrer Bautista i Alcalde D^{n} Marcos Ju^{o} in lle moxtintzitzi Ofisiales de Republica titlatzontequi Ma momacatzino in Sr D^{n} Antt^{o} Gonsales tersero inin deliJensias in ipalehuilocatzin mochihuas[13] ahu inic neltilistle nican tictlalia totoca ihuan tofirma y[14] testigos

---

[9]The reflexive verb *quetza* is "to rise." The measurement is apparently based on a person standing with his arms raised in the air.

[10]The word is based on Spanish *pasear*. It is still in today's dialects. See González Casanova, *Cuentos Indígenas*, p. 22.

[11]Literally, "it (or he) was greeted."

González, whom God took away, that now his children have. And in width it measured from north to south 20 brazas. It abuts on the north on lands of the citizens of the district of San Simón Pochtlan, and on the south it abuts on the lands of the citizens of the district of Santo Domingo Huexotitlan. And the land rod with which it was measured is the one that is 2½ yards long, called "one full height."[9] And when the measurement was finished I summoned Señor don Antonio González, member of the Third Order, and with the power of the king our lord I introduced him into possession; he threw stones, mashed down the grass, and strolled about[10] on his purchased land signifying that he took possession properly; no one disputed it, there was acceptance.[11]

Possession.

In the presence of all the aforementioned district citizens, now and here we issue this document, since no one contradicted the possession that the Castilian Señor don Antonio González took, and if anyone should dispute it in any future time, justice will be on his side, wherefore he will have no voice in it, because it was asked if anyone had any demands concerning the aforementioned land, and they answered no, and declared that it was indeed the property of the sellers of the land, as appears in the citation and declaration that the district citizens made. And if any document should appear it is not to be believed, since that which we officers of the law hereby[5] make is to be accepted, and those who come[12] to work are to attend well to our judgment, with which here we put our names and signatures, with witnesses.

As a witness and the proxy, Juan Soriano. Don Marcos Juan, alcalde. Don Vicente Ferrer Bautista, governor. Manuel de Paredes. Before me, don Antonio Bilibaldo y Flores, notary public.

Decree.

On the 20th day of the count of the month of December of the year of 1738, here in the Mexican council building, I the judge and governor don Vicente Ferrer Bautista and the alcalde don Marcos Juan and all the town officials pronounce that Señor don Antonio González, member of the Third Order, is to be given these papers [which will be his support].[13] And as verification we put here our names and signatures [with][14] witnesses.

---

[12]The equivalent, we presume, of *mouicatze*.

[13]It had also occurred to us that perhaps some reference was being made here to the fee González was to pay.

[14]Probably meant to be *ica* as in similar contexts elsewhere in the document.

Por testigo yApoderado Juan Soriano D^{n} Marcos Juan Alcalde D^{n} Vicente ferrer Baptista Govr Manuel de Paredez Juan de Mora Ante mi D^{n} Antt^{o} Bilibaldo y flores Es^{no} de Rep^{ca}

ynomine patri et fili et espiliton s̄ton ame jesos[15]

nehuatl Estepan diegon notlaxillacaltia s̄to tonmigon huexotitla
— ynic ce tlamatlin niquitohua notlantol yn caltzintlin ocan nihuetztoc yn tlaconpapan ytzticac niguimacatiuh yn nopilhua ynhua ynnatzin oca quihuapahuaz canel og choquichtotonti cayamo momapatla ça nima ama yn tlacahuiz yn notlatol yn[te]tzinco pohuiz ynotatzin miSan
— ynic otlamatlin niguitohua notlatol notlalcohual onpan mani chinmalchiuhCan niguimacatiuh yn nopilhua donmigon jusep ynhua jua matheo cocanhuizgue ça nima amo ac tla[ca]huiz yn notlantol
— yniguetlamatlin niguitohua notlatol yn oc cepohualli tlalcohuallin nechmomaguillitiuh nonatzin me yn ça no opan chimalchiuhcan ayamo nicchihua miSan nicchihuazquia miSan auh yn ascan yehuatin guichihuazque yn nopilhua ce miSan niguimacatiuh yn tlaltzintl
— ynic 4 tlamatlin niguitohua metzintzinti cepatlin ni[gui]guinomaguillia yn notlaçonthatzin S.do tomigon ynhua yehuatzin notlaçomahuinatzin [Solitaria?] quimoCahuilizgue oncan yn [achitillilahua . . . qui] oncan ica guiahuac
— yc macuillalamatlin niguitohua ynnomoteneh metzintili ça oca motlapanazque notech pohuiz yn[h]hua nonatzin dios oquimohuigui yntla ninomiguiliz miSa yc topa mito motlapanaz

[15]This, the will of the sellers' grandfather referred to in the text above, was pasted onto the last leaf of the record of the proceedings. It appears to have been written by

As a witness and the proxy, Juan Soriano. Don Marcos Juan, alcalde. Don Vicente Ferrer Bautista, governor. Manuel de Paredes. Juan de Mora. Before me, don Antonio Bilibaldo y Flores, notary public.

In the name of the Father and the Son and the Holy Spirit, amen. Jesus.[15]

I, Esteban Diego, my district being Santo Domingo Huexotitla:

— The first order I declare (is that) I am giving the small house where I lie, which faces Tacuba, to my children and their mother who is to raise them there, since they are still little boys who cannot yet take care of themselves; let no one go against my order; they are to [be responsible for] a mass for my father.

— The second order I declare (is that) I am giving my purchased land there at Chimalchiuhcan to my children Domingo, Josef, and Juan Mateo. They are to have it; no one is to go against my order.

— The third order I declare (is that with) another twenty (rods) of purchased land that my mother gave me, [. . .] also there at Chimalchiuhcan, I am not yet making masses, (though) I would like to make masses; but now (if) my children will have one mass said I will give them the land.

— Fourth, I declare that I am giving a row of maguey to my dear father Santo Domingo and my dear honored mother [Solitaria?]; they are to have it; [. . .][16] there with entryway.

— Fifth, I declare that (from) the aforementioned maguey that they will divide there will be a mass for me and my mother whom God took away, if I die, and when it is said it will be divided.

Esteban Diego himself, in a very idiosyncratic style, and the latter part gives clear evidence of the extremity of the writer's condition.

[16]We cannot further decipher this partially torn and perhaps garbled section.

18. Don Juan de Guzmán donates land to chapel singers, Coyoacan, mid-sixteenth century[1]

Ynican yn icuyliuhtoque y capilla y cuycanime y teopa oniquinotlahlmaquili ynevatl yni don juº ynic mochipa cuycazque y teopa yvan quitemachtizque y cuycatl yn iuh onicçotec[2] onouh quiçotec[2] yn don pablo çacancacintli yxpa don luys acuecuexco yxpa luys cuauhnochtli yxpa bartasal teyolcocova yxpan juº de san lazaro yxpa yezvavacin apçolco yxpa amatecatl tequiva chicome tlacatl ymixpa yn onitlaçotec ayac vel quixitiniz ynotectlatul ynevatl yni don juan ynic oniquinotlalmaquili y teopan y cuycanime

— caxtolli tlacatl onavi yn omotlahlmacac y vel omotlahlmacaque yn ipampa y capilla y vel cuycazque yn ayc y quicavazque ça quimotequipovilizque[3] mochipa

— y coçalo lopez yn itlahl epovalcoyavac macuylpovali ynic viyac

— migel de mexico yn itlalh epovalcoyavac napovalviyac
— andres de sant agusti yn itlahl epovalcoyavac napovalviyac
— anto de san juº pabtista yn itlahl necoc epovali
— franᶜº de logena yn itlahl necoc epovali
— juº leo yn itlahl necoc epovali
— pº paz yn itlahl epovali ynic viyac ytech yn atlauhtli
— toribio motoliniya yn itlahl opovali ynicoyava[4]
— xp̄oval de san gabriel yn itlahl opovali ynicoyavac
— domigo de san lazaro yn itlahl opovali ynicoyavac
— domigo de san pablo yn itlahl opovali ynicoyavac
— anlonso de san gerculiyo yn itlahl opovali ynicoyavac
— marcos yn itlahl

---

[1]AGN, Tierras 1735, exp. 2, f. 113. A Spanish translation of 1681 is on f. 148. In this writer's script *u* and *o* are so similar that they might well be considered the same character.

[2]The equivalent of standard Nahuatl *onictzontec* and *quitzontec*.

[3]The *-tequi-* in *quimotequipovilizque* is an intensifier sometimes inserted in this position (Siméon, p. 458); we take the verb root to be *poa*, of whose many meanings we have somewhat arbitrarily chosen the one in the text. "To give account of" would

Here are inscribed the church choir singers to whom I, don Juan, have given land so that they will always sing in church and teach singing. As I pronounced it, don Pablo Zacancatl was present (at the) pronouncement, in the presence of don Luis (of) Acuecuexco, Luis Quauhnochtli, Baltasar Teyolcocoua, Juan de San Lázaro, Yezuauatzin (of) Apçolco, Amatecatl Tequiua; in the presence of seven people I pronounced it. No one may abrogate the royal command of me, don Juan, in giving land to the church singers.

— Land was given to 19 persons. They were indeed given the land so that they will sing well in the choir and never cease, but are to [esteem it greatly][3] always.

— Gonzalo López' land is 60 wide, 100 long.

— Miguel de México's land is 60 wide, 80 long.
— Andrés de San Agustín's land is 60 wide, 80 long.
— Antón de San Juan Bautista's land is 60 square.
— Francisco de Lucena's land is 60 square.
— Juan León's land is 60 square.
— Pedro Paz' land is 60 long, near the ravine.
— Toribio Motolinia's land is 40 wide.[4]
— Cristóbal de San Gabriel's land is 40 wide.
— Domingo de San Lázaro's land is 40 wide.
— Domingo de San Pablo's land is 40 wide.
— Alonso de San Herculio's land is 40 wide.
— Marcos' . . . land is . . .

---

perhaps do as well. The Spanish translator took the interpretation that the root was *poui*, so that the burden of the latter part of the sentence would be that the land was always to belong to the singers and they would never leave it. As reasonable as this rendition is, it goes against the nature of the intransitive *poui* and the usual construction with *itech*.

[4]The Spanish translator interpreted *coyauac* to mean both dimensions like *necoc*. This may well be, though we have no further evidence for it.

19. Donation of land to church, Coyoacan, 1621[1]

Sabato 7 dias de agusto 1621 año
yn yehuatzin s.tissima drinidat[2] yn nican onicnotlachpanililiaya auh yn axcan ompa mohuicaz yn ichantzinco[3] s. ju^{o} bap^{ta} yn onpa escuela ca umpa quimotlachpanililizque yn pipiltzitzinti yn ompa mohuapahua yn ichantzinco yn notecuio dios auh yhuan yn nocaltzin ca ychantzinco yez ynic centetl huel oncan ymmoyetztica tonatiuh ycalaquiyampa ytzticac ynic ontetl hueitepeccopa ytzticac yhuan yn icallalo çan mocemmattimani ayac tle quitoz oncan tlatoz ynic ocan mani milli yn itechtzinco puhui yn dios notlaçotatzin ymiltitlan p^{o} comez yniquexcan mani tlalli calpilco yhua ycaltitlantzinco mani aluar coca ypan ycac yhuan yzquitlan mani ymiltitech ju^{o} mateo
Auh yn yehuatzin yn notlaçotatzin s. fran^{co} yhuan s. nicolas yhuan yecce homo sta cricifixus yhuan yehuatzin notepantlatocanantzin asumptio maje yhuan s. jacinto yhuan crucifixu maje[4] yn intechtzinco puhuiz nocaltzin hueitepeccopa ytzticac çan itech çaliuhtica tonatiuh yquiçayanpa ytzticac yhuan xucotzintli membrilo cempantli yhuan tzapuquahuitl yey matlactli peso yc nicouh niccohuili m^{a} 4 p^{o}s nicmacac p^{o}nila nicmacac 6 p^{o}s

20. Juan Alvaro sells or donates land to church, Coyoacan region, 1575[1]

Lunes yc xx dias Del mes de junio de 1575 años
NEhuatl ju^{o} aluaro nican nichane apçolco tlaxillacalpan yn ascan cenca noyonlocopa nicnomaquilia yn isquich ymanian yn nocal mochi yn calnepanolli yhuan yn isquich yn nocanlal yn yehuatzin yn totlaçotatzin padre fray fran^{co} de loaysa vic^{o} yn quimopielia santa yglesia yn ipatiuh omochiuh yn nocal yhuan yn

Document 19

[1]McAfee Collection, UCLA Research Library, Special Collections. The name of the person issuing the document is nowhere given.

[2]Or possibly cofradía.

[3]Presumably the large church referred to in Doc. 4.

Saturday, 7th day of August of the year 1621.

I have been sweeping up here at the (church)[2] of the Most Holy Trinity, and now it is to be moved there to the house of San Juan Bautista,[3] where there is a school, and the boys who are brought up there are to sweep the house of my Lord God. And also my houses are to be his home; the first one lies there facing well toward the west, the second facing toward Hueytepec all together with its house-land; no one is to claim anything or bring suit there. And a second field that belongs to God my dear father is near the field of Pedro Gómez. And a third piece of land is at Calpilco and near where the house is in which Alvar Coca lives; and on all sides it is next to the fields of Juan Mateo.

And to my dear father San Francisco, and San Nicolás, and (the cofradías of) Ecce Homo, the Holy Crucifix, and also to my intercessor and mother the Assumption of Mary, and San Jacinto, and [Mary at the Cross],[4] to them will belong what goes with my house toward Hueytepec on the eastern side, with fruit trees, a row of quince, and three zapote trees. I bought it for 10 pesos. I bought it from María; I gave her 4 pesos, and I gave Petronila 6 pesos.

Monday, the 20th day of the month of June of the year 1575.

I, Juan Alvaro, citizen here in the district of Apçolco, now very voluntarily give everything found at my house, all the subsidiary buildings and all my house-land, to our dear father fray Francisco de Loaysa, vicar, who guards the holy church. I have taken the price my house and house-land made, 140 pesos in money; I have very gladly

Document 19 (cont.)

[4]These entities appear to include a monastery, a church, some cofradías, and perhaps some chapels or images.

Document 20

[1]McAfee Collection, UCLA Research Library, Special Collections.

nocanlal ynnoniccuic chicompoalli p^{o}s yn t^{o}s huel noyonllocopa ynnoniccelli yn isquich yn t^{o}s auh ynnoncate nopilhuan omentin ynic ce ju^{o} aluaro yhuan ana Elvilla ayc ceppa tlatozque yehica ca oc mochi nomac ca yn notlatqui nehuatl nicmati yn tlein niquimmacaz yehica ca amo ymascauh yntlətqui Ca huel nehuatl nociahuiliz notlapalihuiliz ynic onicnesti notlaçaçalol omochiuh yn isquich ymanian yn nocal yhuan yn notlal oniccouh ynic ce tlacatl notlal nicpatilti cihuapilli doña juana xochmilco omatzaqualli[2] ynic ome nictlalcohuilli catherina yllamatzin chane omac chicome p^{o}s nicmacac yn imon yniquei nictlalcohuilli a^{o}l pz apçolco nacamicti nahui p^{o}s nicmacac ynic nahui migl cortes huecamecatl tenanitlan nictlalcohui nicmacac xxii p^{o}s t^{o}s ynic nahui lorenzo ypiltzin diego chane omaxac ompantli yn notlal nicpatilti ynic macuilli tlacatl ytoca margos feliciano chane apçolco cempantli yn notlal nicpatilti macuilistinin[3] yn tlalleque ynnoniquintlalcohuilli yhuan oniquintlalpatilli yehica ayac oc ceppa aquin tlein quitoz yn tepilhuan yn oc huecauhtica ca huel mochi nascauh notlatqui ynnonicnamacac yn tlacpac omoteneuh huel nomatica oniccuic onicceli chicompohuanlli p^{o}s yn t^{o}s onechmomaquilli yn padre vic^{o} auh yn imispan yn quiz yn t^{o}s testigos omochiuhque yn ica señor anton gomez Español vezino coyoacan yhuan yispantzinco señor don turibio fiscal vicente Ramirez bal^{sar} p̄z alguaziles yglesia margos feliciano Escriu^{o} yglesia anton sanchez tepisqui apçolco Etc̄ auh yn isquich yn nochantlatqui onicpiaya yn puertas cerraduras mochi niccencahua aocmo tleyniccuiz ça isquich ascan ypan ce xihuitl yn nocanlalpan ocatca oc nipiscaz nehuatl ju^{o} aluaro nican nictlalia nofirma cruz ynicneltilia[4] yn notlatol

nicneltilli nehuatl thomas felicia^{o} Escriuano
† ts^{o}g don toribio silvestre vicenten Ramires alguazil yglesia barthasal p̄z alguazil teopan testigos joseph jacobo thomas felicia^{o} Escriuano

[2]Possibly a district of Xochimilco? It can be translated literally as "two dams."
[3]The actual total is six, since two persons were listed as fourth.

received all the money. And there are two children of mine, first Juan Alvaro, and Ana Elvira; they are never again to bring suit, because it is all still in my hand and is my property; I know what I will give them, because it is not their property and possession, for it was with my fatigue and work that I made my living and my fortune was made. I bought everything that is at my house and land; for the first person, I exchanged my land with lady doña Juana (of) Xochimilco [Omatzaqualli].[2] Second, I bought land from Catalina, an old woman, citizen of Omac; I gave her son-in-law 7 pesos. Third, I bought land from Alonso Pérez, butcher at Apçolco; I gave him 4 pesos. Fourth, I bought land at Tenantitlan from Miguel Cortés Huecamecatl and gave him 22 pesos cash. Fourth, I exchanged two strips of my land with Lorenzo, son of Diego, citizen of Omaxac. The fifth person is named Marcos Feliciano, citizen of Apçolco; I exchanged one strip of my land with him. (There are) five[3] landowners from whom I bought land and with whom I exchanged land; wherefore no one is ever again to lay claims, nor their children far into the future, for the above-mentioned that I have sold is all truly my property and possession; and I have indeed taken and received in my hand 140 pesos in cash; the father vicar gave it to me, and the money was brought out in the presence of those who were made witnesses, with Sr. Antón Gómez, Spaniard, citizen of Coyoacan, and in the presence of Sr. don Toribio, fiscal; Vicente Ramírez, Baltasar Pérez, constables of the church; Marcos Feliciano, notary of the church; Antón Sánchez, district officer of Apçolco; etc. And I give up all the household gear I had, the doors and locks and everything and will no longer take anything, except that now for a year I will harvest my former house-land. I Juan Alvaro, put here my signature of a cross in order to verify[4] my words.

I verified it: Tomás Feliciano, notary.

† witness. Don Toribio Silvestre. Vicente Ramírez, constable of the church. Baltasar Pérez, constable of the church. Witness, Joseph Jacobo. Tomás Feliciano, notary.

---

[4]Apparently a slip for *inic nicn̓eltilia*; see the comparable portion of Doc. 21, by the same writer.

21. Baltasar Esteban and wife sell or donate land to church, Coyoacan region, 1575[1]

Sabado a 6 dias del mes De agusto 1575 años

NEhuatl balthasar Estephan nican nichane tlalxopan tlaxillacalpan Auh yn teoyotica nonamic ytoca ysabel chane ycçotitlan yn cecni huel ycihuatlal[2] quicahuilitiuh quimacatiuh yn itatzin ynantzin nican mani ycaltitlan joan aluaro[3] yn itech pouhqui ocatca oquinamacac yn çan ye no oncan yn teopisque yntlaltzin onoc auh yn totlal amo cenca quesquich ynic huiac caxtolli quahuitl yc patlahuac matlacquahuitl huel ochpantli ytenco Ca huel tascauh totlatqui yn tlaltzintli yn tomestin yn teoyotica nonamic ysabel Auh yn ascan toyonllocopa tictomaquilia yn totlaçotatzin padre fray fran^{co} de loaysa vic^{o} yn ipan santa yglesia villa de coyohuacan yn ipatiuh yn totlaltzin ynnoticcuique cempohualli p^{o}s yn t^{o}s huel oticpaccacelique yn imispan yn quiz yn t^{o}s testigos mochiuhque yispan Señor Don turibio siluestre fiscal yglesia yhuan vicente Ramirez balthasar $\overline{pz}$ alguaziles yglesia yhuan yispan ju^{o} aluaro chane apçolco Nehuatl balthasar Estephan ynic nicneltilia yn notlatol ypampa nican amapan nictlalia nomachio nofirma ynic aocmo ceppa aquin tlein quitoz yn çatepan

bal^{sar} esteban don toribio silvestre fiscal balthasar
$\overline{pz}$ teopan topile vicenten Ramirez alguazil yglesia

Ytencopa balthasar Estepha yhuan teoyotica ynamic ysabel yn tlacpac omoteneuhque ynic omotlalnamacaque nicneltilli nehuatl onitlacuillo thomas feliciano Escriuano

---

[1]McAfee Collection, UCLA Research Library, Special Collections.

[2]This special term often hovers, as here, close to the meaning "dowry land.'

Saturday, 6th day of the month of August of the year 1575. I Baltasar Esteban, citizen here in the district of Tlalxopan, and my legitimate wife named Isabel, citizen of Icçotitlan: this parcel is truly her woman's-land[2] that her father and mother bequeathed and gave her which is here near the house of Juan Alvaro,[3] that used to belong to him and he sold, and also right there lies the land of the priests; and there is not much of our land, 15 rods long, 10 rods wide, close to the edge of the highway. The land is truly the property and possession of both of us, my legitimate wife Isabel and myself, and now voluntarily we give it to our dear father fray Francisco de Loaysa, vicar in the holy church of the town of Coyoacan; we have taken the price of our land, 20 pesos in money, we have indeed gladly received it. The money was brought out in the presence of those made witnesses: in the presence of señor don Toribio Silvestre, fiscal, of the church, and Vicente Ramírez and Baltasar Pérez, constables of the church, and in the presence of Juan Alvaro, citizen of Apçolco. I Baltasar Esteban, in order to verify my words, place here on the paper my rubric and signature so that no one will dispute anything again afterwards.

Baltasar Esteban. Don Toribio Silvestre, fiscal. Baltasar Pérez, church constable. Vicente Ramírez, church constable.

At the command of Baltasar Esteban and his legitimate wife Isabel, who were mentioned above as having sold their land, I Tomás Feliciano, notary, have verified and written it.

---

[3]This is the Juan Alvaro and the land referred to in the preceding document.

III. Municipal

22. Municipal council records, Tlaxcala, 1547[1]

Viernes iiii metztli de nuvienbre 1547 Años In nican cabildo mocentlanlique in gou^{or} al̄ldes regidores yn ievatzin mg^{co} señor diego rramirez corr^{or} por su mg^{t} yn nican proūi^{a} tlaxcallan quinmonavatilli in gou^{or} al̄ldes regidores cenpuvallilhuitl quinmonavatilli icihuca quichivazque iztac teocuitlatl iezqui ixquich iezqui in navi tomin oncan neztiiez tlaxcalla atl tepetl itlaviz yc machiyotiloz amatl tlen temacoz ano amatlacuiloli etc yntla oquipanavi cenpuvalilhuitl ic tlaxtlavazque cenpuvalli p^{o}s t^{o}s yn centlacolli itech poviz ycamara de su mg^{t} av in oc no ixquich itech puviz yn tlaxcalla cabildo iehuatl navatlato luis de la torre yn ilhuitl metztli xiuitl aco omito

di^{o} Ramirez luys de la torre ynterpetre Escrivàno de cabil tlsn fabian R^{o}s

çanno yquac yn ilvitl meztli yvan xivitl omihto yn ipan cabildo mocentlalique yn gou^{or} al̄ldes yvan regidores yn nican proui^{a} tlaxcalan ipan mononozque yn ixquich nican tlaxcallan nemi uehcatlaca cholulteca tezco^{ca} mexica tepepulca yvan oc cequin avaque tepevaque quintlaqualtizue yn nican tlaxcallan tlatequipanoua texima quauhxima tlahcuiloque yn iquac ychan atl tepetl tequitizque yn mag^{co} sr^{o} d^{o}i ramirez corr^{or} por su mag^{t} quimitavili oniccac ynic anmononoza lonestica namechnanquiliz quenin mochivaz yehuatl yn quinavatlatavili luis de la torre

yvan yc mononozque yn nican cabildo ipanpa yn tlavanque yeua macozque yn ça nican covalozque[2] ome tomin quimacazque centetl meztli yc tequitizque hau yntla español aca quicouaz aço canah estancia quivicaz yn çan nican proui^{a} tlx̄n ey tomines yvan quitlaqualtiz hau yntla onpa namacoz[2] cuetlaxcouapan[3] navi tomines quimacazque yvan quitlaqualtizque hau yntla aca amantecatl yn intla ytequiuh aço texima quauhxima tlacuilouani yntla nican

---

[1]Museo Nacional de Antropología, document C. A. 340, ff. 1-4.

[2]Throughout this passage *coa*, "buy," and *namaca*, "sell," are used for "hire" and "hire out."

Documentation

Friday the 4th of the month of November of the year 1547, there assembled here in council the governor, alcaldes and councilmen. The magnificent sir Diego Ramírez, corregidor for His Majesty here in the province of Tlaxcala, gave orders to the governor, alcaldes, and councilmen, and ordered them to make quickly, in 20 days, (a seal) to be of silver, (weighing) 4 tomines, on which the arms of the city of Tlaxcala will appear, with which to seal papers that are issued, or letters, etc.; if it goes beyond 20 days, they are to pay 20 pesos in coin; half will belong to His Majesty's chamber, and the same amount will belong to the council of Tlaxcala. The interpreter was Luis de la Torre; the day, month, and year were mentioned above.

Diego Ramírez. Luis de la Torre, interpreter. Notary of the council of Tlaxcala, Fabián Rodríguez.

On the same said day, month, and year, the governor, alcaldes, and councilmen here in the province of Tlaxcala assembled in council and consulted about how all the outsiders, people from Cholula, Texcoco, Mexico City, Tepepulco, and other towns, who live here in Tlaxcala, should (help) feed the masons, carpenters, and painters working here in Tlaxcala when they work on city buildings. The magnificent sir Diego Ramírez, corregidor for his Majesty, told them: I have heard what you advise; Monday I will answer how it is to be done. The person who interpreted for him was Luis de la Torre.

And they consulted here in council about the drunks; those who are hired[2] here will be given 2 tomines for each month they work, and if it is a Spaniard who hires one and might take him to an estate somewhere here in the province of Tlaxcala, (he will give him) 3 tomines and feed him; and if he is hired out[2] in Puebla[3] they will give him 4 tomines and feed him, and if he is a craftsman, if his work is masonry or carpentry or he is a painter, if he is hired here they are to

[3]Cuetlaxcouapan (given as Cuitlaxcoapan, Siméon, p. 126) was the name of the small Indian settlement on the site where the Spanish town of Puebla was founded.

covaloz navi tomin quimacazque auh yntla español quicovaz chiquacentomin quimacaz hau yntla onpa cuetlaxcouapan namacoz ce peso quimacazque ypanpa yn vel tlatequipanoz[4] yuhqui quimitavili yn mag^{co} sr^{o} corr^{or} ypan mofirmatique yvan nochi yntoca mococoua felix tececepozin don julian ylpitic[5]

di^{o} Ramirez blas osorio baltasar cortes don juan m̄scin bn^{ra} vnade diego sanchez don fr^{co} de mendoça don juan de paz lucas hernandes luys de la torre ynterpetre Escrivanos de cabildo yn tlx̄n̄ di^{o} de soto fabian R^{o}s

Lunes Ic chicomilhuitl metztli de nobienbre 1547 años In nican cabildo mocentlalique yn ievatzin mag^{co} señor di^{o} rramirez corr^{or} por su mg^{t} yn nican proūi^{a} tlaxcallan yvan ievan gouernador al̄l̄des regidores quinmolhuilli in corr^{or} in ievan gou^{or} yvan al̄l̄des yvan regidores yn ipanpa mononotzque viernes ipanpa chololteca mexica tetzcoca oc cequin atl tepetl ipan valleva yc queni monavatilli yc quinnaquilli in gou^{or} al̄l̄des regidores quimicuilozque in ixquichime nican motlaiecoltiya atl tepetl ipan valleva yvan ceccan quintlalizque in nican tlalli oquimocovique no ceccan quintlalizque yn amo yntlal ipan catte in iquac oquimicuiloque niman ixpan quintlalizque yn mg^{co} senor corr^{or} niman quinmonavatiliz in quenami yntequihu iezqui in intequihu iezqui macoz yn mayordomo de la ciudad tlaxcallan yn mayordomo navatiloz quenami quinmomaquiliz yn ixquichime tequiti ytech ciudad quichichiva yn ilhuitl metztli xiuitl aco vmito yvan quinnavatizque yn quenami tequitizque yntlaca^{o} quicelizque cuililozque yn ixquich yntlatqui yvan yazque in inchan totocozque

çanno iquac ic mononotzque in ipanpa a^{o} vellanamaco tiianquizco yvan in ievazin mg^{co} señor cor^{o}r niman quimonavatilli ce al̄l̄de baltasar cortes yvan bu^{ra} yvan don Julian yevan oncan quimocuitlavizque tiianquizco quenin tlanamacoz momoztla oncan audi^{a} quichivazque yn teilpiloyan caltenco cecentetl metztli quichivazque yn intequihv in imeixtin Juramento quicelique ynic vel quichivazque yntequihu atle quitlacozque yvan iehatl imescr^{o} iezqui di^{o} de soto

[4]This phrase seems also to be open to the interpretation "for which he will be able to work."

give him 4 tomines, and if a Spaniard hires him, he is to give him 6 tomines, and if he is hired out in Puebla they will give him 1 peso [for which he will work well].[4] Thus the magnificent sir corregidor spoke to them, whereon they signed with all their names. Félix (Mejía), (don Juan) Tececepotzin, and don Julián [Ilpitic?][5] are ill.

Diego Ramírez. Blas Osorio. Baltasar Cortés. Don Juan Maxixcatzin. Buenaventura Uñate. Diego Sánchez. Don Francisco de Mendoza. Don Juan de Paz. Lucas Hernández. Luis de la Torre, interpreter. Notaries of the council of Tlaxcala: Diego de Soto; Fabián Rodríguez.

Monday on the 7th day of the month of November of the year of 1547, there assembled here in council the magnificent sir Diego Ramírez corregidor for His Majesty here in the province of Tlaxcala and the governor, alcaldes, and councilmen; the corregidor said to the governor and alcaldes and councilmen: as to what they talked about Friday concerning the people of Cholula, Mexico City, Texcoco, and others who flee to the town and what is to be ordered about it, he answered the governor, alcaldes, and councilmen that they should inscribe all those who make their livings here who have fled to the town and put down each place they have bought land here and also put down each place where they are on land not theirs; when they have inscribed them, then they are to set them before the magnificent sir corregidor, then he will give them orders how their duties are to be; the person by whom their duties will be given will be the majordomo of the city of Tlaxcala; the majordomo will be ordered how he is to assign to all who perform duties for the city what each will do; the day, month, and year were mentioned above; and they will order them how to perform their duties; if they do not accept it, all their property will be taken from them and they will go to their homelands; they will be driven out.

At this same time they consulted about things being wrongly sold in the market, and then the magnificent sir corregidor ordered an alcalde, Baltasar Cortés, and Buenaventura and don Julián to take care of how things are sold there at the market, and they will hold audience there daily at the side of the jailhouse; they will do it for a term of one month each. The three of them took oath to do their duty well and not commit misdeeds; and their notary will be Diego de Soto.

---

[5]We cannot be sure whether *Ilpitic* is an alternative surname for don Julian Motolinia or don Julian de la Rosa, the name of a fourth person who is ill, a title, or simply a Nahuatl word of unknown meaning.

yvan çanno iquac ic mononotzque yn nican proui^{a} tlaxcallan yn iquac sabadotica chichicovmica acan teiamicoz[6] in atlancatepec tecovac veiutlipan topuianco acan teiamicoz çan nican tlaxcallan teiamicoz tlanamacoz yn ilhuitl metztli xiuitl aco vmito

Ivan otlanavatique yn aca oztomecatl nican vallaz quinamacaquihv cacavatl tilmatli cueitl vipilli tlacallaquilli oc cequi yntla aca pochtecatl nican quicovaz niman quimilhuiz yn deputado ynniquac niman yc tzatzic[7] tecpuyotl yn quenami oquicohv çanno ihvqui yc quinamacaz av in ievan gou^{or} alldes regidores in tlacatl tlatovani[8] oquimotlatlahvtilique yn corregidor ytech oquimocavilique iehuatl quimochiviliz hordenaças ic quinmocneliliz in ixquich tlacatl di^{o} Ramirez blas osorio baltasar cortes don juan mscin bn^{ra} vnade diego sanchez don fr^{co} de mendoça don juan de paz lucas hernandes luys de la torre interpetre Escrivano de cabildo tlaxcallan fabian R^{o}s

Viernes omilvitl meztli de dezienbre yn ixiuh yn t^{o} de 1547 años ipan yn cabildo yn muy mag^{co} señor diego ramirez corr^{or} por su mag^{t} yn nican proui^{a} tlaxcallan yquac quinmopiyaltili yn tlatlapolonime macuiltetl yc mozaqua quappetlacalli cabildo onoc centetl quimopiliya gou^{or} blas osorio centetl quimopiliya ocotelulco allde don julian de la rosa centetl quipia quiyauiztlan allde don a^{o}l maldonado yn ontetl cecentetl ticpia escr^{os} fabian rodrigues di^{o} de soto quimitavili yn sr^{o} corr^{or} yn gou^{or} yvan escrivanos de cabildo nochipa quipiazque yn tlatlapoloni hau yn omen alldes cecexiuhtica quipiazque yn axcan ocotelulco yvan quiyauiztlan yn oc ce xiuitl quipiazque tizatla yvan tepeticpac alldes çan yuh mopapatlataz yn oncan quappetlacalco oncan mopiyaz yn ixquich privilegios yvan prouisiones yvan cedulas yn iquac ytla moquixtiz quappetlacalco ahno ye ytla mocalaquiz yzqui tlacatl yxpan yezqui yn macuilli tlacatl quipiah tlatlapoloni yvan yuh quimitavili yn sr^{o} cor^{or} yn tlatlapoloni ayac quimacazque çan uel yehuan quipiazque ipanpa juramento quicuique yehuatl navatlato luys de la torre nochin ymixpan yn cabildo povy yn ilvitl meztly yvan xivitl tlacpac omitoh

---

[6]*Teiamicoz* = *tiamicoz*. Compare *ceyaliztica* = *cializtica* in Doc. 1, also from Tlaxcala.

[7]It appears to us that *tzatziz* is called for.

And at this same time they discussed that here in the province of Tlaxcala on Saturday each week markets are not to be held[6] anywhere, at Atlancatepec, Tecoac, Ueyotlipan, or Topuyanco; nowhere are markets to be held, only here in Tlaxcala will they be held and things be sold; the day, month, and year were mentioned above.

And they ordered that any trader who comes here to sell cacao, cloaks, skirts, women's shirts, or other goods he brings, if any merchant here buys it, then he is to tell the deputy; then right away the crier will proclaim[7] how he bought it, and likewise what he will sell it for; and the governor, alcaldes, councilmen, and the lord ruler[s?][8] turned to the corregidor and left it to him to make ordinances to benefit everyone.

Diego Ramírez. Blas Osorio. Baltasar Cortés. Don Juan Maxixcatzin. Buenaventura Uñate. Diego Sánchez. Don Francisco de Mendoza. Don Juan de Paz. Lucas Hernández. Luis de la Torre, interpreter. Notary of the council of Tlaxcala, Fabián Rodríguez.

Friday, the 2nd day of the month of December of the year of our Lord 1547, in council the very magnificent sir Diego Ramírez, corregidor for His Majesty here in the province of Tlaxcala, appointed guardians for the five keys with which the wooden chest that is in the council is closed: governor Blas Osorio keeps one; the Ocotelulco alcalde don Julián de la Rosa keeps one; the Quiyauiztlan alcalde don Alonso Maldonado keeps one; we the notaries Fabián Rodríguez and Diego de Soto keep two, one each. The sir corregidor told the governor and notaries of the council always to keep the keys, and the two alcaldes will each keep one for a year: now Ocotelulco and Quiyauiztlan; the second year the Tizatla and Tepeticpac alcaldes will keep them, and in this manner it will be exchanged. There in the wooden chest are to be kept all the concessions and provisions and decrees; when something is taken out of the wooden chest, or something is put in, each of the five persons who have keys is to be present; and the sir corregidor told them not to give the keys to anyone, but they alone are to keep them, wherefore they took oath, with Luis de la Torre as interpreter, before all the council members; the day, month, and year were mentioned above.

---

[8]The rulers of the four cabeceras of Tlaxcala, as distinct from the governor and alcaldes, held the title *tlatoani*. Presumably the reference is to them, but the passage is puzzling because *in tlacatl tlatovani* is grammatically singular, though easily pluralized, and more than one of the rulers were present.

di^{o} Ramirez Escr^{os} de cabildo yn tlaxcallan fabian R^{o}s di^{o} de soto

çanno iquac in ilhuitl metztli yvan xiuitl In tlacpac vmito ypan i cabildo vmononotzque in gou^{or} yvan alcaldes yvan rregidores quicentlalique in intlatol in ipanpa yc teiamico tiianquizco iquac sabado ipan centetl semana av in ievan gou^{or} al̄ldes Regidores iehuatl ic mononotzque in ipan centetl semana oppa in teiamicoz in cepa iquac lunes Av inic opa yquac sabado yn ihvqui mochiva sabado yn novia valyallova[9] yn izquican tiianquizco yn nican novian tlaxcallan Ahu niman ic quimotlatlahutilique yn mu mg^{co} señor diego rramirez corr^{or} por su mg^{t} yn nican prouincia tlaxcallan niman oquimitavilli vniccac nicvellitta in ihuqui mochivaz in ipan Centetl semana oppa in teiamicoz inovian valyalovaz yquac lunes yvan sabado nitenavatiya ynnihvqui mochivaz yc tzaziz tecpoyotl yn ihuqui ipan catqui centetl nenonotzalli yvan notenavatil yvan hordenaças yn oncan catqui pena çanno ihvqui ic tlaxtlavaloz yn aquin quitlacoz yn ixquich oncan icuilihutoc çanno ihvqui ic nitenavatiya

di^{o} Ramirez Escrivanos de cabildo tlaxcallan fabian R^{o}s di^{o} de soto

chicunavilvitl meztli dezi^{e} de 1547 años ypan yn cabildo mocentlalique yn gou^{or} alldes regidores yn nican proui^{a} tlx̄n ipanpa namacozque atl tepetl ychcavan yehuan carnellos cenzontli ipan ix tecpantli[10] niman ticnavatique yn don ju^{o} tececepozin regidor onpa ychcapiya amalmalco ynic quincequixtiz yn quexquich carnellos niman quixpantiz yn cabildo mocacoua tlapiyalzintly tenavati don ju^{o} de paz[11] tlacpac omihto yn ilvitl meztly yvan xivitl

blas osorio baltasar cortes don juan m̄sc don julia motolinia felix de mexia bn^{ra} vnade diego sanchez don fr^{co} de mendoça lucas hernandes Escrivanos de cabildo di^{o} de soto fabian R^{o}s

xxxi ilvitl meztli dezienbre de 1547 años yxpan yn mag^{co} señor di^{o} ramires corr^{or} por su mag^{t} yvan ymixpan yn tlaxcallan guardian

---

[9] We take *valyallova* to be an impersonal of the verb *uallauh*, "to come," from the roots *ual* and *yauh*. The impersonal given by Simeon is *ualuiloa*, formed on the imperfect *ualhuia*. There is, however, an alternative imperfect *uallaya*. If its constituents were left unassimilated, it would by the same process yield the impersonal *ualyaloa*.

Diego Ramírez. Notaries of the council of Tlaxcala: Fabián Rodríguez; Diego de Soto.

Likewise on the day, month, and year above mentioned, in the council the governor and alcaldes and councilmen directed their discourse to the matter of how the market is held on Saturday each week, and the governor, alcaldes, and councilmen discussed holding it twice each week, once on Monday and the second time on Saturday, as is done (already) on Saturday, when people from all around come here,[9] from all the markets here around Tlaxcala. And then they asked the very magnificent sir Diego Ramírez, corregidor for his Majesty here in the province of Tlaxcala, about it; then he told them: I have heard it, I approve so doing, that it be held twice each week and people come from everywhere around on Monday and Saturday. I order it so to be done, and for the crier to proclaim it as is in a decree with my command and ordinances; as the penalty is there, such is to be paid by anyone who violates it; I likewise order all that is written there.

Diego Ramírez. Notaries of the council of Tlaxcala: Fabián Rodríguez; Diego de Soto.

On the 9th day of the month of December of the year 1547, the governor, alcaldes, and councilmen here in the province of Tlaxcala assembled in council because the town's sheep are to be sold, 580 muttons. Then we ordered don Juan Tececepotzin, councilman, to collect however many muttons are at Amalmalco where they keep sheep, and then report to the council. (Alejandre) Tlapialtzintli is ill; don Juan de Paz notified [him].[11] The day, month, and year were mentioned above.

Blas Osorio. Baltasar Cortés. Don Juan Maxixcatzin. Don Julián Motolinia. Félix Mejía. Buenaventura Uñate. Diego Sánchez. Don Francisco de Mendoza. Lucas Hernández. Notaries of the council: Diego de Soto; Fabián Rodríguez.

On the 31st day of the month of December of the year 1547, in the presence of the magnificent sir Diego Ramírez, corregidor for His

---

[10]At the end of the paragraph is a note *ça tlazalan actica tecpantli*, "twenty is between the lines" (where it was inserted after having been omitted by oversight).

[11]It is by no means clear who is being notified. Don Juan Tececepotzin seems most likely, but it could also be Tlapialtzintli, or the people at Amalmalco, or people in general.

fray m$\overline{in}$ de hojacastro yvan fray ju^{o} de ribas fray andres de olmos fray p^{o} de torres ynniquac pepenaloque yn gou^{or} a$\overline{ll}$des regidores matlactecpantli onze yn tlapepenque ynic moquez gou^{or} a^{o}l gomez quiyauiztlan ychan yn quipepen ynic tlapanavy chiquacentecpantly oncaxtolli omey niman yehuan moquezque a$\overline{ll}$des pablo de galicia felix mexia gaspar de luna alexandre tlapiyalzintly regidores don fran^{co} de tapia don di^{o} de paredes tiburcio albino don ant^{o} calmecava ju^{o} de avalos calisto portugues don m$\overline{in}$ coyolchiuhqui dg$\overline{o}$ malmolejo ant^{o} tellez lucas gr^{a} ant^{o} flores di^{o} ______ yn imixpan mochiuh blas osorio gou^{or} catca don di^{o} de guzman a$\overline{ll}$de catca yvan fabian rodrigues nehuatl niescrivano di^{o} de soto yn quinavatlatavili sr^{o} corr^{or} yehuatl m$\overline{in}$ diaz español alguazil

xxxi ilvitl meztli dezi^{e} de 1547 años cabildo quichiuhque mocentlalique yn yancuic gou^{or} a$\overline{ll}$des regidores yxpan yn mag^{co} sr^{o} di^{o} ramires corr^{or} por su mag^{t} yn nican proui^{a} tlx$\overline{n}$ quimixquezque quinpepenque yn izquitlamatin tequitizque atl tepetl yalguazilvan Ju^{o} quapilli gaspar daniel andres tlachmazin ant^{o} zoton niman yehuan tiyanquizco tlapiyazque alexandre xaxal ant^{o} chauacue leonardo couazin di^{o} tlacuilozin niman yehuatl alcayde mochiuh vrban meneses niman yehuan atl tepetl ymayordomos don Juan de paz yvan don Julian de la rosa

23. Agreement between Mexica and Tarascans as to allotment of tasks, Nombre de Dios, Durango, later sixteenth century[1]

Yn axca tonatiuh lonestica cepohuali omacuili metzintli marzo mani [. . .][2] titocetlalia ticchihua capilton titononotza tichaneque ynica yn ipan yn altepetl yn itocayoca a la villa del nombre de dios

[1]Bancroft Library, Mexican Ms. No. 93, item 2B, ff. 30-31. The Bancroft item is not the sixteenth-century document but a very late copy; it contains various mistakes, and its orthography deviates considerably from the original. A transcription and

Majesty, and in the presence of the Tlaxcalan prior fray Martín de Ojacastro, and fray Juan de Ribas, fray Andrés de Olmos, fray Pedro de Torres, at that time were chosen the governor, alcaldes, and councilmen, with 201 electors, with the result that Alonso Gómez, whose home is Quiyauiztlan, was elevated to governor; (he was) the one they chose, he won with 138; then those raised to alcaldes were Pablo de Galicia, Félix Mejía, Gaspar de Luna, Alejandre Tlapialtzintli; councilmen, don Francisco de Tapia, don Diego de Paredes, Tiburcio Albino, don Antonio Calmecaua, Juan de Avalos, Calisto Portugués, don Martín Coyolchiuhqui, Domingo Marmolejo, Antonio Téllez, Lucas García, Antonio Flores, Diego ____. Done in the presence of Blas Osorio, former governor; don Diego de Guzmán, former alcalde; and Fabián Rodríguez. I was the notary, Diego de Soto. The person who interpreted for the sir corregidor was Martín Díaz, Spaniard, constable.

On the 31st day of the month of December of the year of 1547, the new governor, alcaldes, and councilmen held council and assembled before the magnificent sir Diego Ramírez, corregidor for His Majesty here in the province of Tlaxcala, and elected and placed in office all those who are to serve: the city's constables, Juan Quapilli, Gaspar Daniel, Andrés Tlachmatzin, Antonio Tzoton; then those who are to guard the market, Alejandre Xaxal, Antonio Chauacue, Leonardo Coatzin, Diego Tlacuilotzin; then the person made jailor, Urban Meneses; then the city's majordomos, don Juan de Paz and don Julián de la Rosa.

Today, Monday, 25th day of the month of March of [. . .][2] we congregate, make council, and consult together, we citizens here in the town called the town of Nombre de Dios, concerning the tasks to be

---

translation into English and Spanish have been published in Barlow and Smisor, eds., *Nombre de Dios, Durango*, pp. 46-49.

[2]Barlow and Smisor, p. 47, estimate the year as 1585, on the basis of calendrical computations.

yn ipampa yn itlatequipanilhuiloca y tote dios yhua y tohueytlatocatzin y rey tonecetlaliliz y timochtin[3] y timexica yhua y timichihuaque ynic tictomaca y totlatequipanolis qu[4] christianoyotica netlazotlalistica ynich[5] tiquitohua yn ispatzinco y tote dios nica tinescayotiani ini[5] ticselohua y totequiuh

— Mexicatlacatli quipiasque yey metzintli yn ichcame

— Michihuacatlaca ome metzintli quipiasque yn ichcame

— Yhua y teopa tlaxcalchihualistli yey metzintli quichihuasque y mexicatlaca

— Yhua y michihuatlaca ome metzintli quichihuasque ytlaxcalchihualis

— Y mexicatlacatli yey semana teopa tlatequipanosque y quauhcalaquisque yn atecasque yhua tlaqualtzintli quicalaquisque yhua teopa tlachpanasque yhua cavayo quipiasque

— Yhua y michihuacatlaca ome semana quauhcalaquisque yhua atecasque yhua tlacualtzintli quicalaquisque yhua tlachipanasque ihua cabayopiesque yhua

— Yhua yn ichantzinco y toueytlatocatzin y rey inic tictopalehuilisque ini[6] alcalde mayor y mexicatlatli[7] yey semana tlatequipanosque y motitlanisque[8] y tlachipanasque

— Yhua y michihuacatlaca ome semana tlatequipanosque in ichantzinco y tohueytlatocatzin y motitlanisque[8] y tlachipanasque

Y axca ticcemitohua y tonecetlalilistlatol yn ispantzinco yni[6] alcaldesmen mexicapa partolome de los angeles yhua tomas filipe alcalde michihuacapan yhua regidortin jua damiya yhua pedro adres yhua mochintin tetahua y mechicapa yhua michihuacapan

Ynica quitlalia yfilma in itoca[9] fracisco martin jua de sa pedro pablo de sa fracisco yhua y mochintin altepehuaque yhua y michihuaque domingo sepastia yhua mochintin yn altepehuaque ini[6] michihuaca[10] yn tonecetlalistlatol ca uel tlayeyecoli tlacetlali in ispantzinco y tote dios yn ayac quitlacos y totlatol ini[6] taltepehuaque

---

[3]For *timochintin*.

[4]For *qualli*; perhaps abbreviated in the original.

[5]For *inic*, presumably.

[6]Four occurrences of *ini* in this document seem to be the equivalent of the simple article, rather than the article plus the possessive pronoun. The sense seems to dictate this solution for *ini michihuaca*; note also that neither this phrase nor *ini alcaldesmen* show the plural possessive ending (see *tetahua*, just below *alcaldesmen*).

[7]For *mexicatlacatli*, as above.

done for our Lord God and our great sovereign the king; all of us, Mexica and Michoaca, are agreed to assign ourselves our tasks with good Christianity and friendship; thus we say before our Lord God, here we indicate how we are dividing our tasks.

— The Mexica people will watch the sheep for three months.
— The Michoaca people will watch the sheep for two months.
— And the Mexica people will do the baking at the church for three months.
— And the Michoaca people will do their baking for two months.

— The Mexica people will work at the church for three weeks; they will deliver firewood, carry water and deliver food and sweep the church and watch the horses.
— And for two weeks the Michoaca people will deliver wood and carry water and deliver food and sweep and watch horses and . . .

— And as to how we will help the alcalde mayor at the house of our great sovereign the king, the Mexica people will work for three weeks; they will be sent as messengers[8] and sweep.
— And the Michoaca people will work for two weeks at the house of our great sovereign; they will be sent as messengers[8] and sweep.

Now we declare firmly our agreement in the presence of the alcaldes; for the Mexica Bartolomé de los Angeles, and Tomás Felipe, alcalde for the Michoaca, and the councilmen Juan Damián and Pedro Andrés, and all the heads of families, Mexica and Michoaca.

Here Francisco Martín, Juan de San Pedro, Pablo de San Francisco place their signatures and names[9] (for) all the (Mexica) townsmen, and Domingo Sebastián (for) all the Michoaca townsmen.[10] Our agreement is firmly decided and determined before our Lord God; no one is to go against the words of us townsmen.

---

[8]Or "will do errands." See Doc. 27, first numbered paragraph, where *titlani* is used for sending fish rather than a message.

[9]The formula (*in*) *ifirma* (*in*) *itoca* is encountered so frequently that we have tentatively decided on the present translation. The passage would also be open to the interpretation "those named . . . place their signatures," particularly since *in* precedes only *itoca*.

[10]This whole passage seems considerably garbled.

24. Sample of records of collection of royal tribute at the local level, Tehuacan, 1642–44[1]

1.

Don fran^{co} hernandez gobernador yhua antonio perez a$\overline{\text{ll}}$de ortinaria ju^{o} pablo ju^{o} ximeo a$\overline{\text{ll}}$des andres bunefacia regitor mayor fran^{co} juares rexitor alexu martonato rexito ju^{o} pablo rexitor fran^{co} di^{o} mayorto jua çacarias escripano ynica ypa aldepetl probicia deohuaca tiquitohua nica tocopehualtia y ticnechicohua yn itlacalaquil y tohueytlatocantzin Rey noestro s^{or} y sumagestad yn itech pohui xihuitl de 1642 años yn idech pohui dercio de april yc ce tonatiuh mopohua

san sebastian tzinnacatepec

toston 47 p^{o}s 4 ser^{o} 23 p^{o}s 6	yn oquicalaquicon yn itlacalaquil toston[2] onpohuali yhuan chicome peso yhua nahui tonmines serbicio[2] cenpohuali yhua yey ps^{o} yhua chiquace tomi yc tlami ymatica onquicalaquico ju^{o} antonio[3]

san sebastian xiquetzpalco

toston 8 p^{o}s 2 ser^{o} 4 p^{o}s 1 ts	yn oquicalaquicon yn itlacalaquil toston chicuey p^{o}s yhuan omme tomines servicio nahui p^{o}s yhuan ce tomi yc tlami ymatica onquicalaquicon sebastia calpixquin[4]

---

[1]UCLA Research Library, Special Collections. We present only a small sampling of the substantial volume, which covers several years by *tercios*, each section containing entries in the same style for the settlements in the Tehuacan district (though not all are recorded every time). Our selection includes the headings of the three sections for the first year, with the first few entries in each and, in our section 4, some entries chosen for their mention of a maize tribute. The rest of the volume contains no further variations other than the specific names and amounts mentioned, except that some entries have a marginal notation such as *itech ca 7 t^{o}s m^{o}*, which is then crossed out. The meaning seems to be "he (or they) owes 7½ tomines," that is, the village did not pay that much of what it nominally delivered. The crossing out presumably occurred when the amount was actually paid.

[2]The normal tribute was one silver peso per tributary annually, plus a so-called *real servicio*, an additional levy of one-half peso (a *tostón*) instituted in 1592 (see

1.

Don Francisco Hernández, governor, and Antonio Pérez, alcalde ordinario; Juan Pablo, Juan Jimeno, alcaldes; Andrés Bonifacio, chief councilman; Francisco Juárez, councilman; Alejo Maldonado, councilman; Juan Pablo, councilman; Francisco Diego, majordomo; Juan Zacarías, notary here in the town and province of Tehuacan: we declare that here we begin to collect the tribute of our great sovereign king, our lord His Majesty, corresponding to the year 1642, corresponding to the third of (the year ending with) April on the first day of the month.

San Sebastián Zinacantepec

Tostón, 47 pesos, 4 Service, 23 pesos, 6	Its (the town's) tribute that they came to deliver was, for the Tostón,[2] 47 pesos and 4 tomines; for the Service,[2] 23 pesos and 6 tomines, with which it is completed. The person who came to deliver it was Juan Antonio.[3]

San Sebastián Xiquetzpalco

Tostón, 8 pesos, 2 Service, 4 pesos, 1 tomín	Its tribute that they came to deliver was, for the Tostón, 8 pesos and 2 tomines; for the Service, 4 pesos and 1 tomín, with which it is completed. The person who came to deliver it was Sebastián the steward.[4]

Cook and Borah, *Essays in Population History*, I, 32). In this document, the word *tostón* appears to be applied to the one-peso head tax, and the *servicio* is consistently one-half the amount of the *tostón*.

[3]The Nahuatl sentence is a gem of succinct expression. Literally it is "with-his-hand-he-came-to-deliver-it Juan Antonio." English can say "it was delivered by the hand of Juan Antonio," or "it was Juan Antonio who came to deliver it," but cannot combine both without undue emphasis on the hand delivery. Hand delivery may have been important, but was also an expected and conventional element, as seen in other entries.

[4]It is noteworthy that the stewards delivering the tribute from the subject villages are mainly called by the traditional Nahuatl term *ċalpixqui*, while the equivalent person at the head-town level is called *mayordomo*. In a few other entries not given here, the person who delivers the tribute has the title *tlayacanqui*, "leader, head man," or *tecpoyotl*, "crier."

s. juseph elocotla

tosto 21 p^{os} ser^{o} 10 p^{os} 4	yn oquicalaquico yn itlacalaquil toston cepohuali yhua ce p^{os} ser^{o} matlactli p^{os} yhua nahui tomi yc tlami ymatica oquicaquico [*sic*] calpixquin baltasar melchior

san ju^{o}n bau^{ta} [tepochco]

yn oquicalaquico yn itlacalaquili y tosto castoli yhua 3 p^{os} yhua chiquacen tomi auh y serbicio chicunahui p^{os} yhua ey tomi yc tlami ymatica oquicalaquico calpixqui diego felipe

san ju^{o}n bau^{ta} tepetlala

totos 2 p^{os} ser^{o} 1 p^{os}	yn oquicalaquico yn itlacalaqui fran^{co} alhuacil mayor tosto 2 p^{os} yhua y serbicio 1 p^{os}

2.

Don fran^{co} herz gu^{or} Antonio Perez al̄de ordinario Ju^{o}n Pablo al̄des Ju^{o}n ximeo al̄des Andres Bunibancion Regidor mayor fran^{co} Ju^{o}rez Regidor alexon maldonado Regidor Ju^{o}n Pablo Regidor fran^{co} Diegon mayordomo miguel Di^{o} escri^{o} ynica ypan altepetl probincian teohuanca tiquitohua nican tocanPehualtia yn ticnechicohua yn itlacalaquil yn tohueytlatocatzin Rey nuestro señor y Sumagestad yn itech Pohui xihuitl 1642 años yn itech pohui tercion Augusto yc [ce]milhuitl.

santa maria nativitas teopochco

tosto 6 p^{os} 4 ts ser^{o} 3 p^{os} 4 ts	yn oquicalaquico yn tlacalaquili tosto chiquacen p^{os} yhuan nahui tomi auh ser^{o} ey p^{os} yhua ome to yc tlami ymatica oquicalaquico Antonio calpixqui

San Josef Elocotla

Tostón, 21 pesos Service, 10 pesos, 4	Its tribute that they came to deliver was, for the Tostón, 21 pesos; for the Service, 10 pesos and 4 tomines, with which it is completed. The person who came to deliver it was the steward Baltasar Melchor.

San Juan Bautista [Tepochco]

	Its tribute that they came to deliver was, for the Tostón, 18 pesos and 6 tomines, and for the service, 9 pesos and 3 tomines, with which it is completed. The person who came to deliver it was the steward Diego Felipe.

San Juan Bautista Tepetlala

Tostón, 2 pesos Service, 1 peso	Francisco, chief constable, came to deliver its tribute: for the Tostón, 2 pesos, and for the Service, 1 peso.

2.

Don Francisco Hernández, governor; Antonio Pérez, alcalde ordinario; Juan Pablo, alcalde; Juan Jimeno, alcalde; Andrés Bonifacio, chief councilman; Francisco Juárez, councilman; Alejo Maldonado, councilman; Juan Pablo, councilman; Francisco Diego, majordomo; Miguel Diego, notary here in the town and province of Tehuacan: we declare that here we begin to collect the tribute of our great sovereign king, our lord His Majesty, corresponding to the year of 1642, corresponding to the third (of the year ending with) August, on the first day.

Santa María Nativitas Teopochco

Tostón, 6 pesos, 4 tomines Service, 3 pesos, 2 tomines	The tribute they came to deliver was, for the Tostón, 6 pesos and 4 tomines, and for the Service, 3 pesos and 2 tomines, with which it is completed. The person who came to deliver it was Antonio the steward.

san Ju^{o}n bauh^{ta} Yyeteohuanca

tosto 2 p^{o}s ser^{o} 1 p^{o}s	yn oquicalaquico tlacalaquili tosto ome p^{o}s auh ser^{o} ce p^{o}s yc tlami ymatica oquicalaquico p^{o} Ju^{o}n calpixqui

san mateo tlacochcalco

tosto 9 p^{o}s 2 ts ser^{o} 4 p^{o}s 5 ts	yn oquicalaquico tlacalaquili tosto chicunahui p^{o}s yhuan ome tomi ser^{o} nahui p^{o}s yhuan macuili tomi ymatica oquicalaquico gabriel miguel calpixqui

3.

Don fran^{co} hernandez gouernador yhuan Antonio perez al̄l̄des ordinario Ju^{o}n Pablo al̄l̄des Ju^{o}n ximeo al̄l̄des Andres Bunibancio Regidor mayor fran^{co} Juarez Regido Alexo maldonado Regidor Ju^{o}n Pablo Regidor fran^{co} Diegon mayordomo miguel Dịegon escri^{o} ynican ypan altepetl probincia teohuaca tiquitohua nican toconPehualtia yn ticnechicohua yn itlacalaquil yn tohueytlatocatzin Rey nuestro Señor i Somagestad yn itech pohui xihuitl 1642 ãs yn itech pohui tercio Decienbre yc cemilhuitl mopohua

San Juseph tozpanco

tosto 42 p^{o}s ser^{o} 21 p^{o}s	yn oquicalaquico tlacalaquili tosto Vnpuali yhuan ome p^{o}s ser^{o} cenpuali yhuan ce p^{o}s y[c] tlami ymatica oquicalaquico fran^{co} miguel calpixqui Aluso Ju^{o} calpixqui

San Juseph elocotla

tosto 21 p^{o}s ser^{o} 12 [*sic*] ps 4	yn oquicalaquico tlacalaquili tosto cenpuali yhuan ce p^{o}s ser^{o} matlactli p^{o}s yhuan nahui tomi yc tlami ymatica oquicalaquico baltasar melchior

San Juan Bautista Yyeteohuacan

Tostón, 2 pesos Service, 1 peso	The tribute they came to deliver was, for the Tostón, 2 pesos, and for the Service, 1 peso, with which it is completed. The person who came to deliver it was Pedro Juan the steward.

San Mateo Tlacochcalco

Tostón, 9 pesos, 2 tomines Service, 4 pesos, 5 tomines	The tribute they came to deliver was, for the Tostón, 9 pesos and 2 tomines; for the Service, 4 pesos and 5 tomines. The person who came to deliver it was Gabriel Miguel the steward.

3.

Don Francisco Hernández, governor, and Antonio Pérez, alcalde ordinario; Juan Pablo, alcalde; Juan Jimeno, alcalde; Andrés Bonifacio, chief councilman; Francisco Juárez, councilman; Alejo Maldonado, councilman; Juan Pablo, councilman; Francisco Diego, majordomo; Miguel Diego, notary here in the town and province of Tehuacan: we declare that here we begin to collect the tribute of our great sovereign king, our lord His Majesty, corresponding to the year of 1642, corresponding to the third (of the year ending with) December, on the first day.

San Josef Tozpanco

Tostón, 42 pesos Service, 21 pesos	The tribute they came to deliver was, for the Tostón, 42 pesos; for the Service, 21 pesos, with which it is completed. The persons who came to deliver it were Francisco Miguel, steward, and Alonso Juan, steward.

San Josef Elocotla

Tostón, 21 pesos Service, 12 pesos, 4	The tribute they came to deliver was, for the Tostón, 21 pesos; for the Service, 10 pesos and 4 tomines, with which it is completed. The person who came to deliver it was Baltasar Melchor.

San Agusti

tosto 2 p^{o}s ser^{o} 1p^{o}s	yn oquicalaquico tlacalaquili tosto ome p^{o}s ser^{o} 1 p^{o}s yc tlami ymatica oquicalaquico Ju^{o}n miguel

4. Selected entries with maize tribute, April 1644

san matheo tlacochcalco

tosto 9 p^{o}s 6 t^{o}s ser^{o} 4 ps^{o} 3 t^{o}s	yn oquicalaquico yn intlacalaquil tosto chicunaui peso yoan chiquacen tomi seruicio naui ps^{o} yoan yei tomi ymatitica oquicauaco bal^{r} miguel calpixqui tlaoltequitl ome aneca yoan yei tomin[5]

san gabriel Viexoloc

tosto 2 p^{o}s 4 ts ser^{o} 1 ps^{o} 1 ts	yn oquicalaguico yn intlacalaquil tosto ome peso yoan naui tomi seruicio ce peso yoan ce tomi ymatica quicauaco ju^{o} xp̄oal calpixqui ytlaoltequiuh ce quauacali 3 t^{o}s

sancta m^{a} del munte

tosto 6 p^{o}s 3 t^{o}s ser^{o} 3 ps^{o} 2 t^{o}s	yn oquicalaguico yn intlacalaquil tosto chiquacen ps^{o} yoan ei tomin seruicio yei peso yoan ome tomin ymatica oquicauaco fran^{co} juan calpixqui tlaoltequitl 2 f^{a}s 2 t^{o}s m^{o}

Tolan tlacochcalco

tosto 1 ps^{o} ser^{o} 4 t^{o}s	yn oquicalaguico yn intlacalaquil toston ce peso seruicio naui t^{o}s ymatica oquicauaco pedro olibaris calpixqui tlaoli 3 t^{o}s

[5] In this case a grain measure, apparently one-eighth of a fanega, is meant rather than a unit of coin.

San Agustín Tostón, 2 pesos Service, 1 peso	The tribute they came to deliver was, for the Tostón, 2 pesos; for the Service, 1 peso, with which it is completed. The person who came to deliver it was Juan Miguel.

4.

San Mateo Tlacochcalco Tostón, 9 pesos, 6 tomines Service, 4 pesos, 3 tomines	Their tribute that they came to deliver was, for the Tostón, 9 pesos and 6 tomines; for the Service, 4 pesos and 3 tomines. The person who came to deliver it was Baltasar Miguel the steward. The maize tribute was 2 fanegas and 3 tomines.[5]
San Gabriel Viexoloc Tostón, 2 pesos, 4 Service, 1 peso, 1	Their tribute that they came to deliver was, for the Tostón, 2 pesos and 4 tomines; for the Service, 1 peso and 1 tomín. The person who came to deliver it was Juan Cristóbal the steward. Its maize tribute was a half fanega, 3 tomines.
Santa María del Monte Tostón, 6 pesos, 3 tomines Service, 3 pesos, 2 tomines	Their tribute that they came to deliver was, for the Tostón, 6 pesos and 3 tomines; for the Service, 3 pesos and 2 tomines. The person who came to deliver it was Francisco Juan the steward. The maize tribute was 2 fanegas, 2½ tomines.
Tolan Tlacochcalco Tostón, 1 peso Service, 4 tomines	Their tribute that they came to deliver was for the Tostón, 1 peso; for the Service, 4 tomines. The person who came to deliver it was Pedro Olivares the steward. The maize was 3 tomines.

25. Local market tax records, Coyoacan, mid-sixteenth century[1]

1.

nican icuiliuhtoc in tiaquiztequitl in tlacalaquilli in teocuitlatl

— copeualtian Sanct agustin quauhnecuillo innitequiuh macuiltomi

— antliztaca quauhnecuilloque in itequiuh onme tomi

— antocon quauhnecuiloque in itequiuh ce tomi

— panamacac innitequiuh centomi

— chamalochiuhqui[2] in itequiuh onme tomi

— chilnamacaque mexica in itequiuh onme tomi

— chiquipatlacan[3] in itequiuh naui tomi

— çoquichiuhqui in itequiuh melio

— ochpauaznamacac in itequiuh onme tomi

— cochiuhqui in itequiuh onmentomi

— oncotlapaqui in itequiuh naui tomi

— michnamacac in itequiuh ce tomi

— picienamacac in itequiuh centomi

— comalchiuhqui in itequiuh onme tomi

— tamalnamacac in itequiuh iey tomi

— acaquauhchiuhqui[4] in itequiuh ce tomi

— tzatzachiuhqui[5] in itequiuh melio

— chiquiuhchiuhqui in itequiuh onme tomi

— petlachiuhqui in itequiuh ome tomi

— quauhtepoznamacac[6] in itequiuh ome tomi

— tepozpitzqui[7] in itequiuh ce tomi

---

[1]AGN, Tierras 1735, exp. 2, ff. 117, 118, and 121. On ff. 149-152 are Spanis.. translations of sections 1 and 4, dating from 1681. The dates are unspecified, but seem to fall within the lifetime of the first don Juan de Guzmán, who died in 1571. Sections 1 and 2 appear on the same page, written in the same hand. Section 3 is separate but adjacent. Section 4 is located at some distance and is in a quite different hand and style. We cannot say whether the assessments are for different years or not, nor do we know the interval of payment; section 3 speaks of a yearly payment, while section 4 mentions payment every 30 days.

We have presumed that each category of taxpayers is a group rather than a single individual (though conceivably some of the groups consist of only one individual);

1.

Here is written the market tax paid in gold.

— The San Agustín wood dealers begin it; their tax is 5 tomines.

— The Atliztaca wood dealers' tax is 2 tomines.
— The Atonco wood dealers' tax is 1 tomín.
— The medicine sellers' tax is 1 tomín.
— The garment[2] makers' tax is 2 tomines.
— The Mexica chile sellers' tax is 2 tomines.
— The color sellers'[3] tax is 4 tomines.
— The clay-vessel makers' tax is ½ tomín.
— The broom sellers' tax is 2 tomines.
— The stewpot makers' tax is 2 tomines.
— The pine-torch splitters' tax is 4 tomines.
— The fish sellers' tax is 1 tomín.
— The tobacco sellers' tax is 1 tomín.
— The griddle makers' tax is 2 tomines.
— The tamale sellers' tax is 3 tomines.
— The smoking-tube[4] makers' tax is 1 tomín.
— The warping-frame[5] makers' tax is ½ tomín.
— The basket makers' tax is 2 tomines.
— The mat makers' tax is 2 tomines.
— The bark-clay-concoction[6] sellers' tax is 2 tomines.
— The metal[7] workers' tax is 1 tomín.

---

singulars predominate in sections 1 and 2, plurals in section 3, and both appear almost equally in section 4. The Spanish translation has only plurals.

[2]*Chamalo* = *chamarro*, a Spanish word for a coarse (upper) garment. The *chamalochiuhqui* may be the same trade as the *ychcamixachiuhqui* in section 4.

[3]*Florentine Codex*, Bk. 10, p. 77, describes the *chiquipantlacatl* as a displayer of wares on a large basket, a seller of colors.

[4]*Florentine Codex*, Bk. 10, p. 88.

[5]I.e., the instrument used in weaving. See *Florentine Codex*, Bk. 2, p. 128.

[6]*Florentine Codex*, Bk. 11, p. 109. In the Spanish translation, *cascara de encina*.

[7]See Doc. 8, n. 7. At this early time, the metal concerned could be equally well copper or iron.

— tlatechiuhqui[8] in itequiuh ce tomi
— ontlachiuhqui in itequiuh melio
— malacachiuhqui in itequiuh centomi
— yztacapan in itequiuh onme tomi
— tlantlapanquin[9] in itequiuh centomi
— tepanecapan acalpan[10] in itequiuh onme tomin
— mexicapan acalpan in itequiuh centomi ipan mellio
— catellachiuhqui in itequiuh chiquacentomin
— tochominamacac[11] in itequiuh naui tomi
— oztomecatl tetitlacalque in itequiuh onme tomi
— mixcouac oztomecan in itequiuh onme tomi
— oztomecan atocon in itequiuh centomi
— oztomecan tequemecan in itequiuh ce tomi
— tominamacac atoiac in itequiuh melio
— oztomeca atoiac in itequiuh melio
— ytzcopeuhqui[12] in itequiuh ce tomi
— palnamacac in itequiuh centomi ic mocouh acallecuextli[13]

— ivinamacac in itequiuh ce tomi
— chienecuilloque[14] coiouaca centomi
— ytztapalapan chienecuilo in itequiuh centomi
— nacanamacac in itequiuh melio
— mecapalnamacac in itequiuh melio
— poquiyenamacac[15] in itequiuh melio
— Ynnomocepouh in teocuitlatl chicuenpexo inpa chiquace tomi ipa melio

2.

nican icuiliuhtoc in tiaquiztequitl innic otlacalaquilli in teocuitlatl
— copeualtia in quauhnecuilloque coiouacan ioa Sanct agustin cololuia in itequiuh opexo ipan ome tomi ipa melio

---

[8]Literally, "maker of the edge or border of something." We have presumed that clothing borders are meant because of the reference to the selling of *cuetentli* and *tilmateṅtli* in a similar market in Mexico City. See Jacqueline de Durand-Forest, "Cambios económicos y moneda entre los Aztecas," *Estudios de Cultura Nahuatl*, IX, 123.

[9]*Tlȧtlapanqui*, "breaker of something," seems to be intended here, as in other instances in this document. What is being broken is unspecified, though doubtless understood at the time. The Spanish translator ventured *hacheros*, "woodcutters."

[10]The Spanish translator gives Acalpan as a place name.

[11]See *Florentine Codex*, Bk. 10, p. 77.

[12]The name of this trade appears twice. In the first compound, we identify the verb

— The cloth-border[8] makers' tax is 1 tomín.
— The cane makers' tax is ½ tomín.
— The spindle makers' tax is 1 tomín.
— Iztacapan's tax is 2 tomines.
— The breakers'[9] tax is 1 tomín.
— The tax of the Tepaneca boat people[10] is 2 tomines.
— The tax of the Mexica boat people is 1½ tomines.
— The candlemakers' tax is 6 tomines.
— The rabbit-hair[11] sellers' tax is 4 tomines.
— The tax of the merchants who live in Tetitlan is 2 tomines.
— The Mixcoac merchants' tax is 2 tomines.
— The Atonco merchants' tax is 1 tomín.
— The Tequemeca merchants' tax is 1 tomín.
— The Atoyac hide sellers' tax is ½ tomín.
— The Atoyac merchants' tax is ½ tomín.
— The obsidian-blade makers'[12] tax is 1 tomín.
— The clay-dye sellers' tax is 1 tomín; with it a heavy reed mat[13] was bought.
— The feather sellers' tax is 1 tomín.
— The Coyoacan chia[14] dealers' tax is 1 tomín.
— The Iztapalapa chia dealers' tax is 1 tomín.
— The meat sellers' tax is ½ tomín.
— The tump-line sellers' tax is ½ tomín.
— The cigar[15] sellers' tax is ½ tomín.

When totaled, the gold is 8 pesos and 6½ tomines.

2.

Here is written the market tax which has been paid in gold.

— The wood dealers of Coyoacan and San Agustín begin it. Their tax amounts to 2 pesos, 2½ tomines.

---

with *cocopeui*, "for dandruff to fall," i.e., "to flake." The verb of the second compound does not appear in the dictionaries, but the form of *itzuipeuhqui* can be found in the *Florentine Codex*, Bk. 10, p. 85 for the act of making obsidian blades.

[13]One might expect this form to be the result of compounding *acalli*, "boat," and *tlacuextli* "mat." However, the context seems to make *acatl*, "reed," preferable as the first element despite the slight grammatical irregularity. Compare with the reed mat bought below at the end of section 3.

[14]Chia is a member of the sage family, whose seeds were used extensively for food.

[15]See *Florentine Codex*, Bk. 10, p. 88. The Spanish translator gives *los que benden pebetes*.

— chamalochiuhqui in itequiuh ome tomi
— chilnamacac in itequiuh ome tomi
— chiquipatlacan in itequiuh onme tomi
— çoquichiuhqui in itequiuh melio
— ochpauaznamacac in itequiuh ome tomi
— cochiuhqui in itequiuh ome tomi
— ocotlapaqui in itequiuh naui tomi
— michnamacac in itequiuh ce tomi
— picienamacac in itequiuh ce tomi
— ytzcopeuhqui in itequiuh ce tomi
— palnamacac in itequiuh ce tomi
— comalchiuhqui in itequiuh ome tomi
— acaquauhchiuhqui ce tomi
— cocoiochiuhqui[16] in itequiuh melio
— tzatzachiuhqui in itequiuh melio
— chiquiuhchiuhqui in itequiuh ome tomi
— petlachiuhqui in itequiuh onme tomi
— quauhtepoznamacac in itequiuh ome tomi
— tepozpitzqui in itequiuh centomi
— tlatechiuhqui in itequiuh ce tomi ipa melio
— iztacapan in itequiuh ome tomin
— tlatlapaqui in itequiuh ce tomi
— mexicapa acalpan in itequiuh ome tomi
— cantelachiuhqui in itequiuh chiquace tomi
— tochominamacac in itequiuh naui tomi
— mixcouac oztomeca in itequiuh ome tomi
— oztomeca tetitlacalque in itenquiuh ome tomi
— oztomeca antoco in itequiuh ce tomi
— tequemecan ozt[eocamo]ca[17] in itequiuh centomi
— tepannecapa acalpa in itequiuh ce tomi
— ytztapalapa chienecuillo in itequiuh ome tomi
— yvinamacac yn itequiuh ce tomi
— chienecuilo coyouacan yn itequiuh centomi
— nacanamacac yn itequiuh melio
— poquiyenamacac yn itequiuh melio
— mecapalnamacac in itequiuh melio

Ynnomocepouh yn teocuitlatl chicuinapexo ynpa macuilli ypa melio

[16]We derive *cocoio-* from *coyolli.* Compare with the *coyolli* sold in Mexico City's market (Durand-Forest, "Cambios económicos," p. 124).

— The garment makers' tax is 2 tomines.
— The chile sellers' tax is 2 tomines.
— The color sellers' tax is 2 tomines.
— The clay-vessel makers' tax is ½ tomín.
— The broom sellers' tax is 2 tomines.
— The stewpot makers' tax is 2 tomines.
— The pine-torch splitters' tax is 4 tomines.
— The fish sellers' tax is 1 tomín.
— The tobacco sellers' tax is 1 tomín.
— The obsidian-blade makers' tax is 1 tomín.
— The clay-dye sellers' tax is 1 tomín.
— The griddle makers' tax is 2 tomines.
— The smoking-tube makers' tax is 1 tomín.
— The small bell[16] makers' tax is ½ tomín.
— The warping-frame makers' tax is ½ tomín.
— The basket makers' tax is 2 tomines.
— The mat makers' tax is 2 tomines.
— The bark-clay-concoction sellers' tax is 2 tomines.
— The metal workers' tax is 1 tomín.
— The cloth-border makers' tax is 1½ tomines.
— Iztacapan's tax is 2 tomines.
— The breakers' tax is 1 tomín.
— The Mexica boat people's tax is 2 tomines.
— The candlemakers' tax is 6 tomines.
— The rabbit-hair sellers' tax is 4 tomines.
— The Mixcoac merchants' tax is 2 tomines.
— The tax of the merchants who live in Tetitlan is 2 tomines.
— The Atonco merchants' tax is 1 tomín.
— The Tequemeca merchants' tax is 1 tomín.
— The Tepaneca boat people's tax is 1 tomín.
— The Iztapalapa chia dealers' tax is 2 tomines.
— The feather sellers' tax is 1 tomín.
— The Coyoacan chia dealers' tax is 1 tomín.
— The meat sellers' tax is ½ tomín.
— The cigar sellers' tax is ½ tomín.
— The tump-line sellers' tax is ½ tomín.

When totaled, the gold is 9 pesos and 5½ tomines.

---

[17]For *oztomeca*.

3.

Nican icuilliuhtoc inniconpehua in ce xiuitl in tiaquiztequitl innic cepa momacan in tlacatl in totlatocauh

— Conpeualtia quauhnecuilloque intomin onpexo inpa chiquace tomi
— tochominamacaque in itequiuh macuiltomin
— catellanamacaque in itequiuh chiquacentomin
— oncotlapaque in itequiuh naui tomin
— Sancta maria tlacan chiquipatlacan in itequiuh naui tomin
— auatlatzaianamacaque[18] in itequiuh iei tomin
— ychchamallochiuhqui in itequiuh onme tomin
— mexicon chilnamacaque in itequiuh ome tomin
— ochpauaznamacaquen in itequiuh onme tomin
— connamacaque in itequiuh ome tomin
— atolnamacaque in itequiuh onme tomin
— chiquiuhchiuhque in itequiuh onme tomin
— petlachiuhque in itequiuh ome tomin
— quauhtepoznamacaque in itequiuh onme tomin
— oztomecan in itequiuh ome tomin
— yztacapan in itequiuh ome tomin
— chienecuilloque itztapalapan in itequiuh onme tomin
— acalpan tepanecapan centomin
— iztatlapanque in itequiuh centomin
— tlatechiuhque in itequiuh centomin
— tepozpitzqui in itequiuh centomi
— oztomecatl nexpilcon in itequiuh centomin
— chienecuiloque tepanecapan in itequiuh centomi
— ihuinamacaque in itequiuh centomin
— acaquauhnamacaquen in itequiuh centomin
— palnamacaquen in itequiuh centomin
— itzcopeuhquen in itequiuh centomin
— picienamacaquen Yn itequiuh centomin
— michnamacaquen in itequiuh centomin
— panamacac in itequiuh centomin
— tecuitlanamacac[19] in itequiuh centomin
— molcaxnamacac in itequiuh mellio
— cocoiochiuhqui in itequiuh mellio
— tzatzachiuhquin in itequiuh melio

---

[18]See *Florentine Codex*, Bk. 11, pp. 108-109.

[19]According to Santamaria (*Diccionario de Mejicanismos*, pp. 42, 1020), *tecuitlatl*

3.

Here is written how one year's market tax begins that is given one time to our sir ruler.

— The wood dealers begin it. Their money is 2 pesos and 6 tomines.
— The rabbit-hair sellers' tax is 5 tomines.
— The candle sellers' tax is 6 tomines.
— The pine-torch splitters' tax is 4 tomines.
— The tax of the Santa María people who sell colors is 4 tomines.
— The split-oak[18] sellers' tax is 3 tomines.
— The maguey-garment makers' tax is 2 tomines.
— The Mexico City chile sellers' tax is 2 tomines.
— The broom sellers' tax is 2 tomines.
— The stewpot sellers' tax is 2 tomines.
— The maize-gruel sellers' tax is 2 tomines.
— The basket makers' tax is 2 tomines.
— The mat makers' tax is 2 tomines.
— The bark-clay-concoction sellers' tax is 2 tomines.
— The merchants' tax is 2 tomines.
— Iztacapan's tax is 2 tomines.
— The Iztapalapa chia dealers' tax is 2 tomines.
— The Tepaneca boat people, 1 tomín.
— The salt breakers' tax is 1 tomín.
— The cloth-border makers' tax is 1 tomín.
— The metal workers' tax is 1 tomín.
— The Nexpilco merchants' tax is 1 tomín.
— The Tepaneca chia dealers' tax is 1 tomín.
— The feather sellers' tax is 1 tomín.
— The smoking-tube sellers' tax is 1 tomín.
— The clay-dye sellers' tax is 1 tomín.
— The obsidian-blade makers' tax is 1 tomín.
— The tobacco sellers' tax is 1 tomín.
— The fish sellers' tax is 1 tomín.
— The medicine sellers' tax is 1 tomín.
— The lake-scum[19] sellers' tax is 1 tomín.
— The mortar (and pestle) sellers' tax is ½ tomín.
— The small bell makers' tax is ½ tomín.
— The warping-frame makers' tax is ½ tomín.

---

is a kind of *ahuauhtli* or water fly eggs floating on the lake surface and forming an edible scum.

— otlachiuhquin in itequiuh mellio
— caueçochiuhquin[20] in itequiuh mellio
— mecapalchiuhqui in itenquiuh melio
— poquiienamacac in itequiuh mellio
— nacatl quinamacan in itequiuh melio
— mallacachiuhqui in itequiuh mellio
Auh in omocepouh matlacpexo inpa naui tomi inpa melio
Auh in mexicanpa acalpa in itequiuh centomin ic mocouh quiiotlecuextli oca monec in ocan ca Juez atoiac oztomecan opa itequiuh ce tomin ic mocouh xochinacaztli[21] melio auh ic mocouh ce melio cuetlaxtli ic mochichiuh inquauhchiquiuh in fray juan lobez

4.

nican pouhtoc yn tiaquizhuaque yc tequiti
— Conpeualtia tlayeualli[22] yn nepapa tlayeualli yc necin macuylli domi
— chiquipantlaca naui domi quimana
— tlaxinqui totoltepec quimana domin ome
— tochomipa quimana yey domi
— quauhnecuylloque tetzcolca quimana ome domi
— mallacachiuhqui atliztacan quimana domi ce
— atliztacan cactzoc quimana ce domi
— abçolco ychcamixachiuhqui quimana ome domi
— tenexnamacac nexpilco ychan quimana ome domi
— abçolco picienamacac quimana ce domi
— acalpantlaca coyoaque quimana ome domi
— acalpantlaca mexicapan quimana ome domi
— abçolco chilnamacac quimana ce domy
— abçolco ocotlapanqui quimana ome domi
— abçolco michnecuylo quimana ce domi
— abçolco cantelachiuhque quimana macuyli domi
— nexpilco chiquiuhchiuhquen quimana ome domi
— nexpilco malacachiuhqui quimana ce domi
— nexpilco acaquauhchivhque quimana ce domi

---

[20]See the item *caveçon*, garment collars, being sold in the Mexico City market (Durand-Forest, "Cambios económicos," p. 123).

[21]An aromatic herb used with cacao. See Hernández, *Historia Natural*, II, 67-68.

[22]In early seventeenth-century cofradía records in the Museo Nacional de Antropología, Fondo Franciscano, Vol. 129, f. 1 ff., *tlayehualli* is equated with the money and

— The cane makers' tax is ½ tomín.
— The collar[20] makers' tax is ½ tomín.
— The tump-line makers' tax is ½ tomín.
— The cigar sellers' tax is ½ tomín.
— The tax of those who sell meat is ½ tomín.
— The spindle makers' tax is ½ tomín.
And when totaled it is 10 pesos and 4½ tomines.

And with the tax of the Mexica boat people, 1 tomín, was bought a heavy reed mat that was needed where the judge is; as to the Atoyac merchants' tax, 1 tomín, with ½ tomín was bought ear-flower herb,[21] and with ½ tomín was bought a cured hide with which Fray Juan López' wooden basket was outfitted.

4.

Here is the account of what the market stewards pay as tax.
— The [contributions][22] begin it. Among the different [contributions] appear 5 tomines.
— The color sellers give 4 tomines.
— The carpenters of Totoltepec give 2 tomines.
— The rabbit-hair sellers give 3 tomines.
— The Tetzcolca wood dealers give 2 tomines.
— The Atliztaca spindle makers give 1 tomín.
— The Atliztaca sandal makers give 1 tomín.
— The Apçolco maguey-fiber-shirt makers give 2 tomines.
— The lime sellers who live in Nexpilco give 2 tomines.
— The Apçolco tobacco sellers give 1 tomín.
— The Coyoacan boat people give 2 tomines.
— The Mexica boat people give 2 tomines.
— The Apçolco chile sellers give 1 tomín.
— The Apçolco pine-torch splitters give 2 tomines.
— The Apçolco fish dealers give 1 tomín.
— The Apçolco candlemakers give 5 tomines.
— The Nexpilco basket makers give 2 tomines.
— The Nexpilco spindle makers give 1 tomín.
— The Nexpilco smoking-tube makers give 1 tomín.

---

cacao donated by members to maintain the organization. It apparently means "contribution," "offering," or the like, and is used in these records wherever Spanish would use *limosna*. The thrust of the term would seem to be "something asked for"; see Molina's *yeua*, "mendigar."

— nexpilco quauhnecuylloque quimana ome domi
— yzquiteca yztatlamana quimana ome domi
— yzquitecan ytzvepeuhque[12] quimana ce domi
— cacalachiuhque quimana ce domi
— aticpac quavhnecuylloque quimana ce domi
— aticpaccalque quimana ce domi tzatzachiuhque
— aticpac otlachiuhque quimana ome domi
— aticpac tepozpitzque quimana ome domi
— aticpac vztomeca quimana medio
— atoyac palnamacac quimana ce domi
— atoyac quauhtepotznamacac quimana ome domi
— atoyac chimalatl[23] cacavanamacaque quimana yei domi

nican ycuylliuhtoque yn acovic[24] yn intianquiztequiuh
— mixcovac comalchiuhque quimana ce domi
— mixcovac vztomecan quimana yey domi
— ocotlapanque acovica quimana ome domi
— atonco petlachiuhque quimana ome domi
— atonco tlatenchiuhque quimana ome domi
— atonco cactzoque quimana ce domi
— San Geronimo tlaxinque quimana ome domi
— tetitlan mallacachivhque quimana ce domi
— atonco ochpanvaznamacac quimana ce domi
— tamalnamacaque quimana ce domi
— vztomeca acovic quimana medio

Yn acovictlaca yn intianquiztequiuh ome peso ypan ey domi

Auh yn tlalnavac[24] ynnintianquiztequiuh chicome peso ypan ome domi

Yn ye mochi omocenpouh chicuhenavi pesu ypa macuyli domi yn quimomaquillitivy señor don Juan yn cenpovaltica ommat[lac]tica yn tianquiztequitl

---

[23]Literally, "shield-water." Many compounds ending in *-atl* refer to beverages, and we presume that this is one, though unidentified.

[24]The terms *acouic*, "upwards," and *tlalnauac*, "next to the land," were apparently used to designate the two major subdivisions of the province of Coyoacan. The *aco-*

— The Nexpilco wood dealers give 2 tomines.
— The Izquiteca salt dealers give 2 tomines.
— The Izquiteca obsidian-blade makers[12] give 1 tomín.
— The clay-bell makers give 1 tomín.
— The Aticpac wood dealers give 1 tomín.
— The warping-frame makers who live in Aticpac give 1 tomín.
— The Aticpac cane makers give 2 tomines.
— The Aticpac metal workers give 2 tomines.
— The Aticpac merchants give ½ tomín.
— The Atoyac clay-dye sellers give 1 tomín.
— The Atoyac bark-clay-concoction sellers give 2 tomines.
— The Atoyac chimalatl[23] cacao sellers give 3 tomines.

Here is written the market tax of the upper region.[24]
— The Mixcoac griddle makers give 1 tomín.
— The Mixcoac merchants give 3 tomines.
— The upper-region pine-torch splitters give 2 tomines.
— The Atonco mat makers give 2 tomines.
— The Atonco cloth-border makers give 2 tomines.
— The Atonco sandal makers give 2 tomines.
— The San Jerónimo carpenters give 2 tomines.
— The Tetitlan spindle makers give 1 tomín.
— The Atonco broom sellers give 1 tomín.
— The tamale sellers give 1 tomín.
— The upper-region merchants give ½ tomín.
The upper-region-people's market tax is 2 pesos and 3 tomines.

And the nearby-land's[24] market tax is 7 pesos and 2 tomines.

When all added together, it is 9 pesos and 5 tomines which are given to señor don Juan every 30 (days) as the market tax.

---

uic may be taken quite literally, since all *acouic* towns that we have located are indeed in the hill country. As to *tlalnauac*, we are not sure whether the basic meaning is "lower" (near the ground) or "central" (near the traditional lands of Coyoacan). See also the use of these terms in Doc. 26.

26. Some perquisites of don Juan de Guzmán, governor of Coyoacan, mid-sixteenth century[1]

1.

ma moyecteneva yn itocatçin in totemaquixticatçin yn iesu xp̄o Amen

nehuatl ni don juan combernador yn coyovacan nicpiellia in iatçin yn itepetçin yn to^o yn d[ios] ca nican ca amixpantçinco nictlallia yn anquimopillia ynnaltepetl in coyohuacan yn a[n]tlatoque yn anpipiltin in antetecuhtin commonequiltia in totlatocauh yn señor visorey ioan ynnamotatçin yn p^e vicario yn momanaz yn tansancion yn coiovacan in tlatocatlacua[lli] yn nimacoz in monequi momoztlaye hetetl totolli yoan onquauhtanatli tlaolli ioan centçont[li] cacahuatl yoan matlacpovalli chilli yoan centlatlapantli[2] yztatl yoan tomatl aiovachtli yoan matlactli tlapixqui chycuei tezqui chycuacen tlamamalli cuavitl yoan cavallo tlacualli çacatl macuillamamalli yn valcallaquiz in momoztlaye yn cenca monequi

— Ioan monequi momavizmatiz nauhcan in milli ynic cecni ocoçacapan ynic ocan milpolco yniquexcan coiotleuhco ynic nauhcan tochco monequi cenca ypan tlatolloz inic mochyhuaz

— Ioan monequi cecni momanaz calli ycal yez yn ton juan quichivillizque yn macehualtin ypan tla[toz]

— Ioan monequi ytech pohuizque matlactli tlaxinque no matlactli tetçotçonque yn tleyn monequiz quichyuazque yehuantin

— Ioan yn tianquiztli ytech poviz yn don juan tecpancalli ytech pohuiz

— Ioan in ixquich yn toltecca yn tlachichiuhque monequi çan oncan cenpohuizque yn te[c]pan in tlein monequiz quichivazque

— Ioan monequi chicuhnauhpovalticca oume domin macoz yn don juan quimacaz yn ixquichtin macehualtin ynic tlatocatiz opan[3] ce xivitl macoz

---

[1]AGN, Tierras 1735, exp. 2, ff. 119, 114, 115, 136, 137, 123, 124, 125, 129. Date c. 1560-70. Don Juan was also, indeed primarily, *tlatoani* or traditional ruler of Coyoacan. The seven parts of Doc. 26 are related, but are individual pieces, not in any certain order, and possibly not from the same year, though parts 2 and 3 are closely

1.

Praised be the name of our redeemer Jesus Christ, Amen.

I don Juan, governor of Coyoacan, who guard our lord God's city for him, I set forth here before you, you who guard the town of Coyoacan, you rulers, nobles, and lords: our ruler the lord viceroy and your father the vicar wish the assessment to be issued for the Coyoacan ruler's provisions that are to be given to me, needed daily: three hens; two baskets of shelled maize; 400 cacao beans; 200 chiles; one piece[2] of salt; tomatoes; gourd seeds; 10 (men to act as) guards; 8 (women to be) grinders of maize; 6 loads of wood; grass for horse fodder, five loads, to be delivered daily, very much needed.

— And it is required that fields in four places be attended to, the first at Ocoçacapan, the second at Milpolco, the third at Coyotleuhco, the fourth at Tochco. It is necessary to urge it greatly so that it will be done.

— And it is required that a separate house be built, to be don Juan's house; the commoners are to make it for him. It is to be urged.

— And it is required that ten carpenters be attached to him, and also ten stonemasons; they are to do what is needed.

— And the market is to pertain to don Juan, is to pertain to the royal household.

— And as to all the artisans and craftsmen, it is required that they all be attached to the royal house to do what is needed.

— And it is required that every 180 days, two tomines be given to don Juan; all the commoners will give it so that he will rule; it is to be given twice[3] a year.

---

associated, as are parts 5 and 6. On ff. 148-157 of the same *expediente* are Spanish translations, dating from 1681, of all parts except the third.

[2]See Molina's entry *centlatlapantli*, "un pedazo de algo."

[3]*Opan* presumably represents standard *oppa*, "twice."

Oca iz catqui yn cenca monequi yn mochivaz cuix iuhqui yez cuix noço amo ma ypan ximononotçacan yn amehuantin Residoresme yoan amalcaldesme tehuatl di don pablo tiçacancatl yoan tevatl ti don luys tecuhtli acuecuexco yoan tehuatl ti juan tlaillotlac[4] yn amevantin yn ammacuillixtin[5] ximononotçacan ximocentlallican yn acaçomo iuhqui yez yn anoço yuhquiez ca ia isquich yn amixpantçinco niquitohuan

2.

Don juan ytech poui tepantlaca[6] centecpantli ipan chicuhnaui tlacatl ioan ycnociuatl

— Chimaliztaca cate chicome tlacatl
— Atlauhcamilpan chicome tlacatl
— mixcouac navi tlacatl
— Xochitenco navi tlacatl
— Chinancaltonco cate nahui tlacatl
— san hieronimo cate matlactlomome tlacatl
— tlaçoyiacan cate caxtolli omey tlacatl
— Vueycalco cate chicuey tlacatl ome telpopochtotonti
— Auacatitlan cate centecpantli once
— Acopilco cate centecpantli omacuilli chicuacentlacatl telpopochtotonti
— pachiocan cate ome tlacatl
— chimalpan cate navi tlacatl
— Amantlan cate chicuacentlacatl
— Couatzonco matlactlomey tlacatl
— Tecouac chicuacentlacatl
— Acolco nauhtecpantli tlacatl
— Tlamimilolpan ontecpantli omatlactli tlacatl once
— Çacamolpan cate centecpantli chicuhnavi tlacatl
— Ocotitlan centecpantli onmatlactli tlacatl vi telpopochtotontin
— tepechp[an] cate chicuacentlacatl
— Auh in ie mochi mocenpova caxtoltecpantli ipan nauhtecpantli iuan ycnociuatl

3.

In elimiquizque in sant agustin çacamozque in imaceualoan señor don juan compeua[l]tia xiuhtlan çacamoz ioan çacamolpan ioan

[4]A title for a high official or judge, as well as apparently being a name in this case.

Here is what is very necessary to be done; confer together whether it is to be thus or not, you councilmen and alcaldes, you, don Pablo Çacancatl and you, don Luis, lord of Acuecuexco, and you, Juan Tlaillotlac,[4] all five of you[5] consult and determine whether it is to be well done or not. This is all I say to you.

2.

There belong to don Juan 29 men who are [people of his household],[6] and widow[s].

— At Chimaliztaca are 7 men.
— At Atlauhcamilpan, 7 men.
— At Mixcouac, 4 men.
— At Xochitenco, 4 men.
— At Chinancaltonco are 4 men.
— At San Jerónimo are 12 men.
— At Tlaçoyiacan are 18 men.
— At Hueycalco are 8 men and 2 youths.
— At Auacatitlan are 21.
— At Acopilco are 25 and 6 youths.

— At Pachiocan are 2 men.
— At Chimalpan are 4 men.
— At Amantlan are 6 men.
— At Couatzonco, 13 men.
— At Tecouac, 6 men.
— At Acolco, 80 men.
— At Tlamimilolpan, 51 men.
— At Çacamolpan are 29 men.
— At Ocotitlan, 30 men and 6 youths.
— At Tepechpan are 6 men.

And it all totals 380, and widow[s].

3.

The vassals of lord don Juan who are to work the land in San Agustín, and clear the ground, they begin to clear the ground at

[5]The five presumably including some unmentioned councilmen.

ocotitlan ioan cou[a]tzonco ioan tepantlacatl[6] ioan auapoltitlan-tlaca in chicomiluitl inpan icaz diego

— Auh in acopilcotlaca quimacazque in iquauh p^{o} de uercala in ixopetl in iquauhtec in chicomilhuitl inpan icaz in uitznacatl

— Auh in atlauhcamilpantlaca tetlacualtizque in chicomilhuitl ic nemizque domingo

— Auh in temiltique in cimatlan ioan mixcouac quipizque trigo in Atepocaapan inpan icaz juan tlanauaua in chicomiluitl

— Auh in tlachichiuhque ioan tlapanauique helimiquizque quelimiquizque in ixquich in tlalcoualli in chachaiacatoc quipeualtizque neçaualcaltitla inic chicomilhuitl inpan icaz Anton vixtopolcatl

— chimaliztaque quiuicatinemizque in helimiquizque in cuacuaueque chicomilhuitl

4.

memoria tlalnauac[8] yn itlaltzin tlatuhuani don Juan gouer^{or} ni[can] pouhtoc ynic cecni onca ompehua

— tecpan tlacomolco ynic huiac lx quavitl ynic patlahuac xxxv quav[itl]

— tepancallon ypan mani vevecalli[9] ynic huiac lxiiii quavitl auh ynic patlahuac onpoualli quavitl

— te[c]panquiyauac Jular[10] ynic viac xi ynic patlauac x ypan cenmatl[11]

— Acuecuexco vevetlalli[9] ynic viac Lv ynic patlahuac xxxvii quahuitl

— tletlepillocan tlillac ueuetlalli ynic huiac lxxxxiiii quavitl ynic patlauac tlatzintlan xx auh quapitzaton ça viii quavitl

---

[6]Possibly for *tecpantlaca*, "palace people," or related to *tepanecatl*, "palace inhabitant" (Siméon, p. 442); or it might mean "supervisors," as *tepan* is given in Molina as "sobre alguno, o sobre algunos."

[7]We view the translation of this whole paragraph as highly provisional. One major ambiguity is whether the series that makes up the body of the paragraph is to be interpreted as a list of people from certain places, or as a list of the places at which the work is to be performed. In the text we have chosen the former alternative. We are fully aware that this necessitates a break in the interpretation without a corresponding break in the external form of the list; that is, the last two items in the series are clearly groups of people, not places.

A second problem is the interpretation of *chicomiluitl*. Literally, a number + day without further modifier should mean duration, while the addition of *yc* would give

Xiuhtlan and Çacamolpan and Ocotitlan and Couatzonco, and the [people of the household],[6] and the Auapoltitlan people (will clear the ground) [for one week];[7] Diego is to be over them.

— And the Acopilco people are to give Pedro de Vergara his wood—his beams, his logs—[for one week]; Huitznacatl is to be over them.

— And the people of Atlauhcamilpan are to feed people [for one week]; Domingo will take care of it.

— And those who cultivate the fields at Cimatlan and Mixcoac are to reap wheat at Atepocaapan [for a week]; Juan Tlanauaua will be over them.

— And the artisans and [advantaged people] will farm; they are to work all the purchased land [which lies scattered about]; they are to commence at Neçaualcaltitlan [the seventh day]; Antón Huixtopolcatl is to be over them.

— The people of Chimaliztaca are to guide the oxen working the land for 7 days.

4.

Memorandum: the lands of the ruler and governor don Juan [in the lower region][8] are recorded here, beginning first with:

— At Tlacomolco [at the palace], 60 rods long, 35 rods wide.

— At Tepancallon, with an [ancestral][9] house on it, 64 rods long and 40 rods wide.

— A lot [outside the palace], 11 (rods) long, 10 (rods) and one braza wide.[11]

— At Acuecuexco an [ancestral] field, 55 rods long, 37 wide.

— At Tletlepillocan and Tlillac an [ancestral][9] field, 94 rods long, 20 wide below and narrowing to only 8 rods at the top.

---

an ordinal meaning. We have followed this in our translations in this section, though we are as yet unable to envision the actual process of rotation of tasks.

[8]For a discussion of the pair of terms *tlalnauac* and *acouic*, see Doc. 25, n. 24.

[9]*Ueuecalli* and *ueuetlalli* seem analogous special terms in which the *ueue*, rather than being literally "old," means something like "traditional" or "patrimonial," something thought of as having adhered, perhaps to the ethnic group, perhaps to the royal line, for a longer time than other houses or lands. See Molina's entry *ueuetlatquitl*, "patrimony."

[10]*Jular* = *solar*.

[11]The braza is here clearly smaller than the *quauitl*, yet apparently larger than half. Perhaps the *quauitl* is the ten-foot measure mentioned in Doc. 9 as being observed by the Coyoacan council; the relation would then be about 6 to 10.

— atlhuelican tecpancalli ypan mani ynic huiac xxvii ypan cenma[tl] auh ynic patlauac xxiiii quavitl

— atluelican tlacopantonco lxxxiiii quavitl ynic patlahuac tlatzint[lan] xxxvii auh quapitzaton ynic patlauac xxv

— xochac huehuetlalli ynic viac Cxi quavitl ynic patlauac tlatzint[lan] ochpantencopa xxxviii auh quapitzaton ynic patlavac xxvi

— quauhcuezcontitlan chinanpan[12] ynic huiac Cxlix ynic patlauac tlatz[in]tlan Cxxiii quavitl auh quapitzaton ynic patlauac xcviii

— amantlan chinanpan ynic huiac Clxxxi ynic patlauac Cxl

— Atecontonco chinanpan ynic huiac xcv auh ynic patlauac x

— Couatzonco ynic huiac matlacpoualli ça necoc yuhqui

— tecouac tescalli[13] ynic viac Cxxx auh ynic patlavac xxvii auh yn tlalmilli yquac tescalli ic viac xxx ic patlauac xx[v]

tlalcoualli nican pouhtoc

— tecpancaltitlan xocotitlan ynic viac xvi quavitl yc patlavac xiiii quav[itl]

— tecpanquiyauac teçoncaltitlan[14] ynic viac xviiii quavitl yc patlauac vii quavit[l]

— Acuecuesco amaxac ynic viac chiquace quavitl ynic patlahuac iii quavit[l]

— çanno oncan acuecuesco ynic uiac vi ynic patlavac v quavitl

— nespilco yquiyauac p^o^ couacuech ynic viac xxiiii ic patlauac xiii

— çan ye oncan nespilco ynic viac vii ynic patlauac iiii

— atenco yquiyauac mecatzin yc viac vi ynic patlauac iii

— çan ye oncan atactli ytech ynic viac ix ic patlauac v

— sandiago[15] yquiyauac vexotitlan ic viac xiii yc patlahuac iii

— san aug^tin^ teocalçoltitlan[16] ynic viac C ynic patlauac xxxiiii quavi[tl]

— abçolco chiquiuhchiuhcan[17] inic viac xv ic patlauac x quavitl

— tecpanquiyauac atlvelican ynic huiac xii ynic patlauac iii quavitl

---

[12]There was a place called Chinampan in the Coyoacan region. The large size of the fields seems inconsistent with the concept of the "floating garden" type of chinampa, to which we have indeed seen no reference in our documents. The word could mean enclosure or quarter as well (Siméon).

[13]Probably some of the volcanic deposits known today as the Pedregal. The Spanish translation has "tecohuac que es en el pedregal."

— At Atluelican, with a palace on it, 27 rods plus one braza long, and 24 rods wide.

— At Atluelican, at Tlacopantonco, 84 rods (long), 37 wide below and narrowing to 25 wide above.

— At Xochac an [ancestral] field, 111 rods long, 38 wide below, toward the edge of the main road, and narrowing to 26 wide above.

— At Quauhcuezcontitlan, [at Chinampan?],[12] 149 rods long, 123 wide below, and narrowing to 98 wide above.

— At Amantlan, [at Chinampan?], 181 (rods) long, 140 wide.

— At Atecontonco, [at Chinampan?], 95 (rods) long, and 10 wide.

— At Couatzonco, 200 (rods) long, the same wide.

— At Tecoac [rocky land], 130 (rods) long and 27 wide, and the cultivated fields above the rocky land,[13] 30 long, 25 wide.

The purchased lands are recorded here.

— [Next to the palace] at Xocotitlan, 16 rods long, 14 rods wide.

— [Outside the palace] at Teçoncaltitlan,[14] 19 rods long, 7 rods wide.

— At Acuecuexco, at Amaxac, 6 rods long, 3 rods wide.

— Also there at Acuecuexco, 6 rods long, 5 wide.

— At Nexpilco [facing the place of] Pedro Couacuech, 24 (rods) long, 13 wide.

— Also there at Nexpilco, 7 (rods) long, 4 wide.

— At Atenco [facing the place of] Mecatzin, 6 (rods) long, 3 wide.

— Also there next to the reservoir, 9 (rods) long, 5 wide.

— [Facing Santiago],[15] at Uexotitlan, 13 (rods) long, 3 wide.

— At San Agustín, at Teocalçoltitlan,[16] 100 rods long, 34 wide.

— At Apçolco, at Chiquiuhchiuhcan,[17] 15 rods long, 10 wide.

— [Outside the palace] at Atluelican, 12 rods long, 3 wide.

---

[14]Possibly literally, "next to the stone house."

[15]Santiago might be a town or a church or perhaps a person.

[16]Perhaps literally, "near the old temple or church."

[17]Perhaps literally, "where baskets are made."

— çan ye oncan atlvelican inic uiac xii ynic patlauac vi quavitl

— çan ye oncan atlvelican atiçacalli[18] ypan mani ynic huiac ix quavitl ynic patlauac chiquacenquavitl

— çan ye no oncan atiçacaltitlan ynic viac vii ic patlavac iii quavitl

— çan ye no oncan nestlatilliytlan[19] ynic viac ix ypan cematl auh ynic patlavac iii ypan centlacotl[11]

— çan ye oncan yquiyauac p^{o} tetometl ynic viac xvi quahuitl ynic patlavac vii ypan cenyollotli[20]

— acallopan ynic viac xx auh ynic patlauac ii quavitl

— tesomolco ynic huiac xi ynic patlauac ii quavitl

— salpan yquiyauac macaval ynic viac x ic patlauac iiii quavitl

— tenescaltitlan[21] ynic huiac xiiii tescalli yc patlavac ix quavitl

— cueçalco ynic huiac[22] xvi ynic patlauac iii quavitl

— sancopincan[23] ynic huiac xii ynic patlavac i ypan cenmatl

— tlalxopan ynic viac xi ynic patlauac iii quavi[tl]

— çan ye no oncan tlalxopan yc viac iiii ic patlauac iii quavi[tl]

— çan ye no oncan tlalxopan ynic viac v quavitl çan necoc iuhqui

— cueçalco[24] salpan ynic viac lxxi quavitl yc patlavac xxxii

— çannitech antican salpan ynic viac lxxxiiii quahuitl ynic patlauac xxxv quavitl

— atlixocan ynic huiac cv quavitl ynic patlavac c quavitl

Acouic[8]
señor don Juan gouer^{or} yn itlalcoualtzin
nican pouhtoc ynic cecni

— atonco xochicaltitlan[25] ynic huiac xvii quavitl yc patlauac xiiii

— auatzalpan iquiyauac Ju^{o} ueiteicuhtzin ynic viac xiii quavitl yc patlauac iii

— çacatetelco yquiyauac marcos ynic viac v quavitl yc patlauac i ypan cenmatl

— yecapan vecamecatl yquiyauac yc viac x quavitl ynic patlauac iii

---

[18]See *Florentine Codex,* Bk. 2, p. 255.

[19]Conceivably a place name.

[20]The distance from the heart to an outstretched fingertip, and hence one half of the braza.

[21]Perhaps literally, "next to the lime oven or lime storehouse."

— Also there at Atluelican, 12 rods long, 6 wide.

— Also there at Atluelican, with a chalk adobe[18] house on it, 9 rods long, 6 rods wide.

— Also there, next to the chalk adobe house, 7 rods long, 3 wide.

— Also there, next to the ash heap,[19] 9 (rods) plus one braza long, and 3 (rods) and a half[11] wide.

— Also there, [facing the place of] Pedro Tetometl, 16 rods long, 7 (rods) and half a braza[20] wide.

— At Acallopan, 20 rods long, and 2 wide.

— At Texomolco, 11 rods long, 2 wide.

— At Xalpan, [facing the place of] Macaual, 10 rods long, 4 wide.

— At Tenexcaltitlan[21] [rocky land], 14 rods long, 9 wide.

— At Cueçalco, 16 rods long,[22] 3 wide.

— At Xancopincan,[23] 12 (rods) long, 1 (rod) plus one braza wide.

— At Tlalxopan, 11 rods long, 3 wide.

— Also there at Tlalxopan, 4 rods long, 3 wide.

— Also there at Tlalxopan, 5 rods long, the same wide.

— At Cueçalco[24] and Xalpan, 71 rods long, 32 wide.

— [Right next to Antican?], at Xalpan, 84 rods long, 35 rods wide.

— At Atlixocan, 105 rods long, 100 rods wide.

Here are recorded the lord governor don Juan's purchased lands [in the upper region];[8] first:

— At Atonco, next to the bathhouse,[25] 17 rods long, 14 wide.

— At Auatzalpan, [outside the place of] Juan Hueyteicuhtzin, 13 rods long, 3 wide.

— At Çacatetelco, [outside the place of] Marcos, 5 rods long, 1 (rod) plus one braza wide.

— At Yecapan, [outside the place of] Uecamecatl, 10 rods long, 3 wide.

---

[22] *Tetzcolco*, presumably a place name, was later inserted after *huiac*.

[23] Perhaps literally, "where adobes are made."

[24] *Ueuetlalli*, "[patrimonial] land," was inserted later, before Cueçalco.

[25] Possibly a place name.

— quauhtlapetzco yquiyauac quauhxochtli ynic viac vi ic patlauac iii

— tolnauac tenanitlan ynic huiac xx quavitl ynic patlauac x quavitl

5.

Nican icuilliuhtoc ynic macoc posicion in tlacatl don juan gouer^or nican onpehua yn acohuic

— Inic cecni[26] callali tlacomolco
— ynic ocan neçavalcaltitlan[27]
— iniquescan tianquiztenco jular
— inic nauhcan oztopolco callali
— inic macuilcan chimaliztacan alauertan
— inic chiquacecan xoxocotlan
— inic chiconcan atlauhcamilpan alauertan
— inichicuescan atepocaapan
— inic chicuhnauhcan cimatlan
— inic matlaccan ocoçacapan
— inic matlactli oce chinancaltonco
— inic matlactli omome citlalcouac
— inic matlactli omei milpolco
— inic matlactli onnavi tzitzicazpan
— inic castolcan quauhcuillotitlan totollapan[28]
— inic castolli once tecocozco
— inic castolli omome tepetlyitic
— inic castolli omey tlacoiyacan tlachquac[28]
— inic castolli onahui o[co]tepec
— inic cenpovalcan atliitic apan[29]
— inic cenpovalcan once [. . .]

Nican pouhtoc in tlalnavac in ipan [. . .] in tlatouani don juan gouer^or

— inic cecni atlhuelican
— inic ocan tlacopantonco
— iniquescan cohuatzonco
— inic nauhcan coiotleuhco
— inic macuilcan tochco

---

[26]"The first place," "the second place," etc.

[27]This, and later items listing only place names, probably refer to specific parcels of land at that place, undoubtedly well known at the time.

— At Quauhtlapetzco, [facing the boundary], 6 (rods) long, 3 wide.

— At Tolnauac and Tenanitlan, 20 rods long, 10 rods wide.

5.

Here is inscribed how possession was given to sir don Juan, governor. Here begins the upper region.

— 1st,[26] house-land at Tlacomolco.
— 2d, Neçaualcaltitlan.[27]
— 3d, a lot at Tianquiztenco.
— 4th, house-land at Oztopolco.
— 5th, an orchard at Chimaliztaca.
— 6th, Xoxocotlan.
— 7th, an orchard at Atlauhcamilpan.
— 8th, Atepocaapan.
— 9th, Cimatlan.
— 10th, Ocoçacapan.
— 11th, Chinancaltonco.
— 12th, Citlalcouac.
— 13th, Milpolco.
— 14th, Tzitzicazpan.
— 15th, Quauhcuillotitlan Totollapan.[28]
— 16th, Tecocozco.
— 17th, Tepetliitic.
— 18th, Tlacoiyacan Tlachquac.[28]
— 19th, Ocotepec.
— 20th, Atliitic Apan.[29]
— 21st, [. . .]

Here is recorded what belongs to the ruler and governor don Juan in the lower region [. . .].

— 1st, Atluelican.
— 2d, Tlacopantonco.
— 3d, Couatzonco.
— 4th, Coyotleuhco.
— 5th, Tochco.

---

[28]Such dual names are fairly uncommon, and in this case one is probably a division of the other. The latter term may be the more general, as Tlachquac is found by itself (section 6).

[29]Or Atliiticapan.

— inic chiquacecan çacamolpan
— inic chiconcan ocotitlan
— inic chicuescan amantlan
— inic chicuhcnauhcan quauhcuezcontitlan
— inic matlaccan xochac
— inic matlaccan once tlillac

yehuatli in oquimomaquilli in mag^t yn ipan can neltilliztli yn oaxcatilloc yn tlatouani don juan gouer^or yn ipan altepetl coyohuacan

6.

Tehuatin in titecuhtlatoque ioan talgaldesme in ticpia innaltepetl in coiovacan ca toconneltillia in ixquich in itecpilal[30] in señor don juan in gunvernador in coyovacan ca in iquac in tlamiz ca quinmacatiaz in ipilvan in itecpillal

— Inic cecni in itecpillal in señor don juan ytocaiocan acopilco

— Inic oncan in itecpilal in señor don juan ytocaiocan avapoltitla

— Iniquexcan in itecpilal ytocaiocan chimaliztacan
— Inic nauhcan in itecpilal ytocaiocan xoxocotlan
— Inic macuilcan in itecpilal ytocaiocan atlauhcamilpan
— Inic chiquacecan in itecpilal ytocaiocan copilco
— Inic chicocan in itecpilal ytocaiocan cimatlan
— Inic chiquexcan in itecpilal ytocaiocan citlalcovac
— Inic chicuhnauhcan in itecpilal ytocaiocan atepocaapan
— Inic matlaccan in itecpilal ytocaiocan tecocozco
— Inic matlaccan honce in itecpilal ytocaiocan tlachquac
— Inic matlacan homome in itecpilal ytocaiocan ocotepec
— Inic matlaccan homey in itecpilal ytocaiocan tepetliitic
— Inic matlaccan honnavi in itecpillal ytocaiocan totollac
— Inic castolcan in itecpilal ytocaiocan amantla
— Inic castolcan once in itecpilal ytocaiocan quauhcuezcontitla

— Inic castolcan homome in itecpilal ytocaiocan atlvellican
— Inic castolcan onnei[31] ytocaiocan xochac
— Inic castolcan honnahui ytocaiocan çacamolpan
— Inic cenpovalcan ytocaiocan xiuhtlan

[30]See Ixtlilxochitl, *Historia Chichimeca*, II, 170.

— 6th, Çacamolpan.
— 7th, Ocotitlan.
— 8th, Amantlan.
— 9th, Quauhcuezcontitlan.
— 10th, Xochac.
— 11th, Tlillac.

This is what His Majesty gave, for which there is verification that it was given to the ruler don Juan, governor in the town of Coyoacan.

6.

We the lord rulers and alcaldes who guard the town of Coyoacan verify all the nobleman's land[30] of señor don Juan, governor of Coyoacan; when he expires, he will give his nobleman's land to his children.

— 1st, señor don Juan's nobleman's land at the place called Acopilco.
— 2d, señor don Juan's nobleman's land at the place called Auapoltitlan.
— 3d, his nobleman's land at the place called Chimaliztaca.
— 4th, his nobleman's land at the place called Xoxocotlan.
— 5th, his nobleman's land at the place called Atlauhcamilpan.
— 6th, his nobleman's land at the place called Copilco.
— 7th, his nobleman's land at the place called Cimatlan.
— 8th, his nobleman's land at the place called Citlalcouac.
— 9th, his nobleman's land at the place called Atepocaapan.
— 10th, his nobleman's land at the place called Tecocozco.
— 11th, his nobleman's land at the place called Tlachquac.
— 12th, his nobleman's land at the place called Ocotepec.
— 13th, his nobleman's land at the place called Tepetliitic.
— 14th, his nobleman's land at the place called Totollac.
— 15th, his nobleman's land at the place called Amantlan.
— 16th, his nobleman's land at the place called Quauhcuezcontitlan.
— 17th, his nobleman's land at the place called Atluelican.
— 18th, at the place called Xochac.
— 19th, at the place called Çacamolpan.
— 20th, at the place called Xiuhtlan.

[31]The writer had originally written *onnavi*, only partially correcting his error to *onnei*. *Omei* was undoubtedly intended.

— Inic cenpovalcan honce ytocaiocan hocotitlan
— Inic cenpovalcan homome ytocaiocan tecovac
— Inic cenpovalcan homey ytocaiocan axochco

7.

— ynoyollocopan nictemacac[32] ynotlal cohuatzoco çancamolpan ynotemilticahuan niquimacac ynic tlapuhualli yehuatl ymatlactlacxitl omomen quav[itl] ynic quipouhque

— yn çacamolpan ynic viac matlacpuhualli yhuan napuhualli ynic patlav[a]c macuilpohualli

— yn cohuantzoco ynic viac caxtolpohualli ypan onpohualli ynic patlahuac opohualli

— yn aocmo nispa otemacoc axochco ocotitlan tecohuac amatlan chimalliztaca atlauhcamilpan ameyalco tiaquiztoco[33]

— yn oquicuique oxochco ynic viac napohualli ypan matlacmatl[34] yc pantlahuac opohualli

— yn oquicuique ocotitlan ynic viac i tzotli ypan macuilpohualli ynic [pa]tlahuac opohualli yn oquicuique temiltique

— yn oquicuique amatlan ynic viac chicopohuanlli yc patlahuac onpohualli

— yn oquicuique chimalliztaca ynic viac chiquacepuhualli yhuan m[a]tlacmatl yc patlahuac opuhualli

— yn oquicuique atlauhcamilpa ynic viac chiquacepohualli yc patlahuac opohualli

— yn oquicuique ameyalco tiaquiztoco[33] ynic viac macuilpoh[ua]lli yc patlahuac opohuall

yn omocepouhque yn itemilticauh señor don juan de guzman y çano can[35] omotlalmacaque yn imilpatzinco macuiltecpatli ypan chicnaui tlacatl

[32]Presumably don Juan de Guzmán.

[33]Tecouac is omitted in the list that follows; perhaps it is implicitly included with either Ocotitlan or Amantlan. Similarly, Ameyalco and Tianquiztonco may or may not be totally distinct localities.

[34]The twelve-foot unit mentioned above is about twice the length of the customary

— 21st, at the place called Ocotitlan.
— 22d, at the place called Tecoac.
— 23d, at the place called Axochco.

7.

— I[32] gave away my land voluntarily at Couatzonco and Çacamolpan; I gave it to my field workers. As to the manner of the count, they counted it with the twelve-foot rod.

— At Çacamolpan, 280 long, 100 wide.

— At Couatzonco, 340 long, 40 wide.

— That which was not given away in my presence is at Axochco, Ocotitlan, Tecouac, Amantlan, Chimaliztaca, Atlauhcamilpan, Ameyalco, Tianquiztonco.[33]

— What they took at Axochco is 90 brazas[34] long, 40 wide.

— What they took at Ocotitlan is 500 long, 40 wide; the field workers took it.

— What they took at Amantlan is 140 long, 40 wide.

— What they took at Chimaliztaca is 130 brazas long, 40 wide.

— What they took at Atlauhcamilpan is 120 long, 40 wide.

— What they took at Ameyalco [and] Tianquiztonco[33] is 100 long, 40 wide.

What señor don Juan de Guzmán's field workers totaled; also where[35] they were given land on his fields. (They totaled) 109 people.

---

braza. The question remains then, as to whether the numbers given throughout this section refer to the six-foot or the twelve-foot measure.

[35]Alternatively, one might divide *yçanocan* into *y çan ocan* (= *yn çan oncan*). This could then be translated "The field workers of señor don Juan de Guzmán who were given land on his fields totaled 109 people."

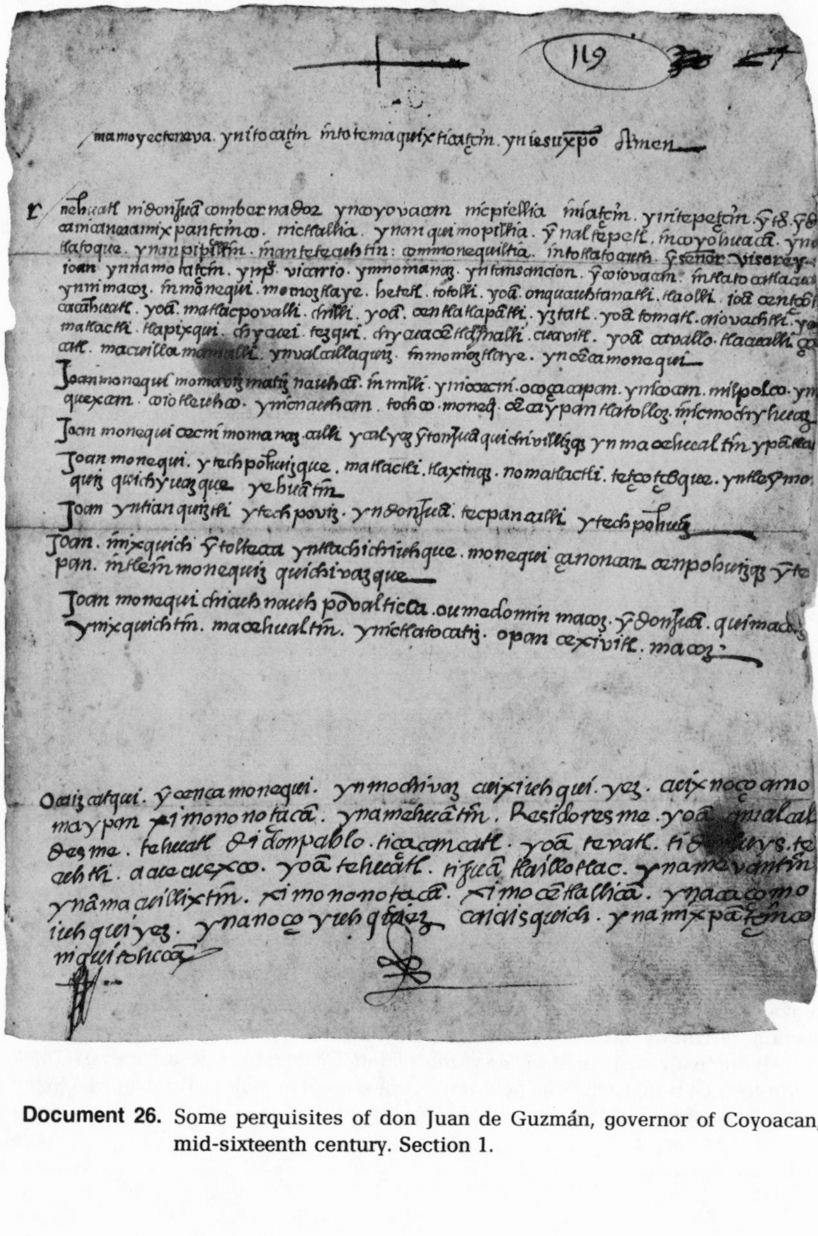

119

/mamoyectenexa. ynitocatzin yntotemaquixticatzin. yniesu xpo Amen

r nehuatl nidon Juan gobernador yncoyovacan nicpielhia ynitlatzin. ynitepetzin. y t8. y
cenquizca ymixpantzinco. nictlalhia. ynnan quimopielhia. y naltepetl. yncoyohuacan. ynn
tlatoque. ynnan pipiltin. yntetecuhtin: connonequiltia. yntotlatocauh. y senor visorey
ioan ynnamotatzin. ynp̃s. vicario. ynnomanaz. yntlamsencion. ycoiovacan. yntlatocatlacua
ynnimacoz. ynmonequi. momoztlaye. hetetl. totolli. yoan. onquauhtlamatli. tlaolli. ioan centecpa
cacahuatl. yoan. matlacpovalli. chilli. yoan. centlatlapalli. yztatl. yoan tomatl. ciovachilli. yo
matlactli. tlapixqui. chycacei. tezqui. chycuacentlacmalli. cuavitl. yoan cavallo. tlacualli. ça
catl. macuilla mamalli. ynvalcallaquiz. ynmomoztlaye. yncecamonequi

Joan monequi momavizmatiz nauhcan. ynmilli. ynicecen. ocoçacapan. yniccan. milpolco. ym
quexcan. coiotlecuhco. ynicnauhcan. tochco. monequi. ceccaypan tlatolloz. ynicmochiyhuaz

Joan monequi cecni momanaz calli ycalyez y Don Juan quichivilizq̃ yn macehualtin ypal

Joan monequi. ytech pohuizque. matlactli. tlaxincq̃. nomatlactli. teçoçoque. yntley mo
quiz quichyuazque yehuantin

Joan yntianquiztli ytech poviz. yn Don Juan. tecpancalli ytech pohuiz

Joan. ynixquich ytoltecaa yntlachichiuhque. monequi çanoncan canpohuizq̃ yte
pan. yntlein monequiz quichivazque

Joan monequi chiucnauhpovaltica. oumadonmin macoz. y Don Juan. quimacaz
ynixquichtin. macehualtin. ynictlatocatiz. opan cexivitl. macoz

Ocaiz catqui. ycenca monequi. ynmochivaz cenixiuhqui. yez. aiix noço amo
maypan ximononotzacan. ynamehuantin. Residores me. yoan [illegible]
des me. tehuatl di don pablo. ticacancatl. yoan tevatl. ti [illegible] luys. te
cuhtli. calcuexco. yoan tehuatl. tijuan tlaillotlac. ynamevantin
ynnamacuilixtin. ximononotzacan. ximocentlallican. ynacacomo
iuhqui yez. ynanoço yuhqui ez. caniaisquich. ynamixpantzinco
niquitohcan

Document 26. Some perquisites of don Juan de Guzmán, governor of Coyoacan, mid-sixteenth century. Section 1.

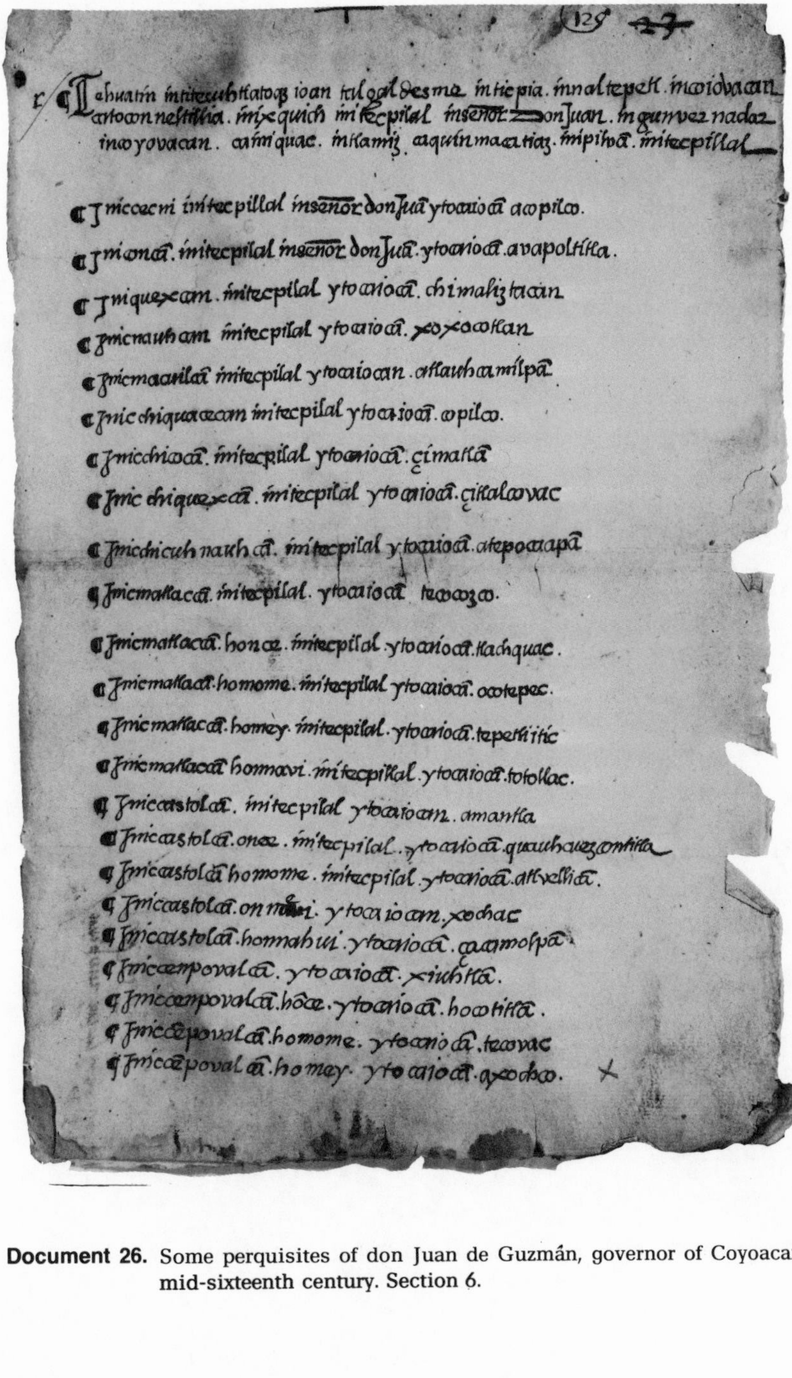

129 27

r ¶ Tehuatin inintecuhtlatocaz ioan tulgaldesma intiepia. innaltepetl. incoiohuacan catocan nestilhia. inixquich initecpilal insenor don Juan. in guernezna dor incoyovacan. caniquac. intlamiz caquinmacatiaz. inipilhoā. initecpillal

¶ Jniccecni initecpillal insenor don Juā ytocaiocā acopilco.
¶ Jnicoņcā. initecpilal insenor don Juā. ytocaiocā. avapoltitla.
¶ Jniquexcam. initecpilal ytocaiocā. chimalhuacan
¶ Jnicnauhcam initecpilal ytocaiocā. xoxocotlan
¶ Jnicmacuilcā initecpilal ytocaiocan. atlauhcamilpā.
¶ Jnicchiquacecam initecpilal ytocaiocā. copilco.
¶ Jnicchicocā. initecpilal ytocaiocā. çimatlā
¶ Jnic chiquexcā. initecpilal ytocaiocā. çitlalcovac
¶ Jnicchicuhnauhcā. initecpilal ytocaiocā. atepocapā
¶ Jnicmatlaccā. initecpilal. ytocaiocā tecocozco.
¶ Jnicmatlaccā. honce. initecpilal. ytocaiocā. tlachquac.
¶ Jnicmatlaccā. homome. initecpilal ytocaiocā. ocotepec.
¶ Jnicmatlaccā. homey. initecpilal. ytocaiocā. tepetlitic
¶ Jnicmatlaccā honnavi. initecpillal. ytocaiocā. totollac.
¶ Jnicca stolcā. initecpilal ytocaiocan. amantla
¶ Jnicca stolcā. once. initecpilal. ytocaiocā. quauhcuezcontitla
¶ Jnicca stolcā homome. initecpilal. ytocaiocā. atlvellicā.
¶ Jnicca stolcā. on[illegible]i. ytocaiocan. xochac
¶ Jnicca stolcā. honnahui. ytocaiocā. caca molpā.
¶ Jniccempovalcā. ytocaiocā. xiuhtlā.
¶ Jniccempovalcā. hōce. ytocaiocā. hoco titlā.
¶ Jniccēpovalcā. homome. ytocaiocā. tecovac
¶ Jniccēpovalcā. homey. ytocaiocā. ayocheco. +

Document 26. Some perquisites of don Juan de Guzmán, governor of Coyoacan mid-sixteenth century. Section 6.

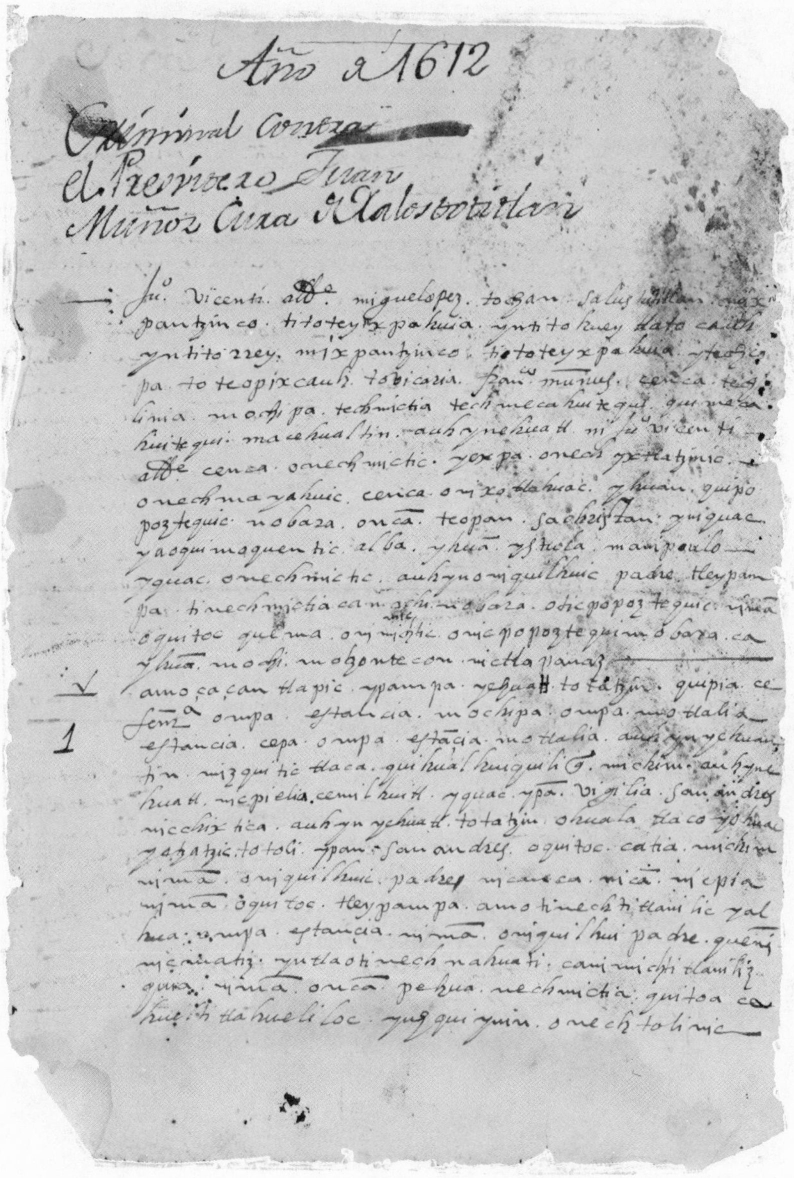

Año d 1612

Criminal contra el Presvitero Juan Muñoz Cura d Xalostotitlan

Ju° Vicente alcalde miguel lopez tochan Xalostotitlan mixpantzinco titoteyxpahuia yntitohuey tlatocauh yntitorrey mixpantzinco titoteyxpahuia yteoticpa toteopixcauh tobicario Juan muñoz cenca techtolinia mochipa techmictia techmecahuitequi quimecahuitequi macehualtin auh yn nehuatl ni Ju° Vicente alcalde cenca onechmictic yexpa onech ... onechmayahuic cenca onixotlahuac yhuan quipopoztequic nobara onca teopan sacristan yniquac yaoquimaquentic alba yhuan ystola manipulo yniquac onechmictic auh yn oniquilhuic padre tleypampa tinechmictia ... nobara ... oquitoc ... ca yhuan mochi mohontecon mictlapanaz

V — amo çaçan tlapic ypampa yehuatl totatzin quipia cefemina ompa estancia mochipa ompa motlalia estancia cepa ompa estancia motlalia auh yn yehuantin ... tlaca quihualhuiquilia michin auh yn nehuatl nicpielia ... yniquac ypan vigilia San Andres nicchixtica auh yn yehuatl totatzin ... totoli ypan San Andres oquitoc ca tla michin ... oniquilhuic padres ... oquitoc tleypampa amo tinechtitlani ... ompa estancia ... oniquilhuic padre ... yn tlaotinechnahuati ... nechmictia quitoa ... onechtolinic

1

Document 27. Petition for removal of the priest of Jalostotitlan, 1611. Page 1.

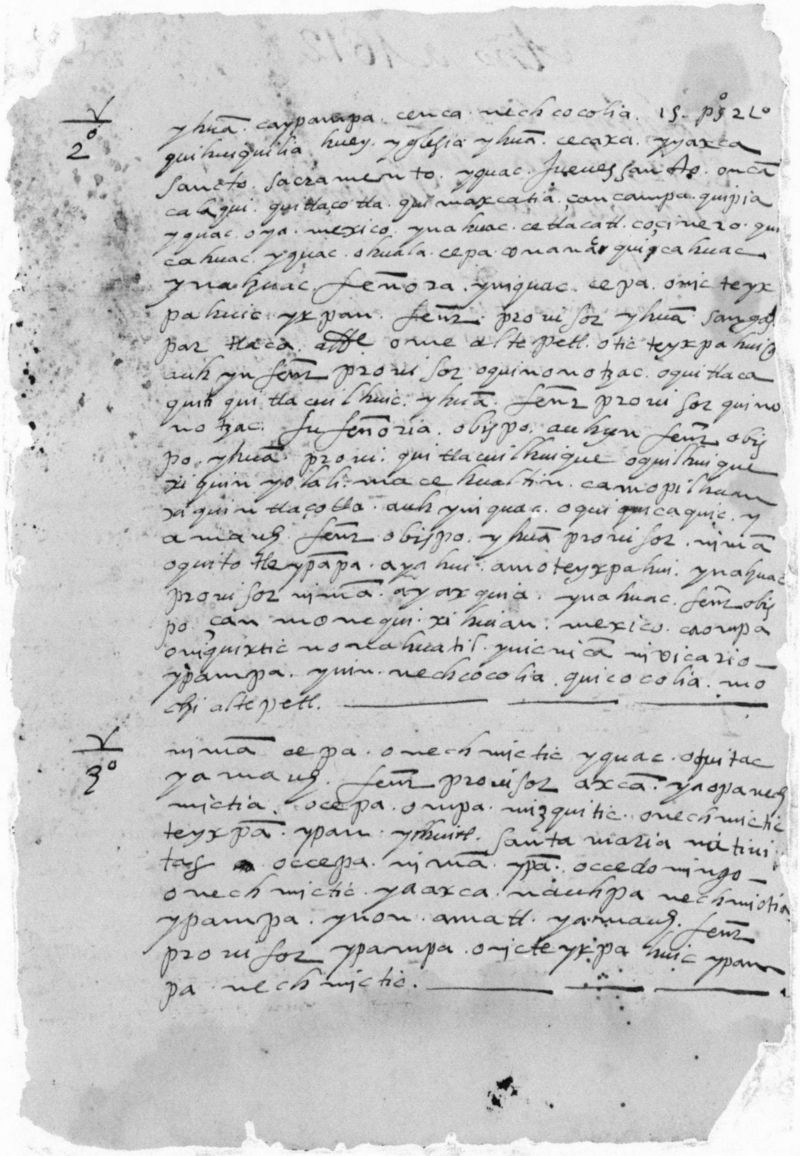

V
2°
yhua. caypanpa. cenca. nechcocolia. 15. p$ 2L°
quihuiquilia huey. yglesia yhua. cecaxa. yyaxca
sancto. sacramento. yquac. jueues santo. omca
caqui. quitlaçotla. quimaxcatia, çan canpa. quipia
yquac. oya. mexico. ynahuac. cetlacatl. coçinero. qui
cahuac. yquac. ohuala. cepa. onanā quiqcahuac
ynahuac. señora. yniquac. cepa. omic teyx
pahuic. yxpan. señr. prouisor yhua sangop
par tlaca. adde onne altepetl. otic teyxpahuiq
auh yn señr. prouisor oquinonotzac. oquitlaca
quiti qui tlacuilhuic. yhua. señr. prouisor quino
notzac. su señoria. obispo. auhyn señr. obis
po. yhua. proui. quitlacuilhuique oquilhuique
xiquin yolali. macehualtin. camopilhuan
xiquin tlaçotla. auh yniquac. oqui quicaquic. y
amauh. señr. obispo. yhua prouisor. ynma
oquito tleypapa. ayahui. amoteyxpahui. ynahuac
prouisor ynma. ayaxquia. ynahuac. señr. obis
po. çan monequi. xihuian. mexico. caompa
omquixtic nonahuatil. ynicnica nivicario
ypampa. ynin. nechcocolia. quicocolia. mo
chi altepetl.

V
3°
ynma cepa. onechmictic yquac. oquitac
yamauh. señr. prouisor axca. yaopanech
mictia. ocepa. ompa. nizquitic. onechmictic
teyxpa. ypan. ybuiel. santa maria natiui
tas. occepa. ynma. ypa. occedomingo
onechmictic. yaaxca. nanhpa nechmictia
ypampa. ynon. amatl. yamauh. señr.
prouisor ypampa. oyicteyxpahuic ypam
pa nechmictic.

Document 27. Petition for removal of the priest of Jalostotitlan, 1611. Page 2.

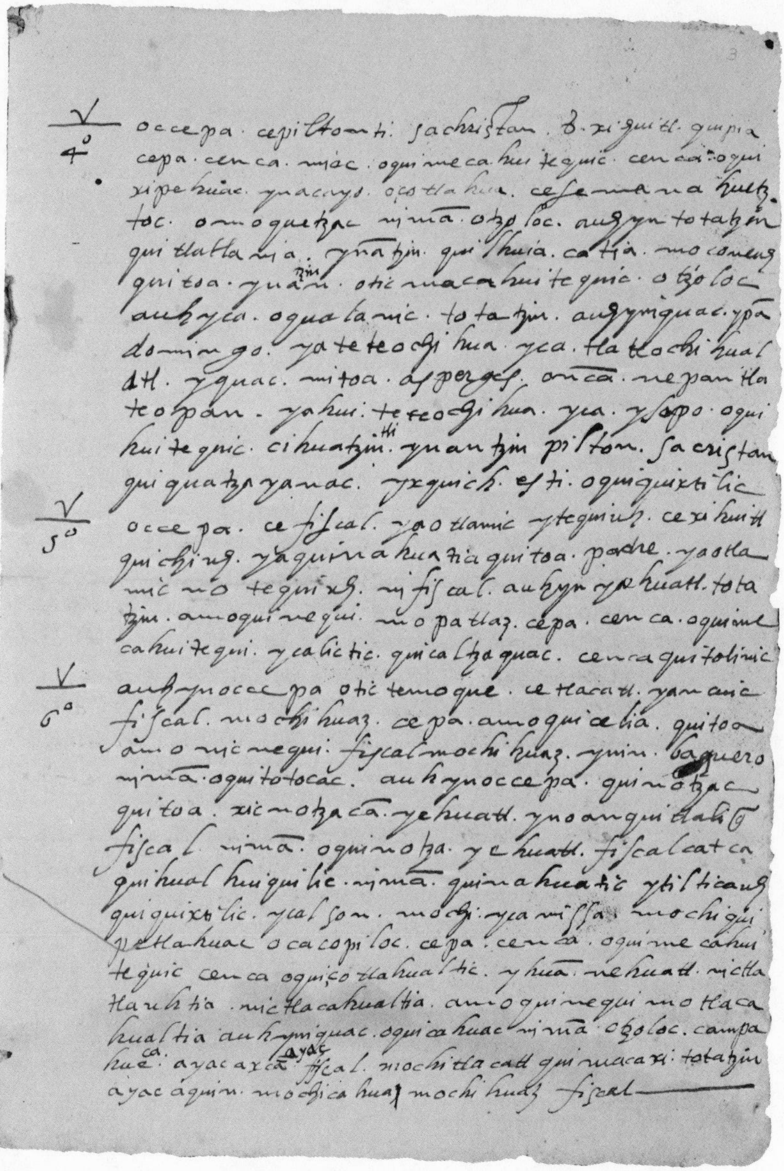

V 4º occepa · cepiltonti · sachristan · 8 · xiuitl · quipia
cepa · cenca · mac · oquimecahuitequic · cencan · oqui
xipehuac · ynacayo · ocotlahua · cesemana huetz
toc · amoquetzac ninma · otzoloc · auh yn totatzin
quitlattania · ynatzin · quilhuia · catlia · mocone
quitoa · ynantzin · otic macahuitequic · otzoloc
auh yca · oquatlanic · totatzin · auh yniquac · ypa
domingo · yateteochihua · yca · tlateochihual
atl · yquac · mitoa · asperges · oncan · nepantla
teopan · yahui · teteochihua · yca · ysopo · oqui
huitequic · cihuatzintli · ynantzin pilton · sacristan
quiquatzayanac · yxquich · esti · oquiquixtilic
V 5º occepa · ce fiscal · yaotlanic ytequiuh · ce xihuitl
quichiuh · yaquinahuatia quitoa · padre · yaotla
nic no tequiuh · ni fiscal · auh yn yehuatl · tota
tzin · amoquinequi · mopatlaz · cepa · cenca · oquime
cahuitequi · ycalictic · quicaltzaquac · cenca quitolinic
V 6º auh ynoccepa otic temoque · ce tlacatl · yancuic
fiscal · mochihuaz · cepa · amoquicelia · quitoa
amo nicnequi · fiscal mochihuaz · yniun · baquero
ninma · oquitotocac · auh ynoccepa · quinotzac
quitoa · xicnotzaca · yehuatl · ynoanquitlalia
fiscal ninma · oquinotza · yehuatl · fiscal catca
quihualhuiquilic · ninma · quinahuatic ytilticauh
quiquixtilic · ycalsom · mochi · ycamissa · mochi qui
petlahuac ocacopiloc · cepa · cenca · oquimecahui
tequic cenca oquiçotlahualtic · yhuan · nehuatl · nictla
tlaulatia · nictlacahualtia · amoquinequi motlaca
hualtia auh yniquac · oquicahuac ninma · otzoloc · campa
hueca · ayac axcan ayac fiscal · mochi tlacatl quimacaxi · totatzin
ayac aquin · mochicahuaz mochihuaz fiscal

Document 27. Petition for removal of the priest of Jalostotitlan, 1611. Page 3.

V

7º yhuan . occepa . cetlacatl quititlanic . ompa . atoto
nilco . quicahuaz . amecaxas . ya mo huicac quihui
cac . caxas . auh ynto tatzin oquilhuic . ygastiaz
ompa . mitic . tinechitas . nimichmaca . ce carta
ticmacaz . ~~atl~~ temayor ompa . atotonilco . auh ynin
tlacatl . qui huica . caxas . acito . mitic . quitemoc . to
tatzin . ayac onca . ca nompa . mocahuato . es
tançia . ynahuac . Señora auh ynquiman
ompa . mo cuepac . mitic . oya . ompa . estançia
ypan acito . totatzin . ynma . oquilhui . tleypam
pa nican . estançia tihuala . oquilhuic . padre
nicomanaznequi . moamas . ynma . ycoquala
nic . oquilhui : xiyauh . ompa . mitic . tinechia
ompa nyaz . nimichmacaz . amatl . ynman
tlacatl . mocuepac . mitic ynma . ohualato
tatzin . mitic . ynma . ~~[illegible]~~ oncan . cepa . niec
oquimictic . quicotahualtic . ypapa . oquitocac
ompa estan . yca . oqualanic totatzin . auh oquine
aquin . quitocaz . yaz . estançia ynahuac
ySeñora . ynquemaman . aquin . motitla
niz . mitic . quitemoz . cepa . yaz . estançia
ynma - ompa . quimictiz ynic quitechtoli
nia .

V

8. cepa . nochpoch . catalina . Juana . ompa
yahui . teopan . teotlac . tlachpanaz . auh ynto
tatzin . ompa . teopan . quitzitzquic . qui ynecoz
nequi . amoquicelia . cepa : oncan . teopanca
litic . oquimictic ynma . ohuala . moteyx
pahuico . nixpan . : ——— ——— ———

Document 27. Petition for removal of the priest of Jalostotitlan, 1611. Page 4.

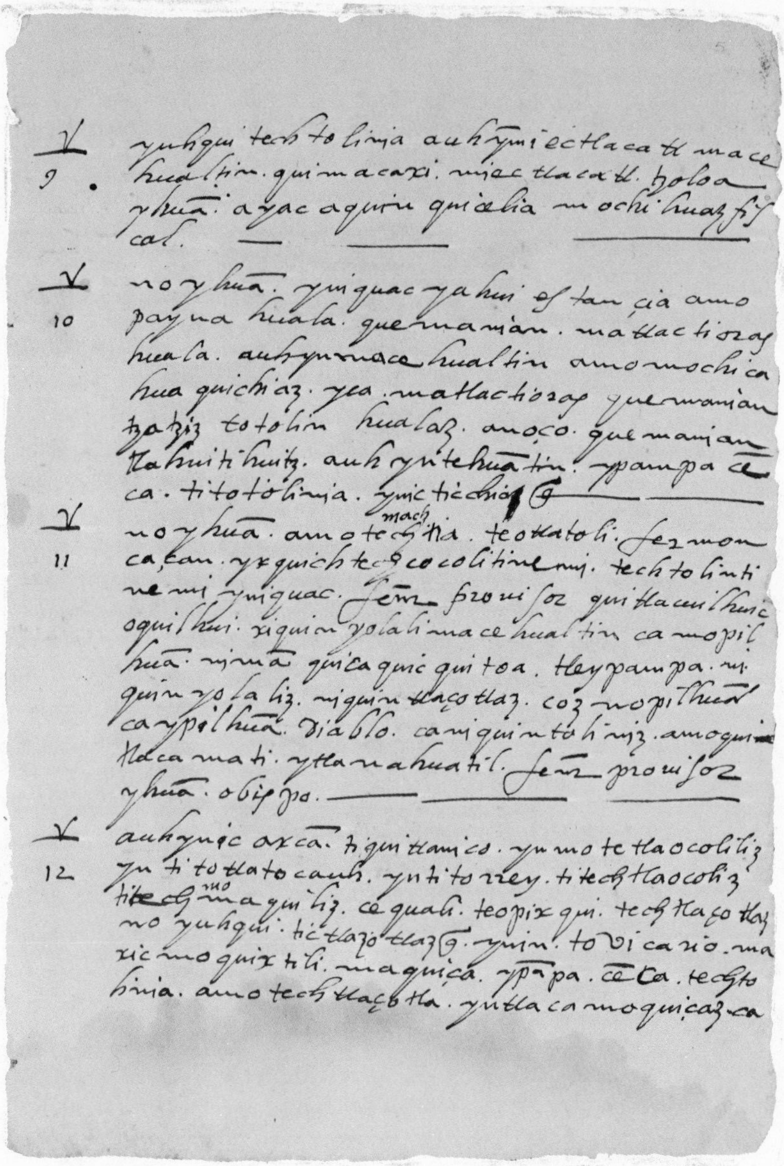

V
9 yuhqui techtolinia auh yniectlacatl mace
hualtin. quimacaxi. ynic tlacatl. yoloa
yhua. ayac aquin quicelia in ochihuaz fis
cal.

V
10 noyhua. yniquac yahui estançia amo
payna huala. quemmanian. matlactiozas
huala. auh ynmacehualtin amo mochica
hua quichiaz. yca. matlactiozas quemmanian
tzatziz totolin hualaz. anoço. quemmanian
tlahuitihuitz. auh yntehuatin. ypampa ce
ca. titotolinia. ynic ticchiaz (?)

V
11 noyhua. amo techmachtilia. teotlatoli. sermon
cacan. yxquich techcocolitinemi. techtolinti
nemi yniquac. señor provisor quitlacuilhuic
oquilhui. xiquin yolali macehualtin ca nopil
hua. nima quicaquic quitoa. tleypampa. ni
quin yolaliz. niquintlaçotlaz. cuix nopilhua
ca ypilhua. diablo. caniquintoliniz. amo qui
tlacamati. ytlanahuatil. señor provisor
yhuan. obispo.

V
12 auh ynic oxca. tiquitlanico. yn motetlaocoliliz
yn ti totlatocauh. yn ti torrey. titechtlaocoliz
titemomaquiliz. cequali. teopixqui. techtlaçotlaz
no yuhqui. tictlaçotlazq. ynin. to vicario. ma
xicmoquixtili. maquiça. ypampa. ceca. techto
linia. amo techtlaçotla. yuhtlaca moquiçaz ca

Document 27. Petition for removal of the priest of Jalostotitlan, 1611. Page 5.

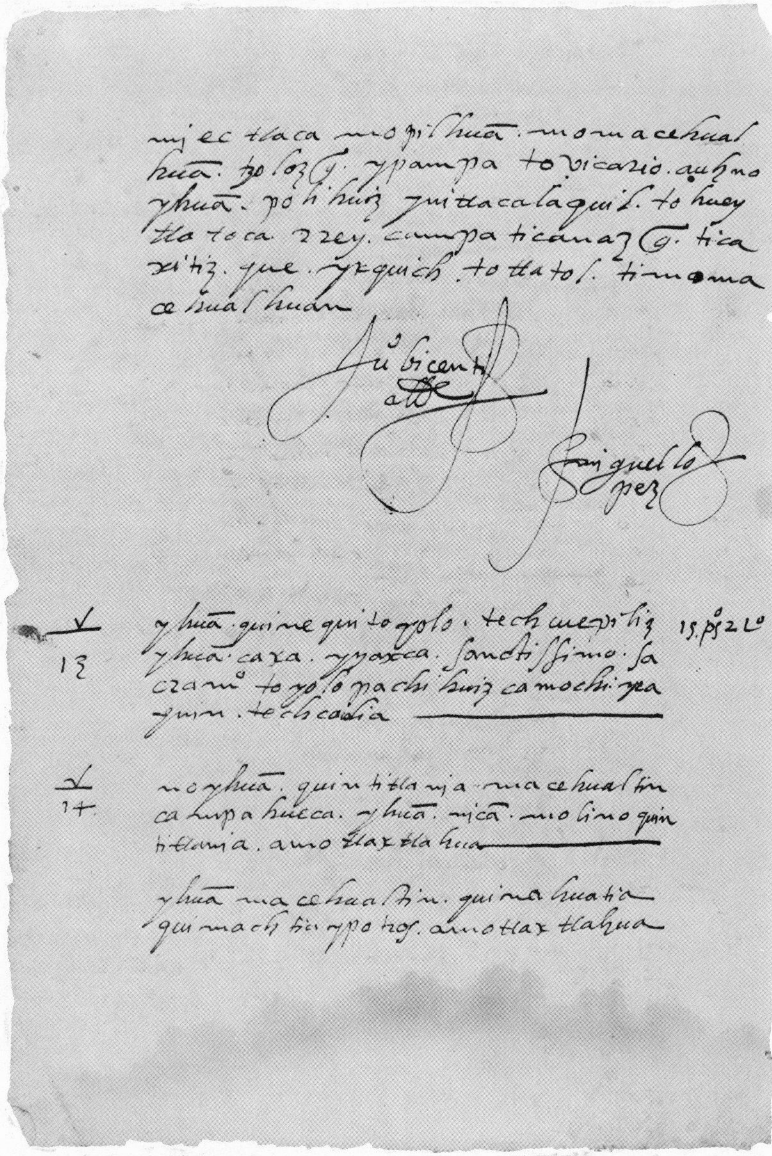
nijectlaca mopilhuã. momacehual
huã. ypolozq. ypampa tovicario. auh no
yhuã. pohihuiz quitlacalaquil. to huey
tlatoca rrey. campa ticanazq. tica
xitiz. que. yxquich. totlatol. timoma
cehualhuan

Juº bicente
alde

miguel lo
pez

V 13 yhuã. quinequi toyolo. techmopilhuiz 15 ps 2 Lº
yhuã. caxa. yyaxca. sanctissimo. sa
cramº toyolo yachihuiz camochipa
quin. techcahua

V 14. noyhuã. quintitlania macehualtin
cahuapahueca. yhuã. nicã. molino quin
titlania. amo tlaxtlahua

yhuã macehualtin. quinahuatia
quimachtin ypotros. amo tlaxtlahua

Document 27. Petition for removal of the priest of Jalostotitlan, 1611. Page 6.

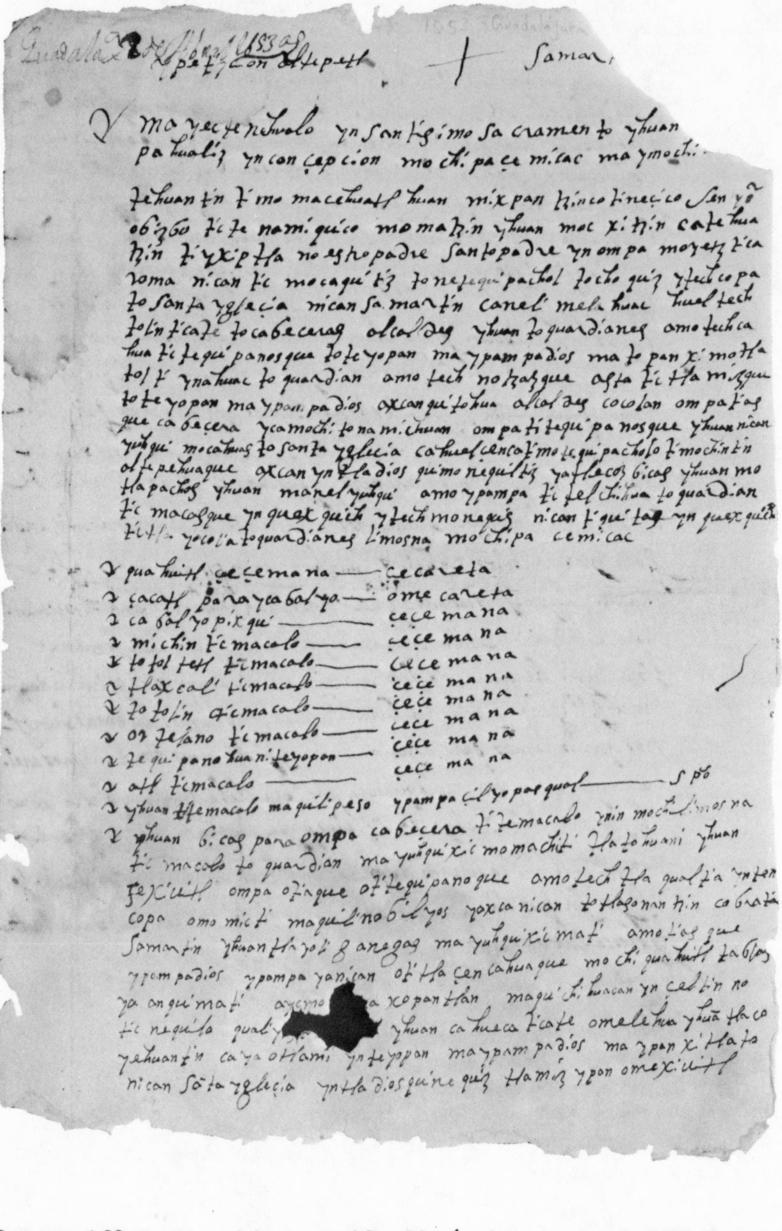

Document 28. Petition of the town of San Martín about its church, 1653. Page 1.

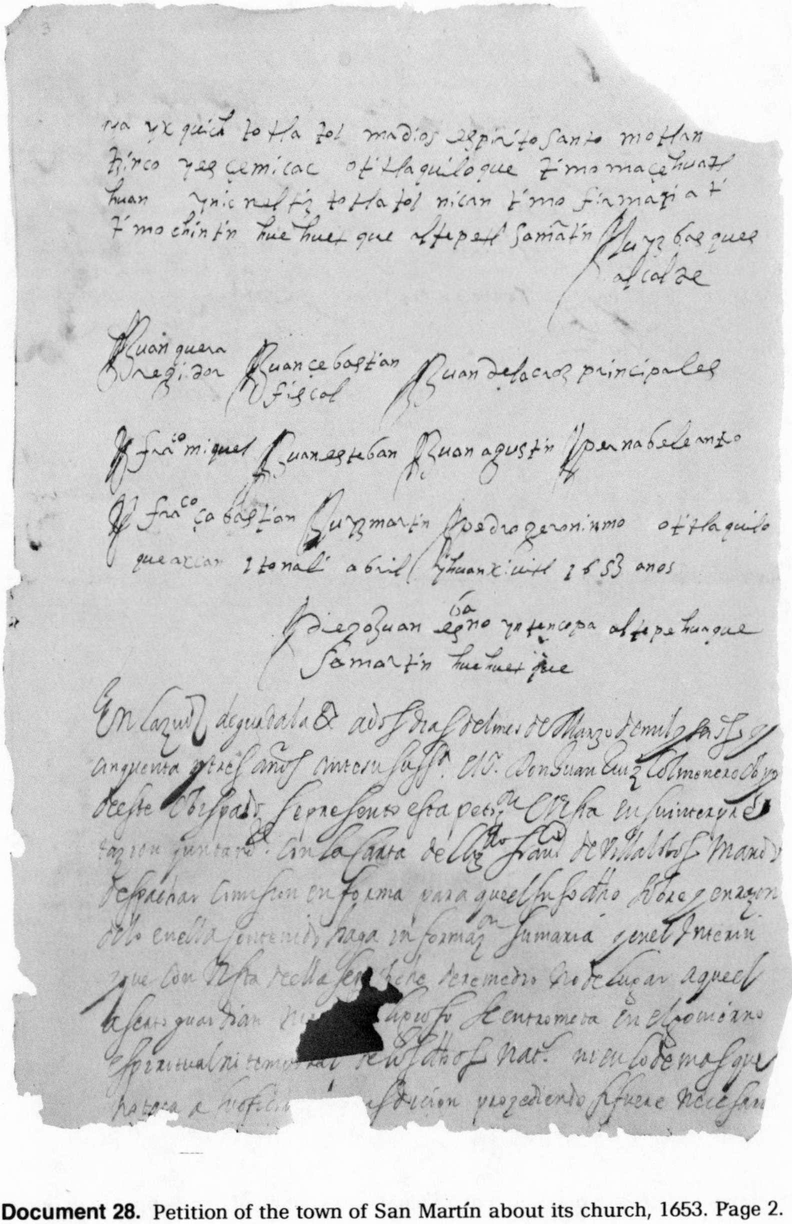

ma yxquich totlatol madios espiritosanto motlan
tzinco ye yeçemicac otitlaquiloque timomaçehualtzi
huan ynic neltiz totlatol nican timofirmatia ti
timochintin huehuetque altepetl samartin luys baezquez
alcalde

juan guerra regidor   juan çebastian fiscal   juan delacros principales

fran.co miquel   juan esteban   juan agustin   pernabe lemus

fran.co çabastian   luys martin   pedro geronimo   otitlaquilo
que axcan 1 tonali abril [illegible] 1653 anos

diego juan escribano [illegible] altepetl [illegible]
samartin huehuetque

En la ciud. de guatemala a dos dias del mes de março de mil y seis[illegible]
cinquenta y tres años ante su Ssa. el Sr. Don Juan [illegible]
deste obispado se presento esta petic.on [illegible]
[illegible]

Document 28. Petition of the town of San Martín about its church, 1653. Page 2.

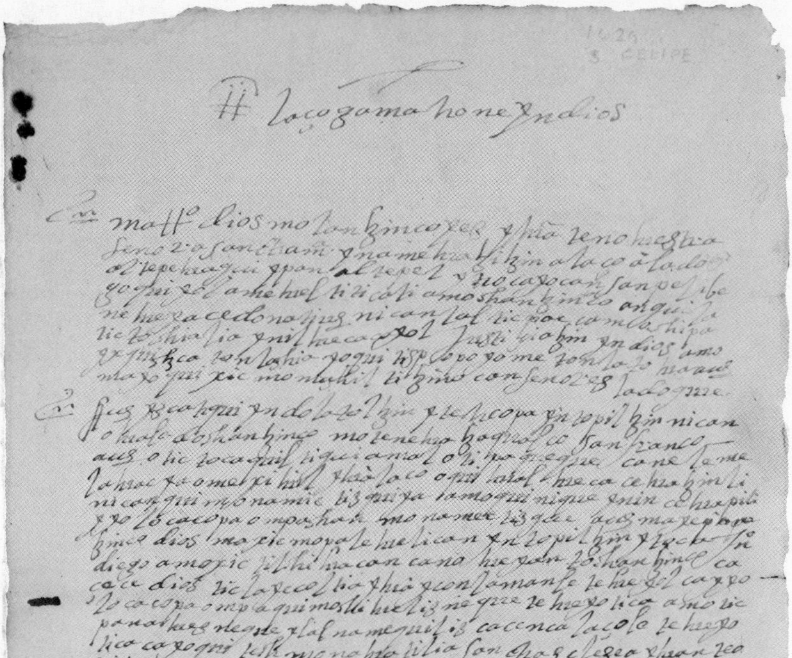

Document 31. Letter of council of Tzacualco to council of San Felipe, 1629. Page 1.

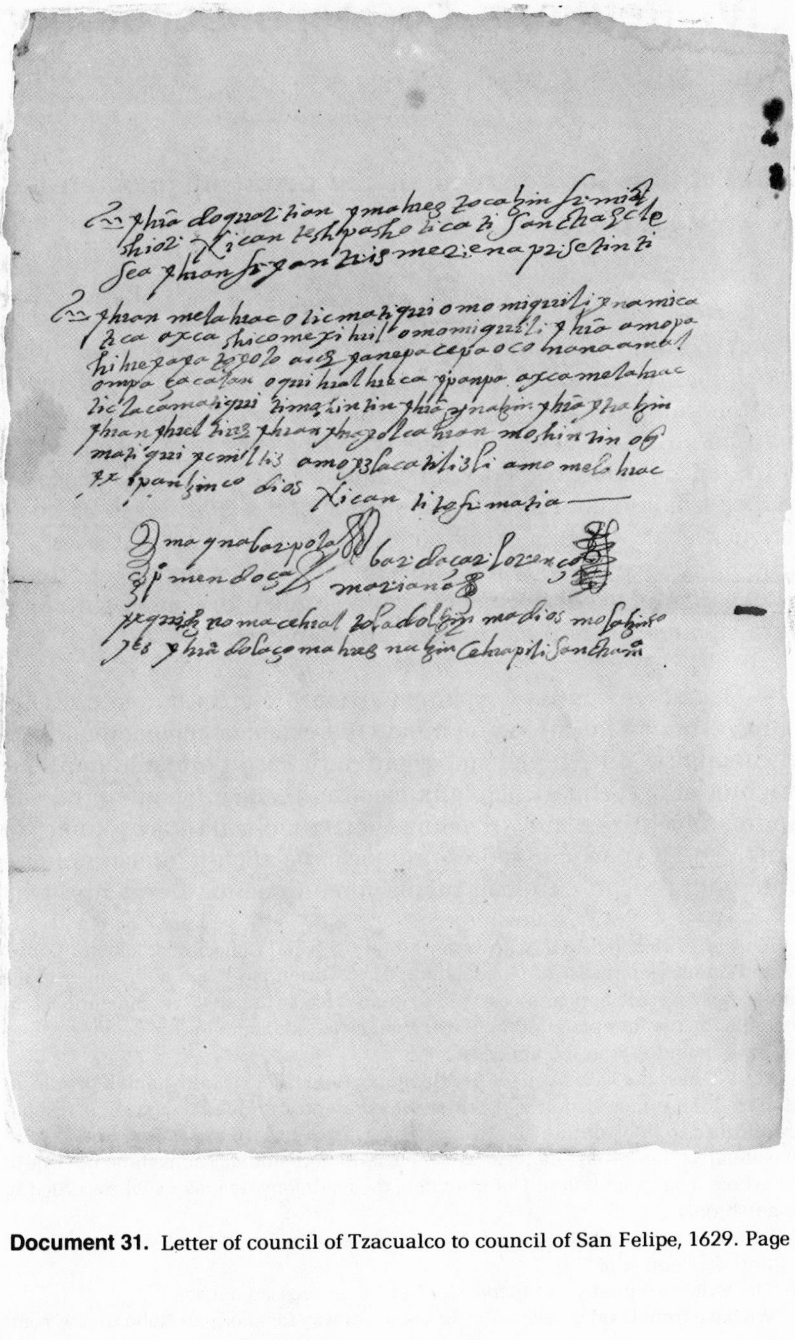

Document 31. Letter of council of Tzacualco to council of San Felipe, 1629. Page 2.

IV. Petitions, Correspondence, and

27. Petition for removal of the priest of Jalostotitlan, 1611[1]

Ju^{o} vicenti a$\overline{\text{ll}}$d^{e} miguelopez tochan[2] Salustutitlan mixpantzinco titoteyxpahuia yn titohueytlatocauh yn titorrey mixpantzinco titoteyxpahuia[3] ytechcopa toteopixcauh tovicaria fran^{co} muñus cenca techtolinia mochipa techmictia techmecahuitequi quimecahuitequi macehualtin[4] auh ynehuatl ni ju^{o} vicenti a$\overline{\text{ll}}$d^{e} cenca onechmictic[5] yexpa onechyxtlatzinic onechmayahuic cenca onixotlahuac yhuan quipopoztequic nobara oncan teopan sachristan yn iquac ya oquimoquentic alba yhuan ystula manipulo yquac onechmictic auh yn oniquilhuic padre tleypampa tinechmictia ca mochi nobara oticpopoztequic niman oquitoc quema onimichmictic onicpopoztequi mobara ca yhuan mochi motzontecon nictlapanaz

— 1 amo ça çantlapic ypampa yehuatl totatzin quipia ce señr^{a} ompa estancia mochipa ompa motlalia estancia cepa ompa estancia motlalia auh yn yehuantin mizquitictlaca quihualhuiquilique michim auh ynehuatl nicpielia cemilhuitl yquac ypan vigilia san andres nicchixtica auh yn yehuatl totatzin ohuala tlacoyohuac[6] ye tzatzic totoli ypan san andres oquitoc catia michim niman oniquilhuic padre nican ca nican nicpia niman oquitoc tleypampa amo

---

[1]McAfee Collection, UCLA Research Library, Special Collections. Jalostotitlan is some 80 miles northeast of Guadalajara. The petition is written and signed in the same hand, to all appearances that of Juan Vicente himself. A translation into Spanish, by the interpreter of the Royal Audiencia, accompanies the document, and we have included it in the appendix.

Nahuatl may not have been the first language of most of the Jalostotitlan people. In January 1612, a month after the petition was presented in Guadalajara, an investigator returned to Jalostotitlan and took testimony from five witnesses who were "fluent in Nahuatl" ("ladino en lengua mexicana"), as though this was something not true of the whole local population. Unfortunately the testimony was, as usual, recorded in Spanish only.

[2]In the accompanying Spanish translation *tochan* is rendered with the phrase *natural de*, "native of."

[3]The writer originally put *tictoteyxpahuia*, then crossed out the *c*.

[4]We have translated *macehualtin* in the usual way for classical Nahuatl, as "com-

Other Formal Statements

We, Juan Vicente, alcalde, and Miguel López, our home[2] being Jalostotitlan, bring a complaint before you, our great lord and king; before you we bring complaint about our priest and vicar Francisco Muñoz, who greatly mistreats us. He is always beating and whipping us; he whips the common people,[4] and he has severely beaten[5] me, Juan Vicente, alcalde. Three times he has given me blows and knocked me down, and I fainted. And he broke my staff into pieces there in the church, in the sacristy; when he was already dressed in the alb, stole, and maniple, then he beat me, and I said to him: Father, why are you beating me, you have broken my staff into bits. Then he said, Yes, I beat you and splintered your staff, and I will break your whole head.

— 1. (The accusation) is not empty, because our father keeps a lady there at the estancia; he is always there staying at the estancia. Once he was staying there at the estancia and the people of Mizquitic came bringing him fish. And I kept it for him for a day while I was observing the vigil of St. Andrew. And our father came very early,[6] when the cocks were already crowing on St. Andrew's day, and said: What has come of the fish? Then I told him: Father,

---

moners" or "subjects," and indeed these senses account for the usage quite well. Yet the Spanish interpreter in most cases translated the word as *naturales*, "natives," or *indios*, "Indians," and once, where the context seemed to demand "subjects," as *tributarios*, "tributaries." Thus in western Mexico at least, *macehualli* seems by the early seventeenth century to have been well on its way to being the referential equivalent of "Indian," as it became in later times.

[5]Note that in contrast to the richly varied preterits of central Mexico, here nearly all the preterits are formed by adding *-c* to the full verb stem, or the verb stem minus final vowel if it ends in two vowels. This is the most striking example we have seen of the regularization of linguistic mechanisms in peripheral areas where Nahuatl might have been a second language or one recently acquired.

[6]*Tlacoyohuac* would seem to be literally "midnight," yet the Spanish translator gives *al amanecer*, "at dawn." On the basis of the verb *yohua*, pret. *yohuac*, "to dawn," one could interpret *tlacoyohuac* as "it was half-dawning," or "at half-dawn." See also Carochi, p. 499, where *yohuatzinco* is given as *de mañana*.

tinechtitlanilic yalhua ompa estancia niman oniquilhui padre quenin nicmatiz yntla otinechnahuati ca nimichtitlanilizquia niman oncan pehua nechmictia quitoa ca huel titlahueliloc yuhqui ynin onechtolinic

— 2º yhuan ca ypampa cenca nechcocolia 15 pºs 2 tº quihuiquilia huey yglesia yhuan ce caxa yyaxca sancto sacramento yquac jueves sancto oncan calaqui quitlaçotla quimaxcatia çan campa quipia yquac oya mexico ynahuac ce tlacatl cocinero quicahuac yquac ohuala cepa conanac quicahuac ynahuac señora yn iquac cepa onicteyxpahuic yxpan señr prouisor yhuan san gaspar tlaca allde ome altepetl oticteyxpahuique auh yn señr prouisor oquinonotzac oquitlacaquiti quitlacuilhuic yhuan señr prouisor quinonotzac su señoria obispo auh yn señr obispo yhuan proui[sor] quitlacuilhuique oquilhuique xiquinyolali macehualtin ca mopilhuan xiquintlaçotla auh yn iquac oquicaquic yamauh señr obispo yhuan prouisor niman oquito tleypampa ayahui amoteyxpahui ynahuac prouisor niman ayaxquia ynahuac señr obispo çan monequi xihuian mexico ca ompa oniquixtic nonahuatil ynic nican nivicario ypampa ynin nechcocolia quicocolia mochi altepetl

— 3º niman cepa onechmictic yquac oquitac yamauh señr prouisor axcan ya opa nechmictia ocepa ompa mizquitic onechmictic teyxpan ypan ylhuitl santa maria natiuitas oc cepa niman ypan oc ce domingo onechmictic ya axca nauhpa nechmictia ypampa ynon amatl yamauh señr prouisor ypampa onicteyxpahuic ypampa nechmictic

— 4º oc cepa ce piltonti sachristan 8 xihuitl quipia[7] cepa cenca miec oquimecahuitequic cenca oquixipehuac ynacayo oçotlahua ce semana huetztoc omoquetzac niman otzoloc auh yn totatzin quitlatlania ynantzin quilhuia catia moconeuh quitoa ynantzin oticmacahuitequic[8] otzoloc auh yca oqualanic totatzin auh yn iquac ypan domingo ya teteochihua yca tlateochihualatl yquac mitoa asperges oncan nepantla teopan yahui teteochihua yca ysopo oquihuitequic cihuatzintli ynantzin pilton sacristan quiquatzayanac yxquich esti oquiquixtilic

---

[7]Note the apparently Spanish idiom, equivalent to *tiene ocho años*, an example which precedes the ones in Doc. 17 (see n. 3) by more than a century.

[8]On the basis of the context and examples elsewhere in the document one may conclude that *a* is a slip, and the intention was *oticmecahuitequic*. The hurried Spanish

here it is, I am keeping it here. Then he said: Why didn't you send it to me yesterday there at the estancia? Then I said to him: Father, how am I to know? If you had notified me, I would have sent it to you. Then and there he began to beat me, and said: You are a great rogue. Like this he mistreated me.

— 2. Also he greatly hates me because of 15 pesos, 2 tomines, that he owes to the main church, and a chest belonging to the (cofradía of the) Holy Sacrament; on Holy Thursday it (the Sacrament) is put in there. He gives it away, he gives it to people who keep it just anywhere. When he went to Mexico City, he left it with a man who is a cook; when he came back he took it again and left it with the lady. At another time I complained about him to the vicar-general along with the alcalde of the people of San Gaspar, and we two towns complained, and the vicar-general admonished him, criticized him, and wrote him, and the vicar-general conferred with his lordship the bishop, and the bishop and vicar-general wrote him saying: Console the commoners, for they are your children; love them. And when he had read the letter of the bishop and the vicar-general, then he said: Why do you go and complain to the vicar-general, and then you would go to the bishop? You really need to go to Mexico City, since there I got my orders to be vicar here. Because of this he hates me; he hates the whole town.

— 3. Then once he beat me when he saw the vicar-general's letter. Recently he beat me again, and another time there in Mizquitic he beat me in public, on the day of St. Mary's Nativity, and another time on another Sunday after that he beat me. Now it is four times he has beaten me on account of that letter, the vicar-general's letter, because I complained of him because he beat me.

— 4. Another time there was a boy, a sacristan, eight years old;[7] he whipped him very severely, he stripped off much of his skin, and he fainted. He lay in bed for a week; when he got up, then he ran away. And our father asked his mother, saying to her: What has come of your son? His mother said: You whipped him[8] and he ran away; and our father became angry at her. And on Sunday when he was already blessing people with holy water, while Asperges was being said, there in the middle of the church he was going along blessing people, and with the sprinkler he hit the woman who is the boy sacristan's mother, and he broke her head and made much blood spurt out.

---

translator arrived at "you gave him much work," presumably on the basis of *maca*, "give," and *tequi(tl)*, "work," but the elements are in the wrong order for this solution, not to speak of other impossibilities.

— 5º oc cepa ce fiscal ya otlamic ytequiuh ce xihuitl quichiuh ya quinahuatia quitoa padre ya otlamic notequiuh nifiscal auh yn yehuatl totatzin amo oquinequi mopatlaz cepa cenca oquimecahuitequi ycalictic[9] quicaltzaquac cenca quitolinic

— 6º auh yn oc cepa otictemoque ce tlacatl yancuic fiscal mochihuaz cepa amo quicelia quitoa amo nicnequi fiscal mochihuaz ynin baquero niman oquitotocac auh yn oc cepa quinotzac quitoa xicnotzacan yehuatl yn oanquitlalique fiscal niman oquinotza yehuatl fiscal catca quihualhuiquilic niman quinahuatic ytilticauh quiquixtilic ycalson mochi ycamissa mochi quipetlahuac ocacopiloc cepa[10] cenca oquimecahuitequic cenca oquiçotlahualtic yhuan nehuatl nictlatlauhtia nictlacahualtia amo oquinequi motlacahualtia auh yn iquac oquicahuac niman otzoloc campa hueca ayac axcan ayac[11] fiscal mochi tlacatl quimacaxi totatzin ayac aquin mochicahua mochihuaz fiscal

— 7º yhuan oc cepa ce tlacatl quititlanic ompa atotonilco quicahuaz ome caxas ya mohuicac quihuicac caxas auh yn totatzin oquilhuic yquac tiaz ompa mitic tinechitas nimichmaca ce carta ticmacaz a$\overline{ll}$d^{e} mayor ompa atotonilco auh ynin tlacatl quihuica caxas acito mitic quitemoc totatzin ayac onca çan ompa mocahuato estancia ynahuac señora auh yniman ompa mocuepac mitic oya ompa estancia ypan acito totatzin niman oquilhui tleypampa nican estancia tihuala oquilhuic padre niconanaznequi moamauh niman yc oqualanic oquilhui xiyauh ompa mitic xinechia ompa niaz nimichmacaz amatl niman tlacatl mocuepac mitic niman ohuala totatzin mitic niman oncan cepa miec oquimictic quiçotahualtic ypampa oquitoccac ompa estanyca[12] oqualanic totatzin amo quine[qui] aquin quitocaz yaz estancia ynahuac yseñora yn quemanian aquin motitlaniz mitic quitemoz cepa yaz estancia niman ompa quimictiz yuhqui techtolinia

— 8º cepa nochpoch catalina juana ompa yahui teopan teotlac tlachpanaz auh yn totatzin ompa teopan quitzitzquic quiyecoznequi

---

[9]For *icalitic*.

[10]Though the sense would make probable that the fiscal was whipped on the same occasion when he was strung up, *cepa* is generally used in the document for some-

— 5. Another time a fiscal had already finished his term and done a year, and he (the priest) still gave him orders. He said: Father, my term as fiscal already ended. And our father did not want him to be replaced. Once he whipped him severely inside his house, closed him up there, and greatly mistreated him.

— 6. And another time we sought a person to be made the new fiscal. Once he did not accept him, and said: I don't want this cow herder to be made fiscal. Then he chased him away. But another time he called him, saying: Call that person you have made fiscal. Then the person who had been fiscal called him (the new fiscal) and brought him back. Then he (the priest) gave orders to his black, who took off his (the new fiscal's) pants and shirt and stripped him completely, and hung him up. One time[10] he whipped him severely and made him faint away, and I begged him and held him back, but he did not want to be held back, and when he let him go then he ran far away. Now no one is fiscal, everyone is afraid of our father, no one dares become fiscal.

— 7. And another time he sent a person there to Atotonilco to deliver two chests. He was already going and taking the chests, and our father told him: When you go there to Mitic, you will see me. I will give you a letter that you will give to the alcalde mayor there in Atotonilco. And this person taking the chests arrived at Mitic and looked for our father. No one was there; he had gone to stay there at the estancia with the lady, and then [was to] return to Mitic. He went there to the estancia. When he arrived, then our father said to him, Why did you come here to the estancia? He told him: Father, I want to take your letter. Then at that he became angry, and told him: Go back to Mitic and wait for me. I will go there to give you the letter. Then the person returned to Mitic. Then our father came to Mitic, then there he beat him severely and made him faint because he followed him there to the estancia, which made our father angry. He doesn't want anyone to follow him and go to the estancia with his lady. When sometimes someone is sent to Mitic and (from there) goes to look for him at the estancia, then he beats him there. Like this he mistreats us.

— 8. Once my daughter Catalina Juana went there to the church in the evening to sweep, and there in the church our father seized

thing like "again" or "another time," and the Spanish translator too rendered this instance as *una vez*.

[11]This second *ayac* was inserted later, above the line.

[12]For *estancia yca*.

amo quicelia cepa oncan teopancalitic oquimictic niman ohuala moteyxpahuico nixpan[13]

— 9 yuhqui techtolinia auh ymmiec tlacatl macehualtin quimacaxi miec tlacatl tzoloa yhuan ayac aquin quicelia mochihuaz fiscal

— 10 no yhuan yn iquac yahui estancia amo payna huala quemanian matlacti oras huala auh yn macehualtin amo mochicahua quichiaz yca matlacti oras quemanian tzatziz totolin hualaz anoço quemanian tlahuitihuitz auh in tehuantin ypampa cenca titotolinia ynic ticchiazque

— 11 no yhuan amo techmachtia teotlatoli sermon ca çan yxquich techcocolitinemi techtolintinemi yn iquac señr prouisor quitlacuilhuic oquilhui xiquinyolali macehualtin ca mopilhuan niman quicaquic quitoa tleypampa niquinyolaliz niquintlaçotlaz coz[14] nopilhuan ca ypilhuan diablo ca niquintoliniz amo quitlacamati ytlanahuatil señr prouisor yhuan obispo

— 12 auh ynic axcan tiquitlanico yn motetlaocoliliz yn titotlatocauh yn titorrey titechtlaocoliz titechmomaquiliz ce quali teopixqui techtlaçotlaz no yuhqui tictlazotlazque ynin tovicario ma xicmoquixtili ma quiça ypampa cenca techtolinia amo techtlaçotla yntlacamo quiçaz ca miec tlaca mopilhuan momacehualhuan tzolozque ypampa tovicario auh no yhuan polihuiz yn itlacalaquil tohueytlatoca rrey campa ticanazque ticaxitizque yxquich totlatol timomacehualhuan

ju^{o} bicenti a$\overline{ll}$d^{e} miguel lopez

— 13 yhuan quinequi toyolo techcuepiliz 15 p^{o}s 2 t^{o} yhuan caxa yyaxca sanctissimo sacram^{o} toyolo pachihuiz ca mochipa ynin techcocolia

— 14 no yhuan quintitlania macehualtin campa hueca yhuan nican molino quintitlania amo tlaxtlahua yhuan macehualtin quinahuatia quimachtia ypotros amo tlaxtlahua

[13]Both the Nahuatl and the Spanish translation seem open to the interpretation that it was the priest, not the daughter, who came to complain, which would surely not be out of character.

[14]We can only speculate that *coz* may be a mistake for the *ca* in the same position

her and wanted to have her. She would not let him, and there inside the church he beat her. Then she came to complain to me.[13]

— 9. Thus he mistreats us, and many of the common people are afraid of him. Many people run away, and there is no one who will let himself be made fiscal.

— 10. And also, when he goes to the estancia he does not return quickly; sometimes he returns at ten o'clock, and the commoners will not exert themselves to wait till ten o'clock. Sometimes he will come when the cocks are crowing, or dawn comes, and because of this we suffer greatly waiting for him.

— 11. And also, he does not teach us the divine words, the sermon, but only hates us and mistreats us constantly. When the vicar-general wrote him, saying: Console the commoners, for they are your children, as soon as he read it, he said: Why am I to console and love them as my children?[14] They are children of the devil, and I will mistreat them. And he did not obey the order of the vicar-general and the bishop.

— 12. And now we have come in order to request your compassion, you our ruler and king, that you do us the favor of giving us a good priest who will love us and whom we likewise will love. Send away this vicar of ours, let him leave, because he greatly mistreats us and does not love us. If he does not leave, many of your children and subjects will flee because of our vicar, and also the tribute of our great ruler and king will be lost; from where will we take enough to complete it? These are all the words of us your subjects.

Juan Vicente, alcalde. Miguel López.

— 13. And our hearts desire that he return us 15 pesos, 2 tomines, and the chest belonging to the Most Holy Sacrament, and we will be satisfied; for he always hates us (for) this.

— 14. And also he sends the commoners far away, and he sends them here to the mill and does not pay for it, and he orders the commoners to break his colts and does not pay for it.

---

within this phrase where it appears just above. Or it may be related to *cuix*, an interrogative marker. The translation would then be "Why am I to console and love them? Are they my children?"

28. Petition of the town of San Martín about its church, 1653[1]

ypeticion altepetl Sa mart[in]

ma yectenehualo'yn santisimo sacramento yhuan [. . .] pahualiz yn concepcion mochipa cemicac ma y mochi[hua]

tehuantin timomacehuatlhuan mixpantzinco tinecico sen ys^{a} obizbo tictenamiquico momatzin yhuan mocxitzin ca tehuatzin tiyxiptla noestro padre santo padre yn ompa moyetztica roma nican ticmocaquitiz[2] tonetequipachol tochoquiz ytechcopa tosanta yglecia nican sa martin ca neli melahuac huel techtolinticate tocabeceras alcaldes yhuan toguardianes[3] amo techcahua tictequipanosque toteyopan ma ypampa dios ma topan ximotlatolti ynahuac toguardian amo technotzazque asta tictlamizque toteyopan ma ypampa dios axcan quitohua alcaldes cocolan ompa tiasque cabecera yca mochi tonamichuan ompa titequipanosque yhuan nican yuhqui mocahuas tosanta yglecia ca huel cenca timotequipacholo[4] timochintin altepehuaque axcan yntla dios quimonequiltiz ya tlecoz bicas yhuan motlapachos yhuan manel yuhqui amo ypampa tictelchihua toguardian ticmacasque yn quexquich ytech monequiz nican tiquitoz yn quexquich titlayocolia toguardianes limosna mochipa cemicac

— quahuitl ce cemana[5]	ce careta
— çacatl para ycabalyo	ome careta
— cabalyopixqui	ce cemana
— michin ticmacalo[6]	ce cemana
— totoltetl ticmacalo	ce cemana
— tlaxcali ticmacalo	ce cemana
— totolin ticmacalo	ce cemana
— ortelano ticmacalo	ce cemana
— tequipanohuani teyopan	ce cemana
— atl ticmacalo	ce cemana

— yhuan titemacalo maquili peso ypampa cilyo pasqual — 5 p^{s}o

---

[1]McAfee Collection, UCLA Research Library, Special Collections. The town involved is San Martín Hidalgo, some 45 miles southwest of Guadalajara; the head town referred to is nearby Cocula. A Spanish paraphrase acccompanies the document. See Appendix II.

[2]This writer often omits the plural in the future.

[3]In this case and some others in this document, the Spanish *-es* ending must be interpreted as a singular.

Petition of the town of San Martín.

Praised be the Most Holy Sacrament and [. . .] the Conception forever eternally, Amen.

We your subjects have come to appear before you, most illustrious lord bishop, we have come to kiss your hands and feet, for you are the representative of our father the Holy Father who is there in Rome. Here we will announce to you our trouble and lamenting concerning our holy church here in San Martín, for it is true and certain that the alcaldes and prior[3] of our head town are mistreating us, and do not let us work on our church. For God's sake, speak on our behalf to our prior, that they not summon us until we finish our church, for God's sake. Now the alcaldes of Cocula say we are to go there to the head town with all our wives and are to work there; and our holy church here will be left as it is, and we townsmen are all very troubled. Now, if God wills it, the beams will be raised and (the church) covered. And though it is so, not for that do we disdain our prior; we will give him whatever he needs. Here we will say how much we always and forever help our prior with contributions:

— wood each week[5]	one cartload
— grass for his horse	two cartloads
— someone to watch horses	each week
— we give him fish	each week
— we give him eggs	each week
— we give him bread	each week
— we give him fowl	each week
— we give him a gardener	each week
— someone to work in the church	each week
— we give him water	each week
— And we give five pesos for Easter candles	– 5 pesos

[4]The writer uses *mo-* as the first person plural reflexive pronoun.

[5]Literally, "one week," but logic dictates a distributive sense. The Spanish paraphraser reached the same conclusion.

[6]These forms in *-lo* resemble passives, yet unlike the regular passive construction, they allow for the expression of the semantic subject as marked by the subject prefix. They may suggest habitual or impersonal action.

— yhuan bicas para ompa cabecera titemacalo ynin mochi limosna ticmacalo toguardian ma yuhqui xicmomachiti tlatohuani yhuan ce xiuitl ompa otiaque otitequipanoque amo techtlaqualtia yntencopa omomicti maquili nobilyos yaxca nican totlasonantzin cobratia sa martin yhuan tlayoli hanegas ma yuhqui xicmati amo tiasque ypampa dios ypampa ya nican otitlacencahuaque mochi quahuitl tablas ya anquimati ayc mo[xtlahua][7] xopantlan ma quichihuacan ynceltin no ticnequilo quali y [. . .] yhuan ca huecaticate ome lehua yhuan tlaco yehuantin ca ya otlami ynteoyopan ma ypampa dios ma ypan xitlato nican santa yglecia yntla dios quinequiz tlamiz ypan ome xiuitl

ya yxquich totlatol ma dios espirito santo motlantzinco yes cemicac otitlaquiloque timomacehuatlhuan ynic neltiz totlatol nican timofirmatia ti timochintin huehuetque altepetl sa martin

luyz basques alcalde juan quera regidor juan cebastian fiscal juan de la croz principales fraco miguel juan esteban juan agustin pernabe leantro fraco çabastian luyz martin pedro geroninmo[8]

otitlaquiloque axcan 2 tonali abril yhuan xiuitl 1653 anos

diego juan esbano yntencopa altepehuaque sa martin huehuetque

29. Letter of the council of Huejotzingo to the king, 1560[1]

C R Mt

Totecuioe totlatocatzine yn tiRey Don felipe nr̄o señor cenca timitzvecapammaviznepechtequilia tocnoteca tocnomati mixpantzinco y vel timavizvecapatlatouani yn ipaltzinco in ixquichivelli in ipalnemovani yn dios Amo tomacehual inic tictenamiquizque mocxitzin ça vecapa timitztonepechtequililia in cenca tivecapa tix̄piano in vel titevellamachticatzin yn dios toteo ca teuatzin vel tixiptlatzin inican tlal-

---

[7]Here the paraphrase has "no se les paga nunca nada."

[8]The notary signed all the names.

Document 29

[1]Doc. 165, Archivo Histórico Nacional, Madrid. A facsimile, neither transcribed,

— And we give beams for the head town. All these contributions we give to our prior, may you so know it, sir. And for a year we went there and worked and they did not feed us; at their command five steers belonging to the cofradía of our dear mother here in San Martín were slaughtered, and bushels of maize. May you know this, and may we not go, for God's sake, because here we have already prepared all the wood and planks. You know it is never (repaid).[7] In the spring let them do it themselves. Also we want [. . .] and they are far away, two and a half leagues. Their church has already been finished. For God's sake, speak about it. The holy church here will be finished in two years, if God is willing.

These are all our words. May God the Holy Spirit always be with you. We your subjects wrote it. To verify our words we sign here, we, all of us elders of the town of San Martín.

Luis Vázquez, alcalde. Juan Guerra, councilman. Juan Sebastián, fiscal. Juan de la Cruz, nobleman. Francisco Miguel. Juan Esteban. Juan Agustín. Bernabé Leandro. Francisco Sebastián. Luis Martín. Pedro Jerónimo.[8]

We wrote it today, the 2d day of April in the year 1653.

Diego Juan, notary, at the request of the townsmen (and) elders of San Martín.

Catholic Royal Majesty:

Our lord sovereign, you the king don Felipe our lord, we bow low in great reverence to your high dignity, we prostrate and humble ourselves before you, very high and feared king through omnipotent God, giver of life. We do not deserve to kiss your feet, only from afar we bow down to you, you who are most high and Christian and very pleasing to God our Lord, for you are his true representative here on

translated, nor commented on, is to be found in the *Cartas de Indias,* and is an excellent example of the orthographic practices of the time. Another letter of this genre, from the council of Tenochtitlan to the king, with a Spanish paraphrase from the same time, is printed in Günter Zimmermann, *Briefe der indianischen Nobilität.*

ticpac yn titechmopachilhuia in titechmoyacanilia yn itechcopa in xp̄ianoyotl in tehuanti in tixquichti in titlachivalhua yn timacehualhuan in ipalnemovani yn dios ihuan in tehuatzin in timomacevaltzitziva in timotetlaecolticatzitziva inican titlaca inican tichaneque yn nueva españa movicpatzinco tocemitztoque movicpatzinco toconcentlazticate yn tix in toyollo timitzotocentemachilia in ixpantzinco in tote[o] dios ca momactzinco otechmotlalili inic titechmopializ ihua motetzinco otechmopouilli ynic timotlacavan tiazque inic timotetlaecolticahuan tiazque ma icatzinco yn to[o] dios ihuan ma ica in cenca maviztic in cenca vecapa motlatocayotzin Xitechmelnamiquili xitechvalmotlaocolithuili ca cenca vei tonetoliniliz tonetequipachol in topan mochiva yn nican nueva espana tichaneque

Totecuioe totlatocatzine yn tirrey don felipe n̄ro señor mixpantzinco totlatoltica tontonextia tontoquetza yn tivexutzinca in timitztlapilia yn mociudad tichaneque Neuatl nigouer[or] ihuan in tial̄desme tirregidoresme ihuan titeteucti tipipilti in timotlacavan timotetlaecolticahuan yn cenca timitztocnotlatlauhtilia omochiuh ototlaueliltic cenca vei cenca etic in topan catqui in tlaocoyaliztli ynetequipacholiztli ancan topan aci ancan totech aci in motetlaocolilitzin in moteicnoitalitzin amo ticmaceva amo tiquicnopilhuia yn motlatocayotzin Auh ca in ixquich cavitl ynic topan acico yn momacevalhua españoles ixquich cavitl movicpatzinco tonitztinemi tontlatemachitinemi yn quemania topan aciquiuh yn motetlaocolilitzin no iuhqui otictemachitinenca oticchixtinenca yn itetlaocolilitzin yn cenca momahuiztlaçotatzin in tlatohuani cemanahuac yn don carlos emperador catca Auh ipampa yn axcan tote[e] totlatocatzine tontocnopechteca yn mixpantzinco ma ticmacevaca yn motetlaocolilitzin ma mitzmoyollotili in cenca huei tetlaocoliani teicnoitani in dios inic topan mochivaz motetlaocolilitzin ca in ticcaqui yn iuh tilhuillo ca cenca ticnovacatzintli titlatlacatzintli in ivicpa in ixquichti momacevalhuan yn iquac ce ticmocnoitilia[2] yn mixpantzinco necih momaceval in motolinia yuh mitoa ca nima ticmocnoittilia yca in cenca mahuiztic motlatocayotzin yhuan in icatzinco yn ixquichivelli in dios ticmochivilia Ma no iuhqui axcan ticmacevaca tiquicnopilhuica ca in momoztlae topan aci topan mochivan ynetoliniliztli yn netequipacholliztli ynic titochoquilia titotlaocoltia omochiuh ototlaveliltic canpa tiazque[3] yn timocnomacevaltzitzivan yn tivexutzinca yn mociudad tinemi intlacamo veca timetztica ca miyacp[o]a

[2]One might suspect that the first *ticmocnoitilia* owes its presence to a slip, in which case *yn iquac ce* could easily and naturally refer forward to *momaceval*. The

earth, you who govern us and lead us in things of Christianity. All of us creatures and subjects of the life-giving God, we vassals and servants of your majesty, we people here, we who dwell here in New Spain, all together we look to you, our eyes and hearts go out toward you; we have complete confidence in you in the eyes of our Lord God, for he put us in your hands to guard us, and he assigned us to you for us to be your servants and your helpers. By our Lord God and by your very honored and very high majesty, remember us, have compassion with us, for very great is the poverty and affliction visited on us who dwell here in New Spain.

Our lord sovereign, king don Felipe our lord, with our words we appear and stand before you, we of Huejotzingo who guard for you your city—we citizens, I the governor and we the alcaldes and councilmen and we the lords and nobles, your men and your servants. Very humbly we implore you: Oh unfortunate are we, very great and heavy sadness and affliction lie upon us, nowhere do your pity and compassion extend over us and reach us, we do not deserve, we do not attain your rulership. And all the while since your subjects the Spaniards arrived among us, all the while we have been looking toward you, we have been confidently expecting that sometime your pity would reach us, as we also had confidence in and were awaiting the mercy of your very revered dear father the ruler of the world, don Carlos the late emperor. Therefore now, our lord sovereign, we bow humbly before you; may we deserve your pity, may the very greatly compassionate and merciful God enlighten you so that your pity is exercised on us, for we hear, and so it is said to us, that you are very merciful and humane towards all your vassals; and as to the time when you pity someone,[2] when before you appears a vassal of yours in poverty, so it is said, then you have pity on him with your very revered majesty, and by the grace of omnipotent God you do it for him. May we now also deserve and attain the same, for every day such poverty and affliction reaches us and is visited on us that we weep and mourn. Oh unfortunate are we, what will happen to us,[3] we your poor vassals of Huejotzingo, we who live in your city? If you were not so far away, many times we would appear before you. Though we greatly wish and desire to reach you and appear before you, we are

translation would then read "when a vassal of yours appears before you in poverty, so it is said, then you have pity on him. . . ."

[3]Literally, "where will we go?"

mixpantzinco tinecizquia tel cenca ticnequi tiquellevia in ma mixpantzinco tacica tinecican ammo tiveliti yeica ca cenca titotolinia ca antle neci in totech monequiz yn otlica yn acalco yn tiquazque yvan inic titetlaxtlavizque ynic huel motetzinco tacizque yeica yn axcan çan totlatoltica mixpantzinco toneci ihuan mixpantzinco tocontlalia yn tocnomacevallatol ma çan ica in cenca vei in mox̅p̅ianoyo ihuan cenca mavizvecapa motlatocayotzin ma xicmohuelcaquiti inin tocnotlatol

Totecuioe totlatocatzine yn ayamo aca techilhui techiximachti yn moteyo ynmotlatollo in ticenvecapamahuiztlatoani ynovian tiRey in titlacenpachoa ihuan yn ayamo ticaquitiloque in timachtiloque yn iteyotzin yn itocatzin in tote^{o} dios yn ayamo topan acic yn tlaneltoquiliztli yn ayamo tix̅pianome yn iquac topan onacico yn motetlaecolticavan españoles inic valla in mocapitan general Don her^{do} cortes yn maçonelivi yn ayamo tictiximachilique in ixquichivelli in cenca tetlaocoliani in sanctissiman trinidad yn ilhuicava yn tlalticpaque yn to^{o} dios techmomacehualtili in ica ytetlaocolilitzin techyolloti ynic timitztotlatocatizque ynic motetzinco tipouizque inic timotlacahuan timomacevalhuan titochiuhque ayac ce altepetl techpanavia ynic nica nueva españa ynic yacuica yacachto movictzinco titotlazque timitztomacaque no ihuan ayac yc techmamauhti ayac techcuitlahuilti ca ça uel yehuatzin yn dios techmomacevaltili toyollocacopa motetzinco titopouhque ynic tiquintopacacelilique in yancuica huallaque españoles in topan acico nica nueva españa ca hueca ticauhque yn tocal inic tiquizque ynic veca tiquinamiquito cenpouali leguas inic tiyaque inic tiquintlapaloto in yehuatl capitan general don her^{do} cortes ihuan oc cequinti quihualyacan vel tiquintopaccacelilique tiquintonahuatequilique vel tiquinchoquiztlapalloque yn macoçonelivi yn amo tiquimiximatia Auh in tothahuan yn tocolhuan yn amo no quimatia ca çan itetlaocolilitzintica yn to^{o} dios ynic huellotiquimixmatque ca tohuanpoua ynic tiquintotlaçotilique oncan[4] tiquinpevaltique ye tiquintlaqualtia in ye tiquintlaecoltia cequinti hualmococotaque inic tiquinapaloque tiquimemeque yn oc cenca miyac ic otiquintlaecoltique yn amo vel nican tiquitozque macihui in yeuatl moteneva mitoa tlaxcaltecatl ca otlapallevi ca ça vel tevan ticuitlaviltique inic tlapalleviz ihuan tevan tictlacavaltique inic amo quiyaochivaz yn maçonelivi tictlacahualtique ca ya iuh ya caxtolilhuitl[5] quiyaochivaya quimicatia[6] Auh yn

---

[4]Though the manuscript has *oncan*, we read it as *ancan*, as in the examples in the second paragraph.

unable, because we are very poor and do not have what is needed for the journey on the boat nor things to eat nor anything to pay people in order to be able to reach you. Therefore now we appear before you only in our words; we set before you our poor prayer. May you only in your very great Christianity and very revered high majesty attend well to this our prayer.

Our lord sovereign, before anyone told us of or made us acquainted with your fame and your story, most high and feared universal king who rules all, and before we were told or taught the glory and name of our Lord God, before the faith reached us, and before we were Christians, when your servants the Spaniards reached us and your captain general don Hernando Cortés arrived, although we were not yet acquainted with the omnipotent, very compassionate holy Trinity, our Lord God the ruler of heaven and possessor of earth caused us to deserve that in his mercy he enlightened us so that we took you as our king to belong to you and become your people and your subjects; not a single town surpassed us here in New Spain in that first and earliest we threw ourselves toward you, we gave ourselves to you, and furthermore no one intimidated us, no one forced us into it, but truly God caused us to deserve that voluntarily we adhered to you so that we gladly received the newly arrived Spaniards who reached us here in New Spain, for we left our homes behind to go a great distance to meet them; we went twenty leagues to greet captain general don Hernando Cortés and the others whom he led. We received them very gladly, we embraced them, we saluted them with many tears, though we were not acquainted with them, and our fathers and grandfathers also did not know them; but by the mercy of our Lord God we truly came to know them. Since they are our neighbors, therefore we loved them; nowhere[4] did we attack them. Truly we fed them and served them; some arrived sick, so that we carried them in our arms and on our backs, and we served them in many other ways which we are not able to say here. Although the people who are called and named Tlaxcalans indeed helped, yet we strongly pressed them to give aid, and we admonished them not to make war; but though we so admonished them, they made war and fought[6] for fifteen days.[5] But

[5]Probably the equivalent of the Spanish *quince días*, "two weeks."
[6]*Quimicatia* must be read as *quimicalia*.

teuan inma çanel[7] ce motollinia español ynman quen ticchiuhque inma itech tacique niman ayac[8] ynin amo tiztlacati ca huel quimati in ixquichti conguistadores yn omomiquilique ihuan axca cequinti monemitia

Auh in iquac yn oconpehualtique yn intepeualiz in inteyaochivaliz ca niman vel no titocencauhque ynic tiquintopallevilique[9] ca ça vel ixquich totech oquiz yn toyaopantlatqui in totlaviz in titac ca huel mochi taxca auh amo çan titlaixquetzque ca vel tonoma tiyaque in titlatocati ihuan in ixquich yn topilloa ihuan in ixquichti tomacevalhua tiquivicaque ynic tiquipallevique yn españoles amo çaniyo yaoyotica in tiquipalevique çano ihuan yn ixquich yntech monec otiquimacaque tiquintlaqualtique tiquintlaquetique Auh in yaopan quincocovaya yn anoço ça vel mococovaya tiquinapallotinenca tiquimemetinenca auh in ixquich yn yaopan tequitl inic tlachichivalloya mochi tehuanti ticchiuhque Auh inic vel quinpeuhque yn mexicatl in acaltica vel tevanti tictequipanoque tiquinmacaque yn quahuitl yvan in ocotzotl ynic quichiuhque acalli yn espanoles Auh in iquac oquinpeuhque yn mexicatl ihuan in ixquich ytech pouia ayc otiquintlalcauique ammo no yc tiquimicapacauhque Auh in iquac tepevato yn michvaca in xalixco in colhuacan yhuan in ompa in panco auh in ompa yn vaxcac yn tequanteopec in quauhtemalla ça ce yn ya ic nica nueva españa in tepeuhque in teyaochiuhque inic quitzonquixtique yn intepevaliz ayc tiquintlalcavique amo no itla tiquimitlacalhuique yn inyaotiliz yn manel ticeme yc tipololoque yn manocen tomaceval niman ayac[8] ca vel ticyecchiuhque yn totequiuh Auh in yehuanti tlaxcalteca ca quezquinti pipiltin yn piloloque ynic amo qualli quichiuhque yn yaoyotl miyacca hualcholloque in miyacpa quitlacoque yn yaoyotl ynin amo tiquiztlacati ca huel yevan quimomachitia yn conguitadores

Totecuioe totlatocatzine no ihuan mixpantzinco tiquitohua ticnextia inic topa acicoh in motatzitziuan p̄resme in matlactli ommome yn sanct fran^co^ ipilhuan in quihualmivali in cenca vecapa teopixcatlatoani s^o^ p̄re iuan in tehuatzin tiquivalmivalli ynic antechmotlaocolilique inic techmachtico yn evangelio inic techmach-

[7]We are here interpreting *inmaçanel* as *inma çanel*, containing *imma* "when" and *çanel* = *çanelli* "without fail," rather than as *in maçanel* "although."

[8]The expression *niman ayac* occurs twice in this document as a relatively independent phrase. By analogy with phrases such as *ayac tlacatl*, "there is no one," *niman ayac* might mean "there is no one at all" (*niman* often serves as an intensifier of negatives). The sense of the first occurrence would be "there was no one who did what we did." The second case would mean "there were none of us left." But the interpretation

we, when a Spaniard was afflicted, without fail[7] at once we managed to reach him; [there was no one else].[8] We do not lie in this, for all the conquerers know it well, those who have died and some now living.

And when they began their conquest and war-making, then also we well prepared ourselves to aid them, for out came all of our war gear, our arms and provisions and all our equipment, and we not merely named someone, we went in person, we who rule, and we brought all our nobles and all of our vassals to aid the Spaniards. We helped not only in warfare, but also we gave them everything they needed; we fed and clothed them, and we would carry in our arms and on our backs those whom they wounded in war or who were very ill, and we did all the tasks in preparing for war. And so that they could fight the Mexica with boats, we worked hard; we gave them the wood and pitch with which the Spaniards made the boats. And when they conquered the Mexica and all belonging to them, we never abandoned them or left them behind in it. And when they went to conquer Michoacan, Jalisco, and Colhuacan, and there at Pánuco and there at Oaxaca and Tehuantepec and Guatemala, (we were) the only ones who went along while they conquered and made war here in New Spain until they finished the conquest; we never abandoned them, in no way did we prejudice their war-making, though some of us were destroyed in it [nor was there a single one of our subjects left?],[8] for we did our duty very well. But as to those Tlaxcalans, several of their nobles were hanged for making war poorly; in many places they ran away, and often did badly in the war. In this we do not lie, for the conquerors know it well.

Our lord sovereign, we also say and declare before you that your fathers the twelve sons of St. Francis reached us, whom the very high priestly ruler the Holy Father sent and whom you sent, both taking pity on us so that they came to teach us the gospel, to teach us the holy Catholic faith and belief, to make us acquainted with the

---

of this passage is highly dubious because of the different possible meanings of *tomaceval*, which could mean either "our subject" or "our merit." The phrase might thus be open to the construction "there was no one deserving as we." Also the analysis of *ynmanocen* is not easy. We have transcribed it as *yn manocen* and identified it with *manoce*, "nor," "or," as in Carochi, p. 516.

[9]The writer originally put *tiquintopallevilizque*, a future, then marked out the *z*, making the preterit.

tico in sancta fe catolica in tlaneltoquiliztli ynic techiximachitico in icel teotl yn dios tote^{o} Auh in teuanti Tivexu^{ca} yn mociudad tichaneque çanoihuin techmocnelili in dios te[c]hyolloti inic tiquintopaccacelilique yn iquac ipan valcallacque yn altepetl vexutzinco Vel toyollocacopan tiquintomaviztilique tiquintotlaçotilique in iquac techmonahuatequilique inic tictlalcavizque yn nepapan tlateotoquiliztli yn tlavelilocayotl ça niman toyollocacopan ticcauhque no ihuan techmocnelilique in tiquintelchiuhque tiquinpopoloque tiquintlatique in tetl in quavitl ticteteotiaya ca oticchiuhque huel toyollocacopa tiquinpopoloque tiquixixinique tiquintlatique yn teocalti no yquac yn ya techmomaquilia yn s^{o} evangelio in sancta fe catolica vel ica toceyaliz totlanequiliz oticuique oticanque ayac ic techmamauhti ayac techcuitlahuilti ça vel tocializtica otictzitzquique ihuan in izquitlamantli s̄cros otechmomaquilique yhuian yocoxcan totech otictlalique totech oticpachoque ça nima aic ce yn ma pilli anoço macevaltzintli yc toliniloc yn anoço yc tlatiloc in ixquich novian omochiuh inic nican nohuia[10] españa in miequi altepeme cuitlaviltiloque yc toliniloque yn aço piloloque yn anoço tlatiloque inic amo quicavaznequia in tlateotoquiliztli ihuan yn amo iyollocacopa quiceliaya in evang^{o} ihua in tlaneltoquiliztli oc cenca yeuanti in tlaxcalteca can[11] quintopevaya quintlaçaya yn p̄reme yn amo quiceliaya in tlaneltoquiliztli ca miyaquinti tlaçopipilti yc tlatiloque ihuan cequinti piloloque inic ocompehualtique in inotzaloca in itlaecoltiloca in to^{o} dios Auh in tevatin in tihuexutzinca in timocnomacevaltzitziuan ayc ytla otimitztitlacalhuilique mochipa otimitztotlaecoltilique in izquitlamantli otiquivalmivalli motecopatzinco tinavatinavatilo Vel ixquich yvian yocoxca ticana ticui ca tel çan itetlaocolilitzintica yn dios ticchivan ca amo tonoma catle tohuelli yeica axcan ma çan icatzinco ma çan ipaltzinco yn dios xitechmocaquilili Inin totlatol in izquitlamantli mixpantzinco ticnextia tiquitoa inic titechmotlaocoliliz inic topa ticmochiviliz yn motlatocayotzin inic titechmoyollaliliz titechmopalleviliz inic cecemilhuitl tichoca titlaocoya cenca tinentlamati tipatzmiqui ihuan iuhqui ya xiniznequi ya poliviznequi in maltepetzin yn mociudad vexu^{co} Iz catqui in topa ya mochiva yn axcan in topan quitlalia in motlapixcatzitzivan yn officiales yoan in fiscal doctor maldonado cenca vey in tlacallaquili yn motetzinco poui cen xiquipilli pesos tomines ihuan caxtoltzontli pesos yhuan ontzontli pesos tomin no ixquich in tlaolli hanegas in totlacallaquil yn ticchivazque

[10]For *nueva*.

single deity God our Lord, and likewise God favored us and enlightened us, us of Huejotzingo, who dwell in your city, so that we gladly received them. When they entered the city of Huejotzingo, of our own free will we honored them and showed them esteem. When they embraced us so that we would abandon the wicked belief in many gods, we forthwith voluntarily left it; likewise they did us the good deed (of telling us) to destroy and burn the stones and wood that we worshipped as gods, and we did it; very willingly we destroyed, demolished, and burned the temples. Also when they gave us the holy gospel, the holy Catholic faith, with very good will and desire we received and grasped it; no one frightened us into it, no one forced us, but very willingly we seized it, and they gave us all the sacraments. Quietly and peacefully we arranged and ordered it among ourselves; no one, neither nobleman nor commoner, was ever tortured or burned for this, as was done on every hand here in New Spain. (The people of) many towns were forced and tortured, were hanged or burned because they did not want to leave idolatry, and unwillingly they received the gospel and faith. Especially those Tlaxcalans pushed out and rejected the fathers, and would not receive the faith, for many of the high nobles were burned, and some hanged, for combating the advocacy and service of our Lord God. But we of Huejotzingo, we your poor vassals, we never did anything in your harm, always we served you in every command you sent or what at your command we were ordered. Very quietly, peacefully we take and grasp it all, though only through the mercy of God do we do it, since it is not within our personal power. Therefore now, in and through God, may you hear these our words, all that we say and declare before you, so that you will take pity on us, so that you will exercise on us your rulership to console us and aid us in (this trouble) with which daily we weep and are sad. We are afflicted and sore pressed, and your town and city of Huejotzingo is as if it is about to disappear and be destroyed. Here is what is being done to us: now your stewards the royal officials and the prosecuting attorney Dr. Maldonado are assessing us a very great tribute to belong to you. The tribute we are to give is 14,800 pesos in money, and also all the bushels of maize.

---

[11]For *çan*.

Totecuiyoe totlatocatzine ca aic yuhqui topan omochiuh yn ixquich cavitl topan acico in motetlaecolticatzitziua in momacevalhuan españoles ca yn yeuatl yn motetlaecolticatzin yn don herdo cortes capitan general catca in margues del valle yn ixquich cavitl o nica monemiti tonavac vel mochipa otechmotlaçotili otechpaccanemiti ayc otechacoma ayc otechcomoni macihuin in ticmacaya tlacallaquili ca çan techixyeyecalhuiaya maçonelli in coztic teocuitlatl yn ticmacaya ca ça vel tepito çaço quexquich çaço quenami in maca nel huel coztic[12] ca çan quipaccaceliaya ayc techavac ayc techtequipacho yeica ca vel ixpan catca ca vel quimomachitiaya inic cenca vei o yc tictlaecoltique ticpallevique no miyacpa techilhuiaya inic mixpantzinco topan tlatoz techpalleviz mitzmomachitiliz in ixquich yc otimitztopallevilique inic otimitztotlaecoltilique Auh in iquac mixpantzinco vya in iquac oticmoneltilili yn oticmotlaocolili yn oticmaviztili ticmotlaxtlavilli inic omitzmotlaecoltilico inica nueva españa auh aço çan techelcauh in mixpantzinco quenoçonel tiquitozque camo tacia camo titlacaquia in mixpantzinco ac nel in topan tlatoz omochiuh ototlaveliltic ypampa axcan tontocencava mixpantzinco totlatocatzine totee Auh in iquac tiquivalmivalli in mixiptlatzitzivan yn presidente obpo don sebastian Ramirez yvan in oydores yn llicendo salmeron yn llicendo cahinos quiluca maldonado ca vel yeuantin quineltilico quichicavaco yn mihiyotzin yn motlatoltzin inic topampa tiquimonavatili inican titlaca yn nueva espana tichaneque cenca miyac tlamantli yc otechpallevique yc otechcaxanique yn cenca vevey totlacallaquil ocatca yvan in miyac tlamantli in totlatequipanoliz catca vel ixquichipa techmaquixtique vel ixquich techpopolhuilique Auh in tevanti timocnomacevaltzitzinva in tivexutzinca yn mociudad tichaneque ca topa ovalmovicac ypan callaquico yn altepetl Vexutzinco yn llicendo salmeron ca niman quimothuili in altepetl inic cenca motolinitica in ica totlacallaquil in coztic teocuitlatl epouallatemantotontin[13] in cexiuhtica ticcallaquia Auh inic techtolinia yehica amo nican neci in coztic teocuitlatl amo nican catqui yn ipan taltepeuh ca ça novia tictemovaya yc niman quipopollo motecopatzinco yn llicendo salmero yc conixiptlacayoti quipatcayoti yn tomines in techtlalili totlacallaquil macuiltzontli pesos ihuan ompovalli ommatlactli pesos tomines Auh ca ixquich cauitl in techtlalili isquich cavitl otiqualchiuhtaque in timitztomaquilitivitze inic timomacevalhuan ynic motetzinco tipoui aic otiquicxicauhque ayc otiquitlacoque Vel mochi oticaxil-

---

[12]We take the literal meaning to be "not very yellow," i.e., "not very high in gold content."

Our lord sovereign, never has such happened to us in all the time since your servants and vassals the Spaniards came to us, for your servant don Hernando Cortés, late captain general, the Marqués del Valle, in all the time he lived here with us, always greatly cherished us and kept us happy; he never disturbed nor agitated us. Although we gave him tribute, he assigned it to us only with moderation; even though we gave him gold, it was only very little; no matter how much, no matter in what way, or if not very pure,[12] he just received it gladly. He never reprimanded us or afflicted us, because it was evident to him and he understood well how very greatly we served and aided him. Also he told us many times that he would speak in our favor before you, that he would help us and inform you of all the ways in which we have aided and served you. And when he went before you, then you confirmed him and were merciful to him, you honored and rewarded him for the way he had served you here in New Spain. But perhaps before you he forgot us. How then shall we speak? We did not reach you, we were not given audience before you. Who then will speak for us? Unfortunate are we. Therefore now we place ourselves before you, our sovereign lord. And when you sent your representatives, the Presidente and Bishop don Sebastián Ramírez, and the judges, Licentiate Salmerón, Licentiates Ceinos, Quiroga, and Maldonado, they well affirmed and sustained the orders you gave for us people here, us who live in New Spain. In many things they aided us and lightened the very great tribute we had, and from many things that were our tasks they always delivered us, they pardoned us all of it. And we your poor vassals, we of Huejotzingo who dwell in your city, when Licentiate Salmerón came to us and entered the city of Huejotzingo, then he saw how troubled the town was with our tribute in gold, sixty pieces[13] that we gave each year, and that it troubled us because gold does not appear here, and is not to be found in our province, though we searched for it everywhere; then at once Licentiate Salmerón pardoned it on your behalf, so that he made a replacement and substitution of the money. He set our tribute in money at 2,050 pesos. And in all the time he thus assessed us, all the time we kept doing it, we hastened to give it to you, since we are your subjects and belong to you; we never neglected it, we never did poorly, we made it all up. But now we are taken aback and very afraid and we ask, have we done something wrong, have we somehow behaved

[13]The form may be analyzed as *epoualli* + *tlatemantli* + *totontin*. Molina has the entry "pieza o moneda de oro. Cuztic teocuitla tlatemantli." Thus we are not sure whether nuggets or coins are meant, or if the latter, what denomination.

tique Auh yn axca cenca titiçahuia cenca titomauhtia tiquitova cuix itla otiquitlacoque cuix itla anq[u]alli ayectlic oticchiuhque in mohuicpatzinco in titotecuiyo in titotlatocauh anoço yeuatzin in ixquichivelli dios itla otiquitlacoque yn ivictzinco aço itla oticmocaquiti in totlavelilocayo inic cenca vei axcan topan vetz inyn tlacallaquili chicopa oquipanavi in ixquich otiqualtequitaque in macuiltzotli pesos Auh in tiquitoa in mixpantzinco ca amo vecahuaz inic cenpopoliuiz inic xixiniz in mociudad Vexu^co yehica ca amo quiximatia tlacallaquili yn totavan in tocolhuan yn tachtouan ayac quitlacallaquiliaya ca çan mixcavica catca Auh in tevanti in tipipilti yn tiquipia momacevalhuan ca cenca ya titotolinia aocmo totech neci in pillotl ya tiquinenevilia in macevalti yn iuhqui quiqua in iuhqui quimoquentia ya no iuhqui totech ca oc cenca telellacic vel otopan tzonquiçaco in netoliniliztli in iuhqui catca totavan tocolhuan tachtouan in iuh motlacamatia yn iuh maviztique catca niman aocmo achi totech ca

O Totecuiyoe totlatocatzine in tiRey ca ipa timitzontomachitian yn ilhuicac moetztica yn icel teotl dios ca vel ipan timitztomachitia in titotatzin ma xitechmotlaocolitivili ma xitechvalmocnoitivili ma oc cenca yevanti xiquimelnamiquilli in çacatla yn quauhtla[14] yn moquixtia yn monemitia ca yevanti in techoctia in techtlaocoltia vel tixpa vel tiquitzticate in inetoliniliz vel yeuanti ypampa in tontlatoan in mixpantzinco inic amo çatepan totech yc tim[o]quallaniltiz In iquac opopoliuhque anoço oxixinque yn momacevaltzitzivan onca tlami y in[15] tocnotlatol

Auh ca cenca miyac inic motolinitica inic motequipachotica in mociudad vexu^co yn amo nican vel timitzticuilhuilizque Auh ca itech ticcaua in totlaçotatzin p̄re fray alonso de buendia sanct fran^co ipiltzin intla yevatzin quimonequiltiz ycel teutl dios inic vellompa aciz yn mixpantzinco Ca huel yehuatl mitzmocaquitiliz yn oc miyac tlamantli In tonentlamachiliz in tonetoliniliz ca huel quimomachitia velloquitac yn cuidad vexutzinco onxihuitl nican guardian ocatca Ma yehuatl mixpantzinco quitoz quipouaz ca huel itech titotlacanequi Vel itech otitocencauhque ya isquich ynic mixpantzinco tonaci toneci ynin Amatl omochiuh ypa cuidad Vexu^co ya ic cenpoualilhuitl omatlaquilhuitl mani metztli De Julio ynic oquichtli in totecuio Jesu x^o ya etzontli xihuitl ypan caxtolpoualli xivitl yvan epoualli xivitl

Yn cenca hueca timitztocnonepechtequilia timocnomacevaltzitzihua

---

[14]Literally, "grasslands and forests"; the entry *desierto* in Molina contains both of these terms.

badly and ill toward you, our lord sovereign, or have we committed some sin against almighty God? Perhaps you have heard something of our wickedness and for that reason now this very great tribute has fallen upon us, seven times exceeding all we had paid before, the 2,000 pesos. And we declare to you that it will not be long before your city of Huejotzingo completely disappears and perishes, because our fathers, grandfathers, and ancestors knew no tribute and gave tribute to no one, but were independent, and we nobles who guard your subjects are now truly very poor. Nobility is seen among us no longer; now we resemble the commoners. As they eat and dress, so do we; we have been very greatly afflicted, and our poverty has reached its culmination. Of the way in which our fathers and grandfathers and forebears were rich and honored, there is no longer the slightest trace among us.

O our lord sovereign king, we rely on you as on God the one deity who dwells in heaven, we trust in you as our father. Take pity on us, have compassion with us. May you especially remember those who live and subsist in the wilds,[14] those who move us to tears and pity; we truly live with them in just such poverty as theirs, wherefore we speak out before you so that afterwards you will not become angry with us when your subjects have disappeared or perished. There ends this[15] our prayer.

We cannot write here for you the very many ways in which your city of Huejotzingo is poor and stricken; we are leaving that to our dear father Fray Alonso de Buendía, son of St. Francis, if God the one deity wills that he should arrive safely before you. He will be able to tell you much more about our anguish and poverty, since he learned and saw it well while he was prior here in the city of Huejotzingo for two years. We hope that he will tell and read this to you, for we have much confidence in him and have placed ourselves completely in his hands. This is all with which we come and appear before you. This letter was done in the city of Huejotzingo on the 30th day of the month of July, in the year of the birth of our Lord Jesus Christ 1560.

Your poor vassals who bow down humbly to you from afar,

---

[15]We take this unusual form to be the equivalent of *ynin*.

don leonardo Ramirez governador don matheo de la corona allde diego alameda allde don felipe de mendoça allde hernando de meneses miguel de aluarado alonso pimentel agustin osorio don fran^{co} vazquez don di^{o} de chavez juan de almo[. . .] di^{o} de niça agustin d. s^{o} thomas di^{o} xuarez tori^{o} d. s. [x^{o}?] val mot^{a}

30. Letter of members of the council of San Pedro Huehuetlan, Soconusco, to Licentiate Francisco Briceño, visitor general, in Santiago de Guatemala, 1565[1]

totlaçomahuiztote^{o}he

totlaçomahuiztilliztlathocauh totecuiyo liciciado don francisco preceno ma mochipa mitictzinco oye yn espiritu ssancto ca ysquichcapa tictenamiqui ymomatzin tehuantin timomacevalvan[2] nican tochan s p^{o} vehuetlan nehuatl nimomacehual don francisco yhuan merchior tapixqui domingo chililicatl domigo aquiyahuacatl totecuiyohe ca yz catqui ticmocaquiltiya yn totlatoll yn ipanpa y yehuatl p^{o} hordonez ca cenca techtolliniya yuhqui yma ytlacauh techihualtiya[3] noviyan quitzacua otli tanavatiya ahu in icuac ompa ohuiya nopiltzin don paltasal mitztlapalloto ca cenca totech cuallani ycuac oazico nopiltzin niman onechtlalli teylpilloyan yvan nopiltzin onicallaqui niman onechtlatolti quitua catli amatl ohualla cuauhtemalla oniquilvi amo tle nicmati niman oquito ca ya cualli aocmo ticpiaz moaltepetl aocmo ticmocuitahuiz çan ximotlalli imochan yuhqui onechilvi ca çan ipanpa momacehualvan niquinpalleuiz-

---

[1]Our text is a transcription of a facsimile published in *Epistolario de la Nueva España*, X, 63-65. A Spanish translation by Wigberto Jiménez Moreno (but no transcription) accompanies the facsimile. Elsewhere Luis Reyes (VIII Mesa Redonda, Sociedad Mexicana de Antropología, 1961, pp. 167-169, 183-185) has published a transcription as well as a translation. Both translations are quite adequate, though varying considerably in detail. Our main purposes in including this item here are, first, to have an example of the written Nahuatl of the far south, which proves to have much

Don Leonardo Ramírez, governor. Don Mateo de la Corona, alcalde. Diego Alameda, alcalde. Don Felipe de Mendoza, alcalde. Hernando de Meneses. Miguel de Alvarado. Alonso Pimentel. Agustín Osorio. Don Francisco Vázquez. Don Diego de Chaves. Juan de Almo[. . .]. Diego de Niza. Agustín de Santo Tomás. Diego Suárez. Toribio de San [Cristó]bal Motolinia.

Our dear honored lord:

Our dear honorable ruler, our lord Licentiate don Francisco Briceño, may the Holy Spirit always be within you. From here we kiss your hands, we your subjects whose home is here in San Pedro Huehuetlan, I your subject don Francisco and Melchor Tlapixqui, Domingo Chililicatl, and Domingo Aquiyahuacatl. Our lord, here are the words we are telling you on account of Pedro Ordóñez, who greatly mistreats us. He makes people do things as though they were his slaves;[3] he orders the roads closed everywhere. And when my son don Baltasar went there to greet you, he became very angry with us. When my son arrived here, he put me in jail; both my son and I went in. Then he interrogated me, saying "What of the letter that came from Guatemala?" I told him "I know nothing." Then he said "Very well, you are no longer to guard your town, you are no longer to care for it; just sit in your house." Thus he spoke to me,

---

in common with documents from the western fringe (as in Docs. 8, 27, 28), and, second, to provide a fully reliable transcription for use in conjunction with the quite easily accessible facsimile of the *Epistolario*.

[2]This may alternatively be read as *timomacevalyan*.

[3]We have taken the root to be *chihua*, although it could as well be *ihua*, "to send on errands;; (*techihualtiya*, "he has us sent on errands"). Even if *chihua* is the root, the object could equally well be "us," with *tech-chihualtiya* intended and one *ch* elided.

quiya y cenca ya motolliniya ymochi anavac soconochco ypanpa yc cenca notech cuallani amo honicnechico y cacahuatl av ini to^{o}he ca yehuatl ypanpa yc cenca moyxpantzinco titopechteca tictenamiqui ymomatzin auh que quinequi yyollo tuveytlatocauh rey campa mochivaz audiencia cuix cuauhtemallan cuix noço mexico yn ompa tachiyaz altepetl anavac soconochco av ini totecuiyohe ca cenca quinequi yn toyollo çan ompa yez cuauhtemalla audiencia ypanpa cenca papaqui mochintin momacevalhuan otihualmovicac omitzvaltitlani tuveytlatocauh rey ca cenca timitztotlatlauh[4] ma ypanpa dios xicmochivilli ma xitlacuillo ynavac toueytlatocauh rey vmpa castillan ma vallauh topallevilloca ca quimati toyollo cenca techtlaçota totecuiyo rey yhuan ticmocaquiltiya totecui^{o}ye y yehuatl pedro hordonez cepa oyahui ytlatol castilla yxpan rey vmpa oquititlani pedro cueto quitataniya navi xihuitl vc cepa tatocatiz ahu inic opa oquichiva tlatolli oquivica licinciado luaysa oquinavati vel nopan titlatoz yxpan rey vel tinechpalleviz yoqui yn quilhui velloquinavati av ini totecuiyohe amo vel campa titochicava ca çan totecuiyo dios tictlatlauhtiya yvan tehuatzin cenca motech timochicava[5] ma mopaltzinco xitechmopallevilli topan ximotlatolti ma ximonotzacan yn ompa moyetztica mexico vixitador ma valcallaqui juez nican anavac soconochco ma quimaviçoqui yn iquich tlachivalliztli nican mochiuhtimani ytlalpan totlatucauh rey cuix ynavatil yn teca mocacayava y yevantin y cenca tetoliniya yntla yuhqui quimonequiltiya tuveytlatucauh rey motolliniz yn imaceval aocmo tleyn tiquitozque Auh yehuatl yc mixpantzinco tictlalliya ticmocaquiltiya yvan oquito y yeuatl p^{o} hordonez yntla oc cepa yaz moamauh vmpa cuahutemallan ynavac vixitador nehuatl nicmati nimitzpilloz niman oniquilvi cenca cualli tleyn quinequi moyollo xicmochivilli yvan yehuantin ymoçovan ytoca diosio yvan joan rotriquiz ycuac vmpa oviya nopiltzin don paltasal mitztlapalloto niman oquitzacua otli oquinechico tochtecatl[6] quitemova amatl y carta ytencopa p^{o} hordonez amo tle no oquitaque vellomopinauhtique niman cepa quinavatiya tochtecatl quitoa amo aquin cepa yaz cuauhtemallan yntla haquin cepa aquin yaz cuauhtemallan cuaquechco callaquiz cenca motlayhyoviltiz av ini totecuiyohe cuix iuhqui quimonequiltia totecuiy^{o} rey av intla ya nimotolinia cuix amo vellitiz nictlatlaniz justicia yxpan noveytlatocauh rey ca velniquitaniz nopallevilloca yvan quinaxcan omochiva ycuac ohazico totatzin dean niman otechtlatoltique quitoa cuix nelli

[4]*Timitztotlatlauhtilli*, as below, was probably intended.

[5]*Timochicava*: we interpret the *-mo* as reflexive.

just because I want to help your subjects who are greatly afflicted, all those of the Soconusco coast. Because he became so angry with me about it, I have not (been able) to gather the cacao. And another thing, our lord, here is something on account of which we bow down very low before you and kiss your hands: what does our great sovereign king's heart desire as to where the Audiencia should be held, whether in Guatemala or in Mexico City, to which the towns of the Soconusco coast should look; and our lord, our hearts greatly desire that the Audiencia be there at Guatemala. All of your subjects rejoice greatly because you have come and our great sovereign king sent you here. We greatly implore you, for God's sake do something: write to our great sovereign king there in Castile that our aid may come, for our hearts know that our lord king loves us greatly. And we announce to you, our lord, that once a message of Pedro Ordóñez went to Castile to the king. He sent Pedro Cueto there, asking that he govern another four years. And a second time he made a statement that Licentiate Loaysa took. He ordered him: "You must speak well on my behalf before the king, you must help me greatly." Thus he spoke to him and gave him full orders. And another thing, our lord; from nowhere can we draw strength, we only pray to our lord God. And we rely greatly on you.[5] Help us, for your sake, speak on our behalf, confer with the visitor general who is there in Mexico City; let a judge come here to the coast of Soconusco, let him come to be amazed at everything done here, at what is being done in the land of our sovereign king. Is it his order that they make sport of people and greatly mistreat them? If our great sovereign king thus desires his subjects to be mistreated, we will say nothing more. And it is that which we put before you and report. And Pedro Ordóñez said "If a letter of yours goes to Guatemala again to the visitor general, I intend to hang you." Then I said to him "Very well, do whatever your heart desires." And when my son don Baltasar went to greet you, his henchmen named Dio[ni]sio and Juan Rodríguez closed the road; they brought together the people of Tuxtla,[6] seeking papers or letters, on the orders of Pedro Ordóñez. They saw nothing, they came completely to shame. Then once he gave orders to the Tuxtla people, saying "No one is to go to Guatemala again; if anyone goes again to Guatemala he will go into the stocks and suffer greatly." And our lord, does our lord king so desire it? And if I am mistreated, may I not demand

[6]Tochtlan, presumably one of the places in the area called Tuxtla today.

ohamoteyxpahuique cuauhtemalla ixpan vixitador mochi anquinextiya ytlachival pº hordonez niman oticnanquilliquilli[7] amo tleyn ticmatizque çan otictlatique tlatolli ypanpa amo tleyn neciz tlatolli[8] niman oquitoque y yevanti tetlatoltiyani ca ya cualli xictlallican amopeticion yxpan tlatoani opispo ycuac moyolceviz pº hordonez amo cepa amotech cuallaniz niman techvica ce cristiano[9] ytoca pº ruyz ça yeuatl oquichichiva peticion amo totlatul çan tlapic oquitlatlalli pirma av in icuac omocauh nima techvica yspan opispo quitoa amevantin xicmacacan av in icuac oticmacaque niman castillan tlatolli ypan omocuepa yehuatl mochi oquimacac [lic] luvaysa oquihuicac vmpa castillan muchi yc moteyspaviya yxpan totlatocauh rey av ini toºhe amo totlatol omochiva peticion ça yehuantin quichichiva tlatolli ynican techpiya amo quinequi neciz mochi ytlachival yn ipanpa ynic [tetannia][10] av ini toºhe macamo xitechtlavellocamati ma [cenca] mopaltzinco xitechmopallevilli yxpan totecuiyo dios yvan totecuiyo rey cenca timitztotlatlauhtiliya tictenamiqui ymomatzin cenca motechtzinco titocahua yvan yehuatl nican toamauh tocarta macamo campa neciz amo aquin quitaz amo haqui quimatiz ca ya ticmati[11] vmpa cate cequinti ycnihuan pº hordonez ypanpa amo tlacuillozque ynavac pº hornez ypanpa amo quicaquiz ca yehuatl yc timitztotlatlauhtiliya vmpa yavi texotecatl momactzinco quitalliz tocarta yvan vallaz motlatoltzin mocarta tiquitazque yc pachiviz toyollo quivalvicazque texotecatl ca yxquich tictenamiqui ymomatzin timitztotlatlauhtilli ma mochipa mitictzinco hoye yn espiritu ssancto otitlacuilloque nican tochan s pº vehuetlan momacevalhuan axcan ypan metztli hefrero 22 tonali mopoa 1565 xihuitl

don francisco atenpaneca   merchior tapixque[12]   domingo aquiyaguacatl   domingo chililicatl

---

[7]Apparently a slip for *oticnanquillique*.

[8]Alternatively, this entire statement may have been their response to the interrogators.

[9]Literally, "Christian."

justice before our great sovereign king? For I can demand my succor. And it recently happened that when our father the Dean came here, they interrogated us, saying "Is it true that you complained to the visitor general in Guatemala, revealing all the deeds of Pedro Ordóñez?" Then we answered "We know nothing." We hid our words, so that no statement would appear.[8] Then the interrogators said "Very well, place your petition before the lord bishop; then Pedro Ordóñez will be placated and will not become angry with you again." Then a Spaniard[9] named Pedro Ruiz took us with him; he prepared the petition, not our words, and falsely placed the signatures. And when it was finished, then he took us to the bishop, saying "You give it to him." And when we gave it to him, it was translated into Castilian, and he gave it all to Licentiate Loaysa, who took it there to Castile. About all of this, complaint is made to our sovereign king. And our lord, the petition that was made is not our words, but those who rule us here arranged the words. They do not want all their deeds to appear [because of the way they are destroying the people].[10] And our lord, do not consider us wretches, by your very life help us before our lord God and our lord king. We greatly implore it of you and kiss your hands; we confide ourselves completely to you. And let this our paper and letter not appear anywhere, let no one see it, let no one know about it, for we[11] know there are some friends of Pedro Ordóñez there, so that they will not write to Pedro Ordóñez, and he will not hear about it. We implore this of you. Some people of Texotlan are going there to place our letter in your hands, and your message and letter will come back; we will see it and our hearts will be content with it; the people of Texotlan will bring it back. This is all. We kiss your hands and implore you. May the Holy Spirit always be within you. We your subjects wrote it here at our home San Pedro Huehuetlan, today, counted the 22nd day of the month of February of the year of 1565.

Don Francisco Atempaneca. Melchor Tlapixqui.[12] Domingo Aquiyahuacatl. Domingo Chililicatl.

---

[10]The verb *tannia* may be read as *tlamia*, which carries the meaning "to destroy."

[11]Alternatively, "you know."

[12]*Atempanecatl* was the title for a high-ranking military commander; *Tlapixqui* means "guardian."

31. Letter of council of Tzacualco to council of San Felipe, 1629[1]

Laçogamatone[2] yn dios

ma tt^{o} dios moLantzinco yez yhuan te[3] nohuestra senora sancta m^{a} yn amehuatzitzin aLaço anladoque aLtepehuaqui ypan altepeL ytocayocan san peLibe goquiyoL[4] amehueltiticati[5] amochantzinco anguiLanehueya[6] ce donatiuh nican Lalticpac ca mochipa tictochiaLia yn iLhuecacayoL justiciatzin yn dios amo yxquich ca tonLachia yoqui tispopoyome tonLatohua auh ma yoqui xicmomachiLtitzinocan senores Ladoque

Auh yzcatqui yn doLatoLtzin ytechcopa yn topiLtzin nican ohuala dochantzinco motenehua tzaqualco san franco auh otictocaquiltiqui amaL otipaqueque ca neLe meLahuac ya ome xihuiL yhuan Laco oquihualhueca cehuatzinLi nican quimonamictizquiya amo quinique[7] ynin cehuapili yyoLocacopa ompa chan[8] monamectizque auh ma ye[pan]tzinco[9] dios ma xicmopaLehueLican yn topiLtzin ytoca Ju^{o} diego amo xictiLchihuacan canahueyan[10] tochantzinco ca ça ce dios ticLayecoLtia yhuan yc onLamanle tehueyoL ca yyoLocacopa ompa quimochihueLizneque tehueyotica amo ticpanahuezneque ylalnamequiLis ca cenca Laçole tehueyotica ca yoqui techmonahuatiLia sancta ecLesea yhuan teopixquime saserdotis yoqui xicmomachiLtitzinocan anLaço aLatoque tehuantin yn damolaçodahuan[11] Nican ticpach̅o̅ticati aLtepeL motenehua tzaqualco san franco yn tixquichtim al̅l̅des Regedores timochintin Nican tictoLaLiLia autincia yn tolatoLtzin amo anquipanahuesque yxquich yn tolatoLtzin ma tt^{o} dios amolantzinco yez yhuan toLaçomahueznatzin cehuapiLi sancta m^{a} axca ypan sabato 20 tonaLi metzLe ocdopre yhuan xihuiL 1629 anos Nican tictoLaLiLia tomachioL tofrma

[1]McAfee Collection, UCLA Research Library, Special Collections.

[2]The writer of this document uses two forms of *l*, one a standard elongated loop, the other more like a *t*. We have reproduced the first as *l*, the second as *L*. In the first part of the document, *L* frequently seems to correspond to standard *tl*, *l* to ordinary *l*. Yet this shifts, until by the end of the document the opposite is more nearly true. There may be no [*tl*] sound, or at least no orthographic representation of it, here at all.

[3]*To-*, "our," would be more appropriate, but the text clearly says *te*. Sudden shifts of person are characteristic of this entire text.

[4]The *g* apparently precludes the otherwise tempting interpretation "Çoquiyotl."

[5]*(Nin)euiltitica*, though not in the dictionaries, is a reverential equivalent of "be,"

Thanks be to God.

May our Lord God and [you][3] our lady Saint Mary be with you, dear lords, citizens of the town named San Felipe Coquiyotl,[4] being at your home.[5] You borrow[6] each day here on earth, for we always await the celestial justice of God; we do not see it all, we speak as the blind, and may you thus know it, sirs and lords.

And here are our words about our son who came here to our home called Tzaqualco San Francisco; we have read the letter; we were glad, for it is true and certain that two and a half years ago he brought a woman here to marry her, (but) this lady does not wish [it];[7] they would like to be married at (your) home,[8] and [before][9] God, help our son named Juan Diego, do not disdain him, for they are dissatisfied[10] at our home, and we serve only one God, and second, (the marriage they plan) is legitimate, they gladly wish to perform it there legitimately; we do not wish to disregard his intention, for legitimate (marriage) is very precious, and thus the holy church and the priestly ministers admonish us; may you thus know it, dear lords; we [your dear fathers][11] who govern here the town called Tzaqualco San Francisco, all we alcaldes and councilmen, we all here in council issue our statement; you will not disregard our words. May our Lord God and our dear honored mother lady Saint Mary be with you; today on Saturday, 20th day of the month of October and the year 1629, we place here our rubrics and signatures.

---

in a locative sense. An example may be seen in *Florentine Codex*, Bk. 6 p. 30. We have seen the word in the Tlaxcalan municipal records as well.

[6]See *Florentine Codex*, Bk.6, p.49, for *tlaneuia* used in connection with transitoriness.

[7]Perhaps it is "him," rather than "it," that the lady does not want.

[8]Some possessive prefix would appear to be required before *chan*.

[9]We take this as the equivalent of *ixpantzinco*.

[10]The Nahuatl seems to be the equivalent of *ca anahuia*.

[11]We interpret this as equivalent to *t(i)amotlaçotahuan*, and presume that "fathers" has the force of "town elders," or the like, while the possessive would be merely a courtesy.

Ju^o bapean escribano p^o Leon al̅l̅de Ju^o ceprean al̅l̅de diego fiLpe Regedor Ju^o agostin Regedor Ju^o miquiL Regedor Ju^o bardasar Regedor p^o Ju^o Regedor[12]

yhuan doquartian ymahueztocatzin fr miLchior Nican techpachoticati sancta eclesea yhuan fry antris meriena prsetinti

yhuan meLahuac oticmatiqui omomiquiLi ynamicatica[13] axca chicome xihuiL omomiquiLi yhuan amo pachihueyaya toyoLo auh ya nepa cepa oconana amaL ompa çacaLan oquihuaLhueca ypanpa axca meLahuac ticLacamatiqui timochintin yhuan ynatzin yhuan ytatzin yhuan yhueltiuh yhuan yhuayoLcahuan mochintin oquimatiqui yc niLtiz amo yzlacatiLizli amo melahuac yxpantzinco dios Nican titofrmatia

maqna barpoLa bardaçar lorenço p^o mendoça mariana

yxquich tomacehuaL toladoltzin ma dios molatzinco yez yhuan dolaçomahueznatzin cehuapiLi sancta m^a

AmatzinLi quimopohuelizqui laçoladoqui al̅l̅des Regedor ypan aLtepeL san peLipe amehueLtiticati amochantzinco[14]

32. Letter of don Pedro Enrique Motecuhçoma in Mexico City to relatives in Iztapalapa, 1587[1]

Ma yehuatzin Spu̅ Sancto ytlan moyetztie yn cenca mahuiztic amotlaçoanimantzin tlaçocihuapipiltine ma xicmomachiltitzinocan

---

[12]The notary signed for all.

[13]This seems to be the meaning, but the form *ynamicatica* is puzzling. One would expect *ynamic catca*.

[14]This line is written separately, on the outside.

Document 32

[1]AGN, Tierras 1735, exp. 2, f. 134.

To understand this letter the reader needs some grasp of complex family relationships and successions which we will try to outline here as well as our sketchy knowledge permits. (See Tezozomoc, *Crónica mexicayotl*, pp. 131-134, 151-152, 161; Chimalpahin, *Annales*, p. 281, and above all *Colección de documentos inéditos* . . .

Juan Fabián, notary. Pedro León, alcalde. Juan Ciprián, alcalde. Diego Felipe, councilman. Juan Agustín, councilman. Juan Miguel, councilman. Juan Baltasar, councilman. Pedro Juan, councilman.[12]

And our prior, whose honored name is fray Melchor, has guided us (in matters of) the holy church, along with fray Andrés [Mariana?], president.

And we found it to be true that his former wife[13] died, she died seven years (ago) now, and our hearts were not yet satisfied, and then once (he) took a letter there to Zacatlan and brought it back, wherefore now we have all recognized it as true, and his mother and father and older sister and relatives all knew the truth of it; it is not a lie or falsehood, before God; here we sign.

Magdalena Bárbola. Baltasar Lorenzo. Pedro Mendoza. Mariana.

These are all of our humble words. May God and our dear honored mother lady Saint Mary be with you.

The dear lords, alcaldes and councilmen in the town of San Felipe, being at your home, are to read the letter.[14]

May the Holy Spirit dwell in your very honored dear souls, dear ladies; know that I heard, I received your message.[2] And very great

---

Document 32 (cont.)

America y Oceanía, VI, 64-112, brought to our attention by Charles Gibson.) Don Pedro Motecuhçoma was a son of emperor Moctezuma; he was (in the common view, at least) the only male heir surviving into Spanish times, and as such he received various honors, posts, and grants, including part of the encomienda of Tula and a pension from the crown. When he died in 1570, his oldest, perhaps only legitimate son, don Martín, succeeded to his position (as can be deduced, indeed, from the present letter). By the time of the letter don Martín had died as well, and there was contention over the inheritance, as to both grants and property. The writer of the letter, don Pedro Enrique Motecuhçoma, calls don Pedro "grandfather" and don Martín "uncle," so

ca onicac onicnomacehui yn amihiyotzin yn amotlatoltzin[2] Auh ca cenca nohueypapaquiliz noneyollaliz omochiuh ynic achitzin tlacahua yn iyollotzin in tlalticpaque totº dios yn amechmochicahuilia[3] Ma quimonequiltitzino ma mochipa yqui amopantzinco mochihuaz yn iuh niquelehuia amohuicopatzinco tlaçocihuapipiltine Ca yehuatl[4] ynic achitzin nocontenamiqui yn amomatzin yn amocxitzin Auh yn ipetl yn icpaltzin[5] yn tlacatl yn tlatohuani señor don Alonso axayacatzin nocoltzin moyetzticatca ca nocontlapalohua yxquichquich noconciauhquetza yn oncan amechomocahuilitiuh Ma yxquich amihiyotzin amotlapaltzin xicmomachiltican[6] tlaçocihuapipiltine macamo y[e]can nichuicaz yn amitzin amoyollotzin[7] auh ma cenca xinechmotlapopolhuilican ypaltzinco yn totº dios

Auh ynin[4] macamo namechnotequipachilhuiz notlaçopiltzintzine ca ye onamechnocaquiltili yuan cayepa ye iuhca amoyollotzin yn itechcopa yn itelpoch cihuapilli nocitzin doña ynes y[n] don francº

---

he as a member of the next generation was presumably a claimant. A rival claimant, don Francisco, is mentioned in the letter as the son of doña Inés, who had been the wife of don Pedro and mother of the late don Martín. Yet we do not find don Francisco in Tezozomoc's list of don Pedro's children nor in don Pedro's will; he must have been the child of another marriage of doña Inés', thus making his claim through her alone, which fully explains his "taking don Pedro for a father." As to don Pedro Enrique, he may have been the son of don Pedro's daughter doña María, who married in Coyoacan, though there was also another daughter, doña Magdalena. (Two other children of don Pedro died young, and another, don Diego Luis, who ultimately succeeded to the position, had been in Spain for years. See also Doc. 33.)

The recipients of the letter were the daughters of don Alonso Axayaca, ruler of Iztapalapa and son of Moctezuma's younger brother Cuitlahuac; by this time don Alonso had died, leaving doña Magdalena as Iztapalapa's "governess." Though the writer of the letter calls don Alonso "grandfather," this need not be taken literally, since kinship terms could be extended to all relatives belonging to the generation of the term's domain; the same holds for the writer's reference to himself as the ladies' younger brother or cousin. At any rate, a relationship existed, and the Axayaca line apparently also had some claim to the inheritance; indeed, the ladies seem at this time to have been in physical possession of some of the original decrees.

The principal (known) relationships relevant here may be schematized as follows:

is the joy and consolation it gave me that in some little way the Lord of the earth, Lord God, grants that he strengthens you.[3] May it be his wish that you always then fare as I desire for you, dear ladies. Now[4] in some measure I kiss your hands and feet; and as to the lord[5] sir ruler señor don Alonso Axayacatzin, my late grandfather, I greet, in every way I salute what he has bequeathed you there. Muster all your strength,[6] dear ladies, may I not at such a time upset you,[7] and (if so) forgive me very much, by our Lord God.

And in this[4] let me not give you pain, my dear ladies, for I already informed you and you already know about the son of the lady my grandmother doña Inés, don Francisco, who wishes and desires

---

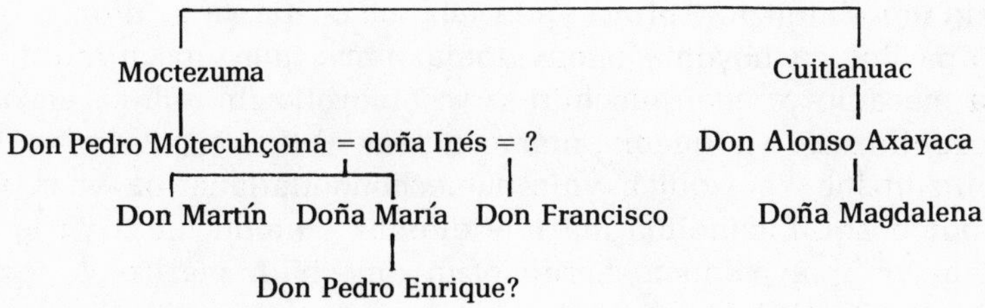

[2]Literally, "your breath, your word," a set formula.

[3]That is, "gives you health."

[4]*Ca yehuatl*, "it is so," and *inin*, "this," are frequently used in this letter to introduce a topic in a general way, and we have translated them variously.

[5]Literally, "his mat, his seat," a formula applied to persons in high authority. At times, indeed, the phrase actually means "authority." If that were the case here, the translation might run as follows: "and as to the governorship of the sir ruler señor don Alonso Axayacatzin, I greet, in every way I salute that he has bequeathed it to you there. May you exercise it fully."

[6]Literally, "realize all your breath and strength."

[7]Literally, "may I not take away your insides and your heart."

yn ontlaixtoca onmotlanectia yn oncan quiztihui[10] yoltihui yn tetecuhtin tlatoque[9] yn techmocahuilitihui yn nican amochantzinco[8] mexico Auh yn inemactzin tlacatl noc[ol]tzin[11] moyetzticatca yuan notlatzin yn nican ommiquiltitiuh señor don Martin motecuhçoma moyetzticatca yn mrd Previlegio iuan cedulas yn quimopialtoca ynquimomactoca auh yn iuh oanquimocaquiltique yn quimotatia tlacatl nocoltzin moyetzticatca Señor don Pº motecuhçoma yn iuh quitohua ca yxocoyouh yetiuh Auh ynin ca ye nocontepotztoquiliz auh ca ye mopinauhtiz ca yehuatl ynic noconpachihuiltia amoyollotzin yn iuhqui y[e yc] quimonmotepotzcomonilia yn techmocahuilitihui yn tetecuhtin tlatoque ca yuhqui nim[an] yn mochihua Auh ynin ma ma xicmomachiltitzinocan ompa amohuictzinco niquimonihua amotlatzitzinhuan yn nican amochantzinco[8] mexico pipiltin quitenamiquizque amomatzin amocxitzin don martin de aguilar don martin Cortes auh ynic amixpantzinco niquimonihua ma xicmomachiltitzinocan ca noconitohua yn Previlegio yuan Cedulas ma tlacahua yn amoyollotzin ma oc hualauh ma oc teyollo onpachihui nican toconteyxpantilizque yn audiencia Real ynic huel teyollopachihuiz tlaçocihuapipiltine ma tlacahuaz yn amoyollotzin ypanpa yn ompa niquimonihua yn amotlatzitzinhuan ma quihualmotquilitiazque[12] ynic amo cana polihuiz canpanel antechmotlaxilia[13] tlaçocihuapipiltine yuan ma achitzin niquicnopilhuiz amihiyotzin amotlatoltzin Auh ca yntlacamo oc onetia yn achiton nonetequipachol ca noyoma ononyazquia namechnoyolpachihuiltilizquia macamo yc quen mochihuaz yn amoyollotzin auh ca anconmocaquiltizque yn quenin ommochihuaz yntla onmoteyxpantilli nopiltzintzine Ye ixquich ynic namechonnotlatlauhtilia yuan yn anconmocaquiltitzinohua ma totº dios amechmomaquili yn igraciatzin yn ipan ySancto Seruiciotzin omochiuh mexico yc 9 de otubre de 87[14] aºs

[8]Don Pedro Enrique appears to mean his own residence, saying "your" out of courtesy; yet we are not quite sure of this, since the Axayaca ladies play some role in the Motecuhçoma inheritance.

[9]That is, don Pedro and don Martín. The house was next to the church of San Sebastián, as appears in don Pedro's will.

[10]*Quiça* as "emerge" could easily mean "be born," and this is the meaning we have preferred. However, the word also has the meaning "to be finished"; in that case the

your[8] house here in Mexico City where the lord rulers[9] were born[10] and lived and that they bequeathed us. And as to the inheritance of my late grandfather[11] and my uncle who died here, the late señor don Martín Motecuhçoma, (don Francisco) considers himself the guardian and holder of (their) grant, concession, and decrees, and as you have heard, he takes for a father my late sir grandfather señor don Pedro Motecuhçoma, as he says that he will be his youngest son. As to this, I will inquire into it and he will surely come to shame. Here is something with which I content your hearts as much as [what the lord rulers left us spreads discord in them, for thus it (will) be done.] And now, know that I am sending there to you your uncles the nobles who are here at your[8] house in Mexico City, who will kiss your hands and feet, don Martín de Aguilar and don Martín Cortés, and as to the reason I am sending them to you, know that I [bespeak] the concession and decrees; may you concede it, may it yet come, may everyone yet be content; here we will make a statement to the Royal Audiencia so that people will be very content. Dear ladies, may you grant it, because I am sending there your uncles to bring it[12] back, so that it will not be lost somewhere; [why should] you reject us,[13] dear ladies? And may I in some way attain your message; and if my illness were not still a little heavy on me, I would go myself to satisfy your hearts. May your hearts not be troubled by this, and you will hear what happens when it has been divulged. My ladies, this is all with which I importune you and which you are to hear. May our Lord God give you his grace in his holy service. Done in Mexico City on October 9, year of (15)87.[14]

---

phrase might convey "lived and died." Also, the related *quixtilia* can mean subsist, so that this might be a characteristic pair of synonyms for "live."

[11]That is, don Pedro.

[12]That is, the papers.

[13]Literally, "Where do you reject us?"

[14]We hesitated for some time between "1" and "7," but decided in favor of the latter on the basis of the very different, well-defined "1" in the date written outside.

Amicuhtzin yquichcapa amechmotlapalhuia[15]
don P^o^ enrrique motecuhçoma

[qu]imotilizque amatzintli tlaçocihuapipiltin doña magdalena axayaca doña p^o^nilla pimentel yuan yehuatzin doña barbula de la Concepcion yn ipan ymatepetzin ytztapalapan yc 12 otubre[16]

33. Letter of don Diego Luis de Moteçuma in Granada to his nieces doña Juana and doña María in Mexico City, 1598[1]

Ca o nican notech onacico yn amamatzin nica granada vnpa oquivalliua yn alonso de solis Aguire yn opa corte madrid onechvallacuilvi y tlen ic oualla yn ixpantzinco y conjeso Real de yndias Ab anoço vel quimotilliz yn axca totlatocatzin yacuic ca omomiquilli yn itatzin catca don felipe auh ca no heuatzin motocayotitzinoua auh cenca miec ynic motetlaocollia y telpochtli y heuatzi catca y principe Auhvin axca ca heuatzin totlatocatzin toRey tote^o^ ma yuh ximomachiltica Auhvin axcan cenca tlamociui ynic movicaz quimonamiquiltiuh yn inamictzin yn opa balcerona ychpoch y Emperador de Roma ca ysuprina y quimonamictitzinoz ca nocyuich[2] ynic amoyollotzin pachivi anel[3] quiniquac aço uellitiz quimotilliz y totlatocatzin auh çanoyvi yneuatl tla oc onquiça y cecuiztli

---

[15]Despite the variance, this seems the same phrase as *ixquichca nimitzonnotlapalhuia* (Siméon, p. 200).

[16]This portion is written separately, outside. Note that only the heiress doña Magdalena bears the Axayaca surname, suggesting that the name accompanies the title.

Document 33

[1]AGN, Tierras 1735, exp. 2, f. 13. The folio immediately following contains a Spanish translation, which we reproduce in Appendix II. Don Diego Luis de Moteçuma was the second son of don Pedro (see Doc. 32, n. 1, and the references there cited). He went to Spain by 1570, the time of his father's death, and lived there the rest of his life. His legitimacy was contested, apparently on very good grounds, since don Pedro's wife doña Inés had only one son by him, don Martín,and doña Inés survived don Pedro by many years. Yet don Pedro, in his will, calls don Diego Luis legitimate (apparently by preconquest notions); after don Martín died, don Diego Luis succeeded, by a decision of the Council of the Indies, to don Pedro's inheritance, including encomienda and royal pension. The recipients of the present letter,

Your younger brother salutes you from here,[15]
Don Pedro Enrique Motecuhçoma

The dear ladies doña Magdalena Axayaca, doña Petronila Pimentel, and also doña Bárbola de la Concepción, in their town of Iztapalapa, are to see the letter. On the 12th of October.[16]

Your letter has come to me here in Granada where Alonso de Solís Aguirre sent it, who wrote me from the court in Madrid why he came to the Royal Council of the Indies. And perhaps he will be able to see him who is now our new king, for don Felipe, who was his father, died, and he too has that name, and many are the favors he grants. The youth is the one who was the prince, and now he is our sovereign king and lord. Consider this; and now there is much concern about his going to meet his wife there at Barcelona, daughter of the Roman Emperor, and it is his (own) niece he is marrying. [. . .][2] in order to satisfy you, then[3] perhaps he can see our king. And I likewise, when the cold leaves the countryside, will take everyone, my wife and children, and will do everything as you

---

Document 33 (cont.)
according to an attached note in Spanish, were living in a house belonging to don Diego Luis next to San Sebastián. It must have been the same house referred to in Doc. 32, which had once belonged to don Pedro.

[2]We have not arrived at any interpretation of the string *canocyuich*; perhaps it is one of don Diego Luis' several slips. The context would seem to indicate the need for words to the effect of "here is something."

[3]The word *anel* is not incorporated into our translation; Molina's *dizque* and Siméon's *de sorte que* seem not to fit the context. This might be the *anel* that turns a statement into a question, like Spanish *verdad* or German *nicht wahr*. However, this also might be one of several examples of don Diego Luis' use of what appears superficially to be an excess *a*. Below, *quin*, "then," would seem preferable to *aquin*, then *auh ma*, "and may," to *auhvama*, and finally *iuhquin atl valvetz*, "like water it fell from above," to *iuhquin atlavalvetz*. This last, it is true, could conceivably be interpreted as equivalent to *iuhquin atlan valvetz*, "it fell as if into the water."

canpania muchinti ynonamic ynopilva niquivicaz nochi no[con]chiuatiuh yn ixquich ynic anhuamonetlamachitia camo yc nonoquelloua ca huel miec ynica nechtequipachoua preytos aquin[3] iyollic aquimocaquiltizque noconicuilloz Auh yn ipanpa ynic oualla y alº de solis cemca nipampaquiz ytla ypanacitiuh y corte ca nicnanamiquiz yn queni conpeualtiz y tlatolli yn ipampa netollinillizyotl he mochiua ynovia altepetl ipa auh ca cenca o no yc nonotequipacho huel mococoua ynollo yniccaqui ynetolinillizyo he mochiua Auh yni ma xicmotlatlauhtillica y totecuiyo dios ma mochiuaz y totlanequilliz y totlaytlanilliz hezqui auhvama[3] nechtlacuillican ymexica yuan in altepeuaque yc pachiuiz ynoyollo yvan ic ninochicauaz yc ninixquetzaz yteyxpa y conjeso auh ytlacamo catel nicnanamiquiz[4] nictlaneltilliliz ynicpatzinco[5] y conjeso auh que ca amotechcopatzinco macamo ximotequipachotzinocan chiua[6] ma uallauh testimonio amopampatzinco y quenin aquimotemaquillia y tequitl cuix yteconpa justicia mahonca vallicuilliuhtiuh yua yn oca no tecpacalco ynic ocanamohetzticate[7] yn opamechmitlanillilia y tequitl tlacallaquilli yuan aquique yn ipa mani y quimocuitlavia ac oquinauati yn atequitizque yuan aquique yn amechmopouilli yeipa calpoualliztli y teycuilloque mochiuhque o heuatli yn aquivalmivallizque auh ytlacamo nel onicquitani yn amamatzin ca he yuh ca noyollo ca ynpa onictlalli ynomemoria ynic ypampa tiazque y corte ca niquispantilli y totl[a]tocatzin yn oc yxquichti yn ixviua ymotecuhçomatzin ymotollinia ca ni[. . .]aniz[8] yn o yuhqui motlaocollique yn ipilva juº gano yn ixviua ca no yuh he yzqui y topampa cacayamo nocopeualtia ynotlaytlanilli ca oc centlamantli yn ipanonemi ynocotepotztoca auhvini tla oc amoyollotzin yc xiqualmochicauillica y que comonequiltiz y toteº dios ma yc xicmotlatlauhtillica amen auh yz ca yua oniccat[9] cuix nelli quichiuaznequi preytos ynic nechixnamiquiz quil quitlaniznequi arimentos yn amohuepol coyouaca catqui auhvini ca çan moztlacauia aço çan aca quiyolleuiltia quiyolcuepa çan ic quitlaquaqualiznequi quipopolviznequi yn itlatqui auh yni ma ça conpeualti ca nicanoconiuaz y memoria ynic amo neltiz y tley quitlaniznequi ytla ça ytla merced mechitlanilli ca nocochiuazquia avini camo yc

---

[4]This seems to be the indicated meaning, though one might expect that don Diego Luis would say instead "if not, I cannot help. . . ."

[5]For *yn ixpatzinco*.

[6]The *c* of *chiua* seems partially marked out, leaving *hiua*, the equivalent of *iuan*, and we have so interpreted it.

[7]The Nahuatl text here might be divided so as to give *ocan amohetzticate* (= *oncan*

mention it. I am not doing this on purpose, because lawsuits occupy me greatly here; later[3] bit by bit you will hear it, I will write it. And on account of what Alonso de Solís came for, I will be very glad if when I arrive at court I can help him in beginning the suit concerning the hardships suffered in the towns everywhere. And I have also been greatly troubled and it pains my heart when I hear of the hardships that have been suffered. And in this pray to our Lord God that our wish and request be fulfilled. And[3] let those of Mexico City and those of the towns write something to satisfy me and with which I can take courage to present myself before the Council; and if not nevertheless I will help[4] and tell the truth before the Council. And as to how things are concerning you, do not worry, and let testimony come on your behalf of how you distribute the tasks, if it is by court order, let it come written there, and [how those there at the courthouse are][7] who demand the work and tribute from you there, and who are in charge and take care of it; who ordered you to work and who counted you at the time of the house-count and those who were the ones appointed to inscribe people. This is what you are to send. And if I had not seen your letter I am certain what I would have put in my memorandum, on account of which we will go to the court, is to inform our king about all the grandchildren of Motecuhçoma who are in poverty. I will [ask][8] for favors such as were given to the children of Juan Cano, his (Motecuhçoma's) grandchildren, since it is also the same on our part. I have not yet begun making my request because I am engaged in another matter that I am following. And so still strengthen your hearts, as our Lord God desires. Pray to him for it. Amen. And also I have heard[9]—is it true?—that your brother-in-law who is in Coyoacan wants to bring suit complaining against me and, they say, wanting to demand sustenance. And in this either he deceives himself or someone is inciting him and influencing him who wants to consume and destroy his property. And let him not begin this, for from here I will send a statement so that what he wants to sue for will not come to pass. If he were only asking me for some favor I would grant it and not be troubled by it. But I am troubled about how both of you are

---

ammoyetzticate), with the translation for the whole passage of "and how you are there at the courthouse," though the meaning of this is no less opaque than the provisional translation we have placed in the text.

[8]The word is partly marked over; by the context and the Spanish translation we imagine it to be some verb like *niquitlaniz*.

[9]For *oniccac*, we presume.

ninotequipachoua ca çan amevati amomexti camoca nonotequipachoua yn quen amomonemilti auh quen amomotlatoctia auh can amomotlamachiltitiui cuix iuhqui çanica aço yvia cana tepaltzinco amoca noueuentiz[10] av ini quenel namechochiuaz ymaçonellivi y quexquich yn onicac yn amopampa ca ça nenoconcaqu[i][11] auhvini tlao yvia yocoxca xocotimalloca ytlay y yovillizyotl y chichinaquizyotl yn iuh otlatoca y cuitlapilli yn atlapalli ca no yuh nopa mochiva ynic yn amomati aço ça nipactinemi ynican auh yn ixquichti ynopilva auh y totla nemi tleyniquimaz tleyniquiqualtiz auh tleyn itech monequiz y tlaquentl yn iquac valla ynopa yn itetlaocoltitzin totlatocatzin çan iuhquin atlavalvetz[3] yn iquac vallauh he teaxca auh nellamo nicaxiltia ynic nitlaxtlaua auhvin axca cenca miec ynonetlacuil mochiuhtica Ahv ini tla oc xomamatica vnpa nocontlacuilvia y jeronimo de castillo amechmomaquilli ynic amoyollotzin oceuiz cedulas aquimomaquillizque ynic amechmomaquilli ytic yauh ynin amatl onca hetic[12] vnpoualli omatlatltli anquimogelvizque cecepoualli ypa mamacuilli pesos yn amomexti hez he yxquich nica granada A 18 de nobienbre de 1598 años

don di^o^ luys de moteçuma

34. List of market prices established by judge, Tlaxcala, 1545[1]

Yo El licenciado gomez de santillan oydor por su mg^t^ En el audiencia E chancilleria Real desta nueva Espania E su visitador En esta provincia de taxcala y en las demas probincias E pueblos desta Comarca por quanto estando visitando Esta ciudad E provincia de tlaxcalla fue[2] ynformado y me fue hecha Re^on^ que avia gran desor-

---

[10]We cannot at present offer a satisfactory rendition of the passage *cuix iuhqui ça nica aço yvia cana tepaltzinco amoca noueuentiz*. The Spanish translation gives *que si estubieramos serca acudiera a saver lo que aviamos de pedir*; this version is so distant from being literal that it is hard to know whether the additional phrase *i asi por la dilacion no se* is meant to correspond to this portion of the Nahuatl, or to the next. Word for word, the passage runs "Perhaps (question word equal to 'is it that?') thus just here perhaps quietly (or gradually) somewhere by someone's means (or for someone's sake) I will grow old on your account."

living and how you are getting along and where your inclination lies. [. . .],[10] how am I to do things for you? Though I have heard something on your part, I hear it in vain.[11] And still quietly and peacefully praise any of this difficulty and pain. As the commoners fare, so it is with me as well, if you think I live in contentment here. And all of my children and those who live with us, what will I gather for them, what will I feed them, and what will be used for clothing? And when the charity of the king came for me, just like water[3] it fell from above. At the moment it comes it already belongs to someone and truly I do not make it suffice to pay back (what I owe), and now my debts are becoming very large. But here, be informed that I am writing to Jerónimo de Castillo there to give you something so that your hearts will be tranquil. You are to give him (my) draft so that it is given to you; it goes inside this letter. It is for 50 pesos.[12] You are to divide it among yourselves; there will be 25 pesos for each of you. That is all. Here in Granada on the 18th of November of the year of 1598.

Don Diego Luis de Moteçuma.

I, Licentiate Gómez de Santillán, judge for His Majesty in the Royal Audiencia and court here in New Spain and his inspector here in the province of Tlaxcala and in the other provinces and towns of this region: since while inspecting this city and province of Tlaxcala I have been informed and report has been made to me that

---

[11]We read this as equivalent to *çan nen noconcaqui*, but the final *i* could be read equally well as *e*.

[12]*Yetic* as "something heavy," (*cosa pesada*) is apparently being used here as the equivalent of "peso."

Document 34

[1]Museo Nacional de Antropología, document C. A. 340, ff. 125-126.

[2]The frequent mistakes in the Spanish sections seem to indicate that the Tlaxcalan copyist did not fully comprehend the sense.

den e carestia en bis[2] cosas que se venden En los tianquez desta ciudad e provincia E para lo proveeis[2] Remediar mande hazer Este Aranzel para que por las cosas en el Conthenidas no se den y lleven A mas precios de los sigui^os segun va asentado declarado En lengua de yndio su thenor del qual Es este que se sigue

— Yn ce tomin matlacpualli cacavatl ipatihv yn tomaoac in patzavac cacavatl matlacpualli ipan cenpualtetl onmatlactli

— Yn centetl çovatotolin yectli macuilpualli cacavatl ypatihu yn chamavac yn patzavac cacahoatl chiquacenpuvalli

— Yn vesulotl matlacpualli cacavatl ypatihu

— yn castillan[3] civatotolin chicavac onpualli cacavatl ipatihv

— yn castilvexolotl[3] cenpualtetl cacavatl ipatihv

— yn castil[3] tepitzin oquichtli castoltetl cacavatl ypatihv

— yn cihtli ahno quahvtochtli[4] mamahcuilpualli cacavatl ypatihu

— yn tochtli tepitzin onpualli onmatlactli ypatihu

— yn centetl nicantotoltecciztli etetl cacavatl ipatihv

— yn castil[3] ytecciz ontetl cacavatl ypatihv

— yn avacatl yancuican necih etetl cacahoatl ypatihv yn ihquac vel onezqui avacatl quinamiquiz in cacavatl

— yn centetl xitomatl quinamiquiz in cacavatl

— yn centetl cacavatl cenpualtetl yn miltomatl

— Yn nicanchilchotl yancuican necih in centetl cacavatl ontetl yn ihquac vel vnezqui in centetl cacauatl nahvtetl

— yn pitzavac chilchotl macuiltetl

— yn chiluactli patlavac in centetl cacauatl Etetl ypatihv in chilacatl macuiltetl ypatihv

— yn yancuican neci nochtli in centetl cacauatl quinamiqui in ihquac vel onezqui Hontetl yn nochtli

— yn tzapotl vei quinamiqui in cacauatl in tepitzi vntetl

— yn quavitl[5] tlatlapanalli quinamiqui centetl cacauatl

— yn tlasipevalli vei macuiltetl cacavatl ypatiho

— yn asolotl[6] vei nahutetl cacavatl ypatihv yn çan tepitzin vntetl Etetl ipatihv in cacavatl

— yn tamalli mopatla in cacauatl

---

[3]*Castillan* is the noun "Castile," though used in effect adjectivally, while *castil* is a noun "chicken."

[4]*Quauh-* might equally well mean "large."

there was great disorder and high pricing in the things sold in the markets of this city and province, in order to provide for and remedy it I ordered this price list made so that for the things contained in it, prices higher than the following will not be paid or taken, as is written, set forth in Indian language, in the wording which follows:

— One tomín is worth 200 full cacao beans, or 230 shrunken cacao beans.

— One good turkey hen is worth 100 full cacao beans, or 120 shrunken cacao beans.

— A turkey cock is worth 200 cacao beans.

— A grown Castilian[3] hen is worth 40 cacao beans.

— A rooster[3] is worth 20 cacao beans.

— A young chicken[3] is worth 15 cacao beans.

— A hare or forest[4] rabbit is worth 100 cacao beans each.

— A small rabbit is worth 30.

— One turkey egg is worth 3 cacao beans

— A chicken[3] egg is worth 2 cacao beans.

— An avocado newly picked is worth 3 cacao beans; when an avocado is fully ripe it will be equivalent to one cacao bean.

— One large tomato will be equivalent to a cacao bean.

— One cacao bean, 20 small tomatoes.

— A local green chile, newly picked, 2 for 1 cacao bean; when fully ripe, 4 for 1 cacao bean.

— A long narrow green chile, 5 (for a cacao bean).

— A wide dried chile, 1 cacao bean is worth 3; a hot green chile, (1 cacao bean) is worth 5.

— A newly picked prickly pear cactus fruit is equivalent to one cacao bean, when fully ripe two cactus fruit (for a cacao bean).

— A large sapote fruit, or two small ones, is equivalent to a cacao bean.

— Chopped firewood[5] is equivalent to 1 cacao bean.

— A large (strip of) pine bark for kindling is worth 5 cacao beans.

— A large salamander[6] is worth 4 cacao beans, a small one is worth 2 or 3 cacao beans.

— A tamale is exchanged for a cacao bean.

[5]It is not clear whether the unit of firewood is a bundle or a log.

[6]The word *axolotl* (to our surprise) is to be found in most English dictionaries.

— yn sasocotl[7] in centetl cacauatl vntetl
— yn michtlapictli Etetl cacauatl ipatihv

Yn isquich nican yhcuilihutoc çan ihv tlacovaloz in tianquizco in aquin çan ichan tlanamacaz quicuilizque in isquich tlen quinamaca yc poliviz ynic oppa ihu quichivaz yeilhuitl teilpiloyan yezqui yvan guimecavitequizque yvan yc poliviz in itlatqui yniquexpa yhv quichivaz quimecauitequizque tianguizco macuilpovallpa yvan quisimazque no yc poliviz yn itlatqui ynic napa yhu quichivaz mexico vicoz onpa quitlatzontequilizque yn tecuitlatoque Audiencia Real çanno ihuqui ypan mochivaz in aquin quipanaviz tlatzontequiliztli yn izquipa yhvqui ypan mochivaz yn ihvqui Aco vmoteneho vmochihv in ciudad de tls̄n̄ cenpualilhuitl metztli março de 1545 xiuitl yn yehoatl isquich cuililozque Hospital pohuiz yntech yn motvliniqueh

Todo lo qual fue declarado E Asentado mediante fran^{co} munoz ynterp^{e} [de] lengua mexicana E de la dicha visita E por su mr̄d fue mandado pregonar publicamente En el tianquez desta ciudad y que dende Aqui adelante hasta tanto que otra Cosa se provea y mande lo guarden E cumplan como En el se contiene so las penas En el Contenidas aplicadas como se q^{e} En el cap^{o} de suso e mando que A los dh̄os prescios den las dhas Cosas a los spañoles que se lo compraren so las dichas penas E a los dichos spañoles mando que no los tomen por fuerça los dichos mantenimi^{o}s sino pagandoles por las tales Cosas que compraren los prescios de suso conthenidos so pena de veinte p^{o}s de oro la mitad para la Camara E fisco de su mg^{t} E de veinte dias de prasion[2] y la otra mitad de p^{o}s de oro para el ospital E pobres desta ciudad fh̄o en tlaxcala A veinte de março de mill E quini^{o}s E quarenta E cinco Años

llicen^{do} santillan por mandado de su mr̄d Joan munoz Rico escriuano de su mg^{t}

En el dicho dia mes e año susodicho fue pregonado todo lo susodicho En el tianquez publico de la ciudad de tlaxcala en haz de mucha Jente que ande[2] Estevan cada cosa por si por boz de penton[8] yndio pregonero En la dicha ciudad mediante del dicho fran^{co} munoz ynterp^{e} el qual lo firmo t^{o}s diego de soto e fabian rr^{o}s y otros muchos yndios paso Ante mi Joan munoz Rico escri^{o} de su mg^{t} fran^{co} munoz

[7]*Sasocotl = xalxocotl.*

— A guava,[7] 1 cacao bean for 2.
— Fish wrapped in maize husks is worth 3 cacao beans.

Everything written here is to be bought only in the market; if anyone sells things at home, everything (the offender) sells will be taken from him and he will lose it;the second time he does it, he will be in jail three days and will be flogged and will lose his property for it; the third time he does it, he will receive 100 lashes in the market and be shorn, and also lose his property for it; the fourth time he does it he will be taken to Mexico City and there the judges of the Royal Audiencia will pass judgment on him; the same will also be done to whoever violates the judgment; each time it will be done with him as mentioned above. Done in the city of Tlaxcala, the 20th day of the month of March of the year of 1545. Everything will be taken for the hospital, to belong to the poor.

All the above was declared and set down through Francisco Muñoz, interpreter of the Mexican language and of the said inspection, and his grace ordered it to be proclaimed publicly in the market of this city, and that henceforth until otherwise provided and ordered, they are to keep and fulfill it as therein contained, under the therein contained penalties, applied as contained in the above paragraph; and he ordered that the said things be given at the said prices to Spaniards who should buy them, under the said penalties, and he ordered the said Spaniards not to take the said foods from them by force, but to pay them the above contained prices for such things that they buy, under the penalty of 20 gold pesos, half for the chamber and exchequer of His Majesty, and 20 days of confinement, and the other half of the gold pesos for the hospital and the poor of this city. Done in Tlaxcala on the 20th of March of the year of 1545.

Licentiate Santillán. By his grace's order, Juan Muñoz Rico, His Majesty's notary.

On the said day, month, and year given above, all the above-said was proclaimed, each item individually, in the public market of the city of Tlaxcala in the presence of many people who were there, in the voice of Penton,[8] Indian crier in the said city, with the aid of the said Francisco Muñoz, interpreter, who signed it. Witnesses Diego de Soto and Fabián Rodríguez and many other Indians. It was done before me, Juan Muñoz Rico, His Majesty's notary. Francisco Muñoz.

---

[8]Possibly from "Benito" or "Pedro."

35. Minutes of viceregal deliberations concerning aqueducts and water distribution in the Coyoacan region, 1557[1]

In ipan Altepetl mex^co^ cempoualli omome ylhuitia yn metztli setiemp^e^ yn ixiuhtz[in] totecuio yetzontli yoan castolpoualli yhoan onpoualli oncastolli omome xiuitl yn y[e]huatl yn tlacatl in tlatoani yn cenca maviztililoni don luis de vellasco visorrey gouern[ador] ytechpatzinco yn toveytlatocauh su magesdad ynic nican yancuic tlalpan yhoan no yehu[atl yn] licenciado maldonado viscal te su mad^dad^ yn nica tecuhctlatolloya otiquimittaque yhoan tiqui[mit]ta yn yehuantin i oticcacque yn intlatol yhoan in tlaneltililiztli yn itechpa yn atl yn onc[an] ytechpa quiça yn tepetl yn cuyuacan Auh yn ce atl huallauh ypan y quauhximalpa[n] yn intlalpan yn españolesme auh çanno oncan mochippa quitoca yn inan yn atlauhtly yeuatl yn iteiccavan[2] yn quitoca yn ompa itztiuh cuyuacan yn imilpan altamirano yhoan oc cequintin españoles yhoan nicantlacan[3] Auh ynnoquimottili yn tlacatl yn cenca maviztililoni yoan yehoatl viscal huel yca imixtelolo quimottilique yn oncan [me]ya in yeuatl ynin atl yhoan inic xexeliuhtoc yhoan in oc cequi ynic cenca tolinillo [in] nicantlaca yn oncan cuyuacan auh ynnic otocontequipanoque yhoan otoconittaque

quittoque yc tlanavatlique yc tlanavatilloc: auh yn axcampa yhoan in oc quexquich cav[itl] ma ytla ye no ceppa mochiuh ma cocuti[4] yn itechcopan ini in axcan ma çan nevivican [tla]matican yn itechcopa yn oncan meya in atl ynic oncan yacachto moxexelloua ynna[tl] ma quitlallican ome apiaztly hueuey cenca chicauaticaz yn oncan moxelloz ynna[tl] yn ce ypiazo ma quixello yn atl yn quitocaz yn inan yn atlauhtly in veveatlauhtli [om]pa yauh cuyuacan auh ynnoc no ce ypiazo ma no yxquich quitocaz yn apantli [i]n ompa yauh quauhximalpan ynic amo yaz ce achi uey çannimomextin neneuhqu[e i]nic yaz ynin xicneltilican ma yuhqui mochioan yn ome apiaztli yhoan xiquitta[can] ynic vel chicavaticaz ynic amo

[1]AGN, Tierras 1735, exp. 2, f. 116. This document must be a translation of a Spanish original. In recording the deliberations, the secretary did not maintain a consistent point of reference, but switched persons frequently. On f. 149 is a Spanish translation of 1681, with several plausible interpretations greatly divergent from our own.

In Mexico City, the 22d day of the month of September, the year of our Lord 1557, the very esteemed sir ruler don Luis de Velasco, viceroy and governor in the name of our great king His Majesty here in the new land, and also Licentiate Maldonado, His Majesty's prosecuting attorney here in the Royal Audiencia: we saw and do see these people; we have heard their words and the proof concerning the water which emerges from the mountain there at Coyoacan. And one stream comes through Quauhximalpan on the lands of the Spaniards, and also there is [its branch],[2] always following the bed of the ravine, which goes toward Coyoacan on the fields of Altamirano and some other Spaniards and local people.[3] And when the very honored sir and the prosecuting attorney had seen it, and saw with their eyes that this water arises there and how it is divided, and also how very afflicted the local people are there in Coyoacan, therefore we concerned ourselves with it and looked into it.

They said and ordered and it was ordered that now and in the future it must not be done again, let [them not suffer?][4] concerning this. Now let some people go with them to trace how the water arises there. In order first to distribute the water let them install two large and very strongly built conduits there to divide the water. Let one of the conduits divide the water which follows the ravine bed of the great ravine going to Coyoacan, and let the other conduit also follow the entire (course of) the canal going to Quauhximalpan so that it will not be any larger, but both of them will run equal. Carry this out, let the two conduits be so made, and see to it that they are very strong so that they will not be destroyed (or) the water leak out. It

[2]Literally, "its younger brothers." We are puzzled by the plural.

[3]The Spanish original was presumably *naturales*, the equivalent of "Indians."

[4]Despite the lack of a reflexive, *ma cocuti* seems to be a vetative plural from *cocoa*.

xixitiniz ynic amo amo[5] moyauaz tepan in icaz ytenexyo yez inic cenca chicauaticaz yn tlatlalili

yc quimonavatillia yhoan quimomaquilique yn huelitiliztli yn don hernando de p[or]tugar desurello[6] regidor ynican ipan altepetl ynic tlanavatilli no ihoan quimote[. . .]tia[7] ynic quittaz quitequipanoz yn yeuatl in ticteneva in tlatlalili yhoan yxpan [mo]chioaz yn apiaztli yeuatl quixexeloz yn atl yeuatl quimati ca oniquittac caquitilloc ynic mochioaz yn yeuatl tlatlalili inic moxexeloz ynnatl auh in ye[uan]-tin yn intech monequi yn atl quitlaxtlavizque in ivicpan cuyuacan ioan quauhximalp[an]

Auh yn itechcopa moxexeloz yn atl yn ompa ytztiuh cuyuacan yn quitoca in inan yn ye uecauh ycac yn yeuatl itech can inecoca yn oncan calle nican chaneque yn quito[ca]iotian çoquiac auh yn oncan yancuican tlalmachioti yn altamirano oncan moxexeloz in atl ynic otlanavatilloc yehoatl quitocaz ynnatl in ye uecauh ycac yn apantly auh no yehuatl yn quitocaz yn atlauhtli yn tomayeccampan yn ixquich ye mochi atl yn quitocaz in atlauhtly inic huel yntech aciz inicantlaca cuyuacan macevaltin yn iuhqui yeppa catca ya in ye uecauh auh ynnoc cecni centlapal ynname ma ompa yauh yn imilco yn ipada in imolino in licenciado altamirano mochi yn ixquich chichioalloni yn tleyn itech monequiz yn atl ytechcopan auh ynnoquiz ynnatl ytech pada yoan molino ynnoontlatequipano ma quicava aocmo quixtocaz ompa contlaçaz yn ompa yauh yn inan yn atlauhtli auh yn yehoatl licenciado altamirano yhoan in yeuantin yn nicantlacan yniquintech vallaciz quitlatequipanilhuiz ma quimmaca ynno yuh quimmacaya ynnixquich cavitl yn licenciado altamirano ynnic huel quicuiz ynnoc cecni atl yn tlacpac yn yeuatl ymixican ynic onca quinequiz ynic tlaavilliz in imilco

O yc titlanavatique ynic ocanixti quicui yn altamirano ma quihoallaça yn ompa yauh yn inan yn atlauhtli auh ynnoc cecni ma yauh ma yc tlaavilli yn ompa imilco ynniuhqui yc onitlanavati ynic amo mocuculizque yhoan inic aocmo ceppa ytla quitozque ma mochi neltia Auh yn oncan tlatzintlan molino oc no oncan moxelloz ynnatl yehoatl quichioaz in altamirano yn tlachichioalli auh in iquac oontlatequipano yn ocanixti in atl auh ynic ome quicui yn itechpa yn inan yn atlauhtli yn licenciado altamirano ayac quicuiliz

---

[5]Apparently inadvertent repetition.

[6]Don Hernando de Portugal held the office of royal treasurer and was councilman by virtue of that. See *Libro del Cabildo . . . de México*, VI (1550-1561), p. 237. We long

will be on stone and its mortar will be so that the construction will be very strong.

They ordered and gave power to don Hernando de Portugal, treasurer,[6] councilman in the city here; (the viceroy) ordered and also [gives notification][7] that he will see and concern himself with the construction we mention, and in his presence is to be made the conduit to divide the water. He knows about it because I saw him and he was advised how the construction is to be done to divide the water; and those who use the water, toward Coyoacan and Quauhximalpan, will pay for it.

And concerning the division of the water toward Coyoacan that follows the bed, and has been there for a long time, it belongs to the local people who dwell on both sides there at the place called Çoquiac; and there recently Altamirano laid claim to land. The water there is to be divided as was ordered: the water is to follow the canal that has stood for a long time, and also it is to follow the ravine on the right-hand side. All the water is to follow the ravine so that it can reach the local people, the Coyoacan commoners, as it had been for a long time before. And on the other side let the waters go to the fields, dam, and mill of Licentiate Altamirano and to the things being established there, as much water as is needed for it, and when the water has emerged from the dam and mill and done its task, let him leave it and not lay claim to it any more, but let it go back to the ravine bed, and it will reach Licentiate Altamirano and the local people for their cultivation. Let him give it to them as he always had given it to them. Licentiate Altamirano may take the other water above; what flows out there he will use to irrigate his fields.

We ordered that if Altamirano takes (water) in both places, let him release that which goes in the ravine bed, and as for the other, let it run, let him irrigate his fields there with it as I have ordered, so that they will not argue and not make further claims; let all be carried out. And there below the mill, there also the water is to be divided, and Altamirano is to do the construction. And when he has built the water (conduits) in both places and Licentiate Altamirano takes the second part from the ravine bed, no one is to seize the

---

imagined that don Hernando had a second surname on the order of Surello, and indeed the Nahuatl writer may have so interpreted the epithet *tesorero*.

[7]This torn space may have originally been occupied by any of several verbs, such as *ittitia, machtia*, or *nauatia*.

çan quimixcaviz ynnatl ayac quixtoquilliz yn yehoantin nican chaneque ynic huel yntech aciz ynic huel yntech monequiz in yehoatl in atl

O yc tlanavatilloc auh no yuh nitlanavatia nicnavatia in licenciado altamirano yhoan ın aqui no yntlanel aca ahuel quicuiz ynnatl Auh yn aqui no oncan hoalmixquetzaz aocmo quicuiz in atl yn omochichiuh auh amo no huel tlaxitiniz yn tleyn motlaliz yn tleyn mochioaz yn itechcopa ynnatl inic moxexeloua nictlalia pena mochi poliuiz yn inemac yhoan quixtlavaz macuilpoualli pesus coztic teocuitlatl yn quezquipa yuh quichioaz yzquipa yuh mochioaz auh occan xelliuiz yn epoualli pesus ytech pouiz in igamarra de su mag^dad ynnopoualli pesos yntech pouiz quicuizque in juezesme in quitlatzontequillizque yn itechpa tlavelilocaiotl yn tlaielleuiliztli yntlacamo quimamatcava yntla nicantlacatl[8] ma momaca macuilpoualli yc mecauitecoz yhoan totocoz ynnipa in altepetl matlactli leguas noviampan ce xiuitl

ynnitechcopa atl yn quauhximalpan ynic tlaavililo in imilpan españolesme in ompa onoque yc tlanauatitiui yhoan ic nitlanavatia yn ipan yuh yetivitz tlatlalili yn ordenaças del capildo yn ipan altepetl mex^co yc tlanavatilo ypammotocaiotitiuh yn yeuatl tlatoani s^or visorrey don antoni^o de menduça Auh yn axcan iyomatzinco oquimottilitzinoto yn tlacatl yn tlatoani yn cenca maviztililoni visorrey ymmomextin quimoviquilitia in yeuatl licenciado maldonado viscal auh quimolhuilli totech monequi cenca monequi ypan tlatolloz yniquehi ma ximotlanavatilli yhoan nitlanavatia ayac huecan ontzatzitz aoc ac apelar quichioaz yntechpan nitlatlatlauhtia don luis de velasco quimolhuilia ynneva omextin licenciado maldonado nixpan mochiuh ni juan de guevas escrivano

[8] I.e., "Indian."

water or take it all for himself; no one is to claim it from the local people, so that the water that they greatly need can reach them.

It was decreed and likewise I decree and order that neither Licentiate Altamirano nor anyone else, no matter who, may take the water, and also anyone who should come to present himself there is not to take the water which has been arranged, and may not transgress against what is ordained and done concerning how the water is divided. I set the penalty that he will lose his whole grant and will pay 100 pesos in gold. For each time he should do this the same will be done, and it will be divided into two parts; 60 pesos of it will go to His Majesty's chamber and 40 pesos will be for the judges to take who pronounce sentence concerning the offense, [if he does not disavow covetousness]. If it is a local person[8] let him be given a hundred lashes and be exiled from the city and the surrounding ten leagues for one year.

Concerning the water at Quauhximalpan, with which the fields of the Spaniards who live there are irrigated, they are ordering and I order that it is to be as established in the ordinances of the council in Mexico City and was ordered during the term of the ruler lord viceroy don Antonio de Mendoza. And now both of them, the very esteemed sir ruler the viceroy and Licentiate Maldonado, the prosecuting attorney, whom he has accompany him, have seen it in person; and (the viceroy) said to him: We need, we greatly need to urge these things. Let it be decreed, and I order that no one is to complain to distant authorities nor to make appeals concerning it. I ask it. Don Luis de Velasco and Licentiate Maldonado both say it together. Done before me, Juan de Cuevas, notary.

Appendix I

Letter of don Francisco de León, governor of Huitzilopochco, to don Juan de Guzmán, governor of Coyoacan, mid-sixteenth century[1]

Several of the early Spanish chroniclers and grammarians commented on the highly metaphorical, allusive nature of Aztec public discourse, which caused difficulties of comprehension even for those most experienced in the language. Here we have an example, a letter of whose import, after much work and thought, we feel that we understand perhaps half. We can identify the majority of the words and follow the contours of the syntax indifferently well, but the true meaning is often fully hidden nonetheless.[2] The text still has great interest because of its genre and because of its very difficulty; we print it here with some background remarks and a paraphrase of certain parts whose meaning we have penetrated, hoping to publish a fully worked out and reliable translation at some future time.

muy magnifico señor

Yn titlatovani don ju^o de coyovanca ca ticaque yn motlatoltçin yn itechcopan ymaltepentçin ca momacenvaltçin omochiva ma yxtlavi yn tecuhyotl yn tlatocayotl ca veyya yn ipan ymaltepentçin y tlatolli y coyovanca auh ca oncate ymotlavan yn pipilti ahu in

---

[1] AGN, Tierras 1735, exp. 2, f. 127. The Spanish translation is on f. 153.

[2] Take the passage *av inic nictlecavia yn tepentitech av [in]natla ynic nicallaquia av in tevatl ca ticpia y quavtla*. Literally, this could be given as "and thus I climb up on the mountain and thus I enter in the water, and you, you have the woodland." Does don Francisco mean himself personally, or is he speaking for the town? Is it that he has expended great effort and Coyoacan *still* has the woodland? Or is it that Huitzilopochco's lands extend from the hill to the lake, and Coyoacan's are beyond, in the woodland? The combination of *atl* and *tepetl*, of course, meant "town," and the two words were the basis of countless poorly recorded metaphors and set phrases. With the expenditure of a little ingenuity one can arrive at an indefinite number of plausible interpretations of this single passage. Only the accumulation of numbers of comparable texts will bring the translation of such passages out of the realm of word games.

tepaneca y vevetque ahu intecopan yn omozcaltique ca nellipan mochiva ca nellimaltepevh y coyovanca yntla yevanti yn oquitlacoque ca quitçalcviltiz yn t^o d. ahu intla tevantçin motollinia yn topilva ca yevaltillotivi mach tepiltçintli nimitçonoyollitlacalviz çan ixquichi yc nimitçonotlatlavhtilia nimitçonixpantillia açanel notlatlavelchiva aça yuhqui yn achi ticmoxictia yn altepetl y vitçillopochco yn tiquivalliva yn tepaneca y vevetque ca miec yniquinolvilli aço yohmitçilvique ca ye miecpa ynimitçnolvillia queni vel ca yn altepetl ca no ticmatiznequi yn tlatocayotl yn icatqui y coyovanca y vitçillopochco ca çanelli y ye toca timocacayava ca vel ticmanti ynica y coyotleuhco otoconcoto çano yuhqui y[e?]ppa ca nechmomaquilique yn tepaneca ahu in ipa yxalcvep[. . .] cvix amo ymil yn tlacatl yn acolvantçin xiquallixiptlati ca oticontemacac canocevantli ynic moxictia y xochmilcatl opan[i?]tlatlaque ychimalcoyoc yn totavan yn imilpa catca oqui[n?]tlatoltique yevantli yniquivaltçatçillia yn testigo ahu i[n?]tla nelli nitlavelliloc aço niquimacaz yn testigo yn toteycavan yn tlatoque cvix noço quipiqui ymantlacxivitl y[o]mey ynopan yn otetlayecolti y tepanecatl y xochimilco c[on]pevalti y quaxochtli amo nevatl amo titonamique yn ac ach[i] y colvanca yn axca yn tlapaltotonti y quavhteca y s.ta aug[. . .] tlaca quecen quitova yn aqui yntech ananto ynopantitla[. . .] y xochmilco cvix onimic ca nicanica ahu inotla y ju^o temillote[catl?] ca nica ca ca opahuiho yn tiquimotemolia ymotechiuhcava y[mix]covatlayllotlac yn acoçacatl yn tocviltecatl yn tepaneca cvix [. . .]tlaquetçal y quaxochtli amo cochpaque y vitçillopochca cammotlatique yn quitlecavi yn tepepan y tlacatecatçi[n] y quiyacatia y vitçillopochca ahu inica yn teyavalco yniquivalyacatia yn antepanecatl y yevatl ymixcovatlayllotlac aca noço telliuhqui mochivh ca ye yuh ticmanti yn tivitçillopochca yn iuh ticmanti thomas delli solis ca omic ahu isoch alparado yn itecviyo y xochmilca ca ymixpan cvix omic y tlatovani ymardonanto aqui quiquetç y quaxochitli amo yevatl yn don mi̅n ychavan tlatova yn tepetechicalqui anoço huehuetlatolli mitoznequi yntlallachco amo no tlacvilloc ypan catqui ynocolco ytçaqualtech av inic nictlecavia yn tepentitech av [in]natla ynic nicallaquia av in tevatl ca ticpia y quavhtla av innima tiquixicauh yn opahui ximititi y tlatolli ymotechiuhcavan y vitçillopochca ca ye yxquichi yn ticmocaquitia ynotlatol atel ticaquizque ymotlatoltçin ma mitçmochicavilli yn t^o d. ye ixquich

nimitçnotlaçotilia nevatl
don fran^co de leo gonvernador s. ma^ot

The letter is from the governor of San Mateo Huitzilopochco, don Francisco de León, to don Juan de Coyoacan (Guzmán), tlatoani and governor of neighboring Coyoacan; the date seems to be the middle of the sixteenth century, certainly during the lifetime of the first don Juan (d. 1569).[3] Don Francisco is defending Huitzilopochco against some jurisdictional claim by Coyoacan; apparently Coyoacan wants areas also claimed by Huitzilopochco in the uplands near San Agustín, Chimalcoyoc, and Tepepan.[4] A possible source of controversy between the two towns can be seen in a passage of Tezozomoc's *Crónica mexicayotl* (pp. 131-134), explaining that Huitzilopochco had no tlatoani until Huitzilatzin, son of a younger brother of Moctezuma I, took office there. Huitzilatzin's daughter married the ruler of Coyoacan, and the first don Juan de Guzmán was their son, with a consequent claim to the succession in Huitzilopochco. Xochimilco is also somehow involved in the dispute. In a letter of 1563 (AGI, Patronato 184, No. 50), the council of Xochimilco asserts that it had traditionally held San Agustín, then lost it to Coyoacan shortly after the conquest, regained it around 1548, and finally lost it again.

To paraphrase, then, don Francisco de León of Huitzilopochco acknowledges receipt of a message from don Juan of Coyoacan, in which the latter said that his rule should be restored; that his noble uncles and the Tepaneca elders of Coyoacan can remember the time when the town (Huitzilopochco? A border town?) was theirs. Don Francisco does not believe them ("if they have sinned, our lord God will punish them") and gives expression to his anger. He rejects Coyoacan's claims, as he has told the Coyoacan elders previously; don Juan must be making sport of Huitzilopochco (*toca timocacayava*). Don Francisco now launches into the justification of his position; certain Tepaneca were given to Huitzilopochco, presumably long ago, in the time of the legendary Acolhuatzin. Xochimilco's claims are to be ignored. Don Francisco then begins to talk about the availability and credibility of witnesses. If he were trying to hide the truth, would he give his noble relatives as witnesses? Are they lying

---

[3]Don Francisco was governor of Huitzilopochco in August 1555, at which time there was an agreement between Huitzilopochco and Coyoacan concerning disputed lands (AGN, Mercedes, IV, ff. 216-218; reference supplied by Charles Gibson). Further documents (1551-56) on disputes over lands at Palpan, Coyotleuhco, and Tzapotitlan are in AGN, Tierras 1735, exp. 2, ff. 34-42.

[4]On the basis of AGN, Hospital de Jesús 329, exp. 2, Charles Gibson has identified Chimalcoyoc as a district of San Agustín.

about the thirteen years for which the Tepaneca served Huitzilopochco? Then the boundary is mentioned, and once again Xochimilco. Whatever the "worthless little woodsmen of San Agustín" say, there are others who know better. "Have I died? Here I am, and here is my uncle Juan Temillotecatl." Don Juan should question his own high Tepanec officials, still given the preconquest titles of Mixcouatlailotlac, Acoçacatl, and Tocuiltecatl, who were present at the setting of the boundary. Nor did the Huitzilopochca revel in sleep (*amo cochpaque*); their official the Tlacatecatl led them up the hill on the occasion. Both sides know what happened, as well as other witnesses, including Judge Maldonado. Don Francisco entreats don Juan to reconsider his position, hopes to hear from him again, and ends wishing him good health and expressing his esteem.

Here we add a Spanish translation made in 1681 by Gregorio Mancio, the official interpreter of the Royal Audiencia of New Spain, for any help it may be, and also to show how little the old rhetoric was understood by that time. Mancio was aiming for a complete and quite literal translation, which he came reasonably close to achieving with some older documents. In this case he limited himself to a paraphrase as brief as ours, and even that is full of dubious points. For example, we feel fairly sure that *ma ixtlavi yn tecuhyotl yn tlatocayotl* means "may the lordship and rule be restored," not "we will pay what is owing to a lord." The translation:

> Mui macnifico Señor Don Juan de Cuyoacan bimos con muncho amor y como Sus Subditos Su carta y estan todos mui obedientez a pagar lo que como a Señor Se debiere pero aduierte Señor que todauia ay munchos Señores Tepanecos tus parientes ci ellos como tuyos i de Cuyoacan no an aduertido que te quieres alcar con todo y que tienes en mui poco al pueblo de chorubusco Sabe senor que los que tienen las tierras las posen mui bien y que alli nacieron y que nosotros queremos saber como es tuyo todo y nada dezte pueblo no te enojen estas palabras porque ablo con sentimiento y saue que todauia uiuen los de Culhuacan los de Xuchimilco y los de palpan que saben asta donde llegan las tierras de Chorubusco y asi ynformate de los tus tepanecos que artos tienes consigo para que te desengañen que ci fueren menester testigos artos ay que digan la uerdad y a ti Senor te desengañen que nosotros buscaremos el remedio y sabremos de una bes todo lo que debemos aser y Salir de Cuidado y que biban con quietud los deste pueblo Dios te de muncha Salud como lo deceo deste pueblo de Chorobusco Te escriue Don Fran[co] de leon Gouernador de San matheo que te estima

Appendix II

Spanish translations

Side by side with many archival documents in Nahuatl, especially petitions, lie Spanish translations which were made by official interpreters of the time. We include here three examples (for Docs. 27, 28, and 33), partially to call attention to the existence of such aids and partially to give readers some sense of their limitations. The advantages of any translation at all are quite apparent; ones like these are especially valuable because they gloss expressions, developed in ordinary usage over the course of the colonial period, which fail to appear in the dictionaries. Thus the translation of Document 27 gives (in item 2) "owe" for *huiquilia*, an important meaning not contained in either Molina or Siméon, and mentioned by Carochi only in passing, in an example illustrating another point (p. 505).

Yet the translations are not to be trusted implicitly. Many were done in a spirit of routine, achieved by that corner of the mind we use today for typing copy or proofreading. The translator of Document 27 left out item 10, translated *molino* (in Spanish in the Nahuatl text) as "city," because the general sense of the expected statement might have run in that direction, and gave the slip *oticmacahuitequic* an interpretation which a moment's thought and comparison with other passages in the same text would have corrected. Then there was simple misunderstanding; some of the translators were native speakers of Nahuatl, some were not. When a translator failed to understand, he might resort to omission of selected passages, or to a literalist piling up of words that yield no true meaning, or to embroidery. All these techniques are illustrated in the translation of Document 33, where the existence of a putatively complete Spanish version has not kept our translation of the text from being, of all those in this volume, the one with the largest remaining questions and ambiguities. When time intervenes between the original and the translation, difficulties mount. The Spanish renditions of the Coyoacan papers, made about a hundred years later, would constitute pernicious misinformation if one had no other knowledge to check them against (see Appendix I for a somewhat atypical example).

Even when intended as complete, Spanish translations are often more succinct than the Nahuatl originals, largely by virtue of reduction of the characteristic duplications, reverential expressions, and circumlocutions. This often led to full-scale paraphrasing, as with the rendition of Document 28.[1] And as here, the paraphrase may frequently contain significant details, of meaning and of substance, that were not in the original text. Such material has its value both for interpretation and for historical-anthropological investigation, whether it came out of the paraphraser's general knowledge or, as appears to have happened often, from an oral interview with the bearers of the petition. Some paraphrases indeed give the impression of resting primarily on oral statements, with little or no reference to the text.[2]

The comparison of Nahuatl and Spanish versions of a document involves the direct confrontation of two points of view and sets of categories; nothing is more instructive than to follow such terms as *indio* and *natural* through the Spanish translations, noting the very different expressions in the originals. And translations like these are prima facie evidence of the culture of the translators, often Indians or mestizos. Of course one or two examples are hardly enough basis for judging whether a certain manner of speech has its origin in the translator's limited Spanish or in the exigencies of translation; whether an *ompa* appears because it was more natural to the translator, or from inertia. All in all, increased attention to these apparently secondary documents promises rewards for intellectual, cultural, and social history as well as materials for the eventual compilation of adequate dictionaries and grammars of colonial-period Nahuatl.

(27.)

muy p^os^ s^or^

Juan uicente Alcalde miguel lopes naturales del pueblo de jalostotitan ante tu precencia nos querellamos que eres gran señor nuestro y nuestro Rey en tu precincia nos Querellamos y quexamos de nuestro clerigo y Uicario fr^co^ muñoz Que mucho nos maltrata y sienpre nos da y nos asota y a todos los naturales y io Juan Uicente Alcalde mucho me dio tres veces me dio de bofetones y me deribo y

[1] For a Spanish version of a Nahuatl letter that is half translation, half paraphrase, see Günter Zimmermann, *Briefe der indianischen Nobilität*, pp. 16-17.

[2] The *Códice Osuna* is an example of how Nahuatl speakers would come to officials with a quite sparse text, then expatiate on it at length. The practice must have continued even as Nahuatl texts grew less pictorial and more detailed.

Quede muy desmayado y me quebro la bara en la sacristia de la yglecia cuando estaba Rebestido con la alua y tanbien la estola y manipulo entonces me aporreo y le Respondi Por que raçon me das y toda mi bara la as quebrado y luego dixo si te aporee y te quebre tu bara y tanbien toda tu cabesa la quebrare

— 1 no es de ualde porQue el padre tiene Una señora en la estancia y sienpre alla se esta en la estancia otra ues estando en la estancia los yndios de mesquitique le trujeron pescado y a mi me los dio a guardar todo un dia el dia de la uigilia de s. andres le estube aguardando y el padre Uino al amaneser cuando Cantauan los gallos el dia de s. andres y dijo que es de el pescado y luego le dije padre aqui esta aqui lo estoy guardando luego le [sic] dijo por que raçon no se lo auian enuiado ayer a la estancia y luego le dije padre Que sauia yo si me lo auisaras te lo enuiara y luego de ay comenso a aporearme y decirme eres gran bellaco de esta manera me maltrato

— 2° Y tanuien Por lo que me quiere mal 15 p^{o}s 2 t^{o} que deue a la yglecia mayor y Una caxa que es del santo sacramento cuando el jueues santo lo ensieran y asi la deja a guardar como quiera cuando fue a mexico la dejo en guarda de un cosinero y cuando Uino la torno a tomar y la dejo Con la señora y cuando otra ves le puse demanda ante el s^{or} proUisor y el alcalde del pueblo de s. gaspar y otro pueblo nos querellamos de el y el s^{or} prouisor le escriuio y el s^{or} proUisor ablo a su señoria oUispo y el s^{or} ouispo y el prouisor le escriuieron disiendole Consolad a esos naturales pues son vuestros hijos y quereldos y cuando acauo de leer la carta del s^{or} o Uispo Respondio y porQue os fuisteis a quejar ante el prouisor y luego al señor oUispo mejor sera Que Uays a mexico Que de alla saque mi recados de Uenficiado y Uicario de aqui y por esto me quiere mal y a todo el pueblo

— 3° luego otra ues me aporeo Quando Uido las cartas del s^{or} prouisor agora dos Ueces me a aporeado otra ues en misquitic me aporeo en presentia de otros el dia de la fiesta de nuestra s^{ar} de la Natiuidad y otra ues domingo adelante me torno a aporear y agora son cuatro ueses las que me a aporeado por Rason de las Cartas y papeles del s^{or} prouisor porQue me queje de el porque me aporeaba

— 4° otra ues Un muchacho sacristan 8 años tenia en grande manera le açoto en grande manera lo desollo sus carnes se desmayo y estubo Una semana en la cama y asi como se leuanto se Uyo y el padre preguntaUa por el a su madre y le desia ques de tu hijo y su madre le respondio distele gran traUajo por eso se Uyo y por esto senojo el padre y luego el domingo cuando enpecso a [e]char agua Uendita que dijo asperges en medio de la yglesia yendo echando agua Uendita Con el ysopo le dio a la muguer madre del muchacho sacristan la descalabro y le saca much sangre

— 5º otra ues Un yndio fiscal Que auia acauado su año de seruirlo le dijo padre ya se acabo mi trabajo de fiscal y el padre no quiso se trocara antes lo asoto mucho alla dentro lo ensero y mucho lo maltrato

— 6º Y otra ues buscamos otra persona de nuebo Que fuese fiscal y no lo quiso Reseuir desia no quiero que sea este fiscal este Uaquero y luego lo corio dee alli y otra ues mando Que lo llamacen dijo llamad al Que a de cer fiscal luego lo fue a llamar el fiscal Que era i se lo tujo el fiscal que era y lugo auiso a su negro que le desnudace los calsones y la camisa todo lo desnudaron y lo colgaron otra ues en grande manera lo asotaron en grande manera lo desmayaron y io le Rogaua y iba a la mano no queria ser rogado ni dejalle y asi cuando lo soltaron luego se Uyo muy lejos y agora no ay fiscal todos los yndios le tienen miedo al padre no ay quien se atreba a cer fiscal

— 7º Y otra ues Un yndio enuio a atotonilco a dejar dos caxas y se fue y lleuo las caxas y el padre le dijo cuando Uayas alla a mitic me ueras que te tengo de dar Una carta que se la as de dar al alcalde mayor alla en atotonilco y el yndio Que lleuaua las cajas llego a mitic y busco al padre y no le allo que alla se fue a quedar A la estancia Con la señora Y luego se torno a boluer a mitic se fue alla onpa estancia fue a dar con el el padre y luego le dijo por que raçon uienes aqui a la estancia padre Uengo por la carta tuya y luego por esto se enojo y le dixo anda alla a mitic aguardame Que alla yre y te dare la carta luego el yndio se Uoluio a mitic y luego fue el padre a mitic y luego alli le enpeso a aporear y le desmayo porQue fue en su seguimiento a la estancia y por esto senojo el padre no quiere que nadie le siga ni uaya a la estancia con su señora y algunas Beces Quando le uan a Buscar a mitic y de alli uan A la estancia alli les aporea y maltrata

— 8º otra ues Una hija mia catalina juana alla fue a la yglesia sobre tarde a barer y el padre alla en la yglesia la cojo Que se lo queria azer no le quiso admitir y dentro de la iglecia la aporeo y luego uino a quejarse a mi

— 9 desta manera nos maltrata y muchas personas naturales le temen y muchos naturales se uyen y no ay persona Que quiera admitir ser fiscal

— 11 Y tanuien no enseña la doctrina sermon sino Que no es mas de por a Querellos mal y maltratarnos y cuando el s^or^ prouisor le escriuo consolaldos a esos yndios pues son tus hijos y asi como lo leyo dixo porQue los e de consolar y Querellos pues son mis hijos Que son hijos de el diablo y los e de maltratar y no obedecio el mandato del s^or^ prouisor y del ouispo

— 12 Y agora uenimos a pedir Tu fabor como a s^or^ y Rey nuesTro y nos agas limosna en darnos un clerigo bueno Que nos Quiera Que asimismo le Queremos y este NuesTro Uicario Quitanoslo mas Que salga porQue en grande manera nos Maltrata y no nos ama y si no sale de aQui mucha guente de tus Yndios se uyran por el nuestro Uicario y asimismo faltara el tributo de nuestro grande Rey de donde lo emos de tomar para cunplirlo con esto se acauan nuestras Raçones somos buestros tributarios

juan bisente alcalde miguel lopez

—13 Y Quiere nuesTro Coraçon Que nos buelua 15 p[o]s 2 t[o] y la caja Ques del santisimo sacramento y quedaremos Contentos y satifechos Que por todo esto nos tiene mala boluntad y nos quiere mal

— 14 Y tanuien enuia a los Yndios lejos y aqui a la ciudad y asimismo no les paga y asimismo ocupa a los Yndios en domalle potros y no les paga

Esta uien Y fielmente sacada y trasUntada en lengua catellana esta petision de ariba Contenida

juan diaz de pangua ynterpete de la R[l] audientia

(28.)

[El] alcayde y naturales del pueblo de San Martin dicen por esta peticion que los alcaldes y p[e] guardian del pueblo de cocula les hacen por fuerza ir a trabajar a la yglesia de otro pueblo teniendo la de su pueblo necesidad de cubrirla como en efecto estan tratando de hacerlo y actualmente cuuierta parte de la capilla mayor y que ansimismo an trabajado por espacio de un año y no se les a dado de comer sino que la han llebado sacandola de su hospital y que ansimismo en el tiempo que an estado alla se les an perdido algunas cosas del hospital como an sido cinco novillos y otros generos y que llebaron para comer mientras trabajaban cinco anegas de maiz por no darles el sustento y que an acudido con lo que a sido necesario para la dicha yglesia con vigas y tablas que an pedido para ella y que ansimismo an acudido al dicho guardian y le acuden todo el año con el tequio en la manera siguiente

— una carretada de leña cada semana
— zacate dos carretadas cada semana
— un indio para guarda de los caballos cada semana
— pescado todas las semanas el que es necesario
— guebos dos dias en la semana
— hortelano cada semana

— indio para trabajar en la iglesia cada semana
— una carga de agua cada semana
y ansimismo nos piden cada año cinco p^{os} para ayuda del cirio pasqual, y lo damos con otras limosnas que hacemos para ayuda de la yglesia como dicho tenemos arriba y que asimismo de lo que toca a la obra de la dicha yglesia como del sustento del religioso no se les paga nunca nada y asi piden a su ss^{a} ill^{ma} sea servido de mandar se les releve de dicho trabajo asi por ser justicia como por estar como dicho tienen la obra de la dicha yglesia entre manos

(33.)

Aqui R^{vi} en Granada una carta de Vmdes por mano de Alonso de Solis Aguirre que me escribio de la corte de madrid a lo que vino al consejo Real de indias no se si podia ver al Rei que es difunto su padre que era D. felipe, del mismo titulo mui amigo de aser mersedes el que antes era Prinsipe que agora es nro Rei defensor de la fe Sepan Vmdes que aora ai muchos cuidados por el viaje a encontrar a la Reina en Barcelona hija del Emperador de Roma sobrina del Rei con quien casa para que lo tengan entendido Vmdes podra ser entonses pueda ber a su Mag. i io tambien pasandose los frios adonde fuere tengo de llebar toda mi familla para entonses are lo que Vmdes me piden no lo ago por no aserlo sino porque tengo muchas ocupasiones de Pleitos que io escribire a Vmdes mui de espasio—por el negocio de Alonso de solis me olgare toparlo en la corte i ver como comiensa el pleito por los trabajos que se pasan en todos los pueblos los naturales i casiques que tengo grandissima pena en el corason por los trabajos que se pasan por alla i esto no ai sino encomendarlo a Dios, i que se aga lo que pretendemos i lo que pedimos i aora que me escriban los mexicanos i los de los pueblos para satisfaser mi corason para que con eso saque la cara a pedir en el consejo para responder con berdad al consejo en favor de Vmdes no teniendo pena i enbiandome testimonio de Vmdes como Reparten los oficios si es por mandado de justicia o si les piden los R^{s} tributos i quienes son los que los cuidan o si les mandan que baian a trabajar i quantos son los que contaron en la cuenta personal i matricula esta es la Rason que an de enbiar escrita si no ubiera visto escritos de Vmdes por lo qual puse en mi memoria i en mi corason i para ir a la corte a satisfaser al Rei n̄ro s^{r} todos los nietos i desedientes del s^{r} emperador montesuma que estan peresiendo i pedirle las mersedes que se les isieron a los hijos de ju^{o} cano i nietos de montesuma pido se les aga a los de mi casa pues les toca el mesmo derecho i asi aun no e pedido ni ni comensado que ando ocupado en otro negozio i con esto tendran satisfacion Vmdes i animo que queriendo dios i suplicandoselo se aga su voluntad i me dixieron no se si es verdad, que queria poner pleito contrandiciendome vro cuñado pidiendo alimentos el que esta en cuiohacan o se engaña o es industria de otra persona por comerle lo que tiene i gastarselo asi comiense que io enviare la memoria como no es verdad lo que pide i si pide alguna mersed lo isiera con toda Voluntad que no me pesara i asi por Vmdes me pesa entreambas a dos como les ba i lo pasan i que es su Voluntad de Vmdes que si estubieramos serca acudiera a saver lo que aviamos de pedir i asi por la dilacion no se lo que tengo de ser que aunque supe que Vmdes pasaban bexasiones i pobresa si Dios fuera servido estubieramos con quietud i sosiego i gosaramos no ai sino paciensia que asi como Vmdes lo pasan lo paso yo con artas nesesidades que estoi cargado de ijos i no tengo con que sustentarlos ni mi familla ni con que darles de comer que quando biene el socorro entra come ahua que sale i entra que tiene ia dueño i muchas veses no alcansa para pagar i con esto mui adeudado i asi sepan Vmdes que ai le escribo a Jeronimo del castillo de a Vmdes sinquenta pesos por esa libransa que ba dentro de su carta de los quales part[an] Vmdes a Ventisico pesos aqui en granada a 18 de noviembre de 1598

de Vmdes Dn Luis de montesuma

Appendix III

Further Types of Colonial Nahuatl Documentation

The exploitation of colonial Nahuatl documents being in such an early stage, we have become aware of further major genres even during the short time while this book was being processed by the press. This is the result of the investigations of others as well as of our own.

In our own explorations, it has come home to us that the entire range of Spanish documents related to litigation had its counterpart in Nahuatl. We had been by no means sure of this. Though briefs, petitions, appeals, and interrogatories with extensive testimony concerning Nahuatl speakers exist by the thousands in the Archivo General de la Nación and other repositories, the vast majority are written in Spanish, even though the Indian testimony was originally given in Nahuatl. When there is Nahuatl material, it is commonly one piece of primary evidence at the beginning, a will or sale, and the rest of the proceedings are in Spanish. It turns out, however, that only those documents produced by outside authorities, in the course of investigations or appeals, were done in Spanish. Inside the towns, at the level of the Indian governor and alcaldes, proceedings were entirely in Nahuatl, from the sixteenth century on into the eighteenth. This is true, at least, of some of the larger and better established towns like Xochimilco, Azcapotzalco, and Amecameca. Such material was rarely sent on to higher authorities, and therefore the volume of what has been preserved may not be large. This remains to be seen, however. For the present we will say only that we have seen examples of the Nahuatl briefs of local Indian lawyers or *procuradores*, in every respect comparable to Spanish texts; notifications, with the spontaneous replies of the persons notified; complaints of a personal nature (such as one of a woman about her unruly daughter-in-law); and full-scale testimony of witnesses. We still need to obtain a better notion of the spread of genres and conventions, and also of the volume of the material. It does appear, however, that especially the testimony represents the closest approximation yet to the ordinary speech of the colonial period, with a potential for cultural history and historical linguistics that is limited only by the number of examples that can be unearthed.

Another type of document of major importance is the Nahuatl census or *padrón*. The most informative ones appear to have been written early in the colonial period. For several years Pedro Carrasco has been describing and interpreting a truly spectacular example of them, three volumes concerning Tepoztlan and other parts of the Cuernavaca region around the late 1530s.[1] They go house by house through entire calpullis, giving the complete membership of households by name, with age, status, place of origin if not local, and duties and degree of kinship to the others. Also included are the amount and type of land held and who in the household cultivates it, as well as the exact amount and type of tribute given, at what times and to whom. Carrasco's analyses and descriptions give a most adequate conception of the nature of the documents. To this he has now added an excellent transcription and Spanish translation of several representative pages.[2]

The potential of the documents for studies of social and economic organization at the urgently interesting microlevel is amply demonstrated by the work of Carrasco. The possibilities are just as great for study of tribute mechanisms, land use, and movement of people, not to speak of names and naming patterns, for the documents contain the names of many hundreds of still unbaptized Nahuatl speakers. Because of the set format, unvarying over large sections, the documents are not hard to understand or use, once some basic terms have been mastered. Other censuses are known to exist, though none nearly so rich. Even if there are no others like them, these volumes alone are material enough for a substantial renovation of the social-economic history of late precolonial and early colonial times in the central regions of Mexico.

---

[1]Museo Nacional de Antropología, Colección Antigua, Vols. 549, 550, 551.

[2]In "La casa y hacienda de un señor tlalhuica," *Estudios de Cultura Náhuatl*, X (1972), 225-244. This also contains a partial bibliography of Carrasco's other articles on the subject. Yet others are forthcoming.

Bibliography

Anderson, Arthur J. O. *Rules of the Aztec Language.* Salt Lake City: University of Utah Press, 1973.

Barlow, Robert H., and George T. Smisor, eds. *Nombre de Dios, Durango: Two Documents in Nahuatl Concerning its Foundation.* Sacramento: The House of Tlaloc, 1943.

Berdan, Frances. "The Matrícula de Tributos: Nahuatl Annotations," in *Matrícula de Tributos.* Graz: Akademische Druck- u. Verlagsanstalt. In preparation.

Carochi, Horacio. *Arte de la Lengua Mexicana.* México: Imprenta del Museo Nacional, 1892.

Carrasco, Pedro. "La casa y hacienda de un señor tlalhuica." *Estudios de Cultura Náhuatl,* X (1972), 225-244.

Cartas de Indias. Madrid: Impr. de M. G. Hernández, 1877.

Chimalpahin Quauhtlehuanitzin, Domingo Francisco de San Antón Muñón. *Annales: sixième et septième relations.* Rémi Siméon, ed. Paris: Maisonneuve et C. Leclerc, 1889.

Códice Osuna. México: Instituto Indigenista Interamericano, 1947.

Códice Sierra. Translation of Nahuatl text by Mariano J. Rojas. México: Museo Nacional de Arqueología, Historia y Etnografía, 1933.

Colección de documentos inéditos relativos al descubrimiento, conquista y organización de las antiguas posesiones españoles de América y Oceanía. Madrid, 1866.

Cook, S. F., and Woodrow Borah. *Essays in Population History: Mexico and the Caribbean.* Vol. I. Berkeley: University of California Press, 1971.

Durán, Diego. *Historia de las Indias de Nueva España e Islas de la Tierra Firme.* México: Editorial Porrua, 1967.

Durand-Forest, Jacqueline de. "Cambios económicos y moneda entre los Aztecas." *Estudios de Cultura Náhuatl,* IX (1971), 105-124.

Epistolario de Nueva España. Francisco Paso y Troncoso, ed. México: Antigua Librería Robredo, 1939-1942.

Florentine Codex: General History of the Things of New Spain. By Bernardino de Sahagún. Translated by Arthur J. O. Anderson and Charles E. Dibble. Salt Lake City: University of Utah Press, and Santa Fe, School of American Research, 1950-1969.

Garibay, Angel María. *Llave del Náhuatl: Colección de trozos clásicos, con gramática y vocabulario, para utilidad de los principiantes.* México: Editorial Porrua, 1961.

Gibson, Charles. *The Aztecs under Spanish Rule.* Stanford: Stanford University Press, 1964.

González Casanova, Pablo. *Cuentos Indígenas.* México: Imprenta Universitaria, 1946.

Hernández, Francisco. *Obras Completas.* Vols. II and III, *Historia Natural de Nueva España.* Universidad Nacional de México. México, 1959.

Ixtlilxochitl, Fernando de Alva. *Obras historicas.* 2 vols. México: Editorial Nacional, 1965.

Libro del Cabildo e Ayuntamiento de . . . México (1550-1561). México, n.d.

Lockhart, James. "Spaniards among Indians: Toluca in the Later Sixteenth Century," in *Creole Societies in Africa and the Americas.* Franklin W. Knight, ed. Baltimore, Md.: Johns Hopkins University Press. In preparation.

Lombardo de Ruiz, Sonia. *Desarrollo urbano de México-Tenochtitlan según las fuentes históricas.* México: Instituto Nacional de Antropología e Historia, 1973.

Molina, Alonso de. *Arte de la Lengua Mexicana y Castellana.* Madrid: Ediciones Cultura Hispánica, 1945.

Molina, Alonso de. *Vocabulario en Lengua Castellana y Mexicana y Mexicana y Castellana.* Mexico: Editorial Porrua, 1970.

Newman, Stanley. "Classical Nahuatl." *Handbook of Middle American Indians,* V (1967), 179-199.

Reyes, Luis. "Documentos nahoas sobre el Estado de Chiapas." VIII Mesa Redonda de la Sociedad Mexicana de Antropología, México, 1961. Pp. 167-193.

Santamaría, Francisco J. *Diccionario de Mejicanismos.* México: Editorial Porrua, 1959.

Siméon, Rémi. *Dictionnaire de la Langue Nahuatl ou Mexicaine.* Graz: Akademische Druck- u. Verlagsanstalt, 1963.

Tezozomoc, don Fernando Alvarado. *Crónica Mexicayotl.* México: Imprenta Universitaria, 1949.

Zimmerman, Günter. *Briefe der indianischen Nobilität aus Neuspanien an Karl V und Philipp II um die Mitte des 16. Jahrhunderts.* Hamburg: Hamburgisches Museum für Völkerkunde, 1970.